MODEL™

VOLUME SEVEN

BY
LEE SO-YOUNG

WITHDRAWN

HAMBURG // LONDON // LOS ANGELES // TOKYO

Model Vol.7
Created by Lee So-Young

Translation - Grace Min
English Adaptation - Stormcrow Hayes
Copy Editor - Peter Ahlstrom
Retouch and Lettering - Joseph Mariano
Production Artist - Bowen Park
Cover Design - Jorge Negrete

Editor - Carol Fox
Digital Imaging Manager - Chris Buford
Production Managers - Jennifer Miller and Mutsumi Miyazaki
Managing Editor - Jill Freshney
VP of Production - Ron Klamert
Publisher and E.I.C. - Mike Kiley
President and C.O.O. - John Parker
C.E.O. - Stuart Levy

A  Manga

TOKYOPOP Inc.
5900 Wilshire Blvd. Suite 2000
Los Angeles, CA 90036

E-mail: info@TOKYOPOP.com
Come visit us online at www.TOKYOPOP.com

ISBN: 1-59532-009-1

First TOKYOPOP printing: August 2005
10 9 8 7 6 5 4 3 2
Printed in the USA

MODEL: SEVEN

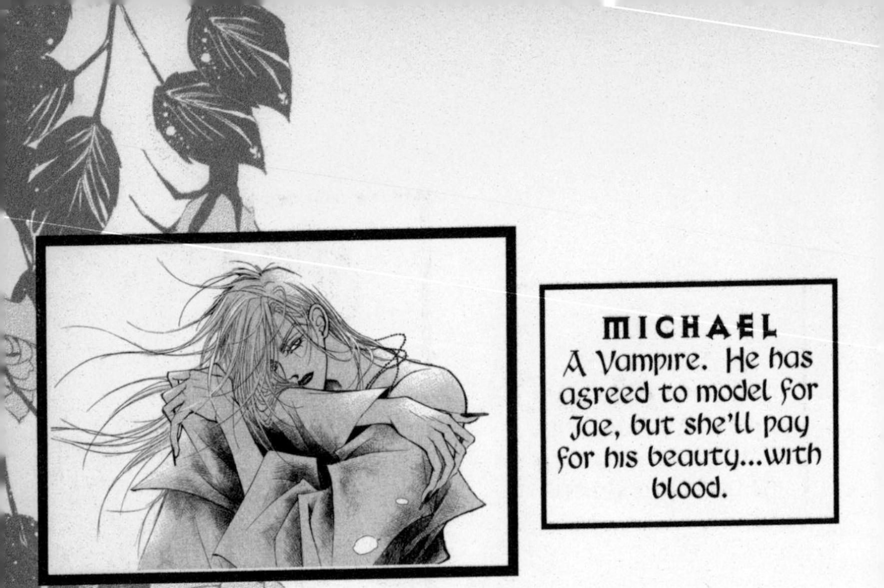

MICHAEL
A Vampire. He has agreed to model for Jae, but she'll pay for his beauty...with blood.

KEN
A Youth. A member of the household who may, or may not, be Michael's prodigal son.

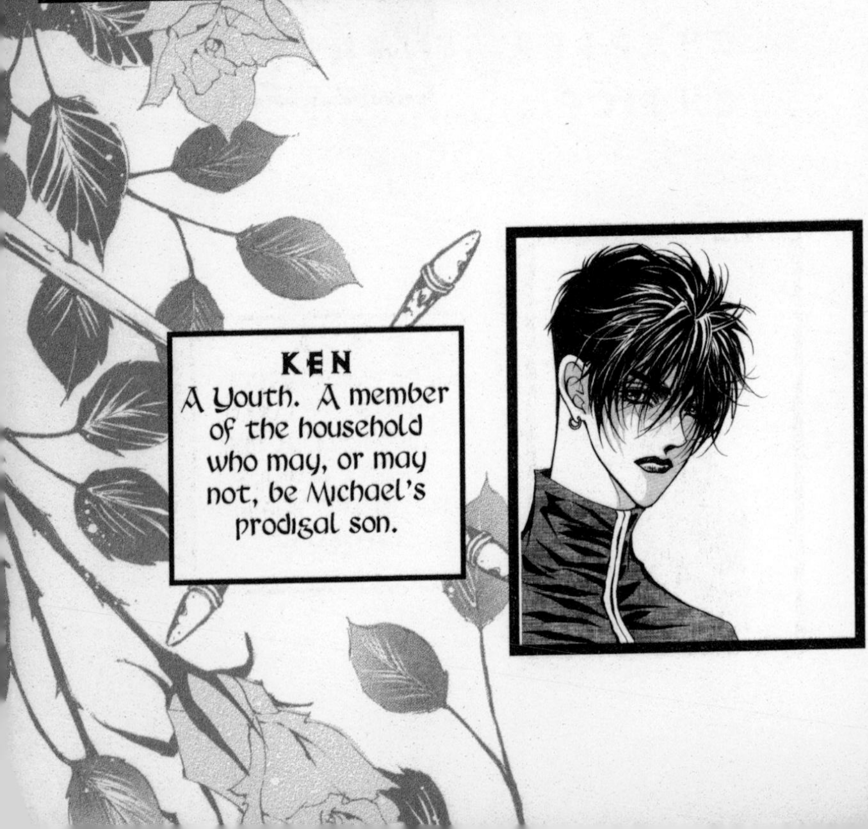

JAE
An Artist. She may have found her muse in Michael, but is he her inspiration or her damnation?

EVA
The Housekeeper. She serves only Michael. But she hasn't always called the Vampire "Master."

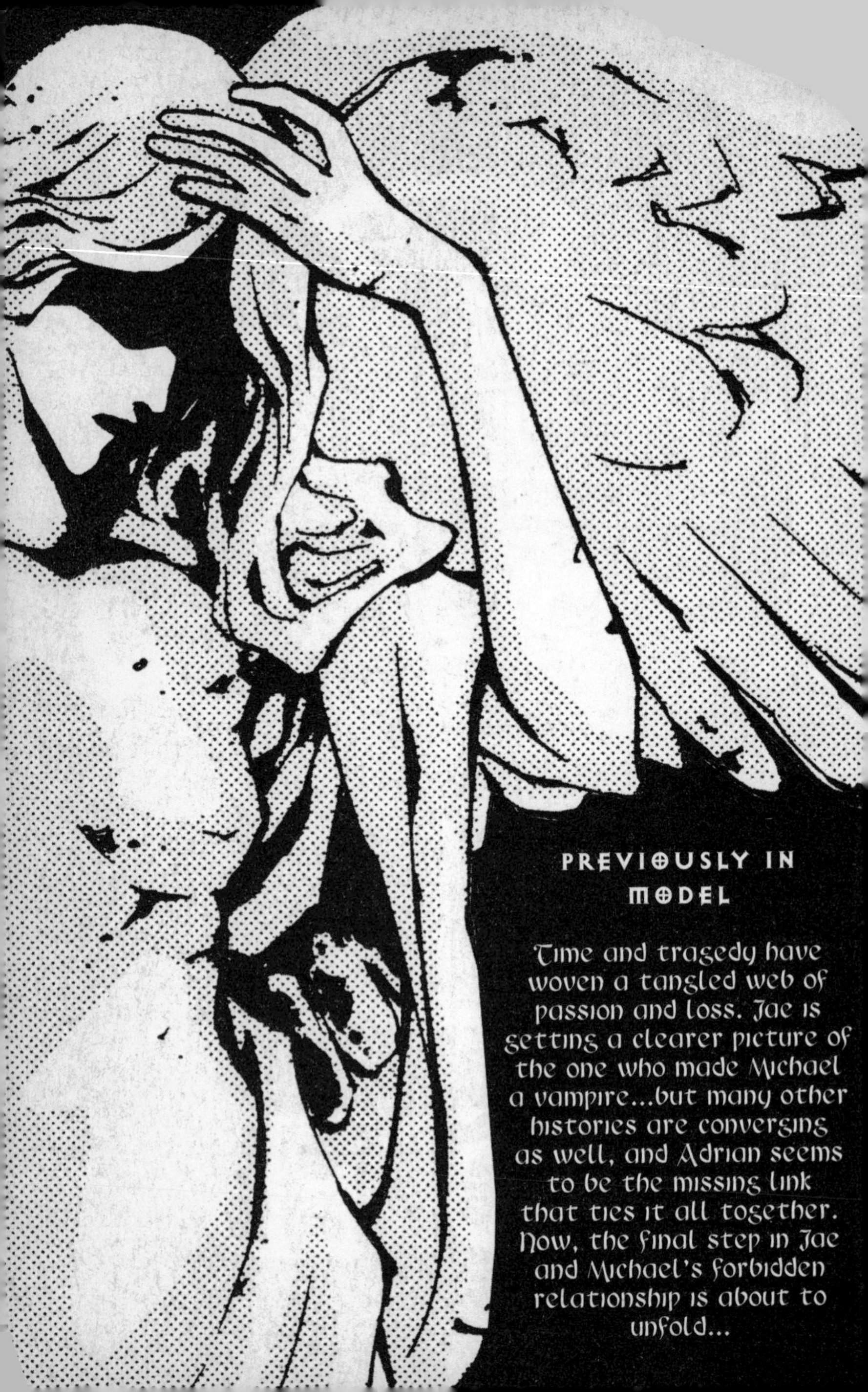

PREVIOUSLY IN MODEL

Time and tragedy have woven a tangled web of passion and loss. Jae is getting a clearer picture of the one who made Michael a vampire...but many other histories are converging as well, and Adrian seems to be the missing link that ties it all together. Now, the final step in Jae and Michael's forbidden relationship is about to unfold...

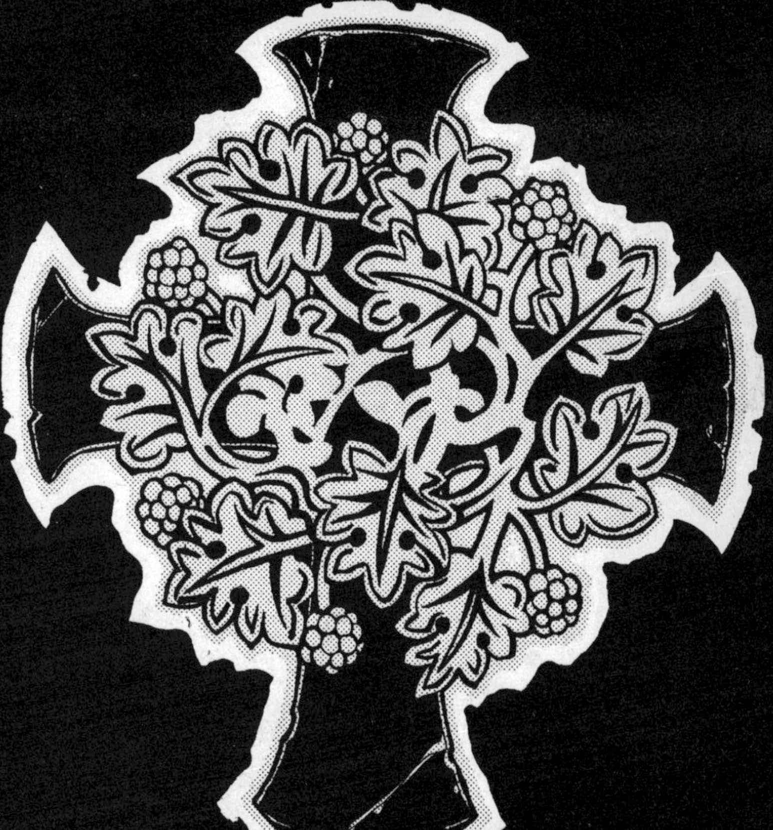

MODEL

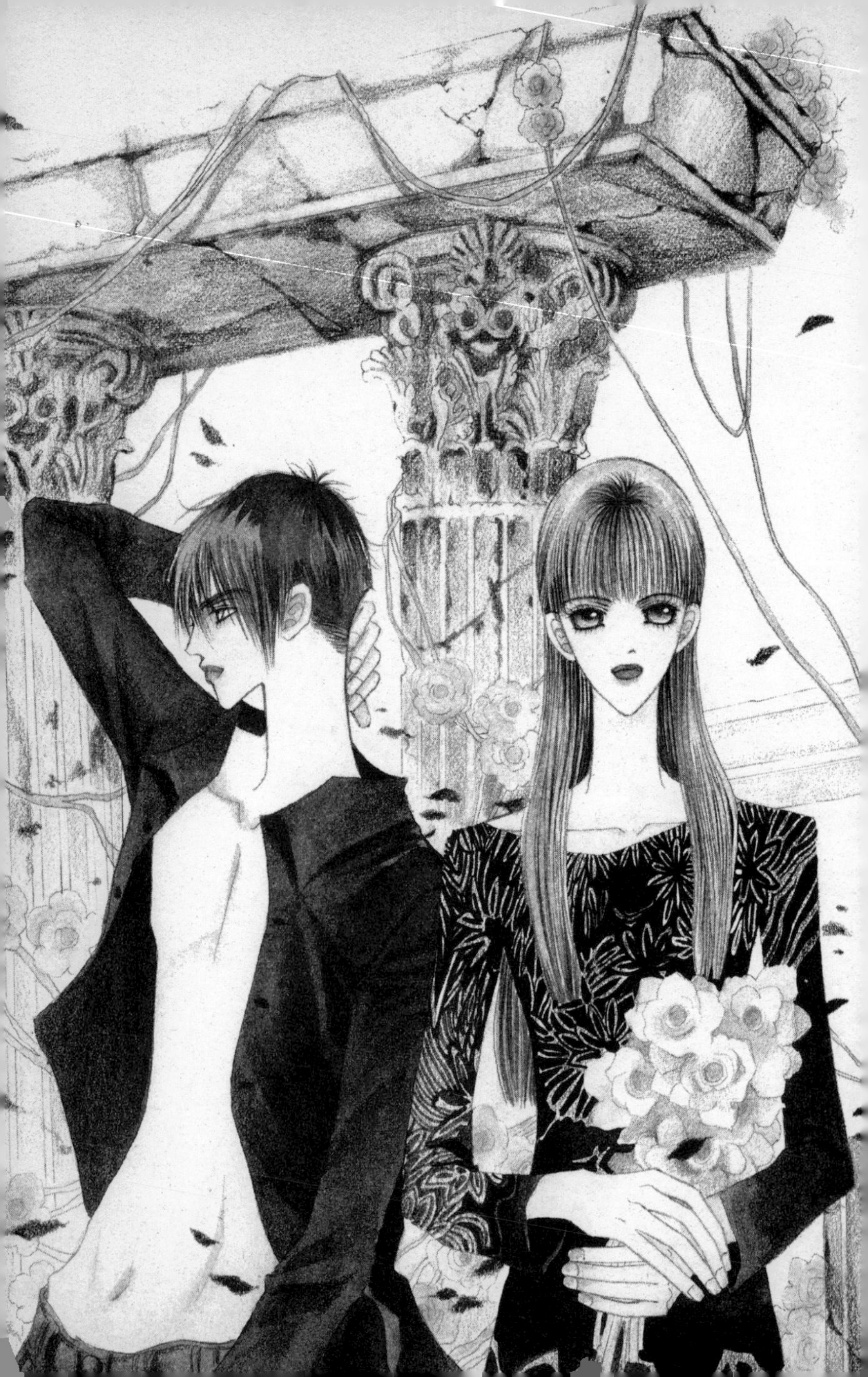

CHAPTER SEVEN
CHOICE

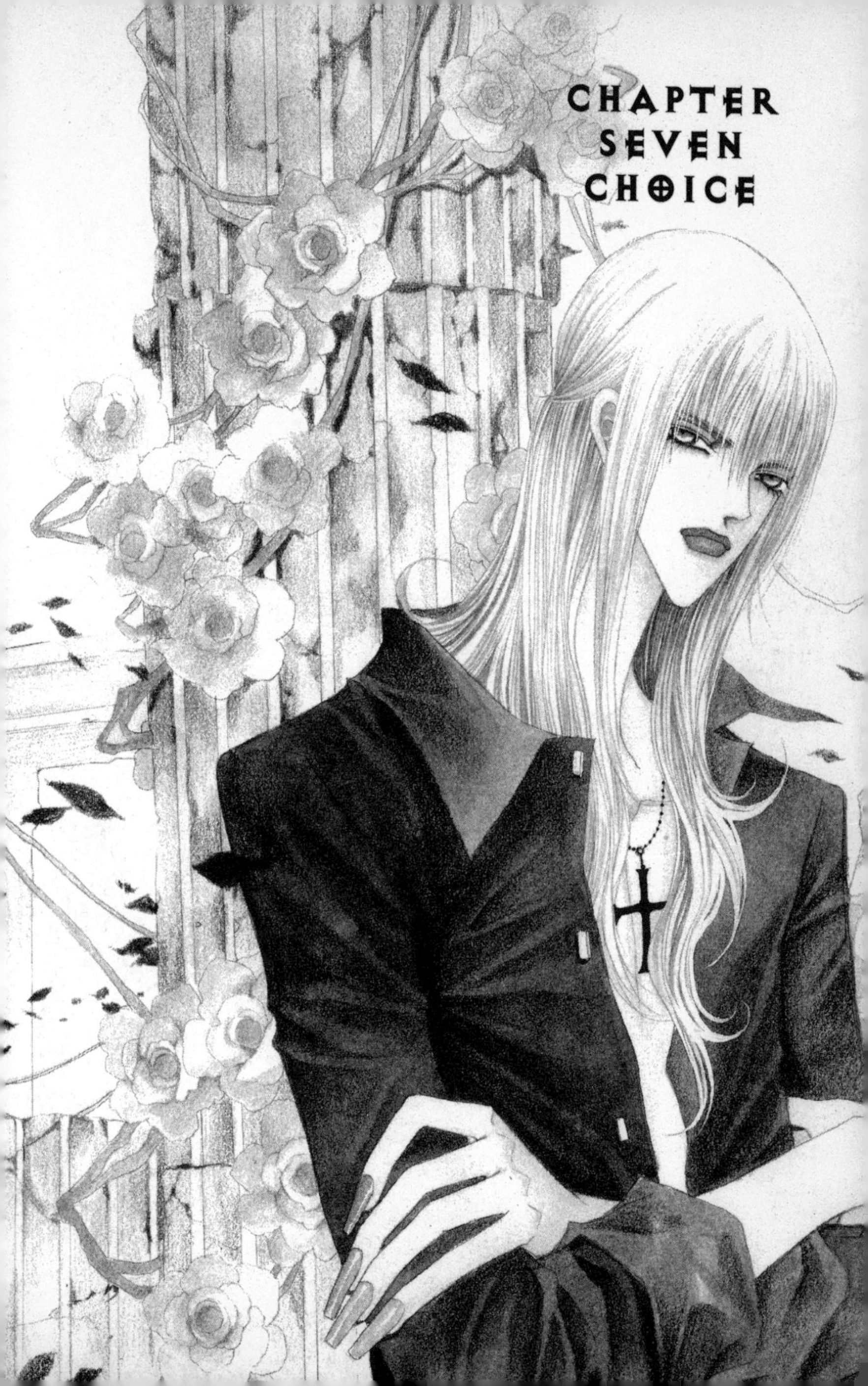

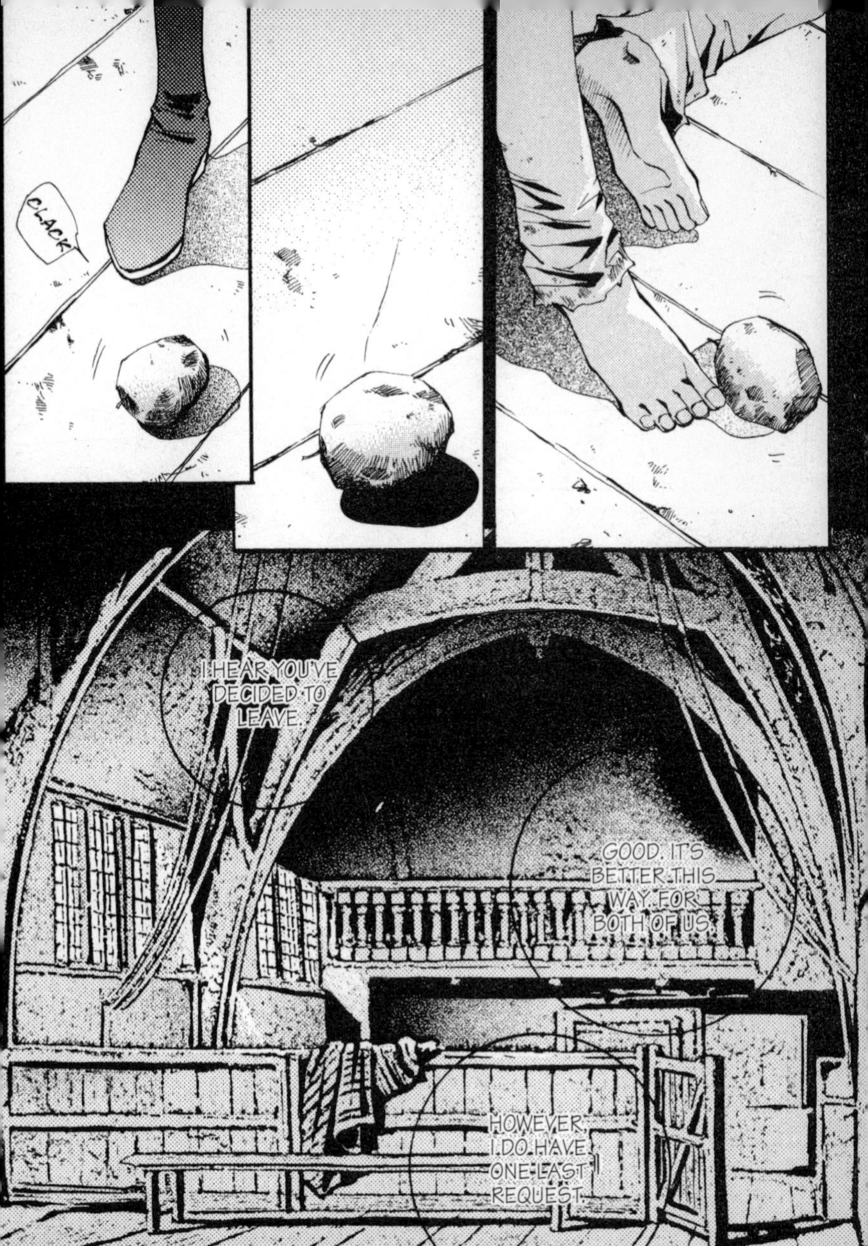
CLACK
I HEAR YOU'VE DECIDED TO LEAVE.
GOOD. IT'S BETTER THIS WAY FOR BOTH OF US.
HOWEVER, I DO HAVE ONE LAST REQUEST.

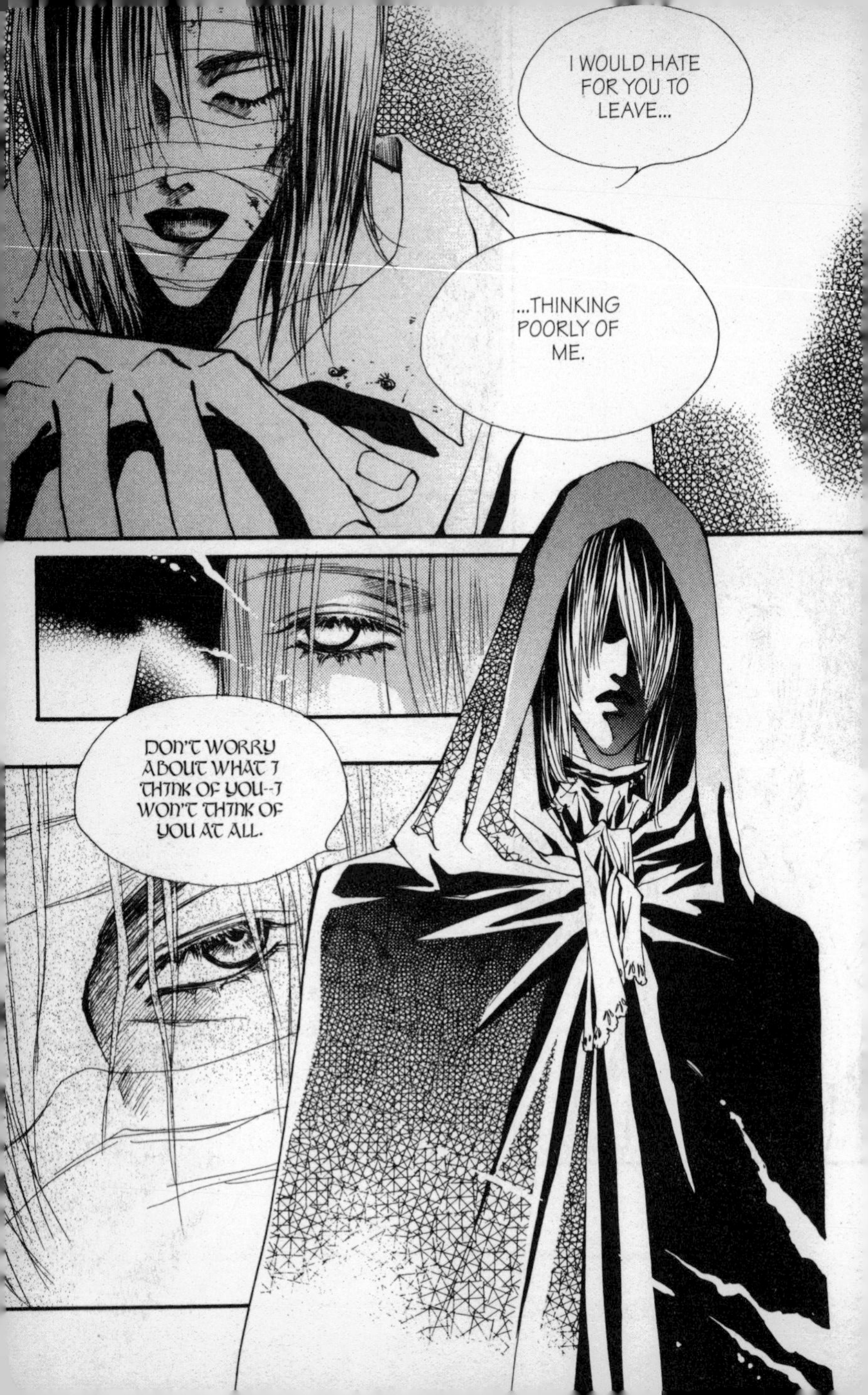
I WOULD HATE FOR YOU TO LEAVE...
...THINKING POORLY OF ME.
DON'T WORRY ABOUT WHAT I THINK OF YOU--I WON'T THINK OF YOU AT ALL.

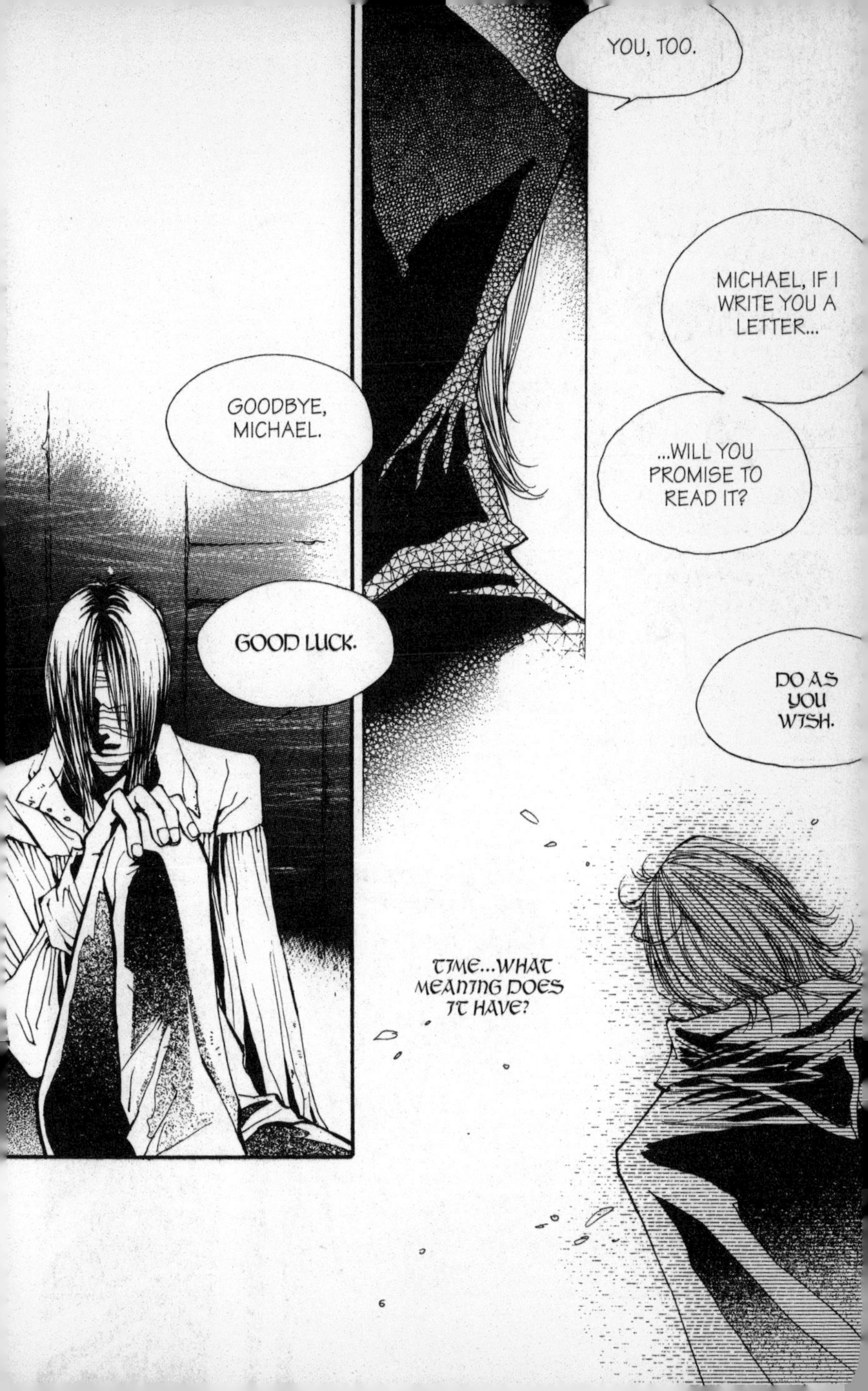
GOODBYE, MICHAEL.
GOOD LUCK.
YOU, TOO.
MICHAEL, IF I WRITE YOU A LETTER...
...WILL YOU PROMISE TO READ IT?
DO AS YOU WISH.
TIME...WHAT MEANING DOES IT HAVE?

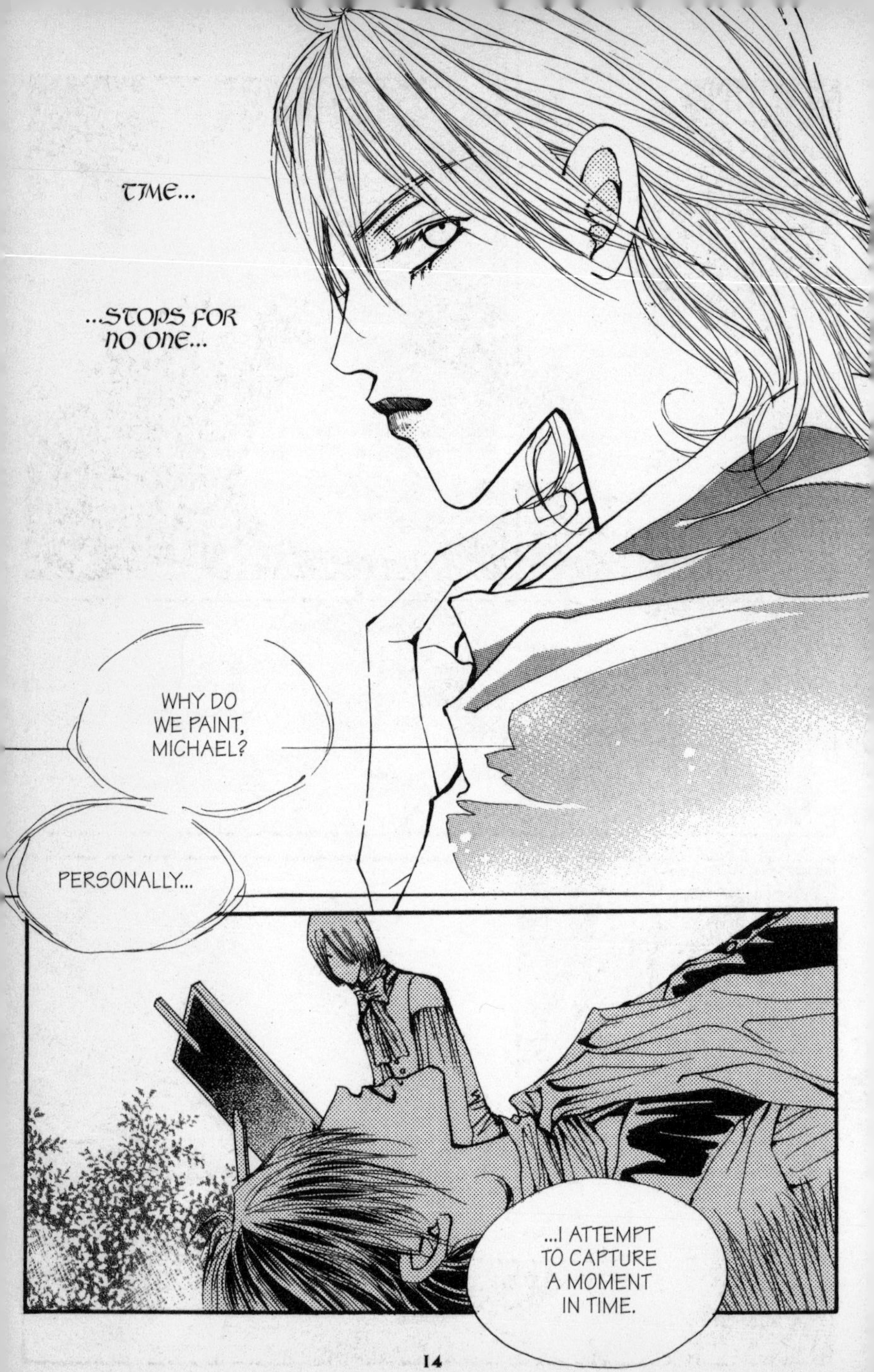
TIME...
...STOPS FOR NO ONE...
WHY DO WE PAINT, MICHAEL?
PERSONALLY...
...I ATTEMPT TO CAPTURE A MOMENT IN TIME.

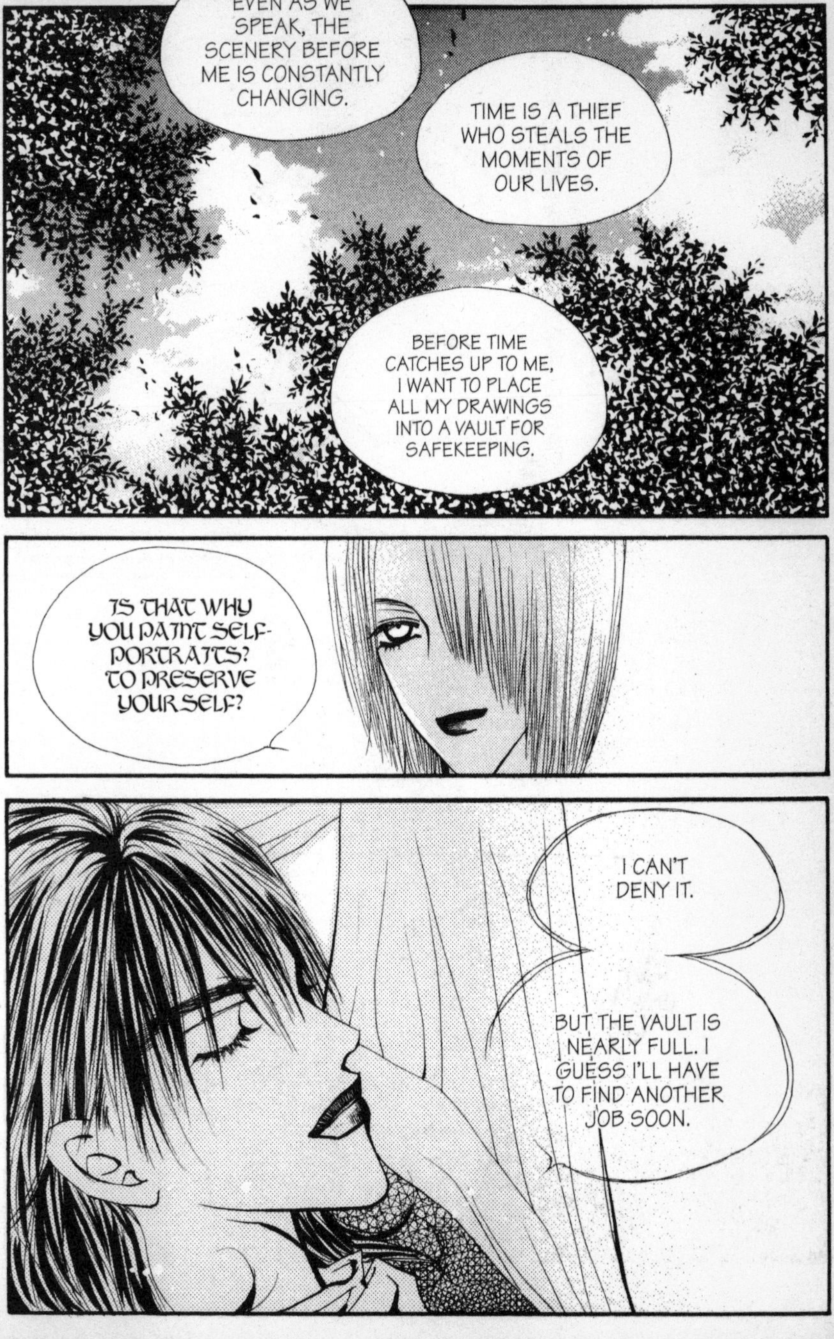
EVEN AS WE SPEAK, THE SCENERY BEFORE ME IS CONSTANTLY CHANGING.
TIME IS A THIEF WHO STEALS THE MOMENTS OF OUR LIVES.
BEFORE TIME CATCHES UP TO ME, I WANT TO PLACE ALL MY DRAWINGS INTO A VAULT FOR SAFEKEEPING.
IS THAT WHY YOU PAINT SELF-PORTRAITS? TO PRESERVE YOUR SELF?
I CAN'T DENY IT.
BUT THE VAULT IS NEARLY FULL. I GUESS I'LL HAVE TO FIND ANOTHER JOB SOON.

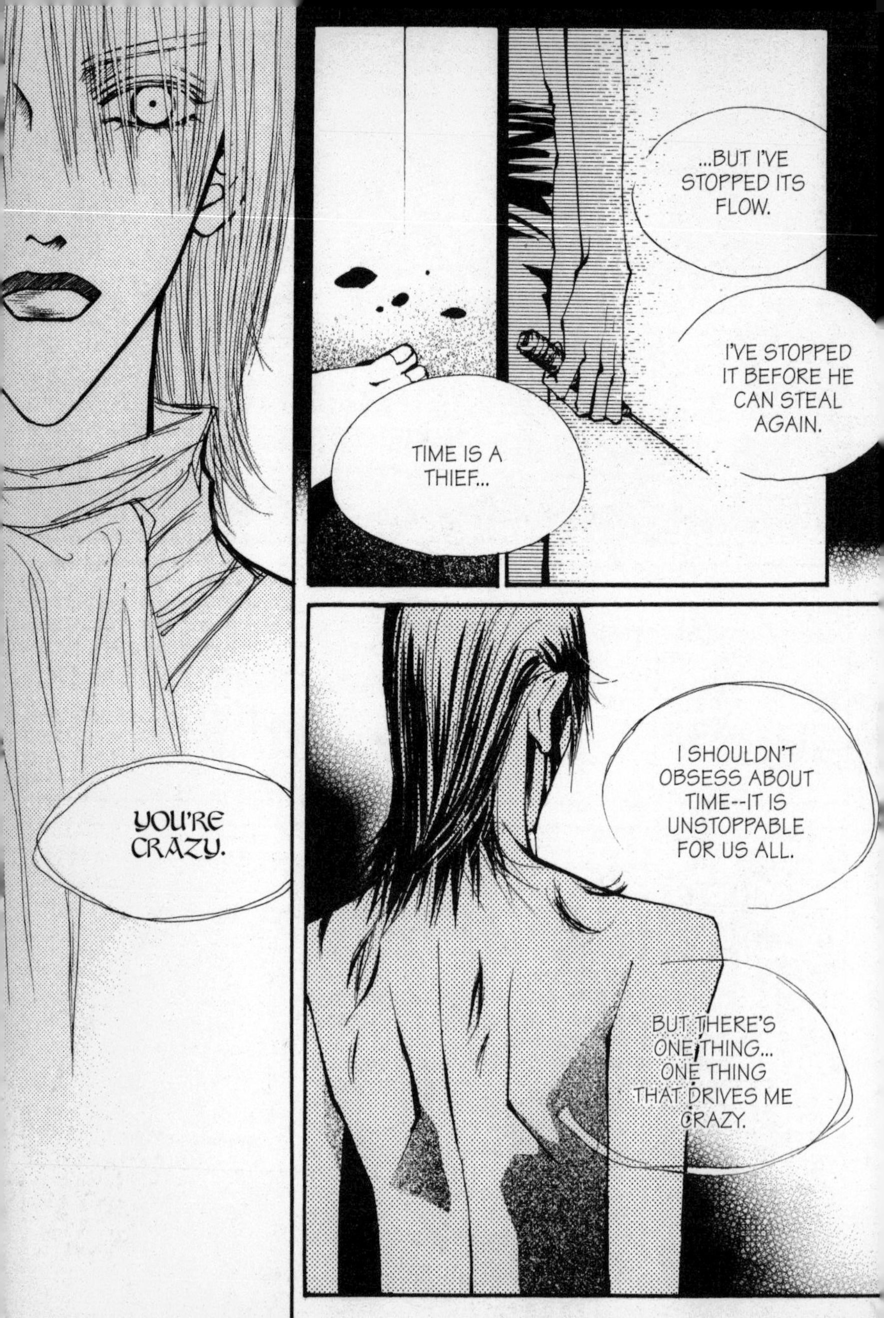
TIME IS A THIEF...
...BUT I'VE STOPPED ITS FLOW.
I'VE STOPPED IT BEFORE HE CAN STEAL AGAIN.
I SHOULDN'T OBSESS ABOUT TIME--IT IS UNSTOPPABLE FOR US ALL.
BUT THERE'S ONE THING... ONE THING THAT DRIVES ME CRAZY.
YOU'RE CRAZY.

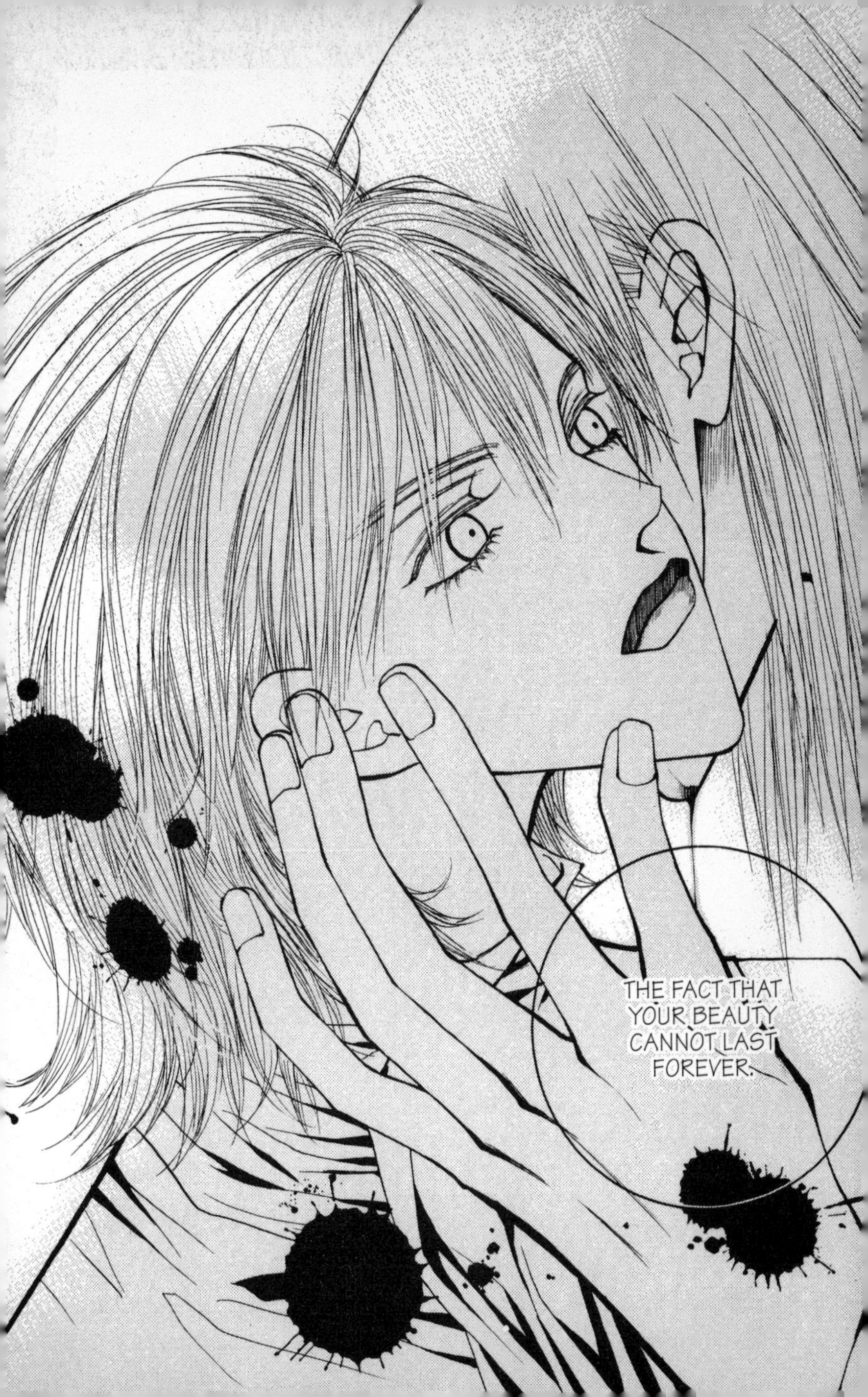
THE FACT THAT YOUR BEAUTY CANNOT LAST FOREVER.

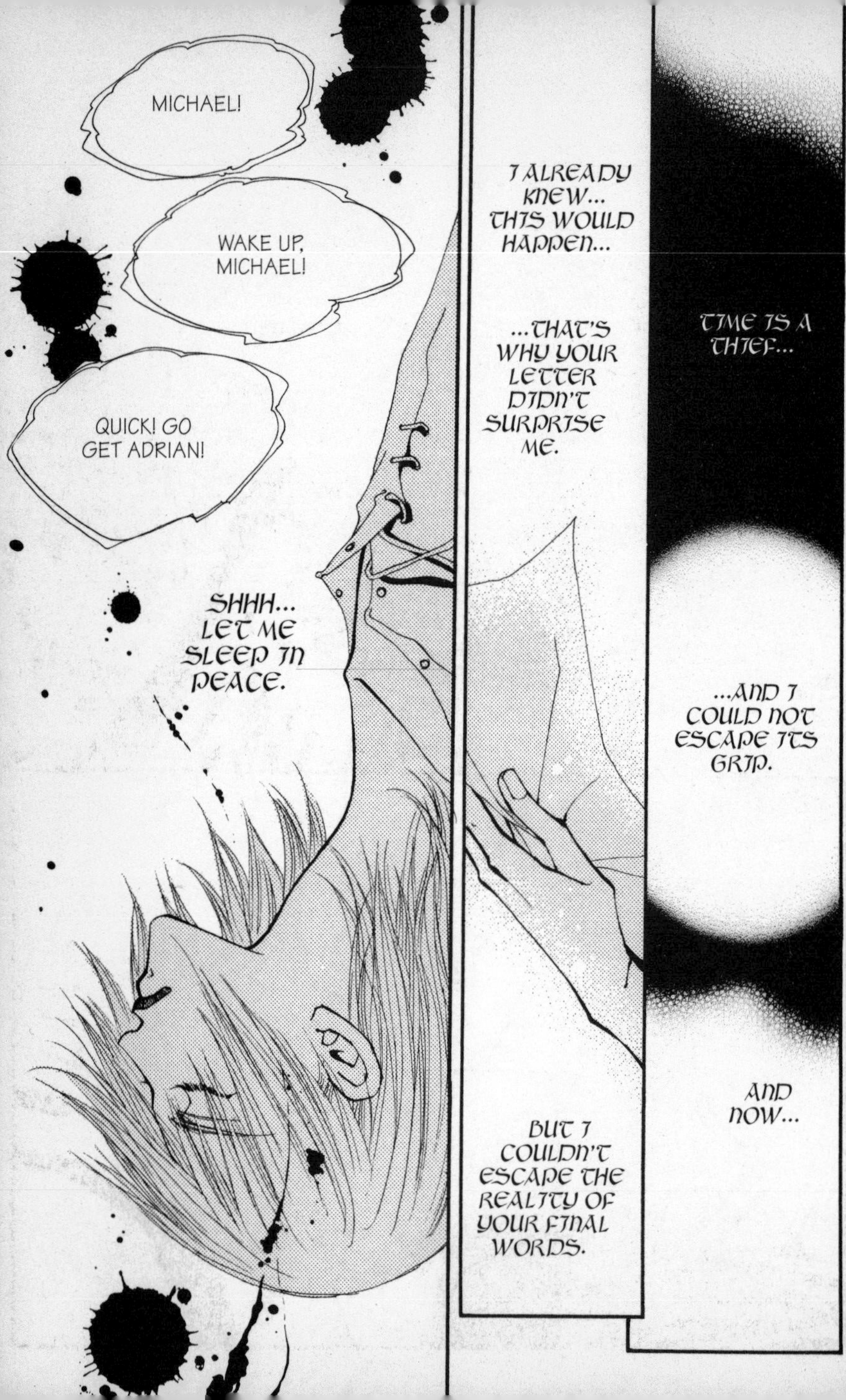
TIME IS A THIEF...
...AND I COULD NOT ESCAPE ITS GRIP.
AND NOW...
I ALREADY KNEW... THIS WOULD HAPPEN...
...THAT'S WHY YOUR LETTER DIDN'T SURPRISE ME.
BUT I COULDN'T ESCAPE THE REALITY OF YOUR FINAL WORDS.
MICHAEL!
WAKE UP, MICHAEL!
QUICK! GO GET ADRIAN!
SHHH... LET ME SLEEP IN PEACE.

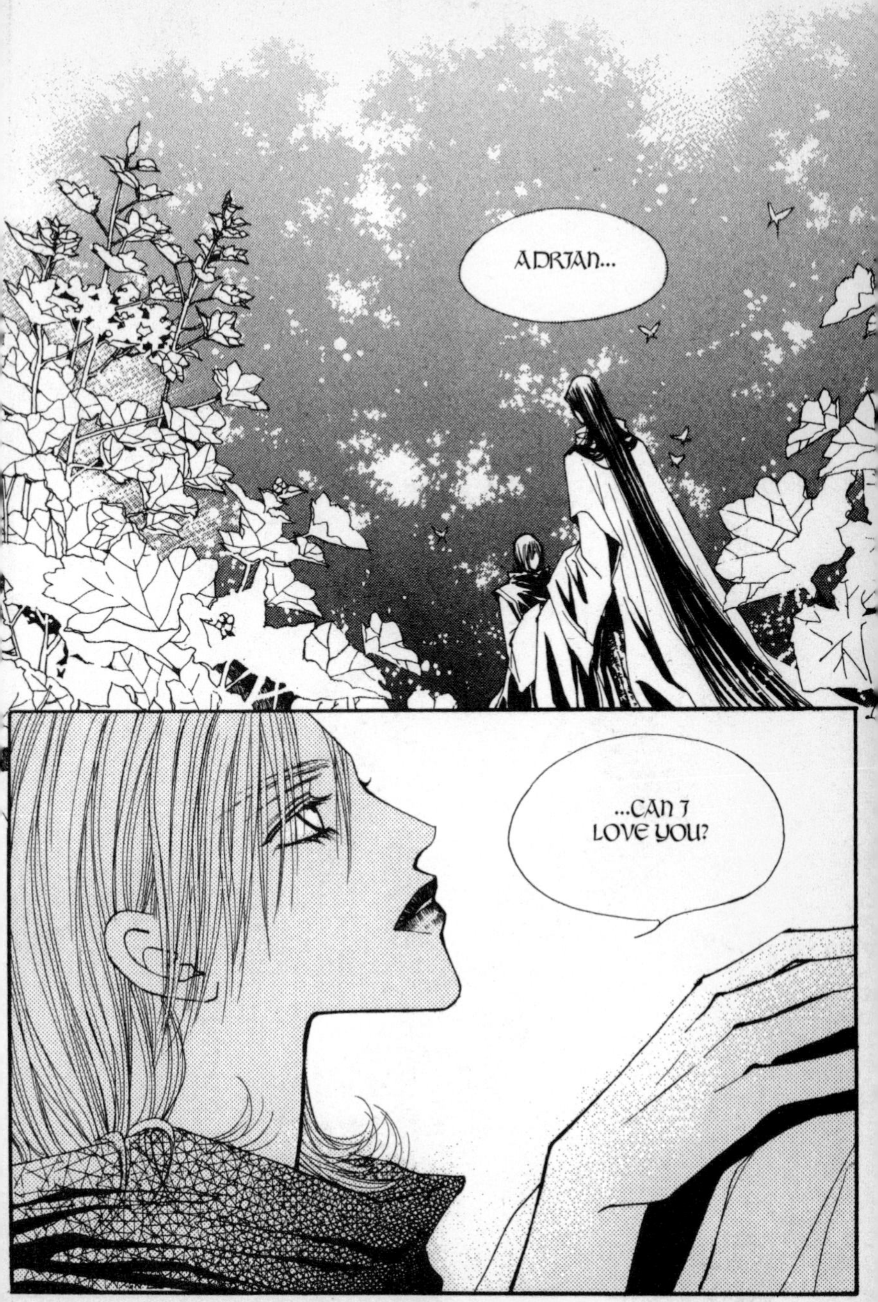
ADRIAN...
...CAN I LOVE YOU?

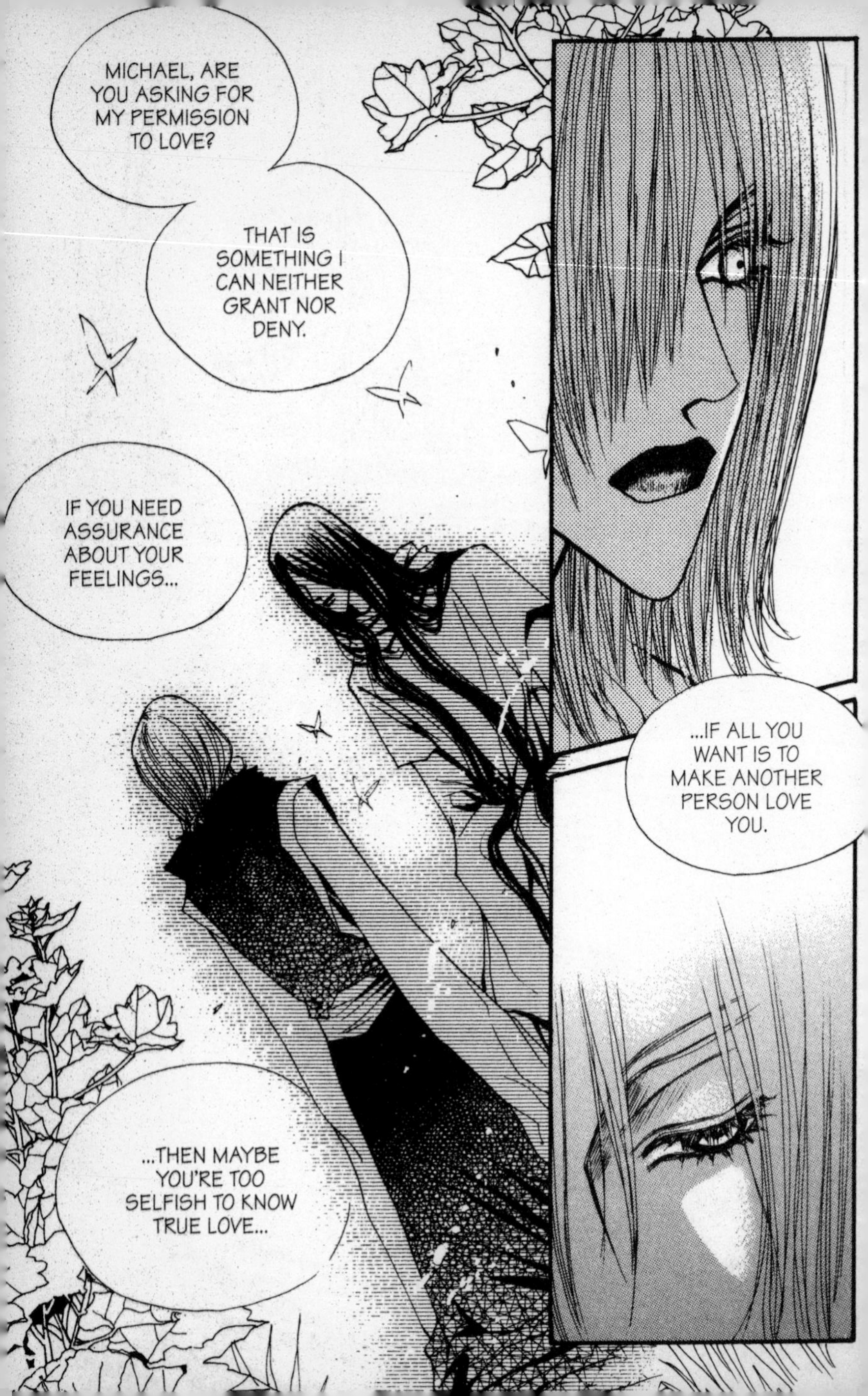
MICHAEL, ARE YOU ASKING FOR MY PERMISSION TO LOVE?
THAT IS SOMETHING I CAN NEITHER GRANT NOR DENY.
IF YOU NEED ASSURANCE ABOUT YOUR FEELINGS...
...IF ALL YOU WANT IS TO MAKE ANOTHER PERSON LOVE YOU.
...THEN MAYBE YOU'RE TOO SELFISH TO KNOW TRUE LOVE...

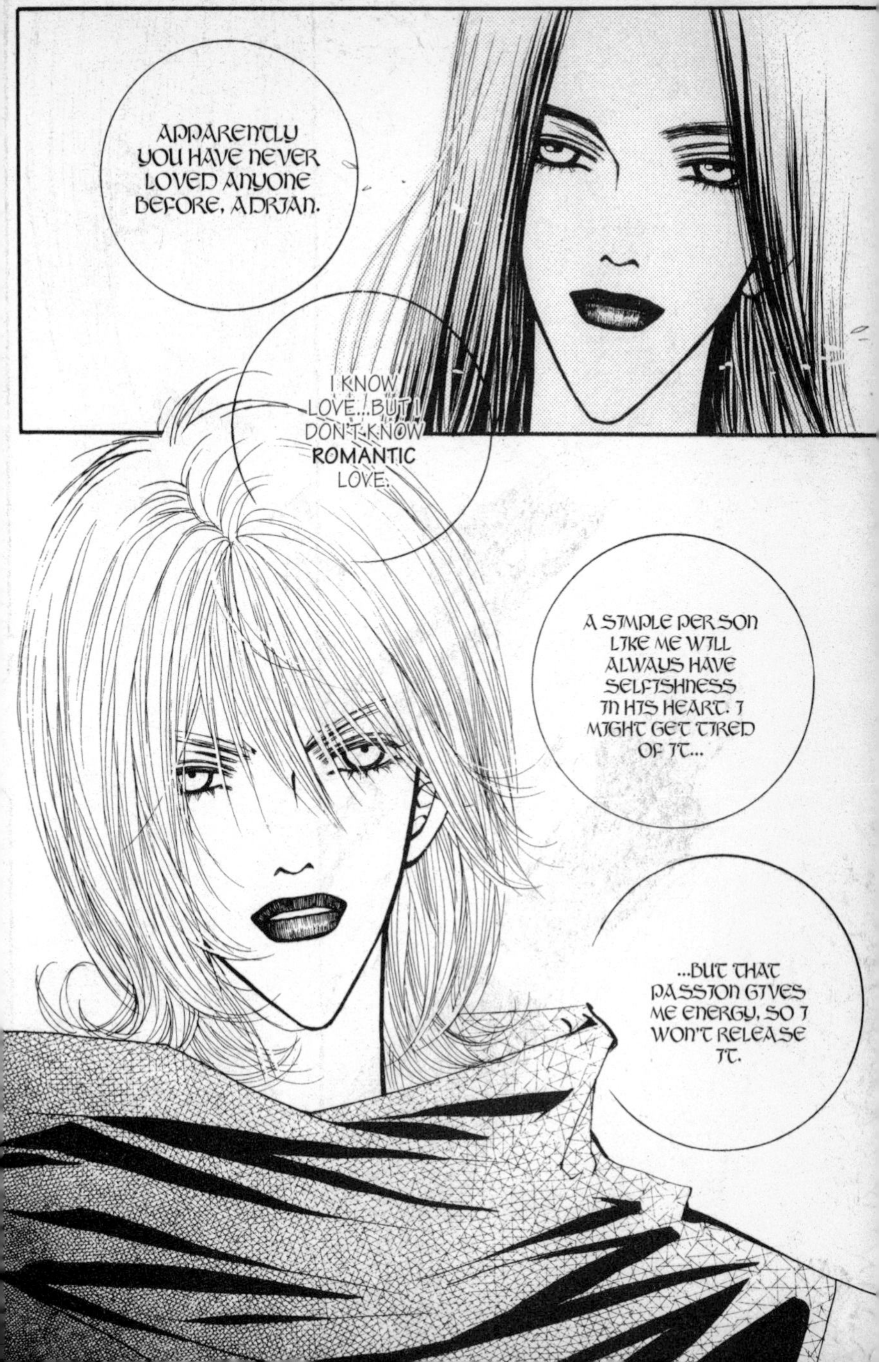
APPARENTLY YOU HAVE NEVER LOVED ANYONE BEFORE, ADRIAN.
I KNOW LOVE...BUT I DON'T KNOW **ROMANTIC** LOVE.
A SIMPLE PERSON LIKE ME WILL ALWAYS HAVE SELFISHNESS IN HIS HEART. I MIGHT GET TIRED OF IT...
...BUT THAT PASSION GIVES ME ENERGY, SO I WON'T RELEASE IT.

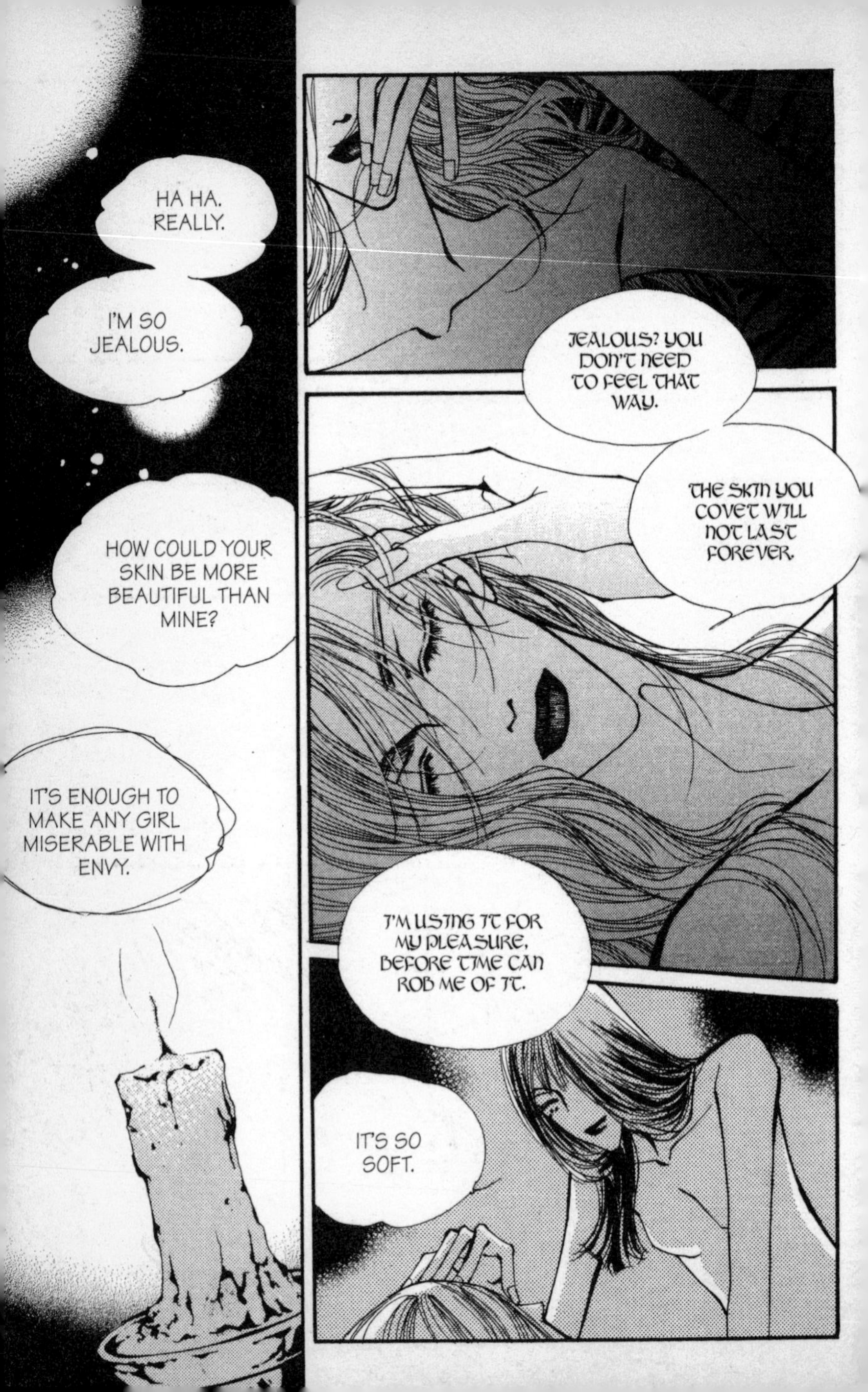
HA HA. REALLY.
I'M SO JEALOUS.
HOW COULD YOUR SKIN BE MORE BEAUTIFUL THAN MINE?
IT'S ENOUGH TO MAKE ANY GIRL MISERABLE WITH ENVY.
JEALOUS? YOU DON'T NEED TO FEEL THAT WAY.
THE SKIN YOU COVET WILL NOT LAST FOREVER.
I'M USING IT FOR MY PLEASURE, BEFORE TIME CAN ROB ME OF IT.
IT'S SO SOFT.

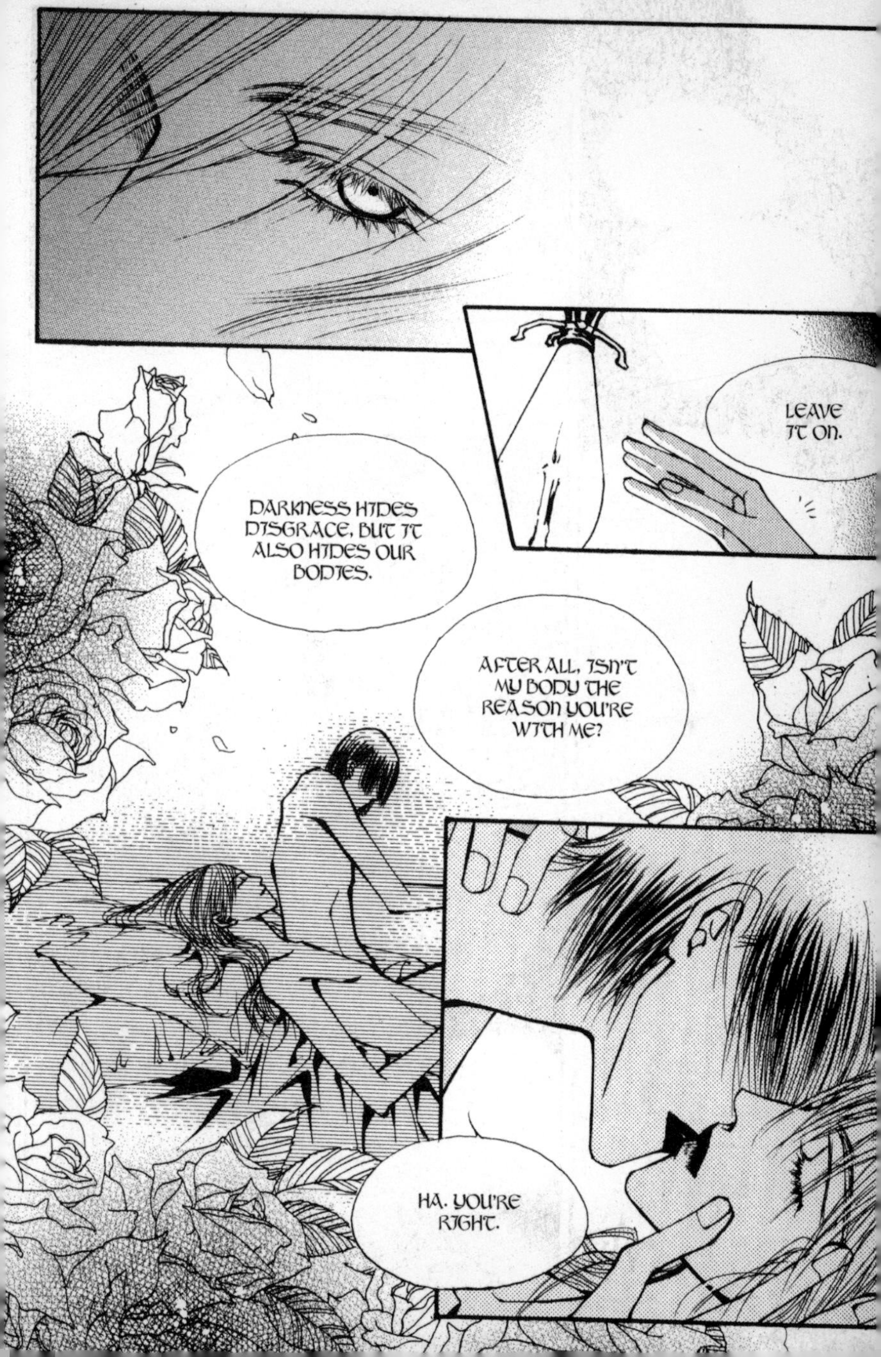
LEAVE IT ON.
DARKNESS HIDES DISGRACE, BUT IT ALSO HIDES OUR BODIES.
AFTER ALL, ISN'T MY BODY THE REASON YOU'RE WITH ME?
HA. YOU'RE RIGHT.

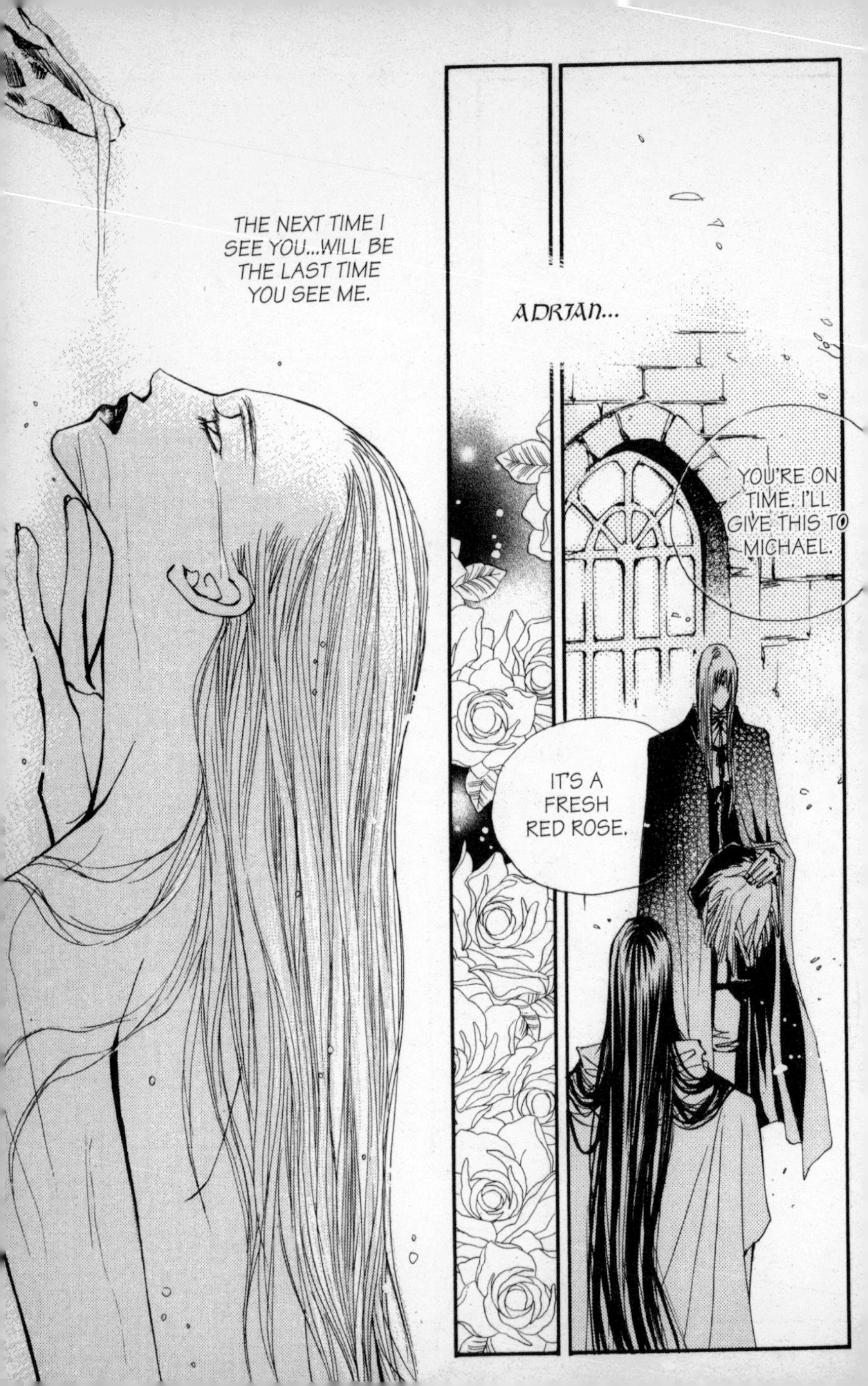
ADRIAN...
YOU'RE ON TIME. I'LL GIVE THIS TO MICHAEL.
IT'S A FRESH RED ROSE.
THE NEXT TIME I SEE YOU...WILL BE THE LAST TIME YOU SEE ME.

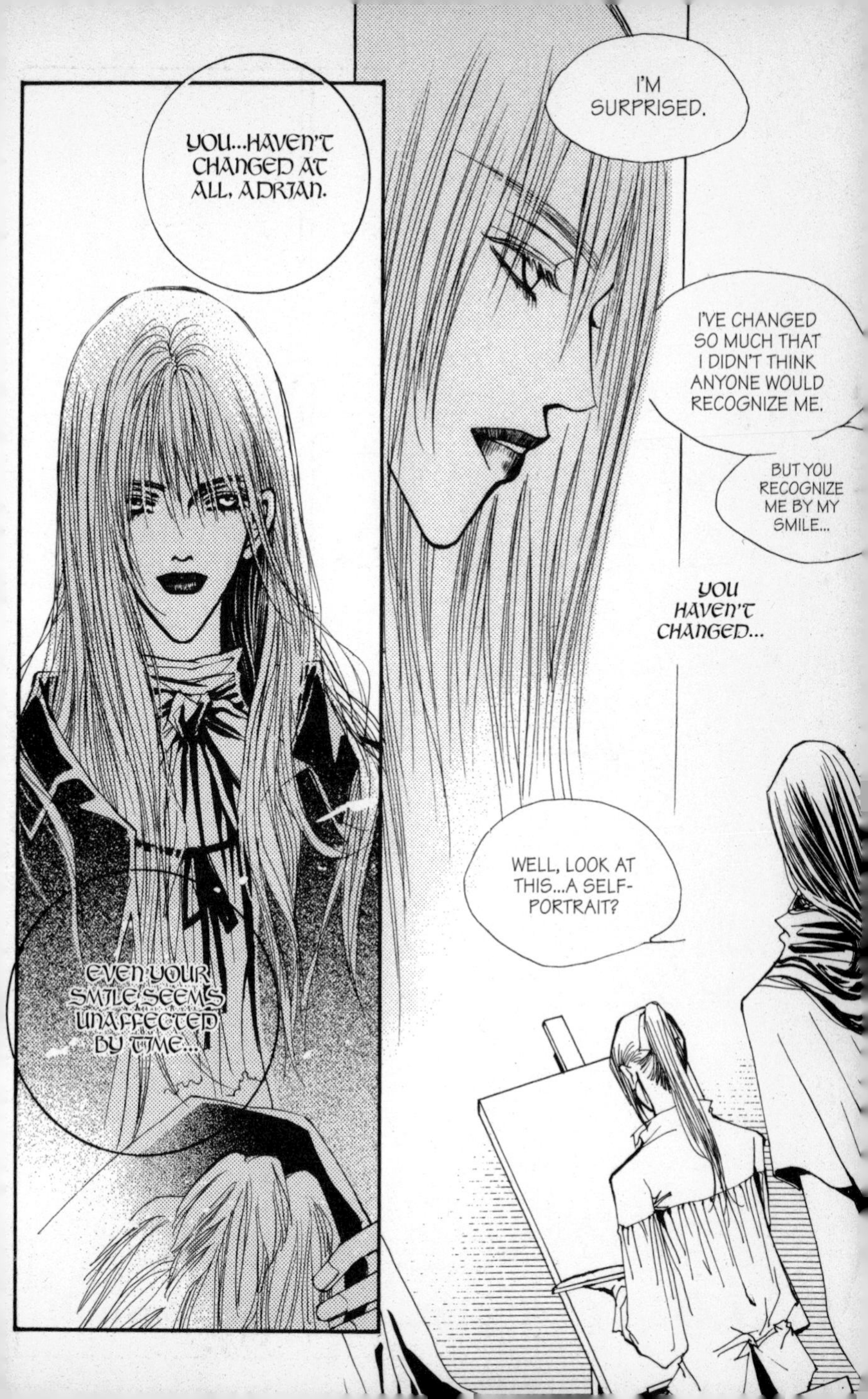
YOU...HAVEN'T CHANGED AT ALL, ADRIAN.
EVEN YOUR SMILE SEEMS UNAFFECTED BY TIME...
I'M SURPRISED.
I'VE CHANGED SO MUCH THAT I DIDN'T THINK ANYONE WOULD RECOGNIZE ME.
BUT YOU RECOGNIZE ME BY MY SMILE...
YOU HAVEN'T CHANGED...
WELL, LOOK AT THIS...A SELF-PORTRAIT?

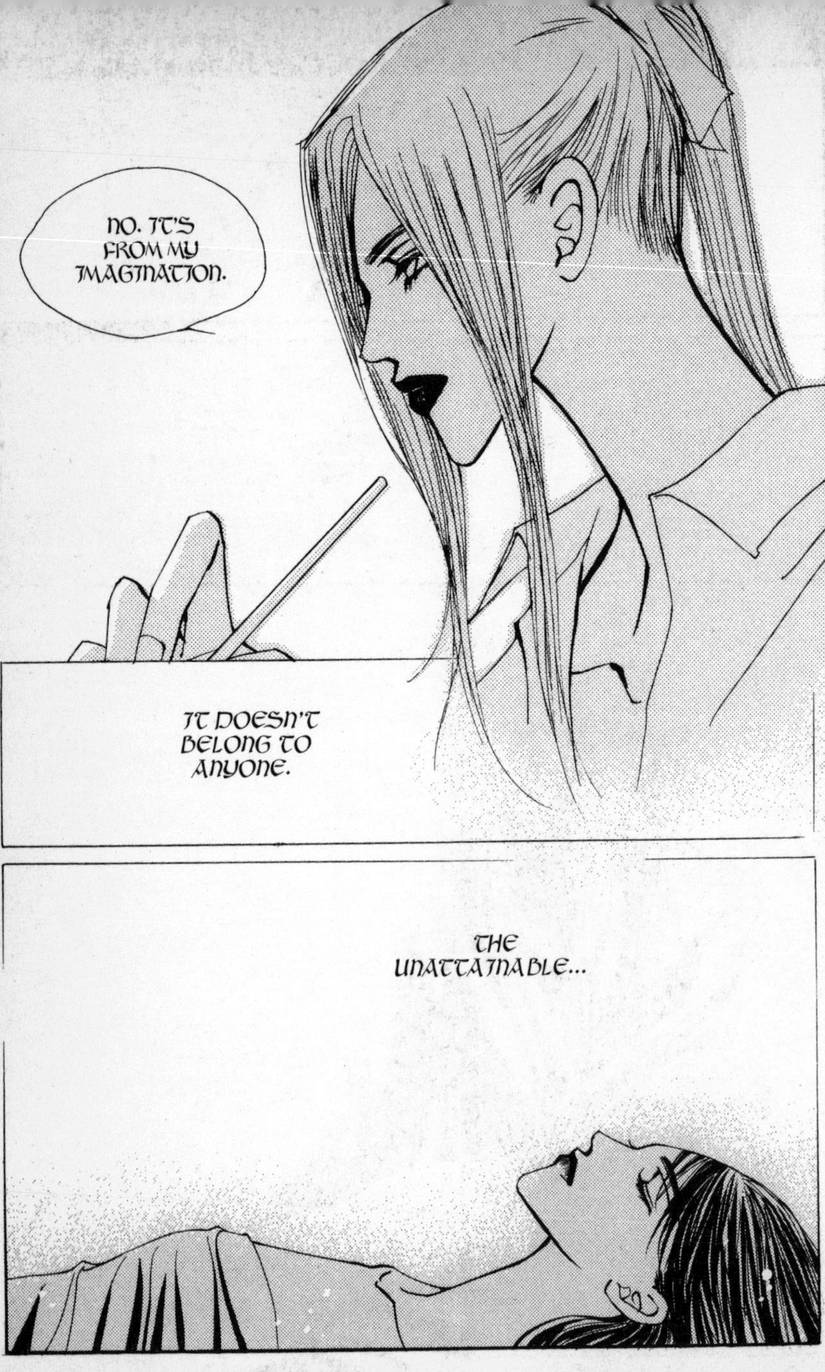
NO. IT'S FROM MY IMAGINATION.
IT DOESN'T BELONG TO ANYONE.
THE UNATTAINABLE...

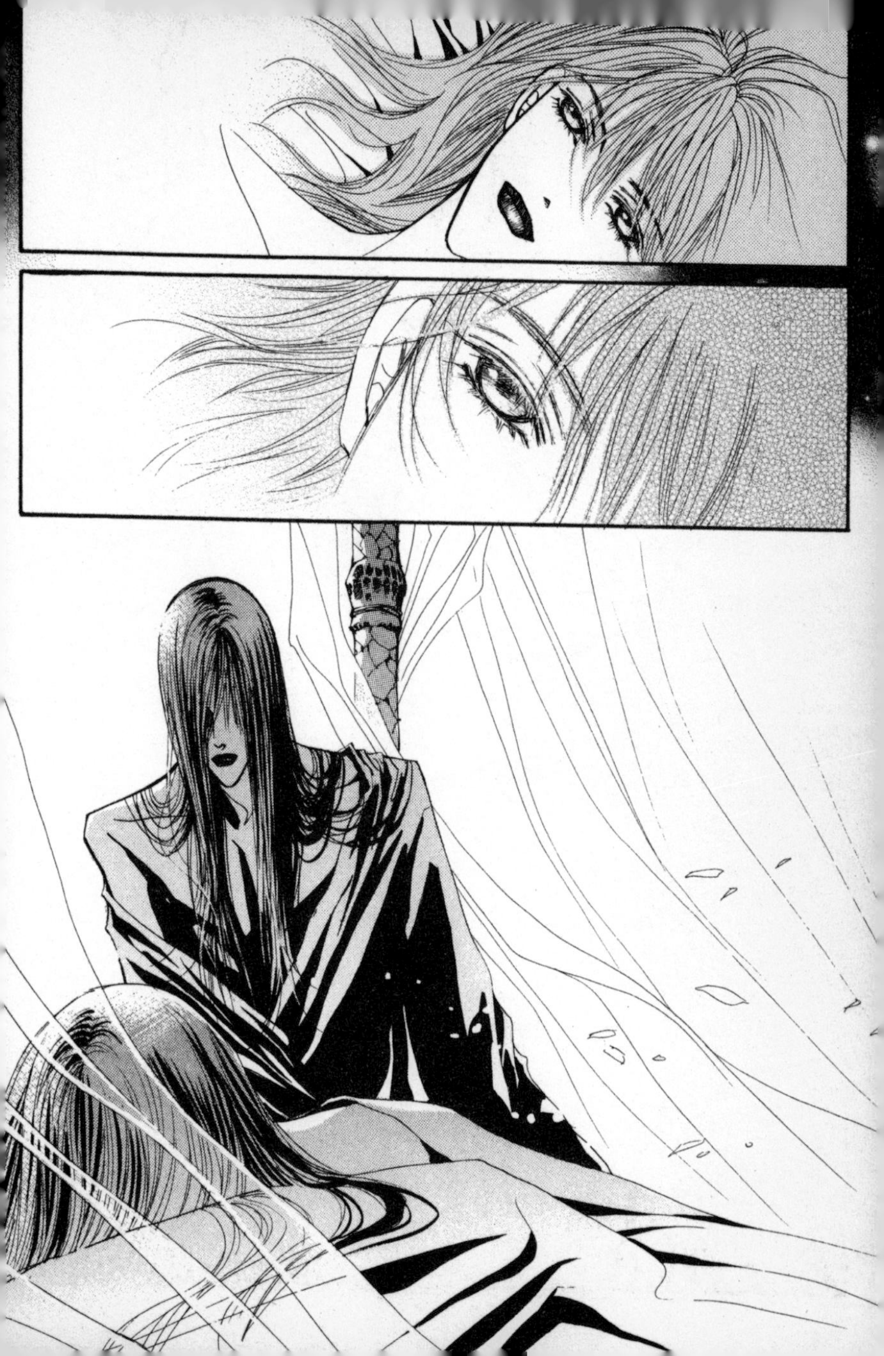

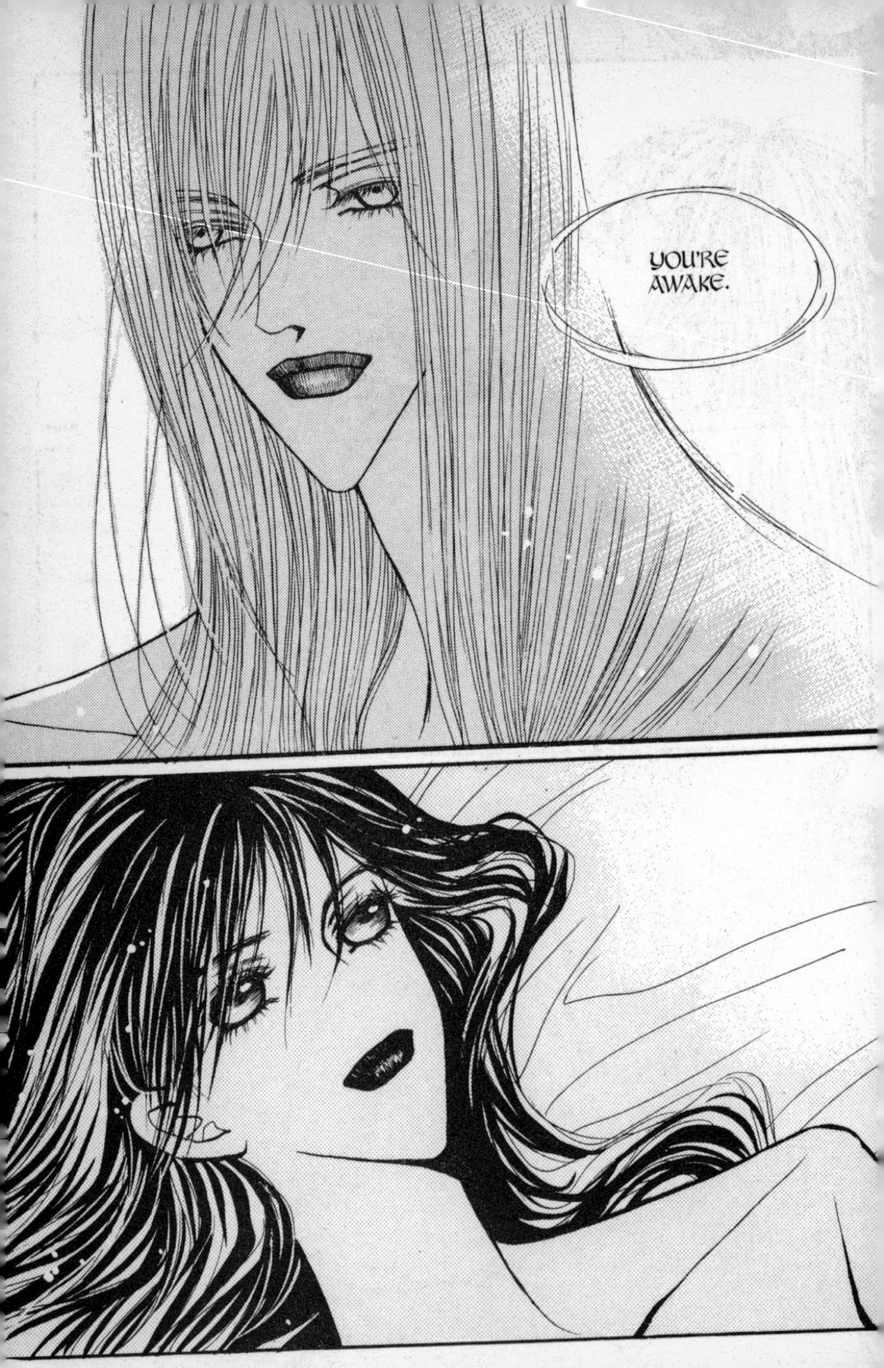
YOU'RE AWAKE.

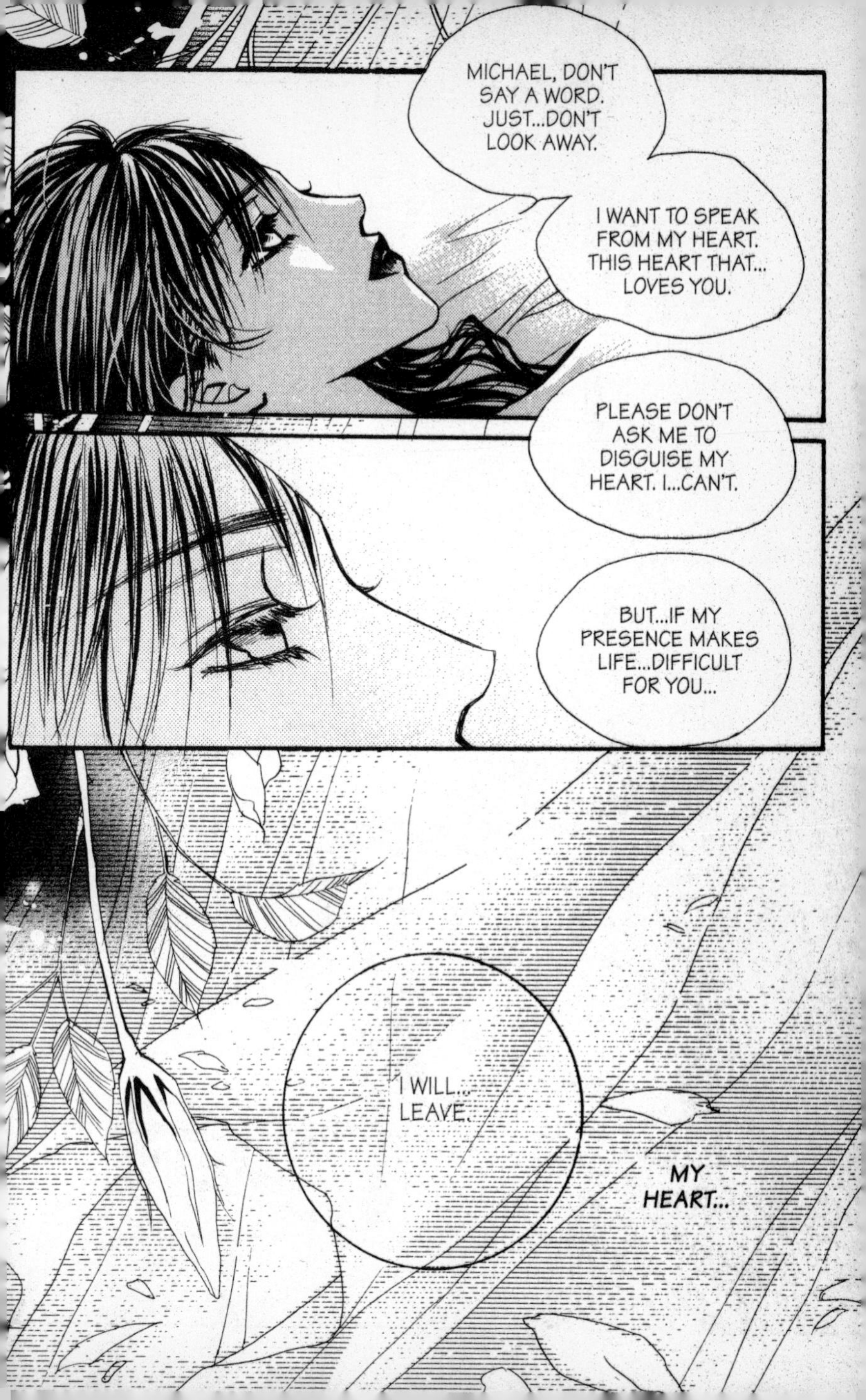
MICHAEL, DON'T SAY A WORD. JUST...DON'T LOOK AWAY.
I WANT TO SPEAK FROM MY HEART. THIS HEART THAT... LOVES YOU.
PLEASE DON'T ASK ME TO DISGUISE MY HEART. I...CAN'T.
BUT...IF MY PRESENCE MAKES LIFE...DIFFICULT FOR YOU...
I WILL... LEAVE.
MY HEART...

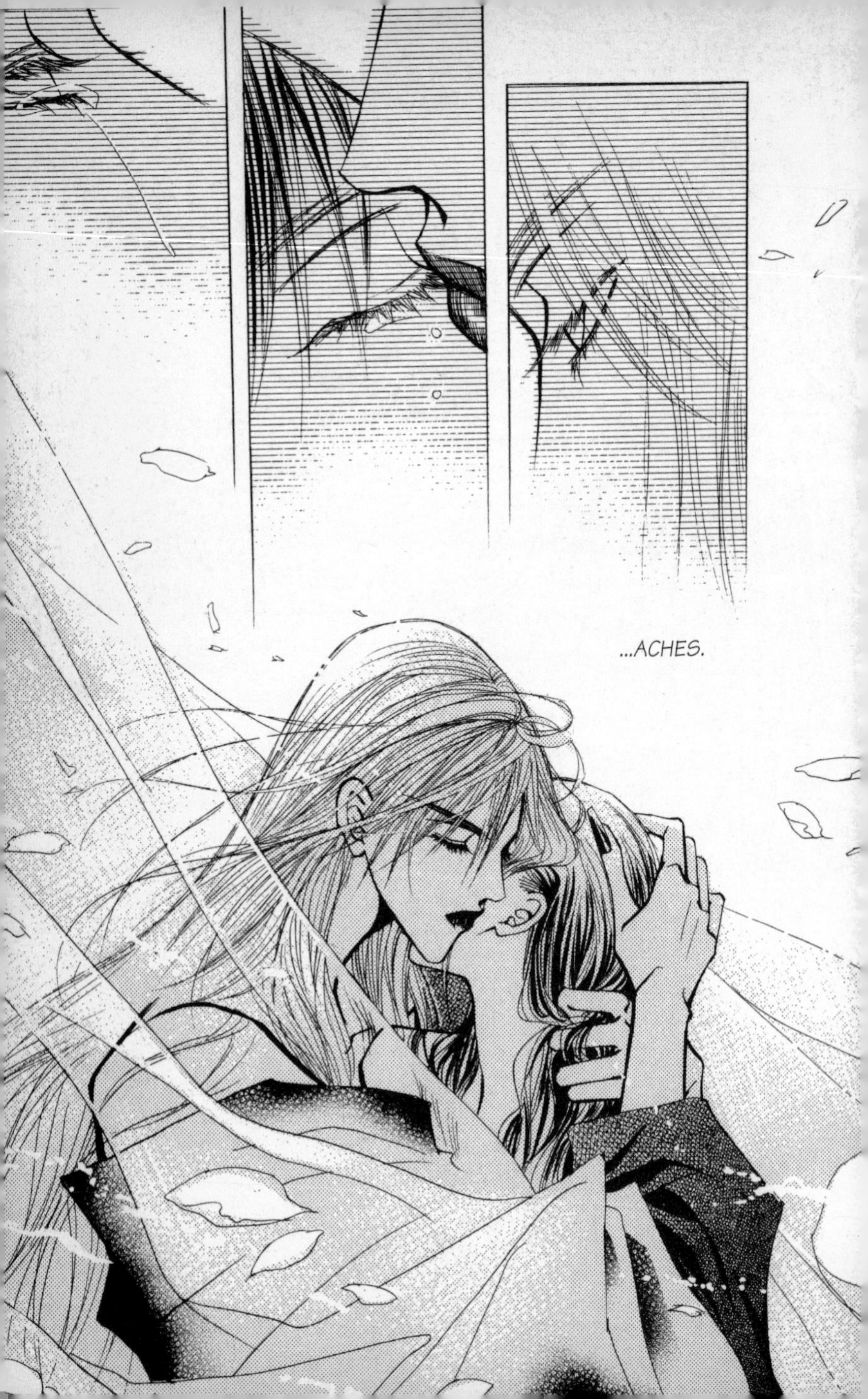
...ACHES.

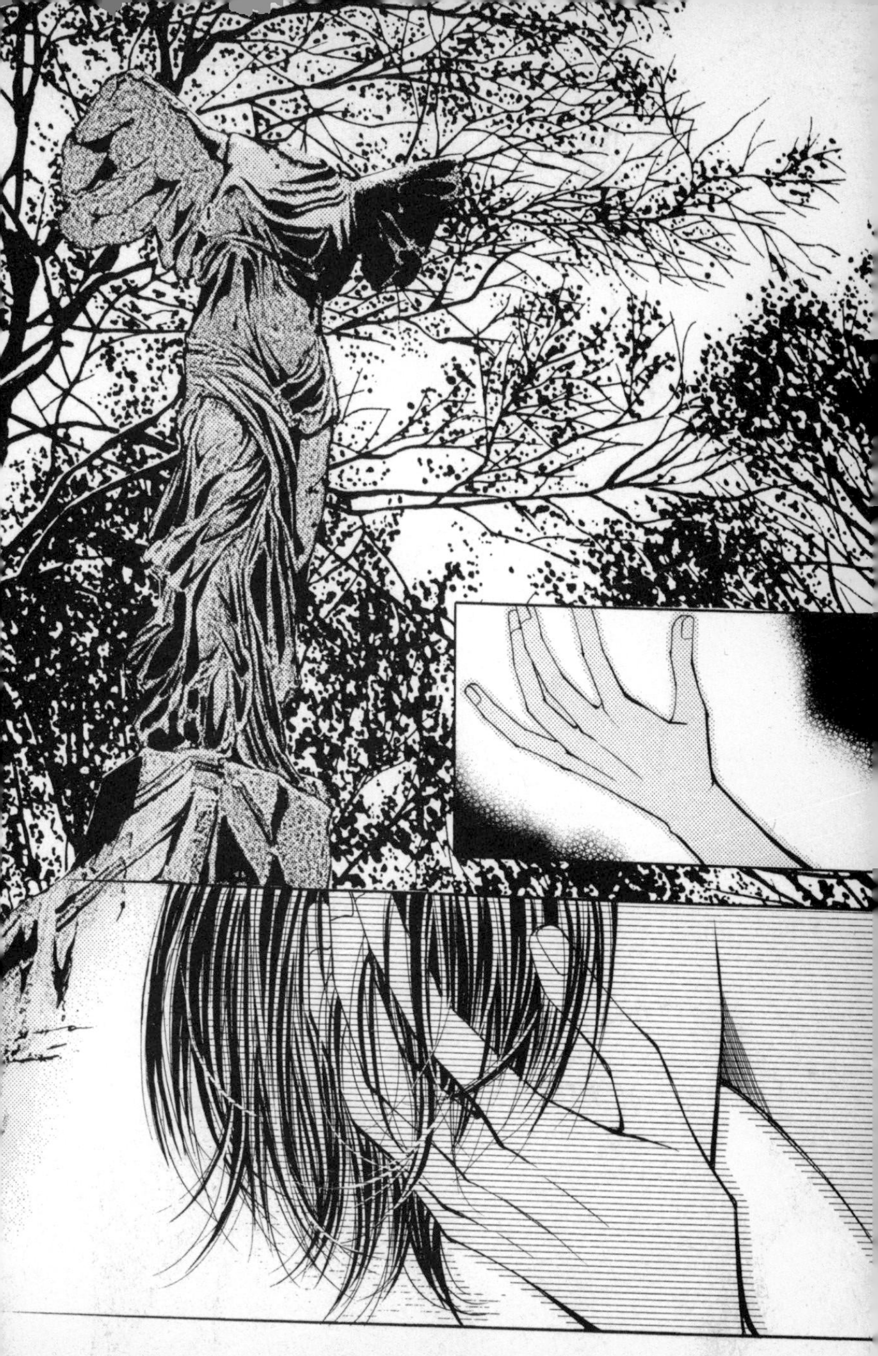

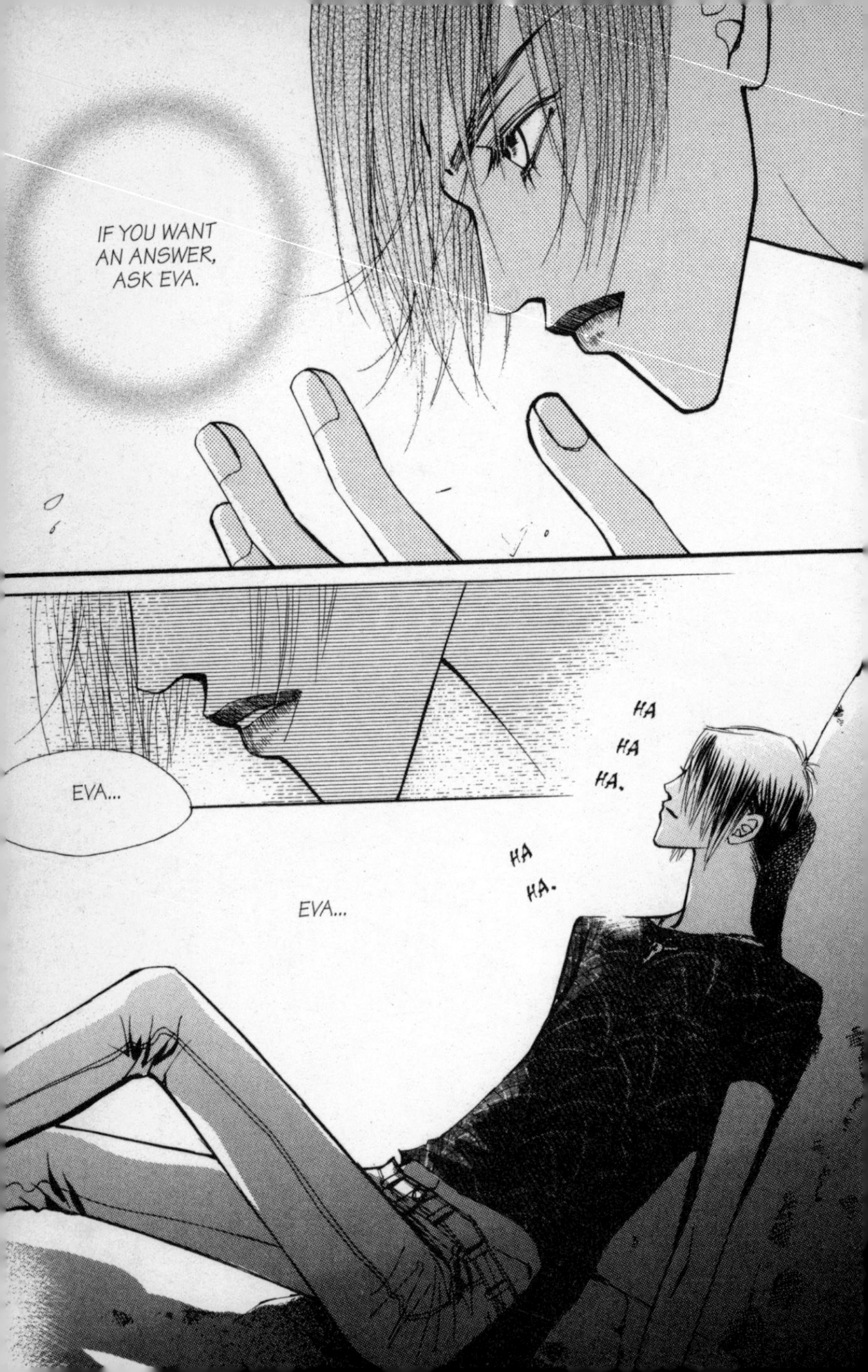
IF YOU WANT AN ANSWER, ASK EVA.
EVA...
HA HA HA.
HA HA.
EVA...

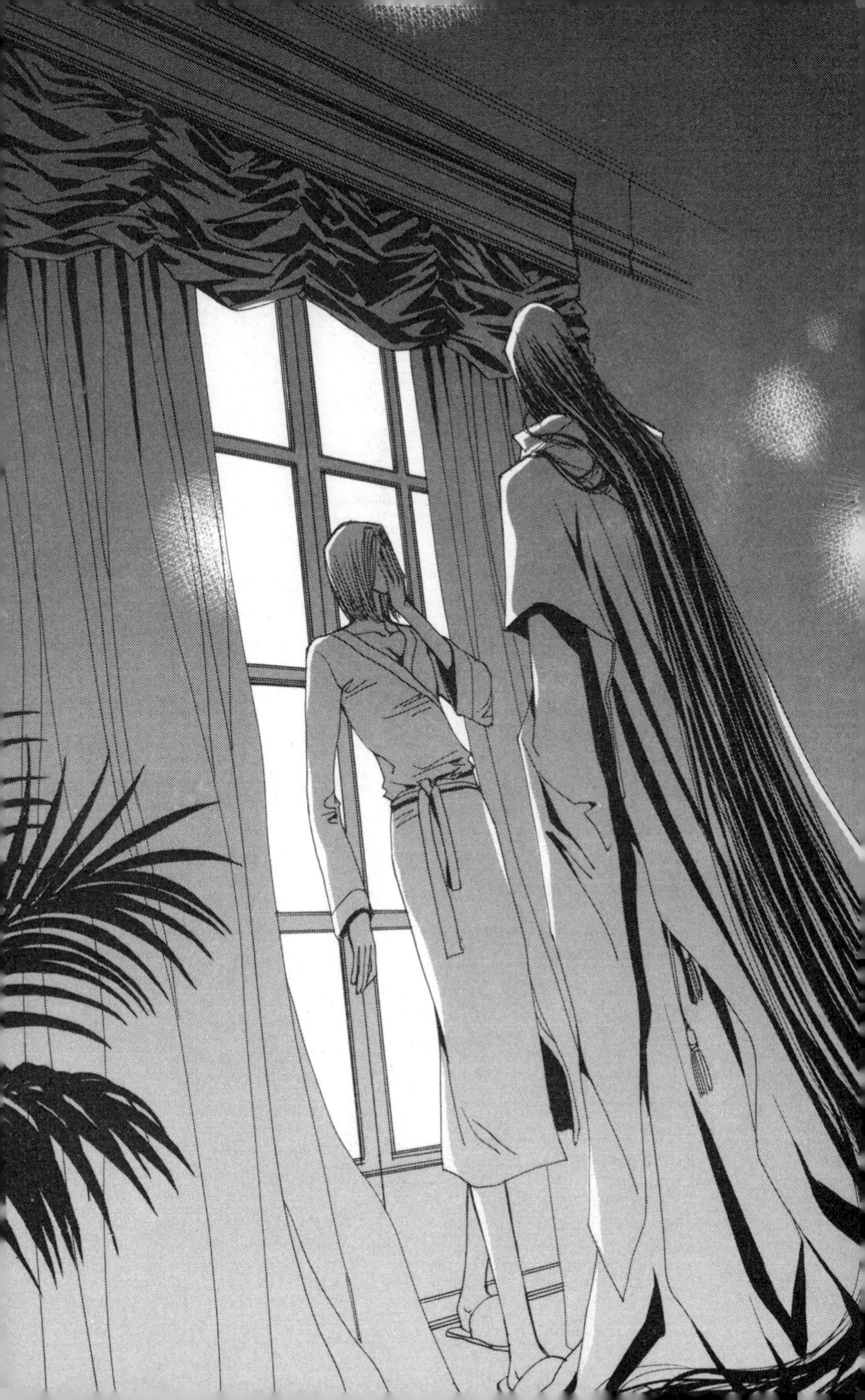

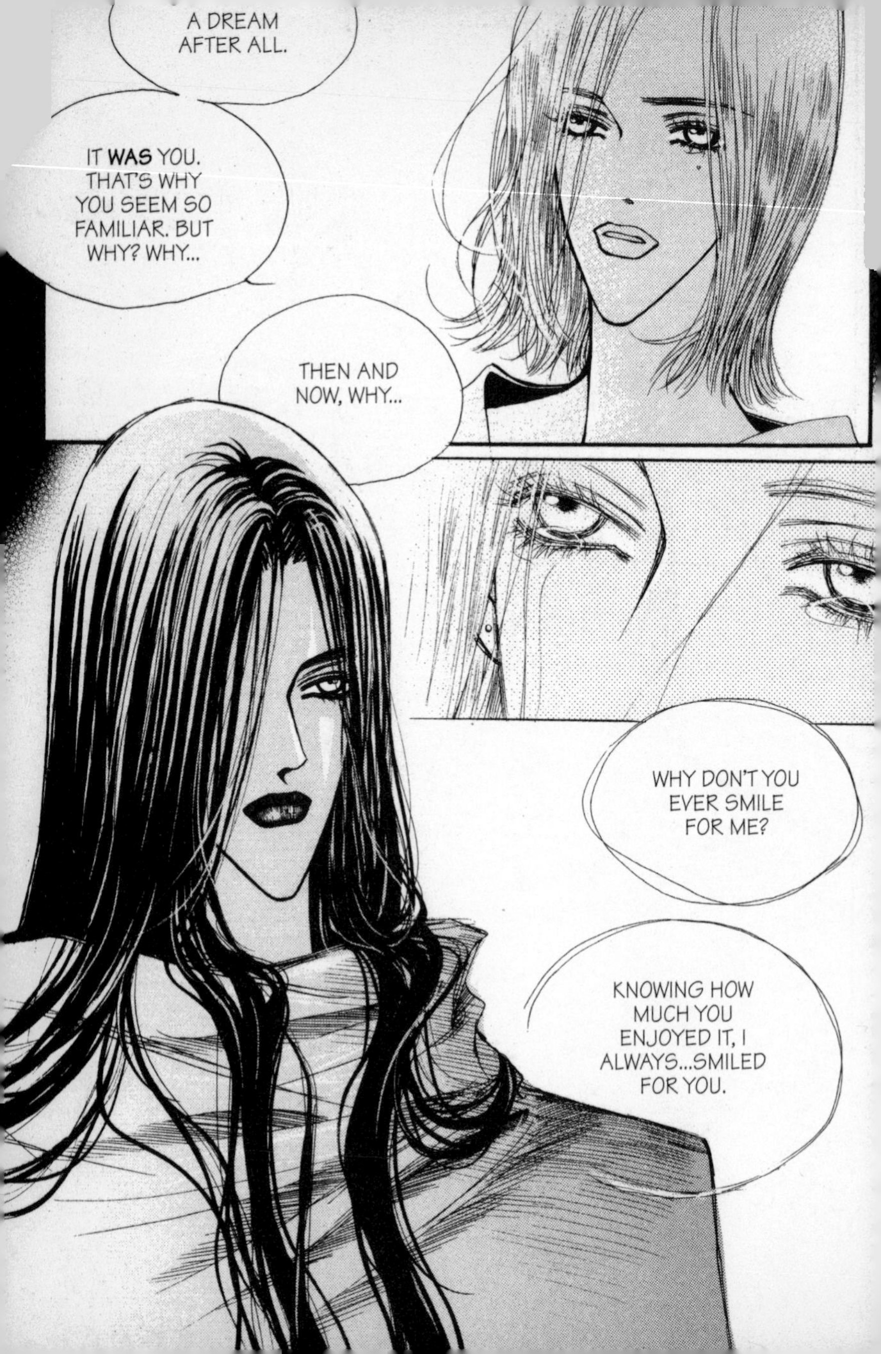
A DREAM AFTER ALL.
IT WAS YOU. THAT'S WHY YOU SEEM SO FAMILIAR. BUT WHY? WHY...
THEN AND NOW, WHY...
WHY DON'T YOU EVER SMILE FOR ME?
KNOWING HOW MUCH YOU ENJOYED IT, I ALWAYS...SMILED FOR YOU.

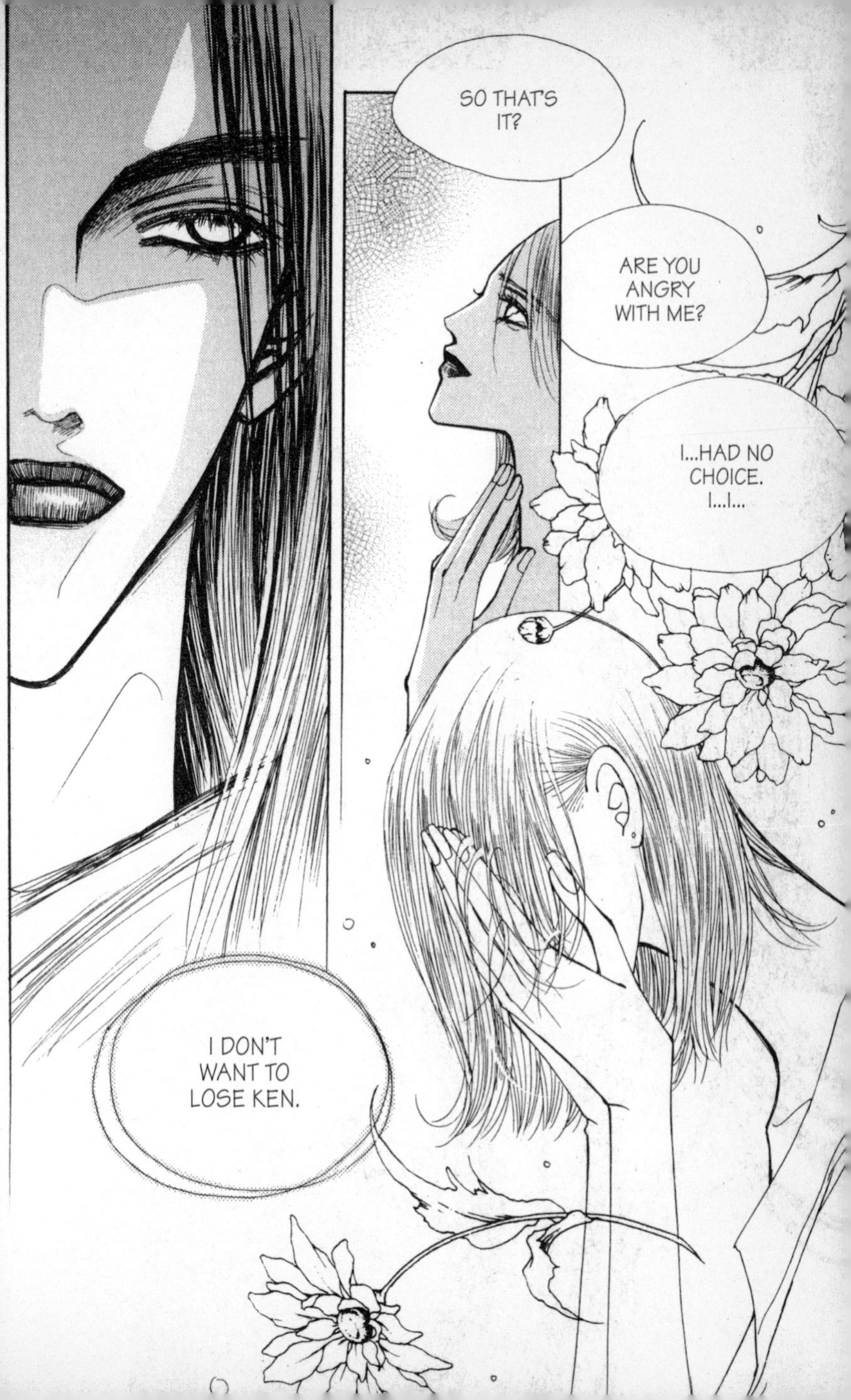
SO THAT'S IT?
ARE YOU ANGRY WITH ME?
I...HAD NO CHOICE. I...I...
I DON'T WANT TO LOSE KEN.

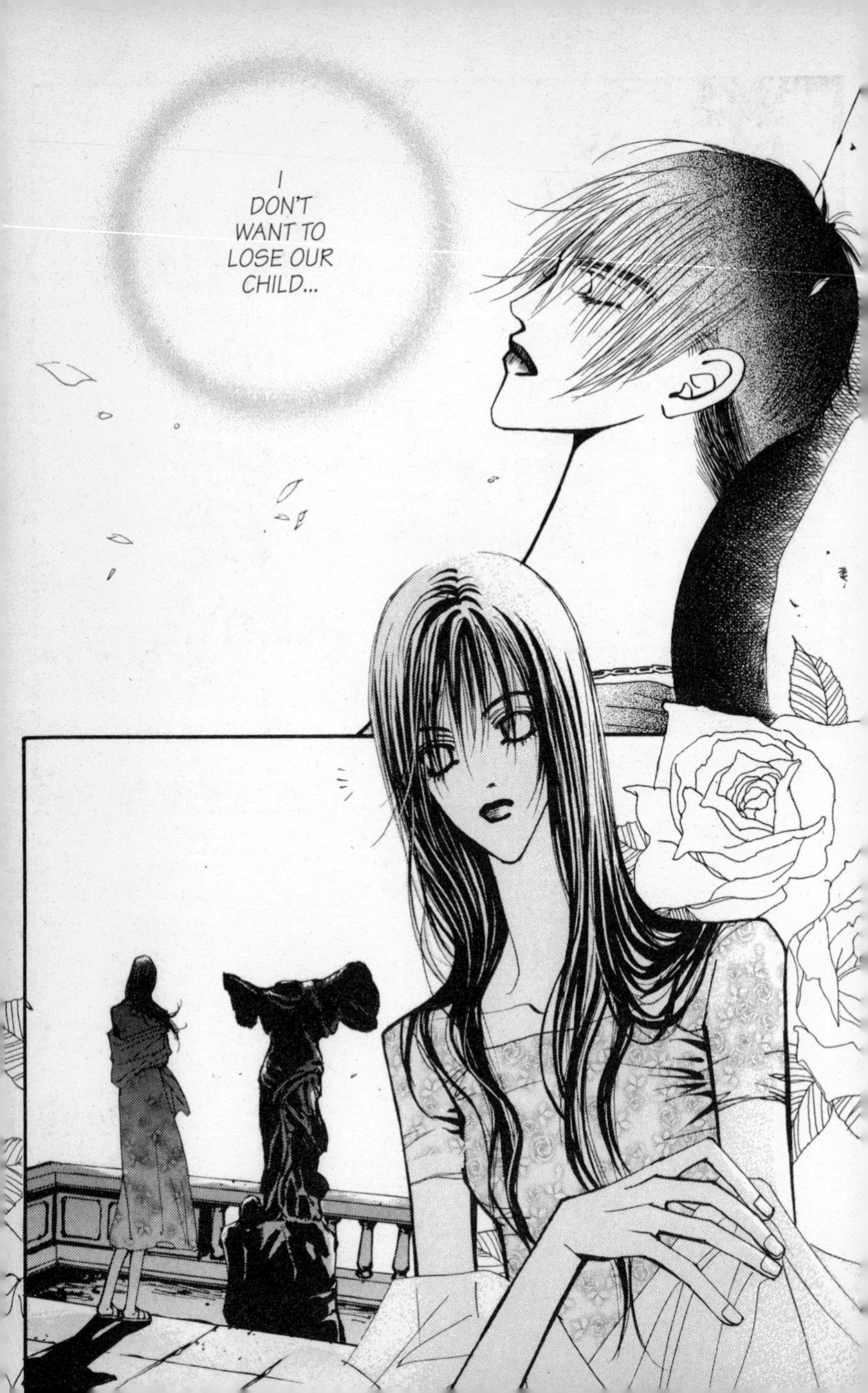
I DON'T WANT TO LOSE OUR CHILD...

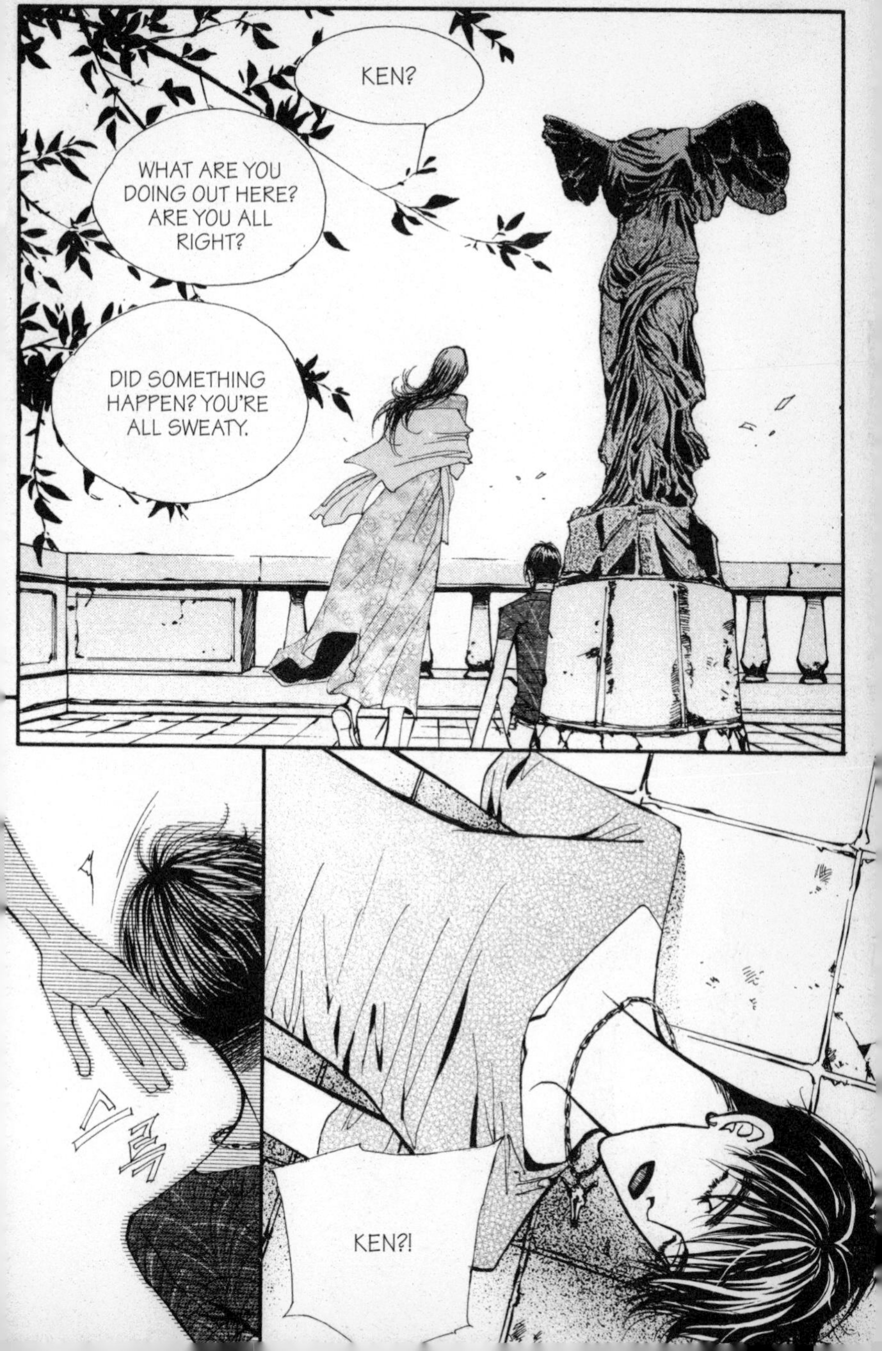
KEN?
WHAT ARE YOU DOING OUT HERE? ARE YOU ALL RIGHT?
DID SOMETHING HAPPEN? YOU'RE ALL SWEATY.
KEN?!

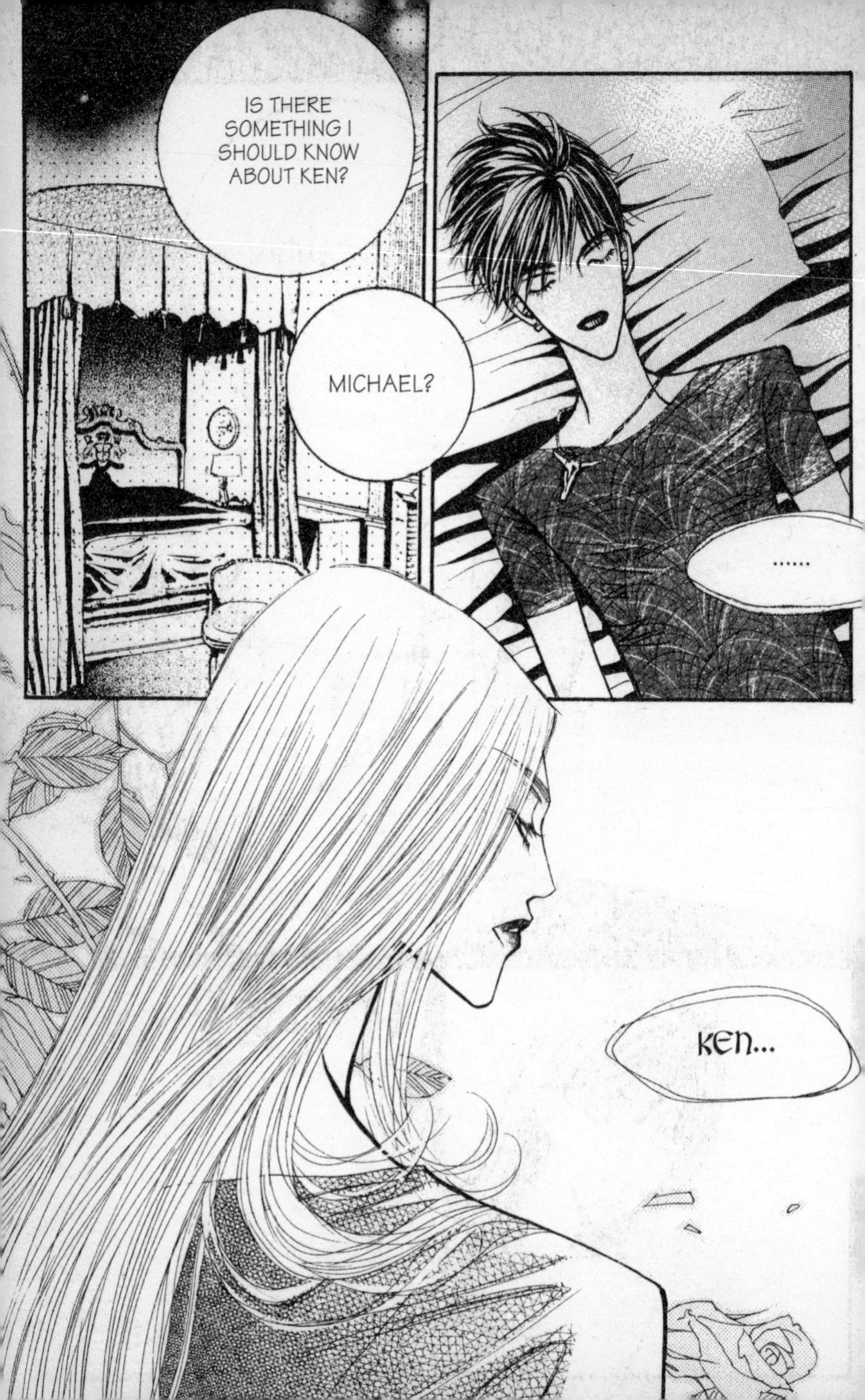
IS THERE SOMETHING I SHOULD KNOW ABOUT KEN?
MICHAEL?
......
KEN...

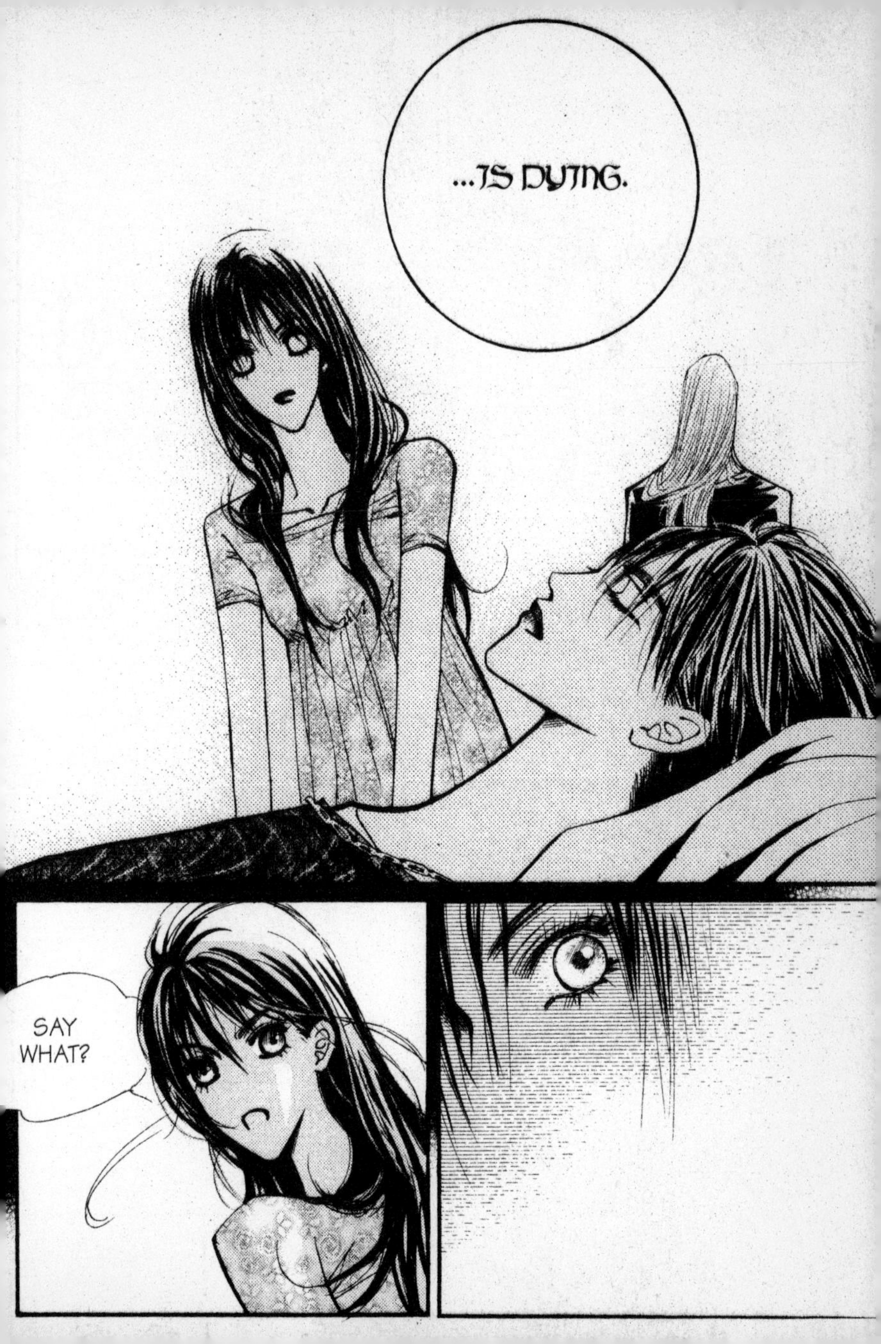
...IS DYING.
SAY WHAT?

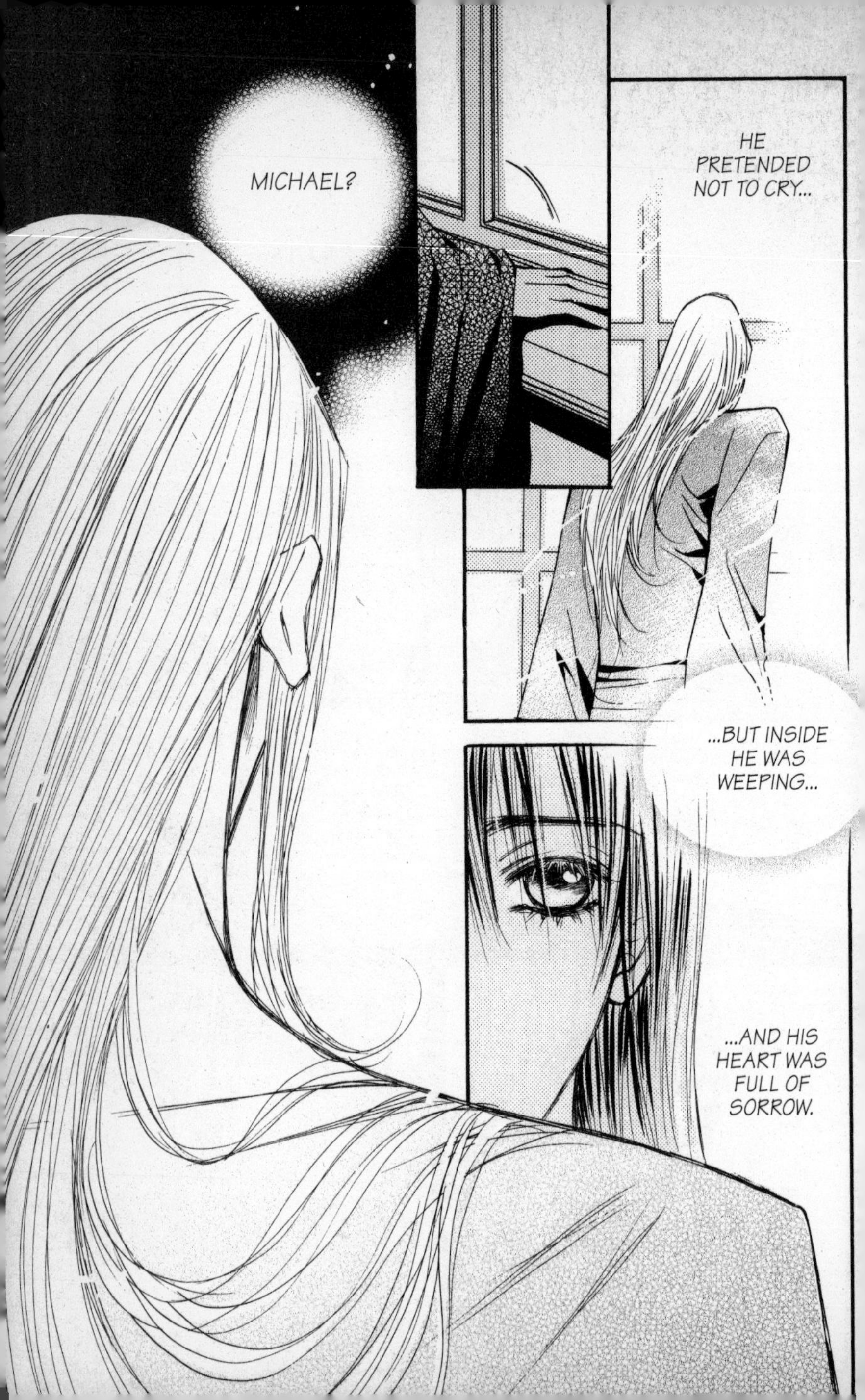
HE PRETENDED NOT TO CRY...
...BUT INSIDE HE WAS WEEPING...
...AND HIS HEART WAS FULL OF SORROW.
MICHAEL?

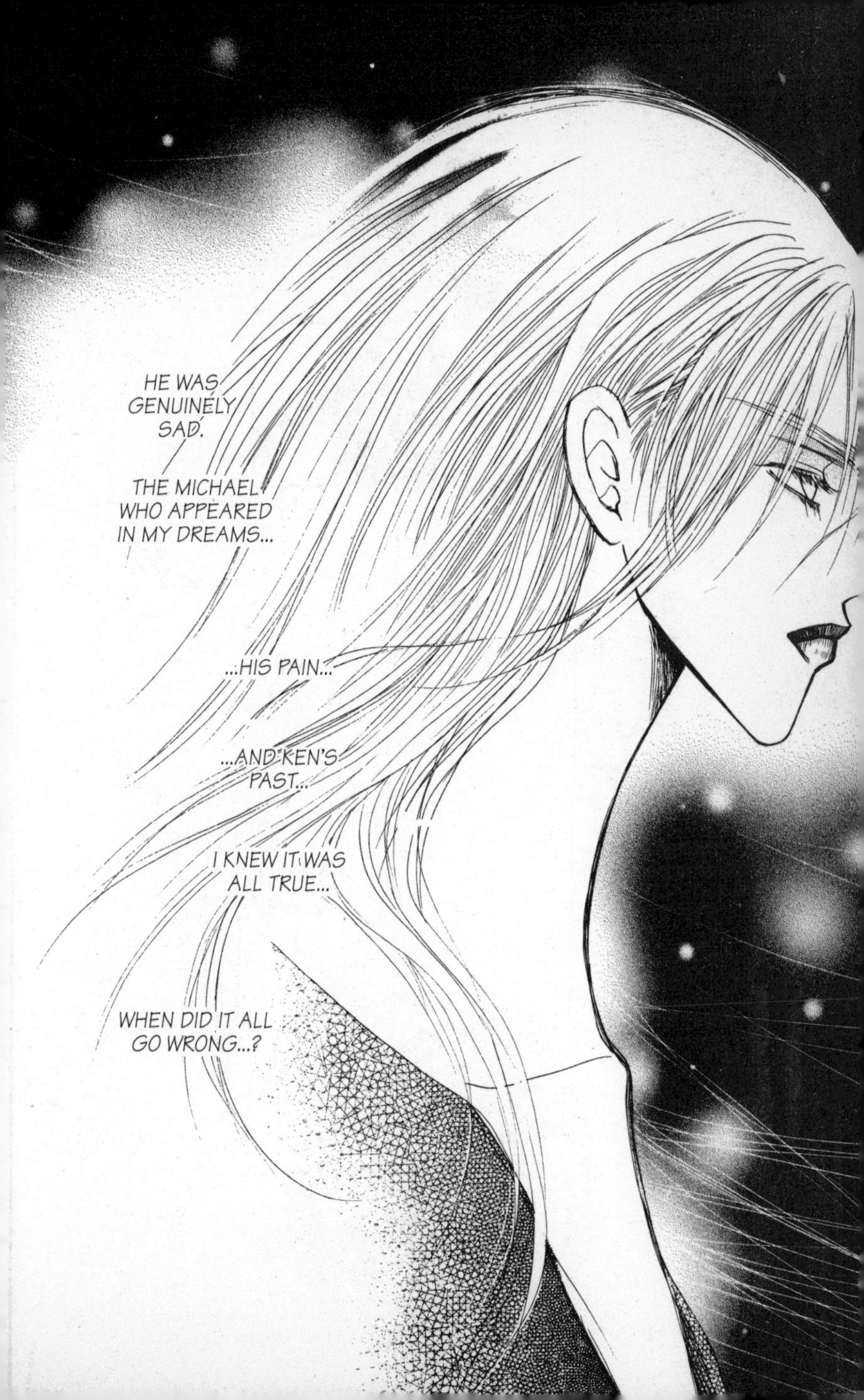
HE WAS GENUINELY SAD.
THE MICHAEL WHO APPEARED IN MY DREAMS...
...HIS PAIN...
...AND KEN'S PAST...
I KNEW IT WAS ALL TRUE...
WHEN DID IT ALL GO WRONG...?

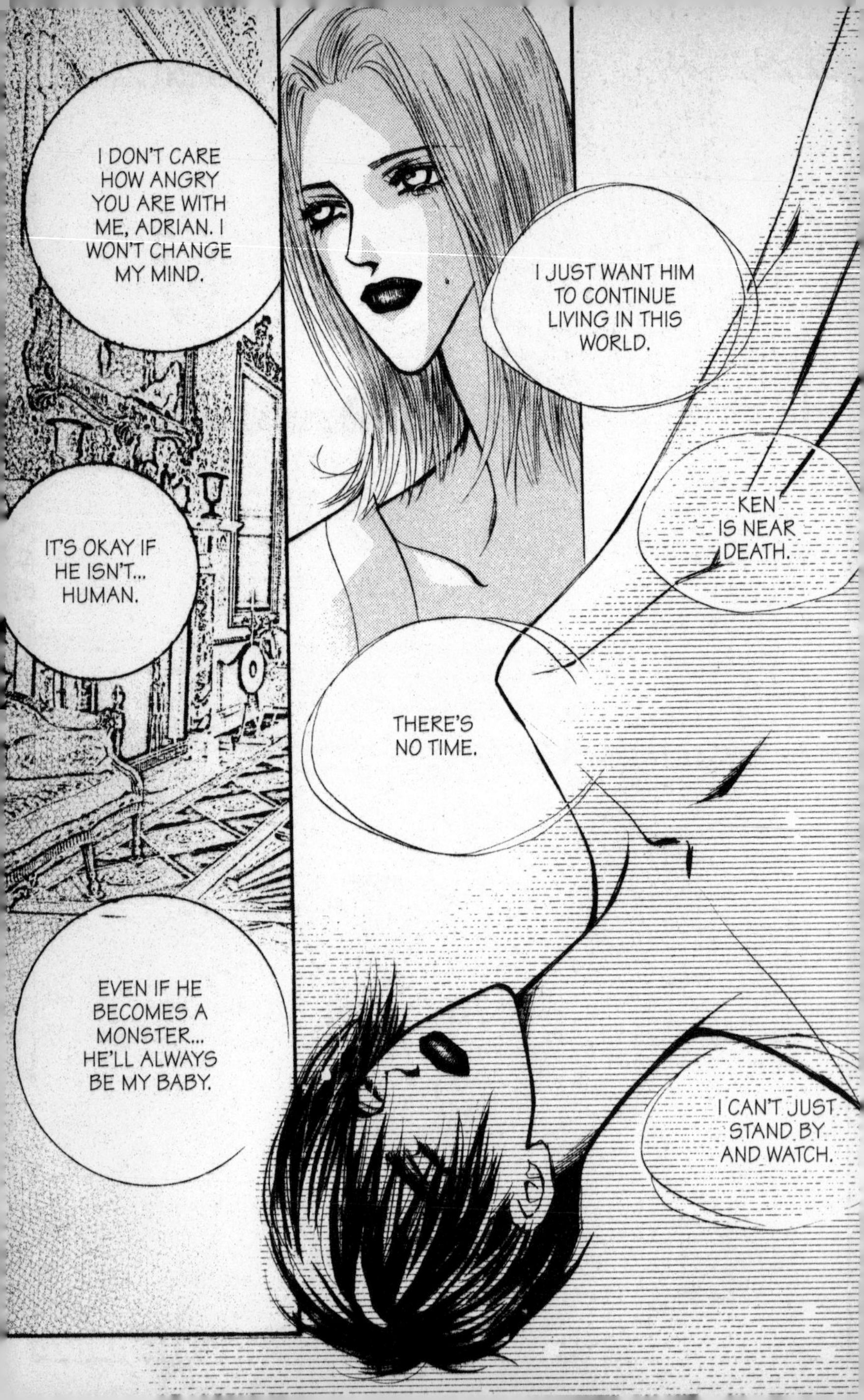
I JUST WANT HIM TO CONTINUE LIVING IN THIS WORLD.
KEN IS NEAR DEATH.
THERE'S NO TIME.
I CAN'T JUST STAND BY AND WATCH.
I DON'T CARE HOW ANGRY YOU ARE WITH ME, ADRIAN. I WON'T CHANGE MY MIND.
IT'S OKAY IF HE ISN'T... HUMAN.
EVEN IF HE BECOMES A MONSTER... HE'LL ALWAYS BE MY BABY.

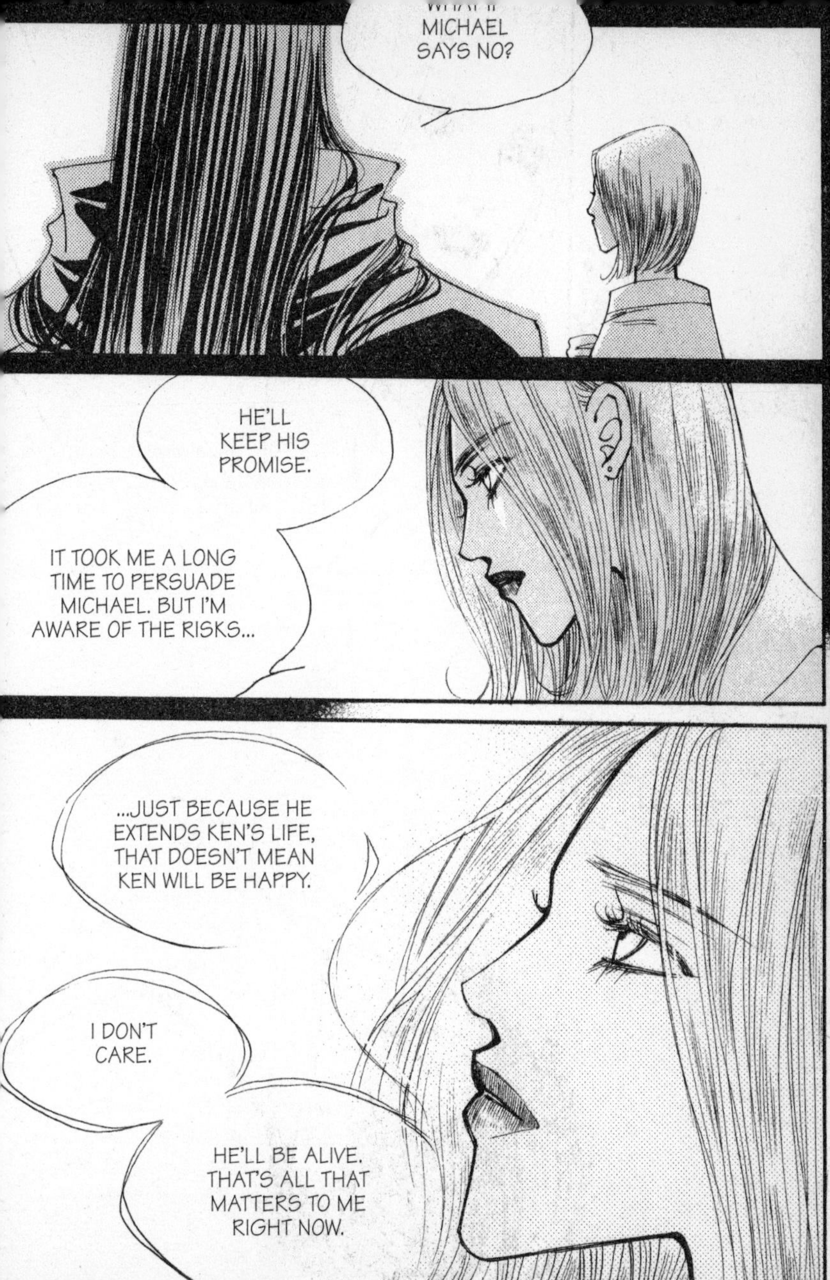
MICHAEL SAYS NO?
HE'LL KEEP HIS PROMISE.
IT TOOK ME A LONG TIME TO PERSUADE MICHAEL. BUT I'M AWARE OF THE RISKS...
...JUST BECAUSE HE EXTENDS KEN'S LIFE, THAT DOESN'T MEAN KEN WILL BE HAPPY.
I DON'T CARE.
HE'LL BE ALIVE. THAT'S ALL THAT MATTERS TO ME RIGHT NOW.

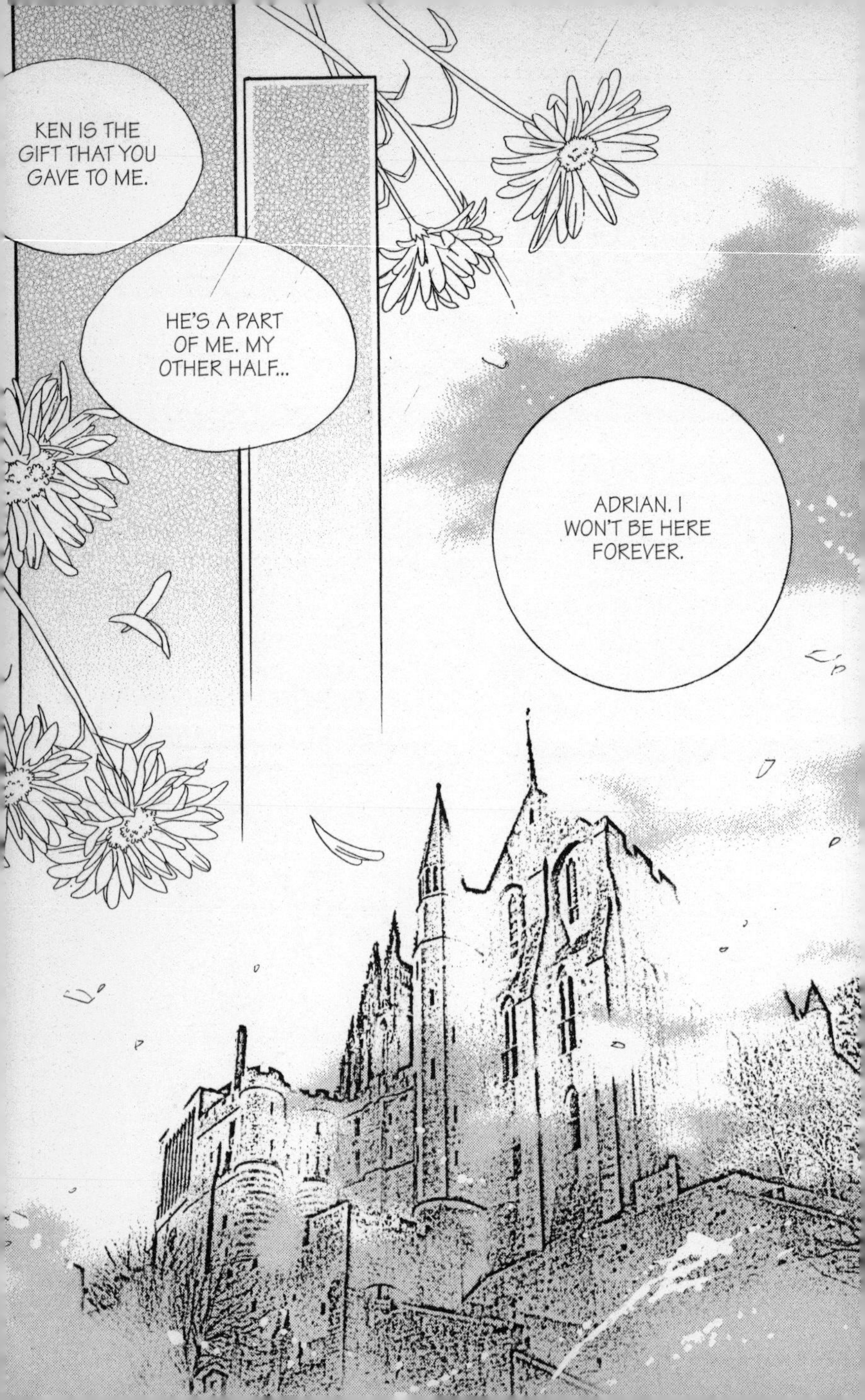
ADRIAN. I WON'T BE HERE FOREVER.
KEN IS THE GIFT THAT YOU GAVE TO ME.
HE'S A PART OF ME. MY OTHER HALF...

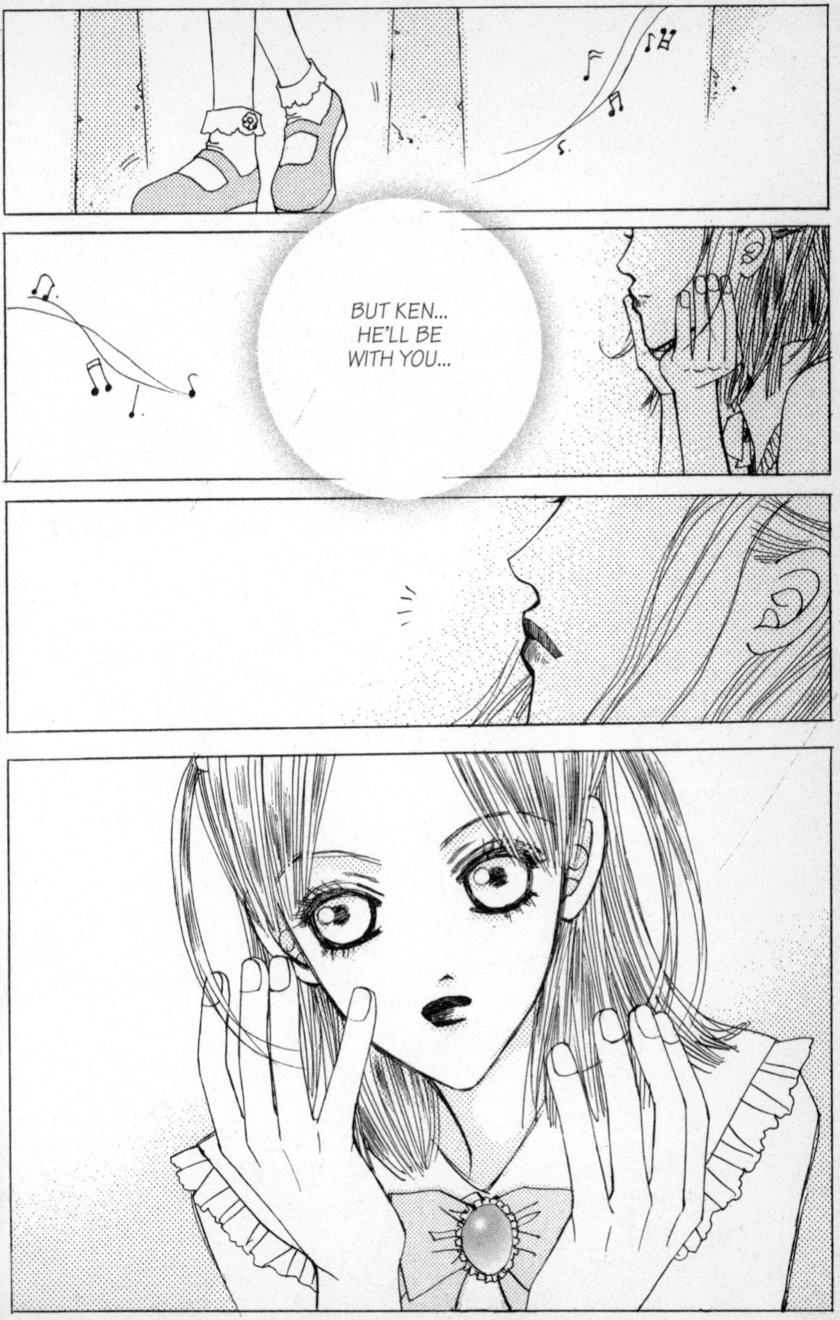
BUT KEN... HE'LL BE WITH YOU...

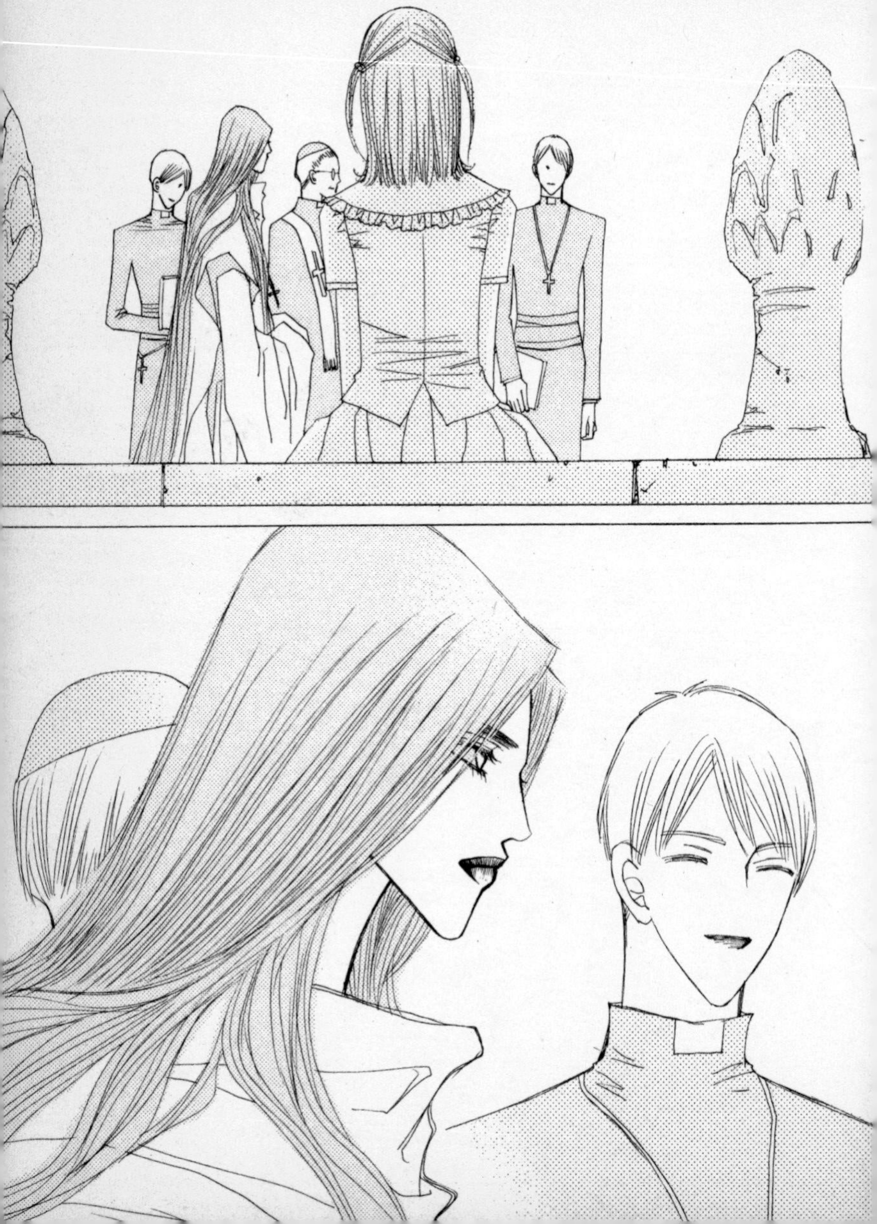

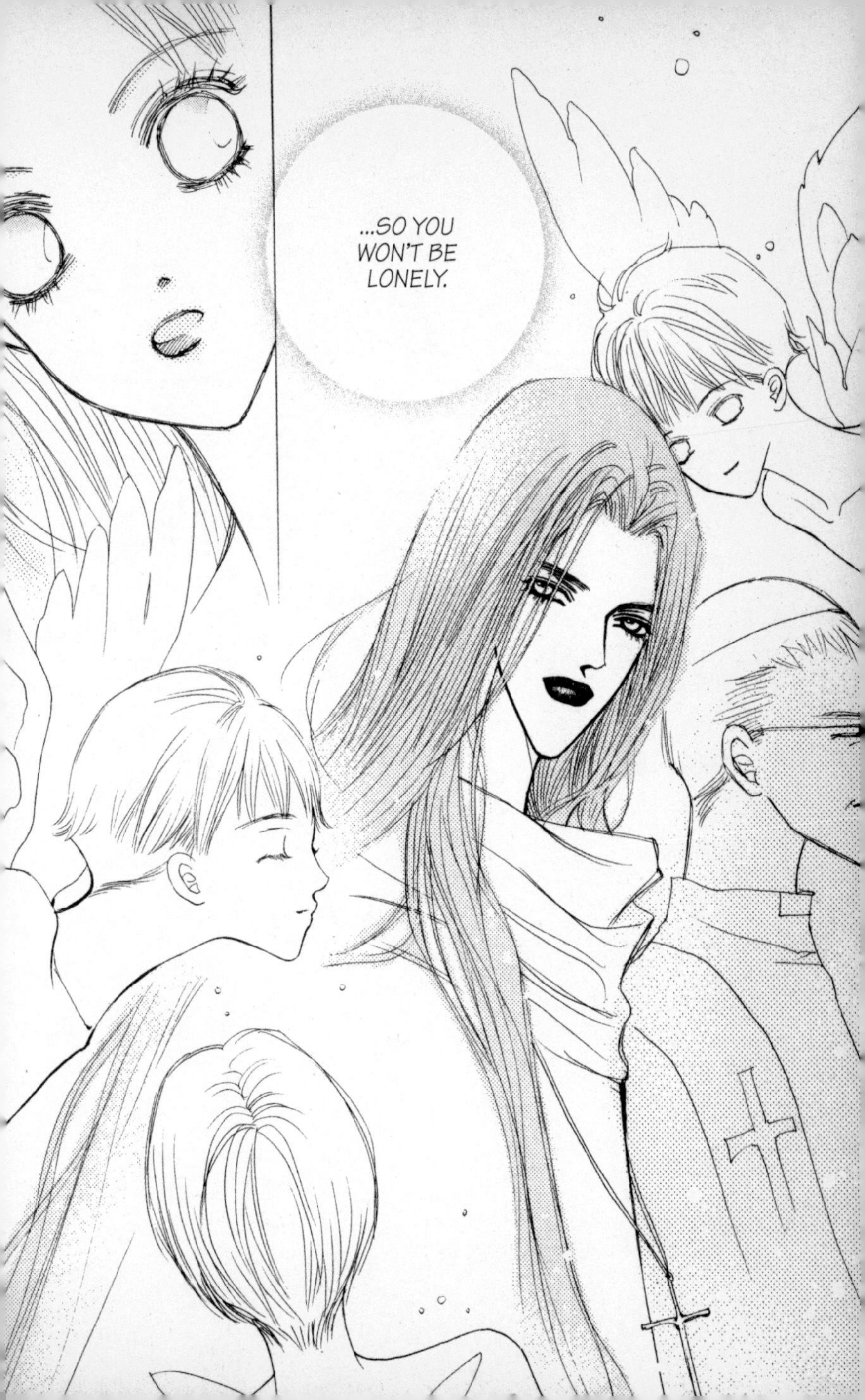
...SO YOU WON'T BE LONELY.

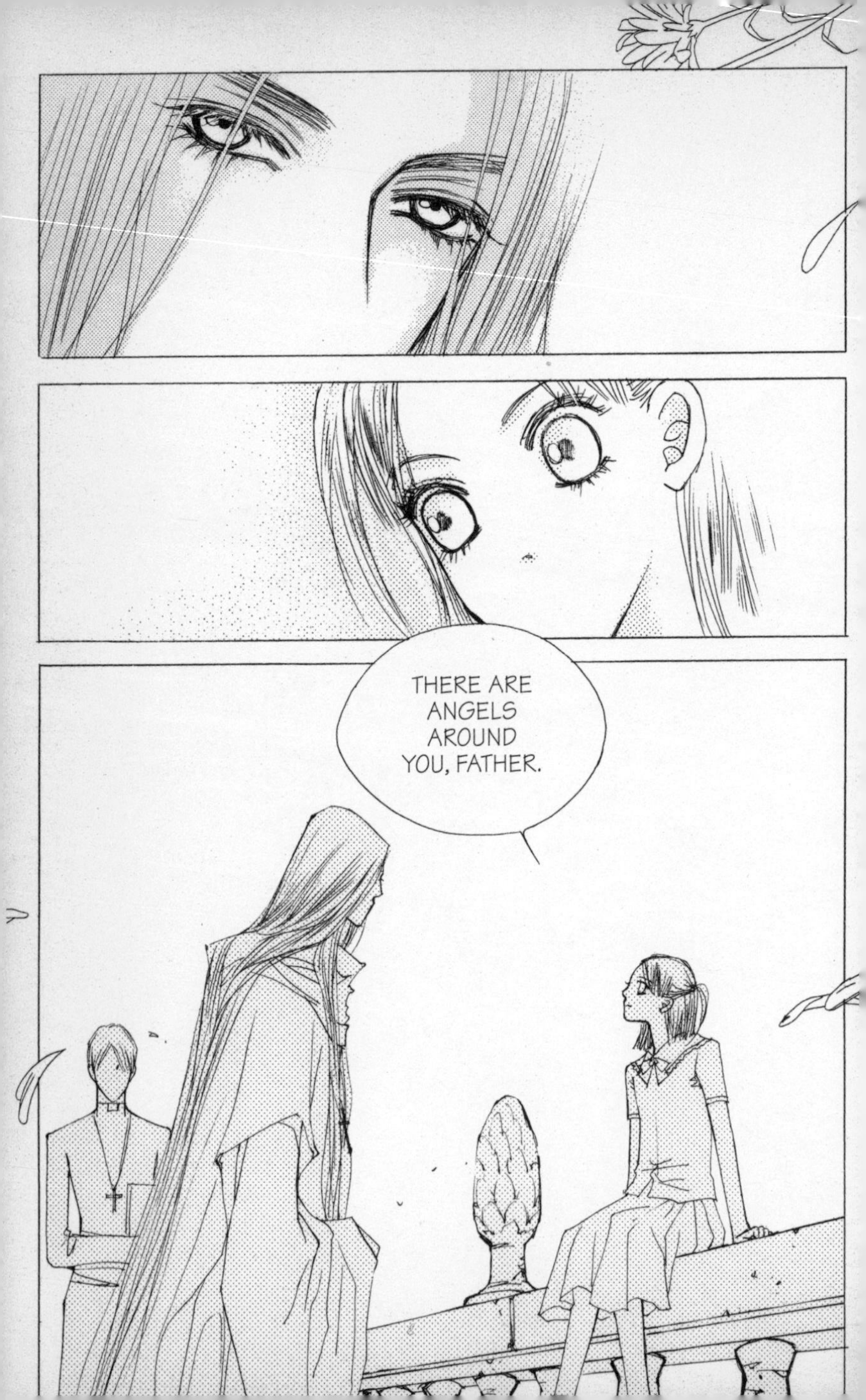
THERE ARE ANGELS AROUND YOU, FATHER.

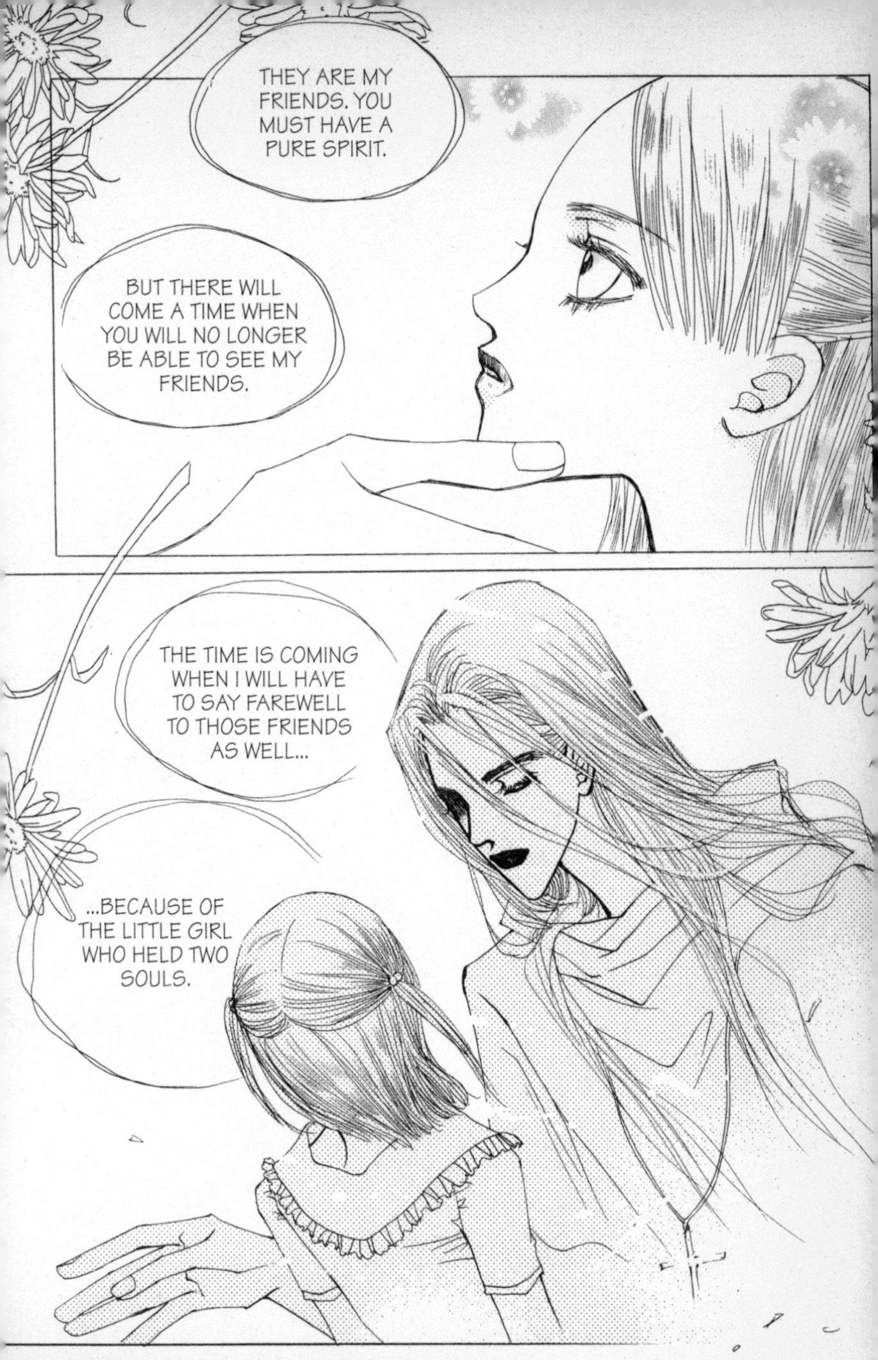
THEY ARE MY FRIENDS. YOU MUST HAVE A PURE SPIRIT.
BUT THERE WILL COME A TIME WHEN YOU WILL NO LONGER BE ABLE TO SEE MY FRIENDS.
THE TIME IS COMING WHEN I WILL HAVE TO SAY FAREWELL TO THOSE FRIENDS AS WELL...
...BECAUSE OF THE LITTLE GIRL WHO HELD TWO SOULS.

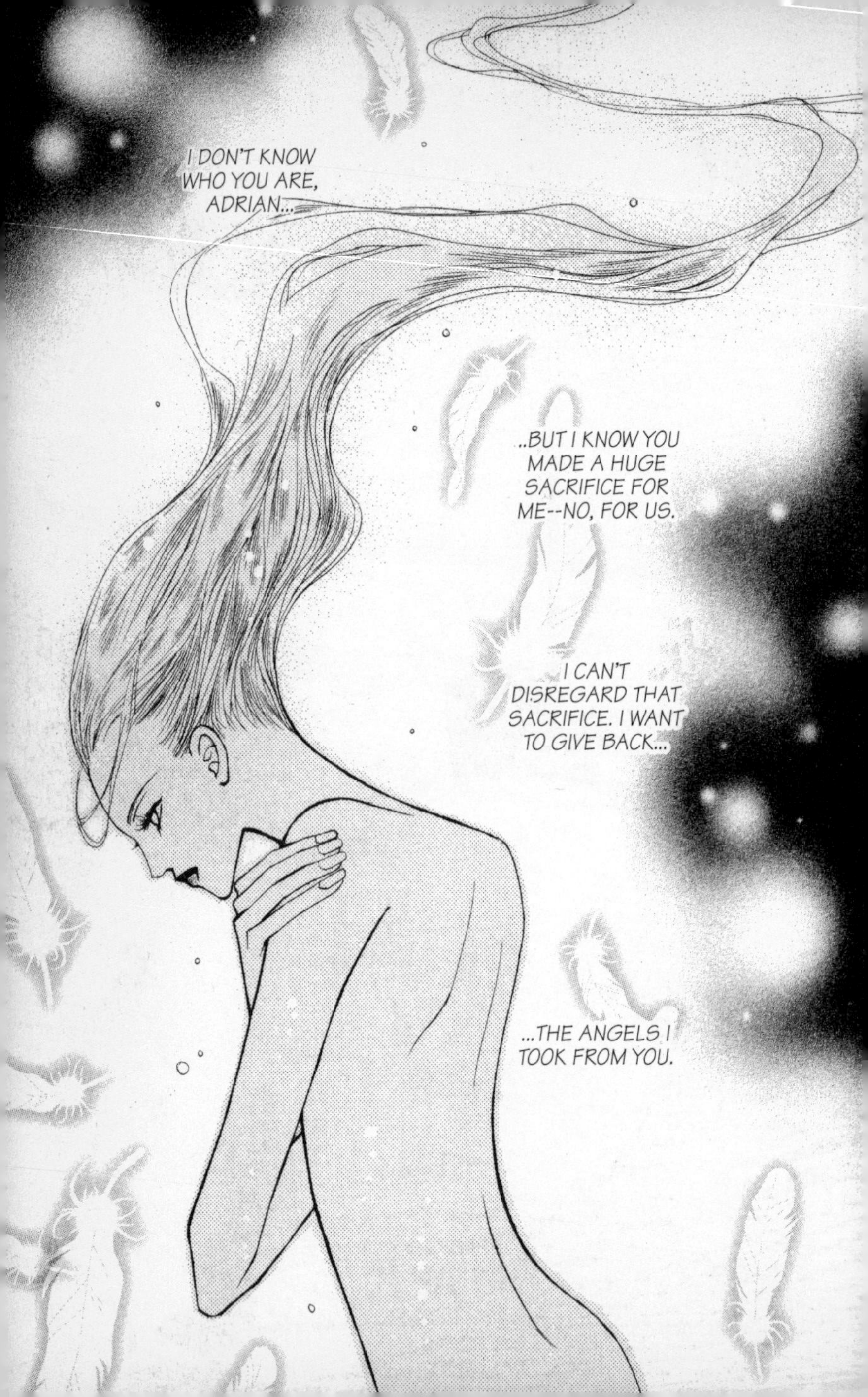
I DON'T KNOW WHO YOU ARE, ADRIAN...
...BUT I KNOW YOU MADE A HUGE SACRIFICE FOR ME--NO, FOR US.
I CAN'T DISREGARD THAT SACRIFICE. I WANT TO GIVE BACK...
...THE ANGELS I TOOK FROM YOU.

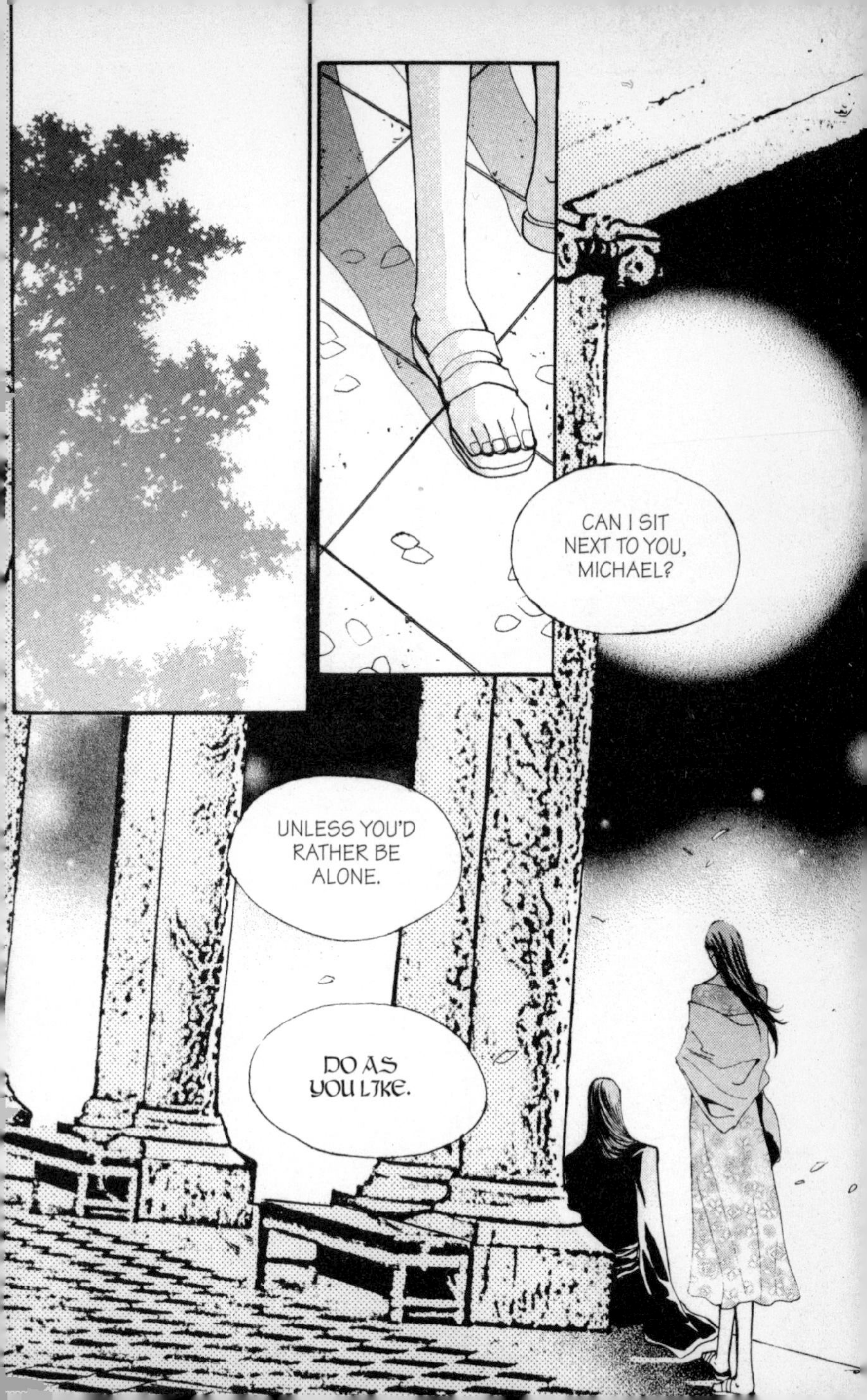
CAN I SIT NEXT TO YOU, MICHAEL?
UNLESS YOU'D RATHER BE ALONE.
DO AS YOU LIKE.

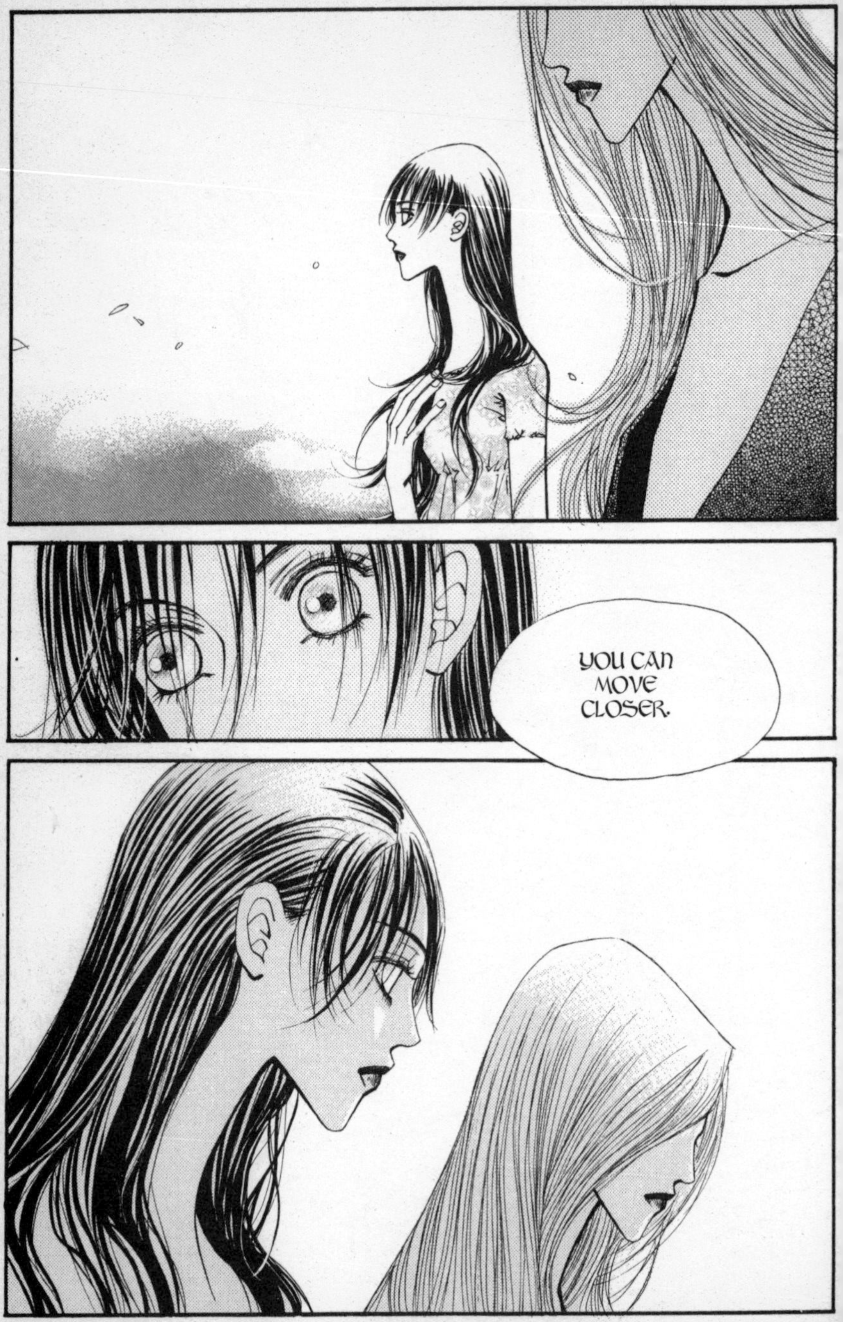
YOU CAN MOVE CLOSER.

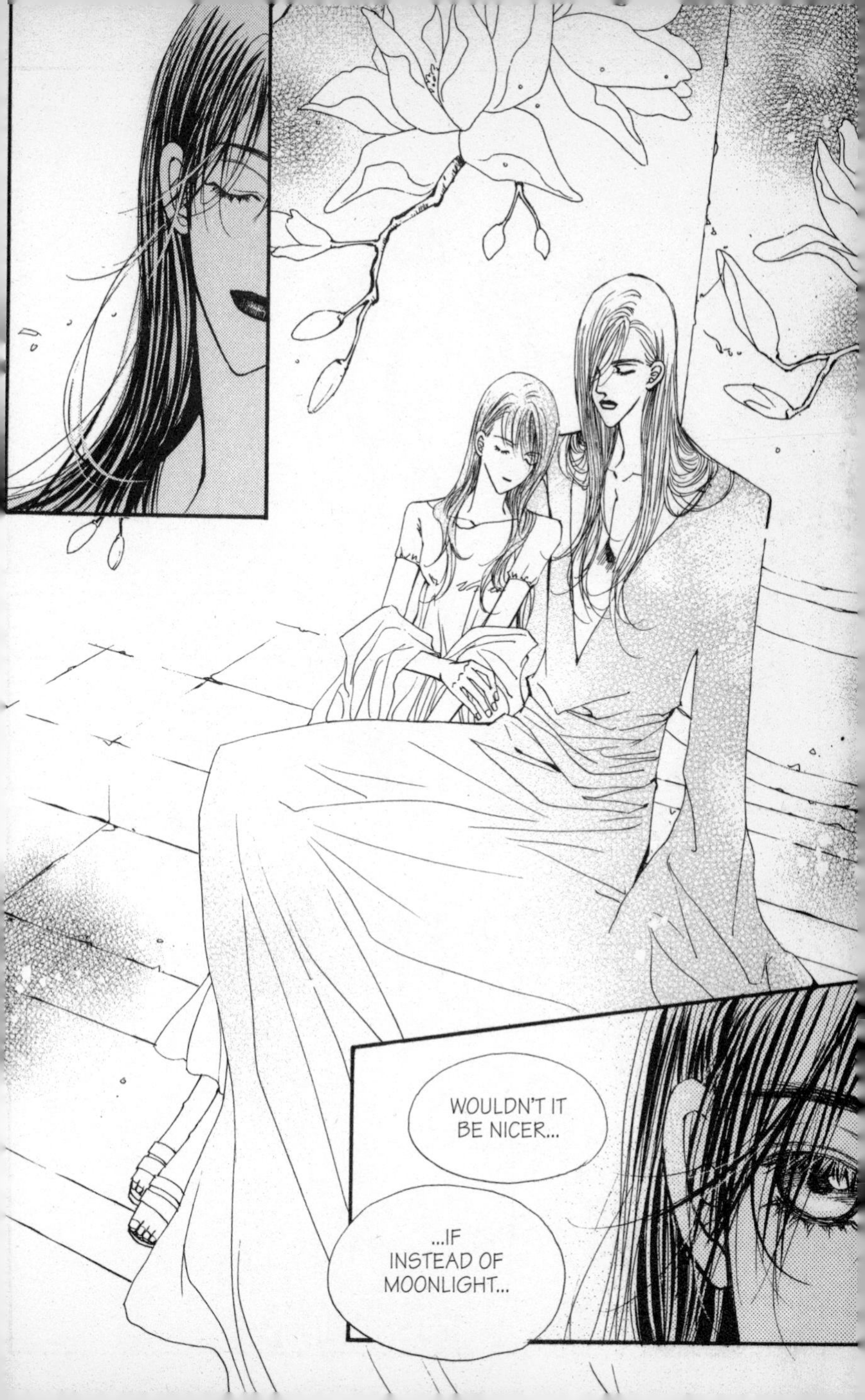
WOULDN'T IT BE NICER...
...IF INSTEAD OF MOONLIGHT...

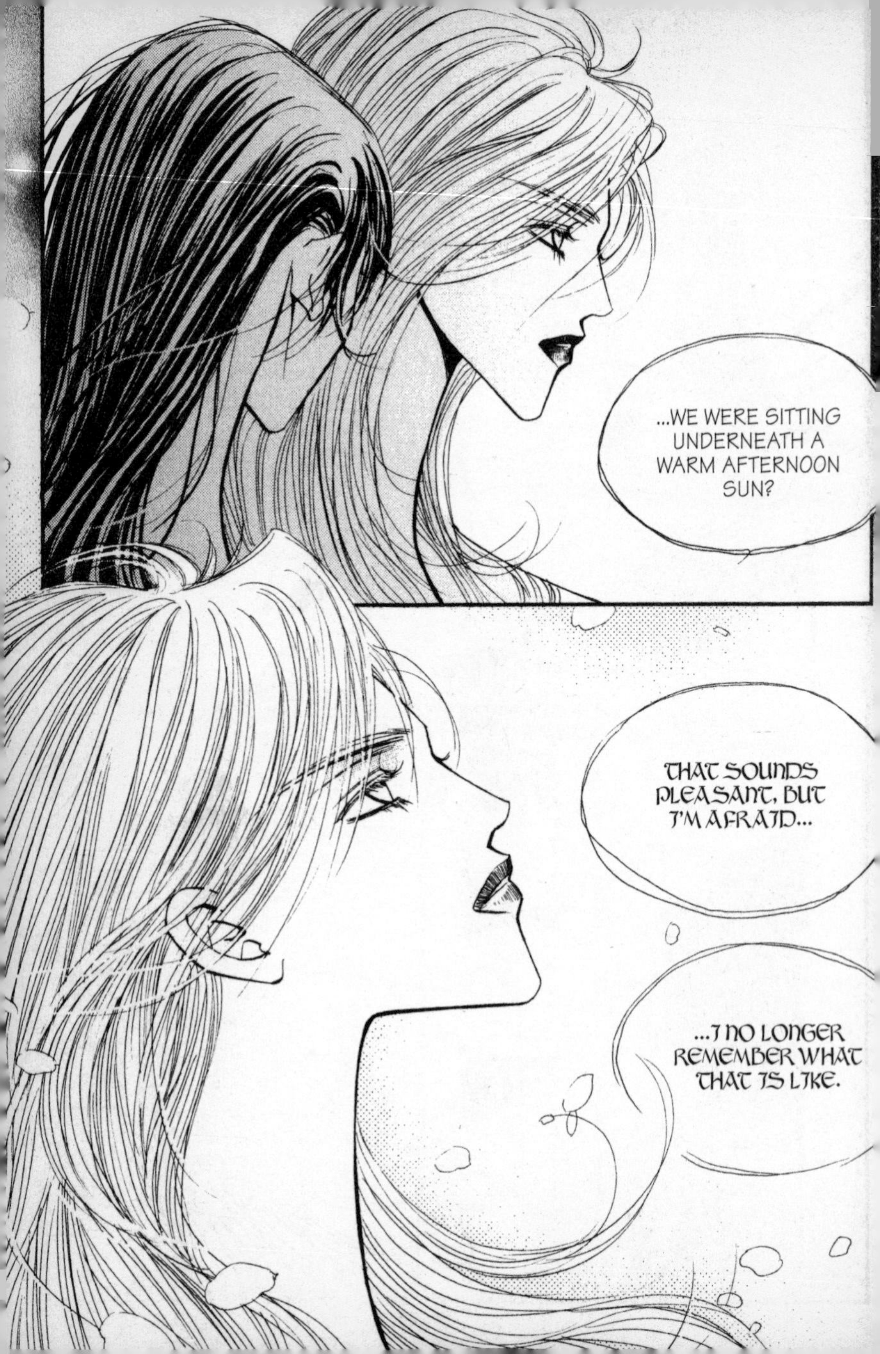
...WE WERE SITTING UNDERNEATH A WARM AFTERNOON SUN?
THAT SOUNDS PLEASANT, BUT I'M AFRAID...
...I NO LONGER REMEMBER WHAT THAT IS LIKE.

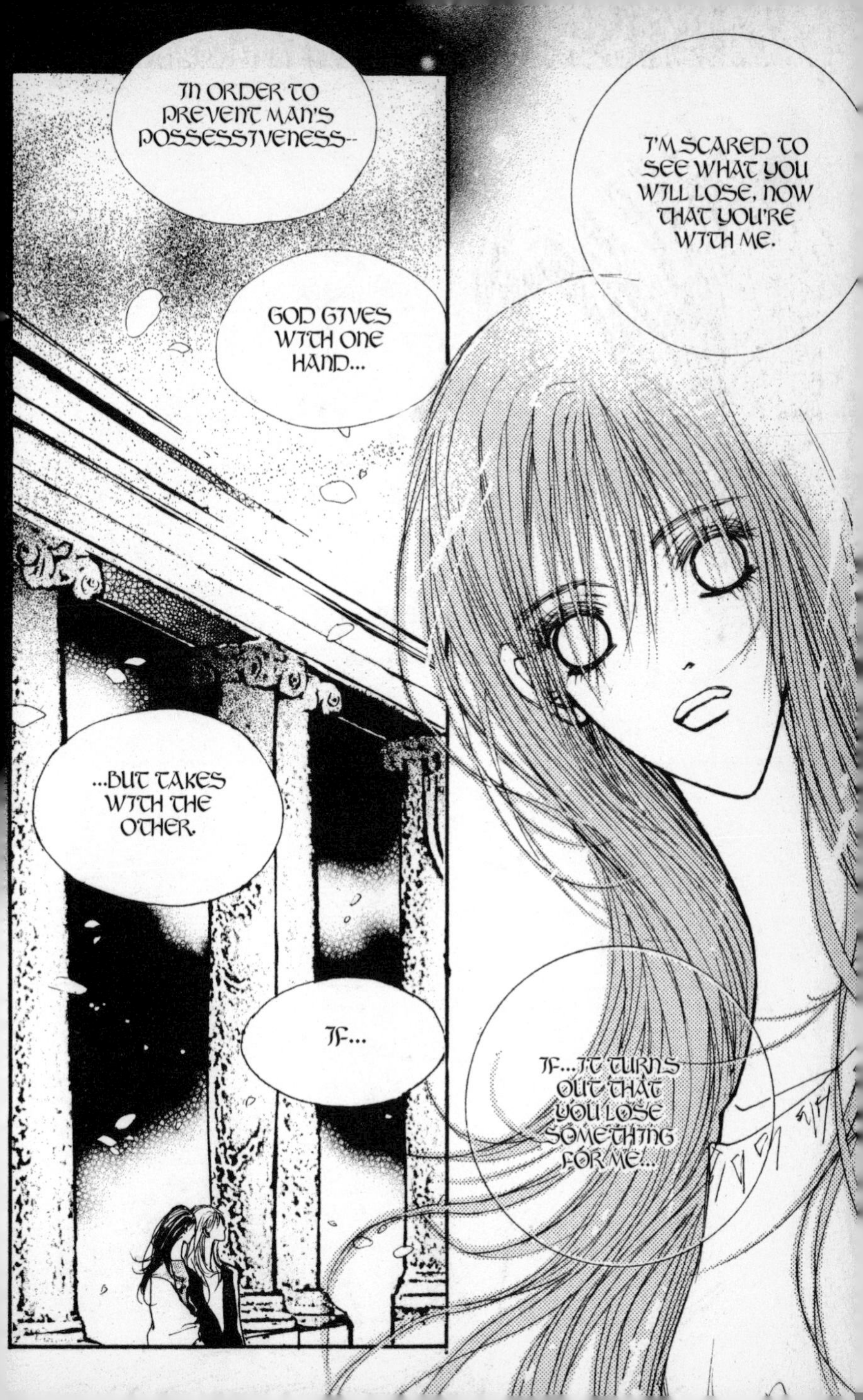
I'M SCARED TO SEE WHAT YOU WILL LOSE, NOW THAT YOU'RE WITH ME.
IN ORDER TO PREVENT MAN'S POSSESSIVENESS--
GOD GIVES WITH ONE HAND...
...BUT TAKES WITH THE OTHER.
IF...
IF...IT TURNS OUT THAT YOU LOSE SOMETHING FOR ME...

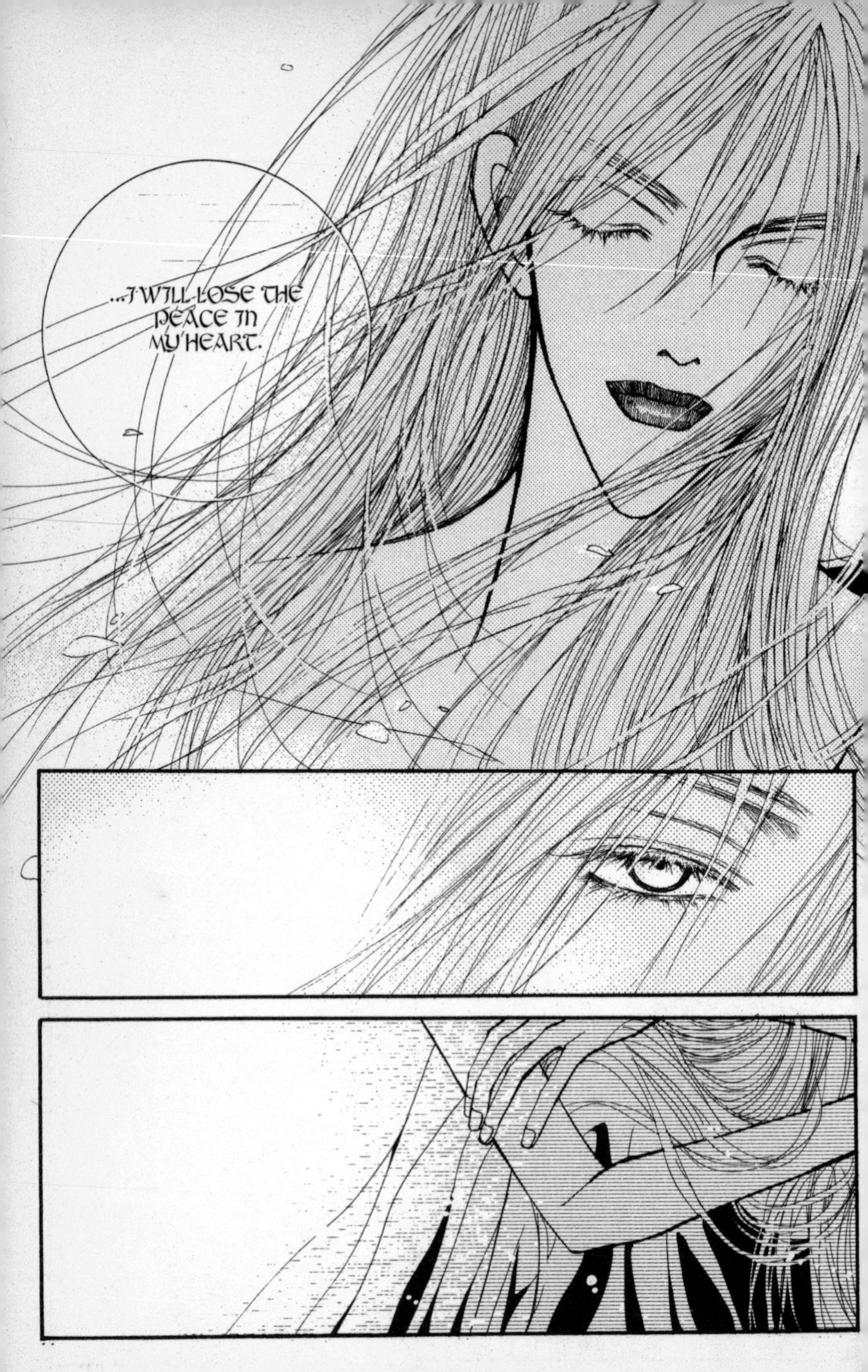
...I WILL LOSE THE PEACE IN MY HEART.

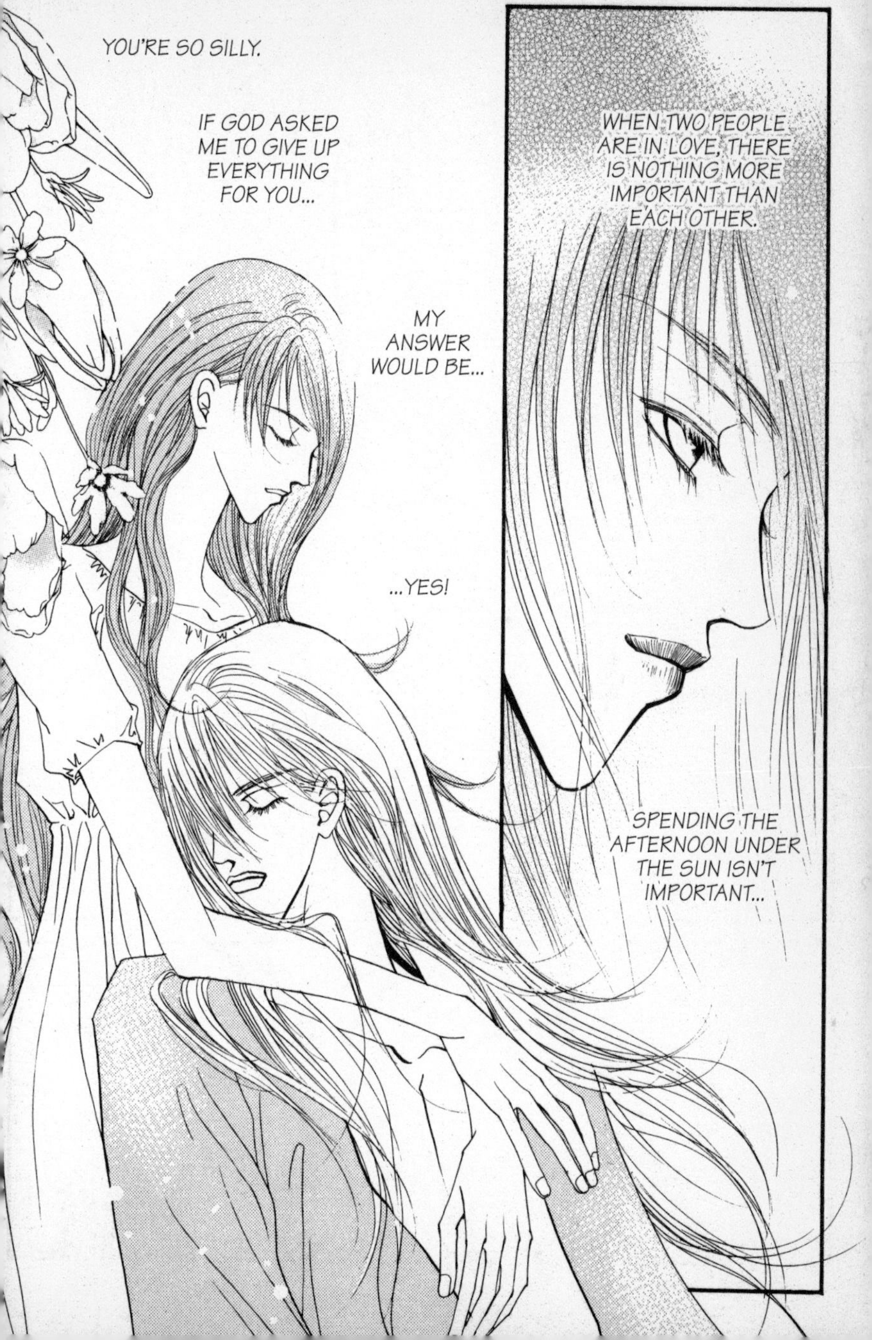
WHEN TWO PEOPLE ARE IN LOVE, THERE IS NOTHING MORE IMPORTANT THAN EACH OTHER.
SPENDING THE AFTERNOON UNDER THE SUN ISN'T IMPORTANT...
YOU'RE SO SILLY.
IF GOD ASKED ME TO GIVE UP EVERYTHING FOR YOU...
MY ANSWER WOULD BE...
...YES!

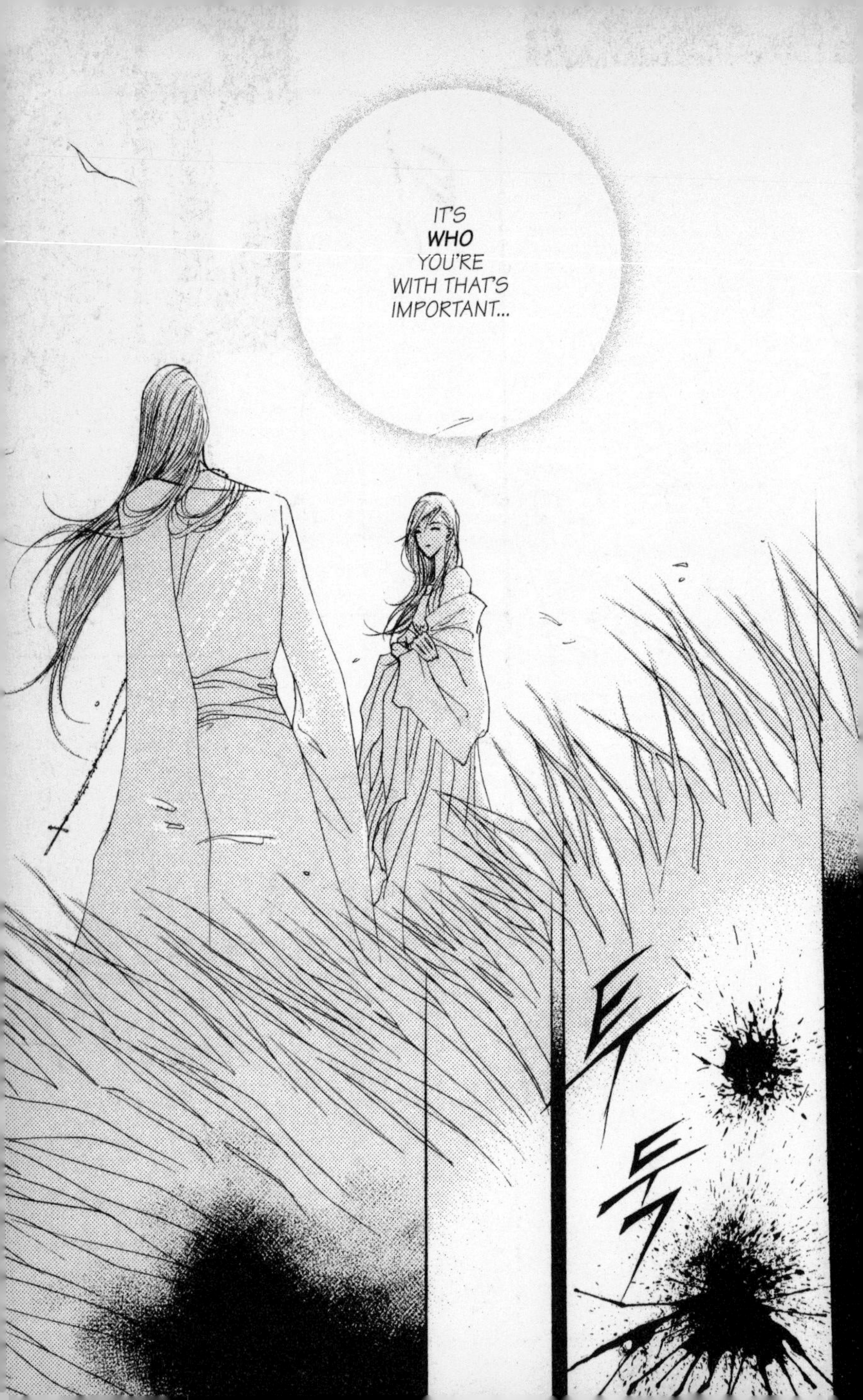
IT'S **WHO** YOU'RE WITH THAT'S IMPORTANT...

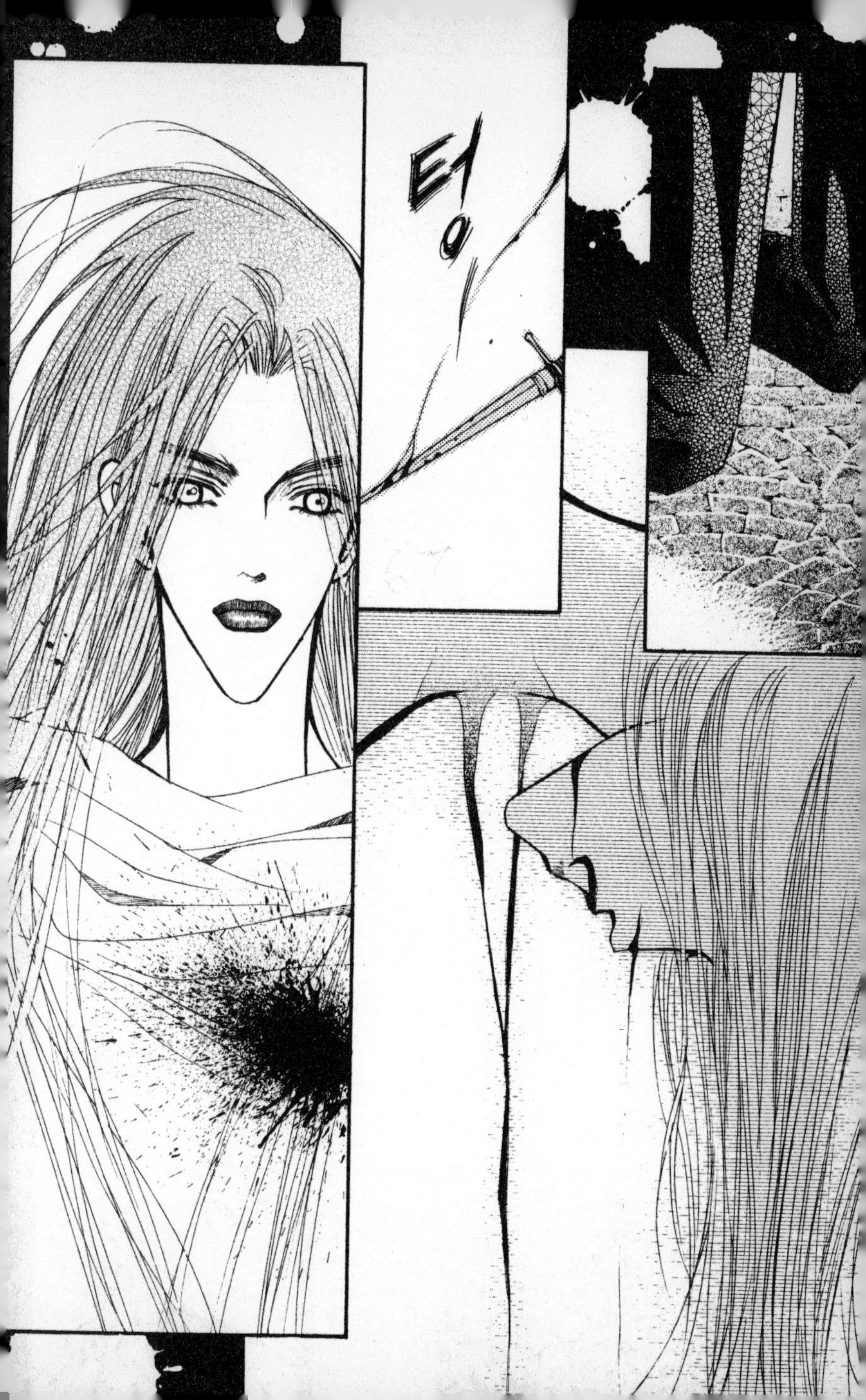
텅

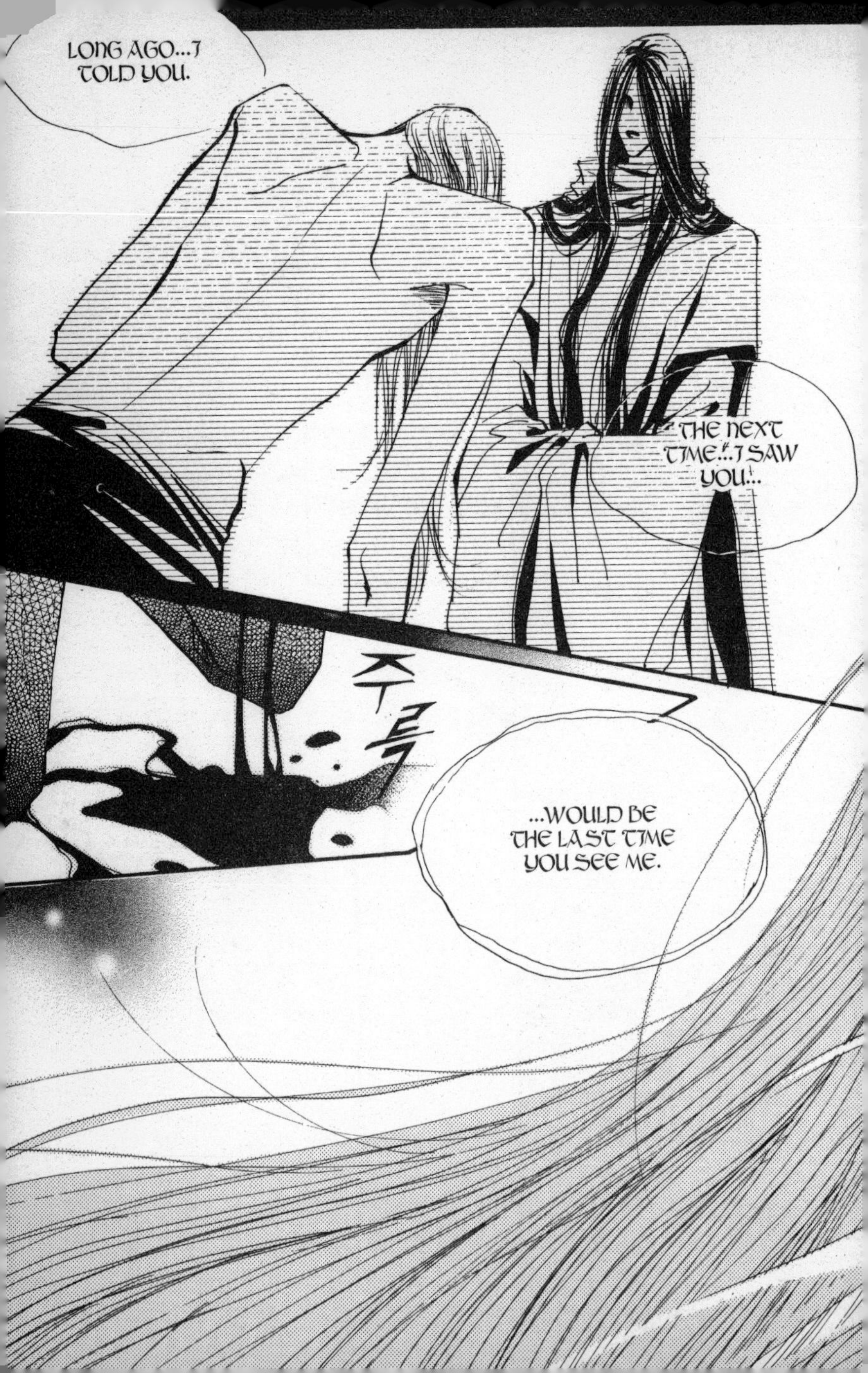
LONG AGO...I TOLD YOU.
THE NEXT TIME...I SAW YOU...
주륵
...WOULD BE THE LAST TIME YOU SEE ME.

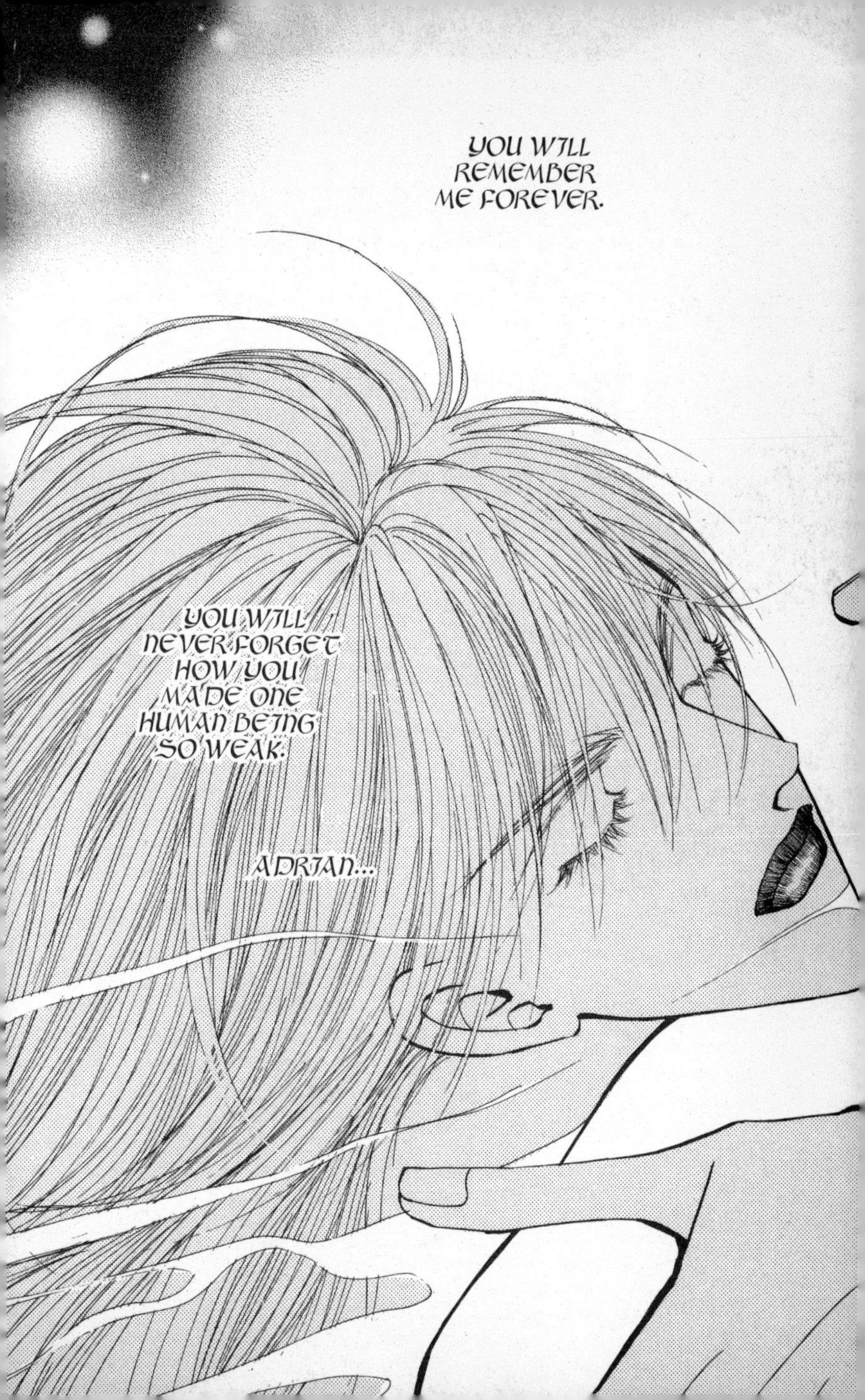
YOU WILL REMEMBER ME FOREVER.
YOU WILL NEVER FORGET HOW YOU MADE ONE HUMAN BEING SO WEAK.
ADRIAN...

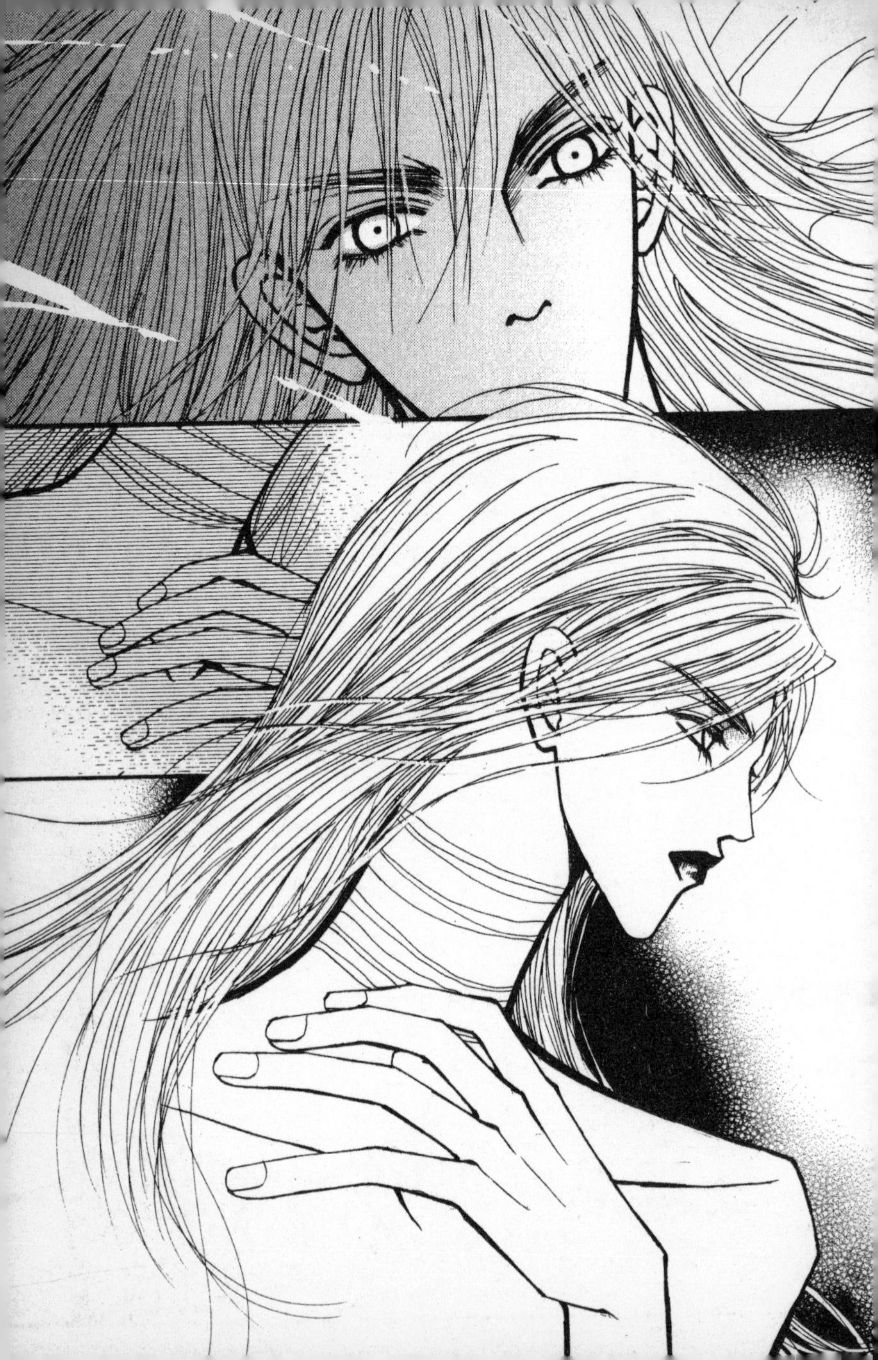

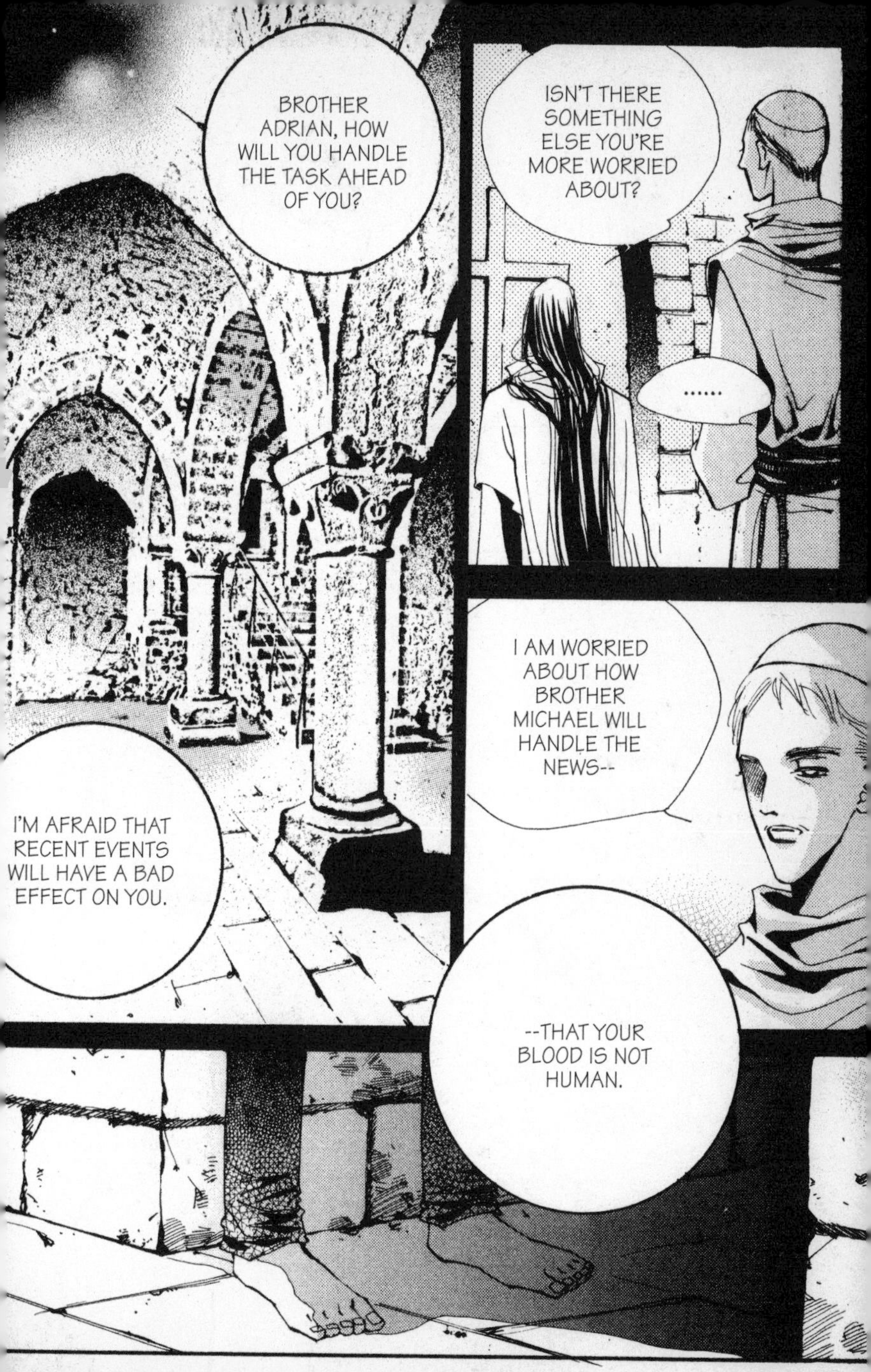
BROTHER ADRIAN, HOW WILL YOU HANDLE THE TASK AHEAD OF YOU?
I'M AFRAID THAT RECENT EVENTS WILL HAVE A BAD EFFECT ON YOU.
ISN'T THERE SOMETHING ELSE YOU'RE MORE WORRIED ABOUT?
......
I AM WORRIED ABOUT HOW BROTHER MICHAEL WILL HANDLE THE NEWS--
--THAT YOUR BLOOD IS NOT HUMAN.

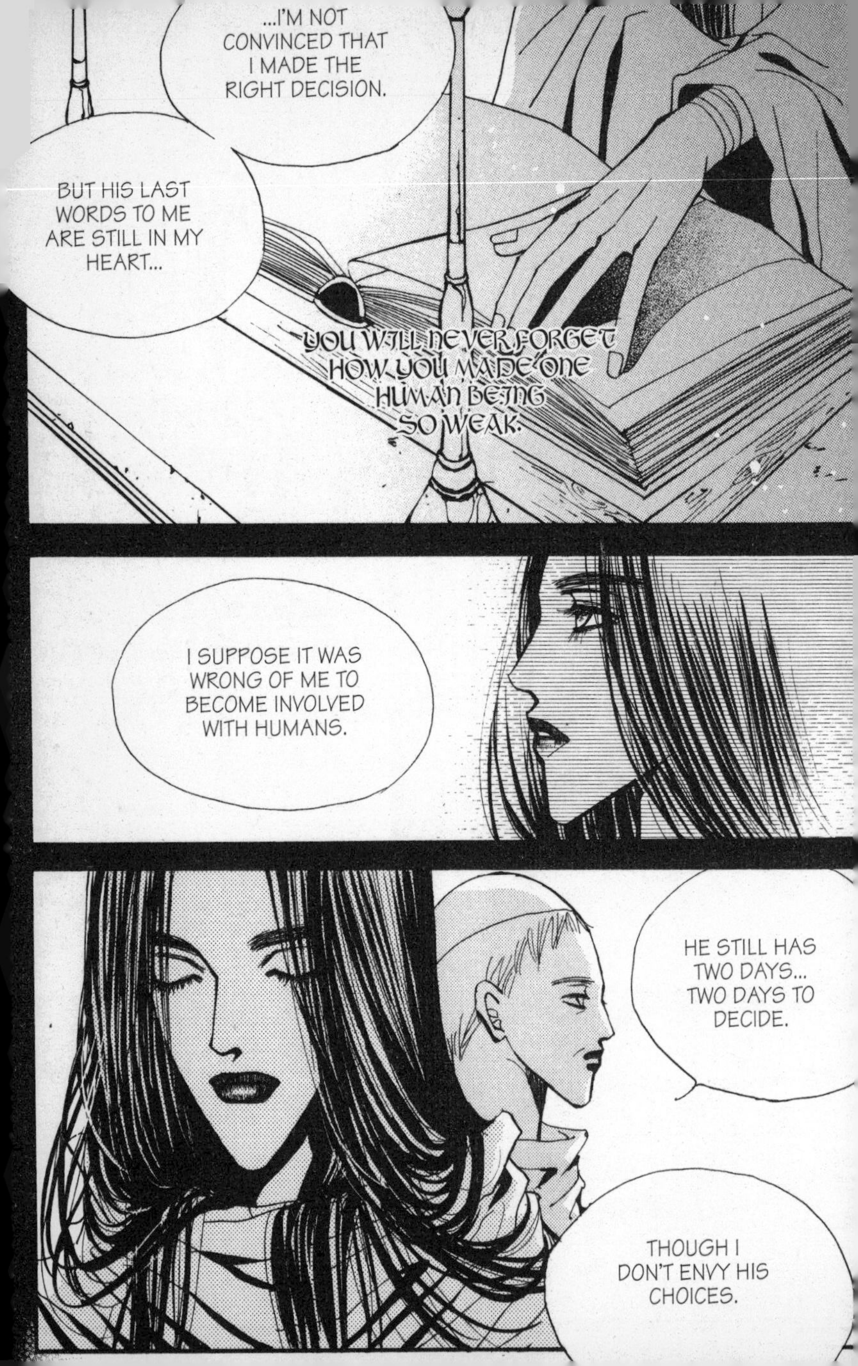
...I'M NOT CONVINCED THAT I MADE THE RIGHT DECISION.
BUT HIS LAST WORDS TO ME ARE STILL IN MY HEART...
YOU WILL NEVER FORGET HOW YOU MADE ONE HUMAN BEING SO WEAK.
I SUPPOSE IT WAS WRONG OF ME TO BECOME INVOLVED WITH HUMANS.
HE STILL HAS TWO DAYS... TWO DAYS TO DECIDE.
THOUGH I DON'T ENVY HIS CHOICES.

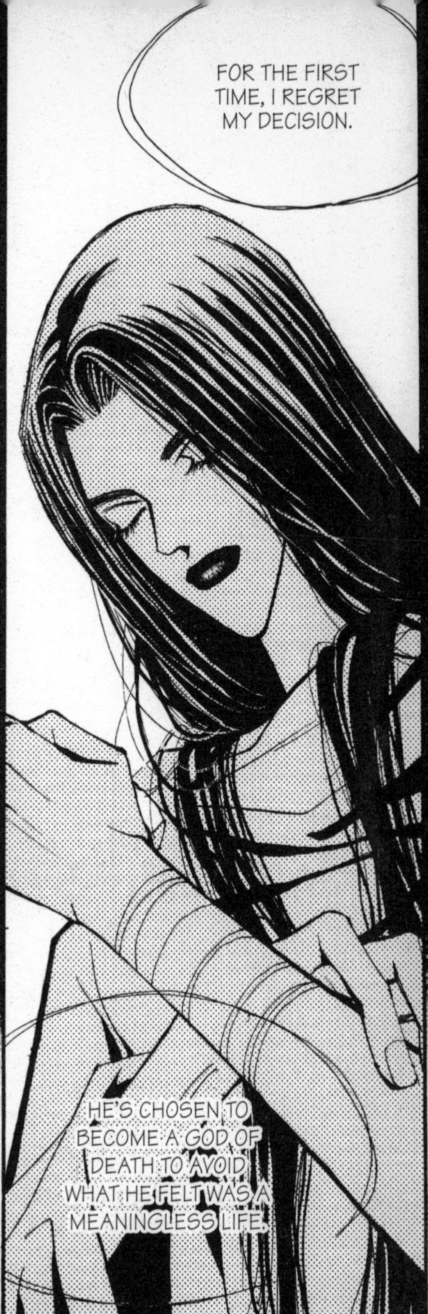
FOR THE FIRST TIME, I REGRET MY DECISION.
HE'S CHOSEN TO BECOME A GOD OF DEATH TO AVOID WHAT HE FELT WAS A MEANINGLESS LIFE.
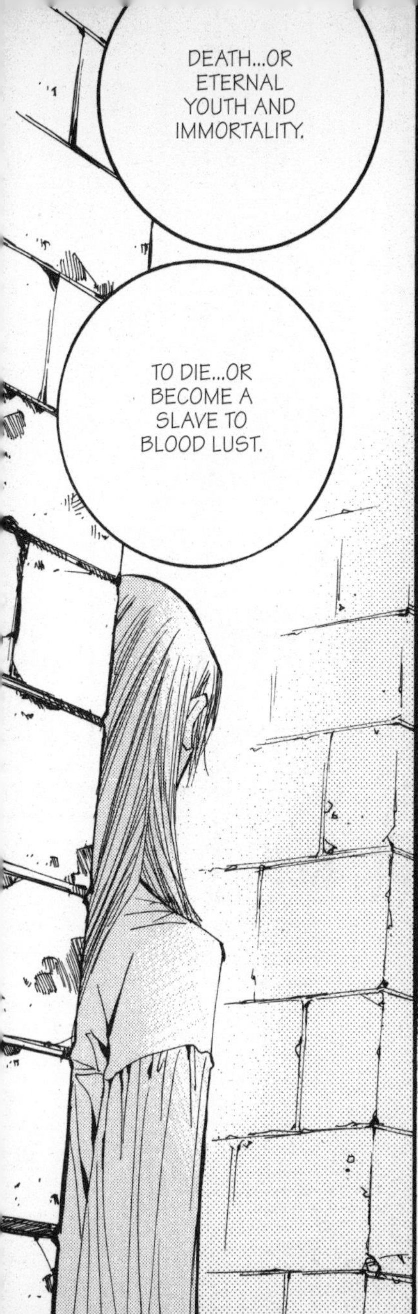
DEATH...OR ETERNAL YOUTH AND IMMORTALITY.
TO DIE...OR BECOME A SLAVE TO BLOOD LUST.

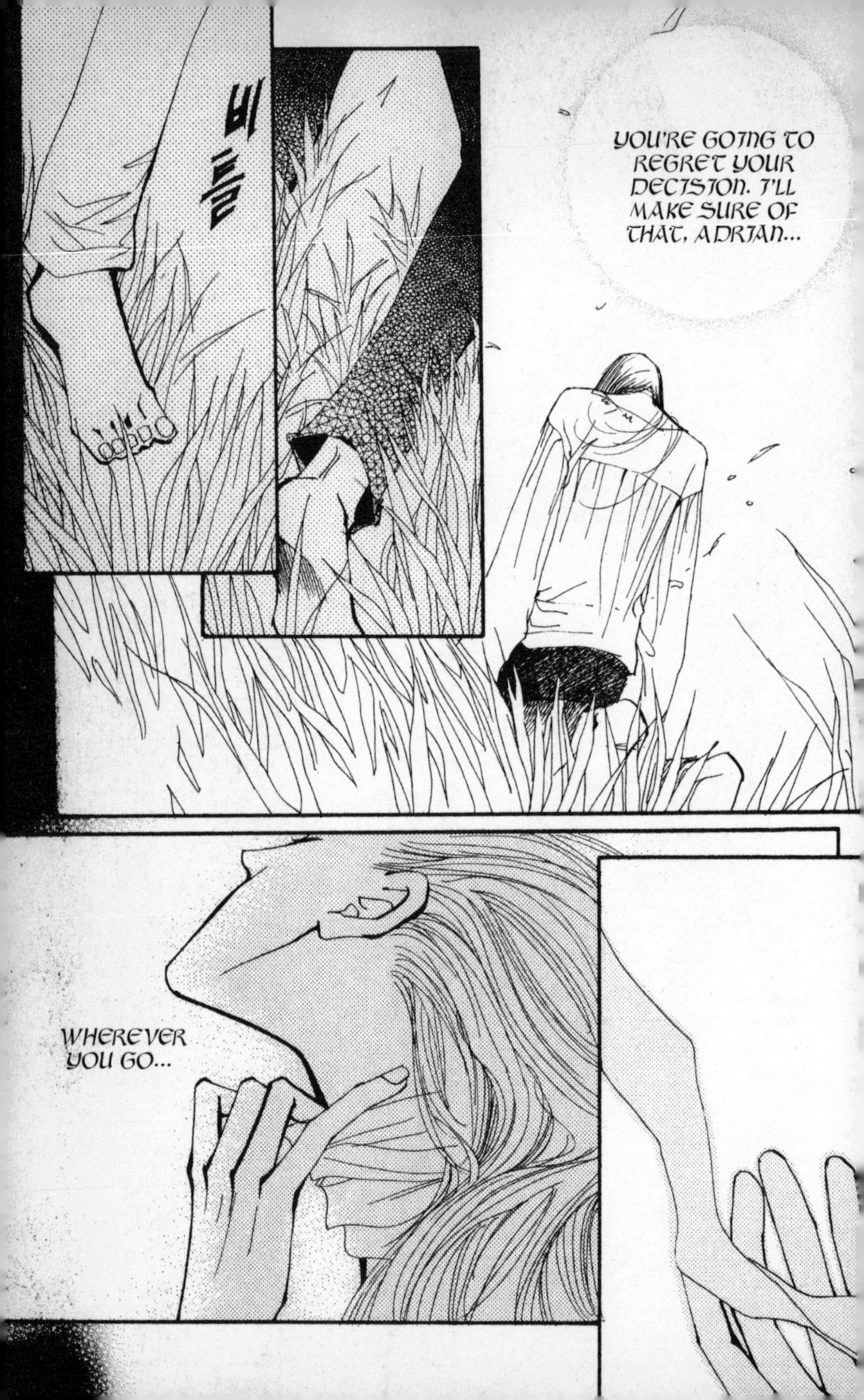
비틀
YOU'RE GOING TO REGRET YOUR DECISION. I'LL MAKE SURE OF THAT, ADRIAN...
WHEREVER YOU GO...

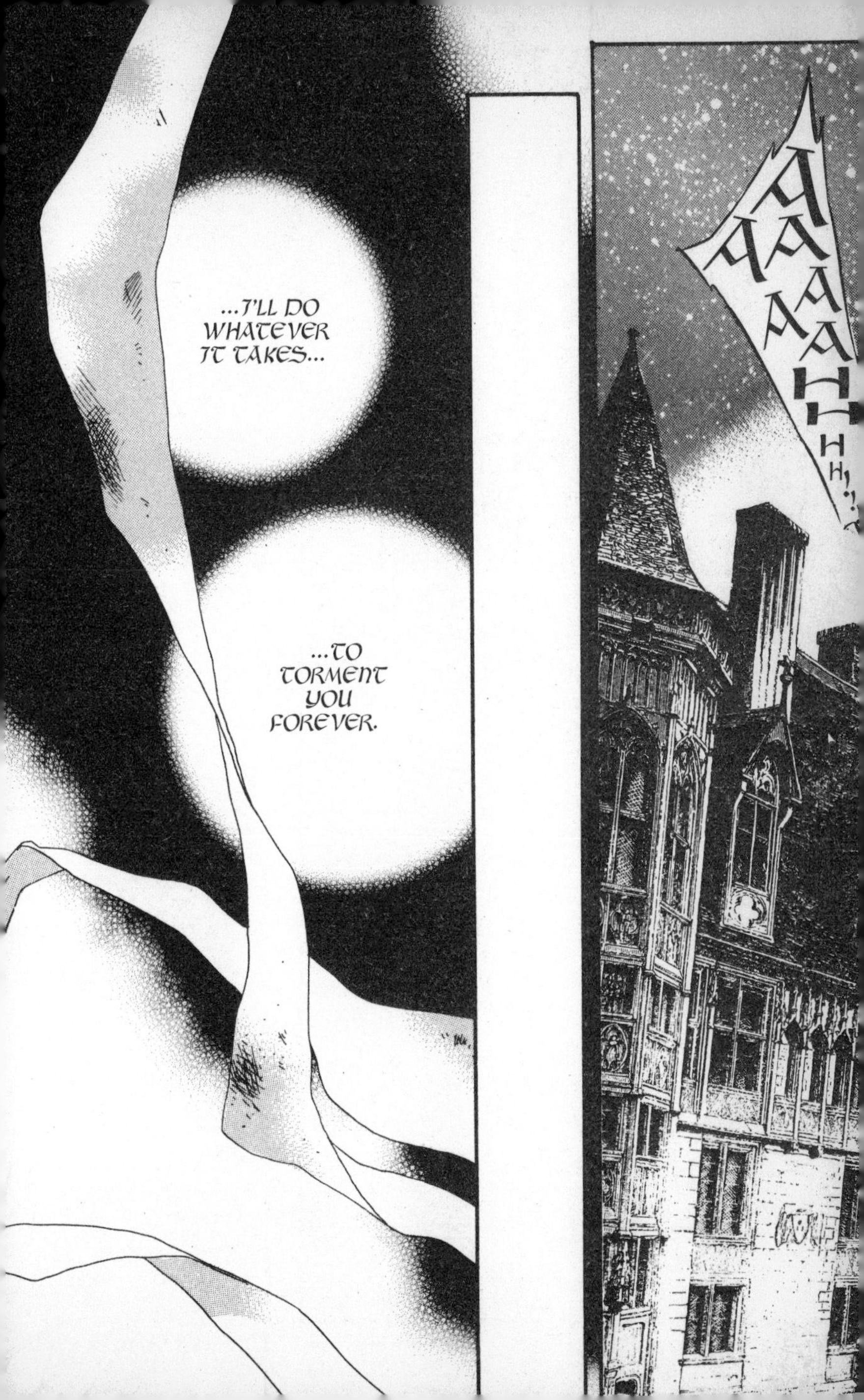
AAAAAAHHHH!!
...I'LL DO WHATEVER IT TAKES...
...TO TORMENT YOU FOREVER.

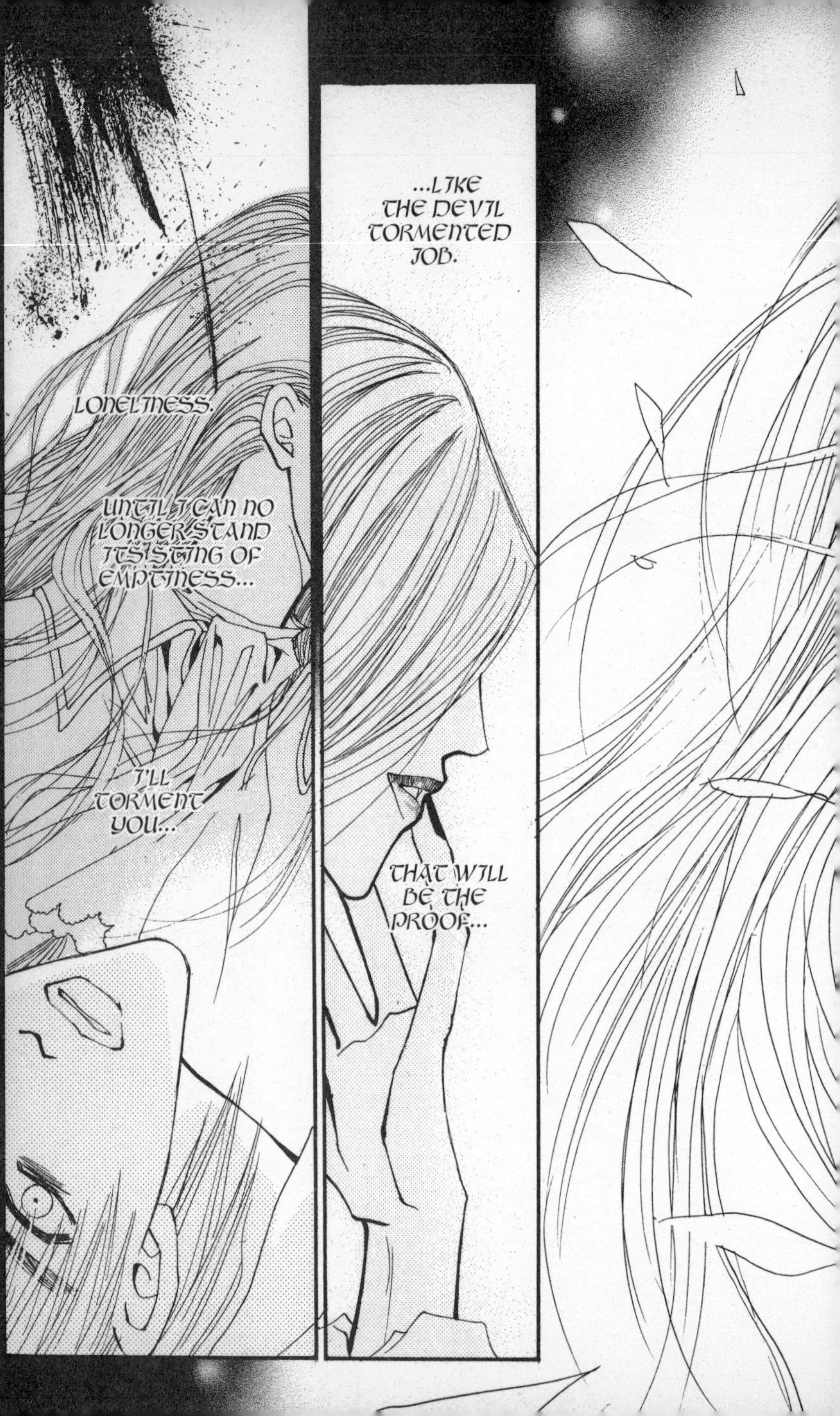
LONELINESS.
UNTIL I CAN NO LONGER STAND ITS STING OF EMPTINESS...
I'LL TORMENT YOU...
...LIKE THE DEVIL TORMENTED JOB.
THAT WILL BE THE PROOF...

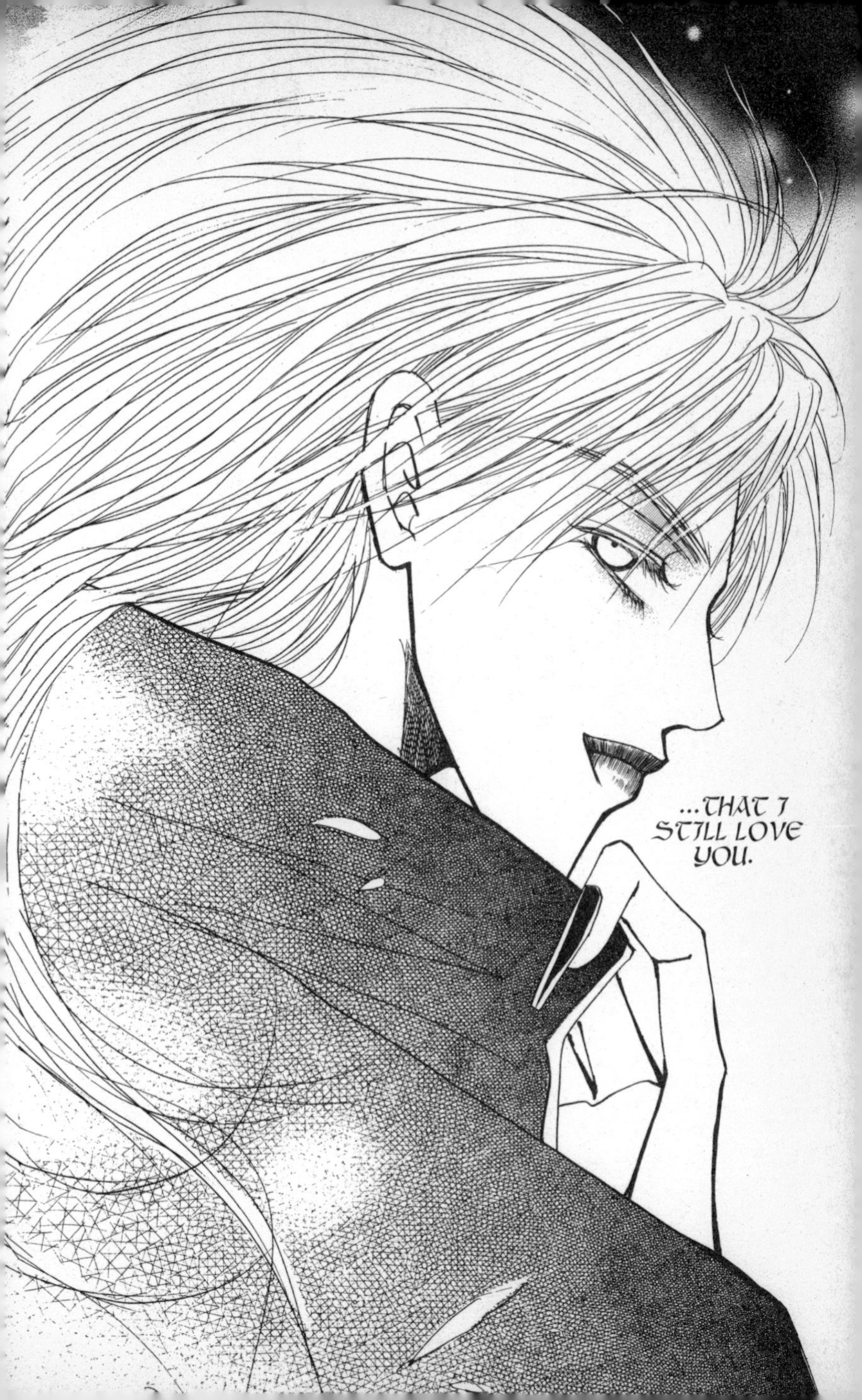
...THAT I STILL LOVE YOU.

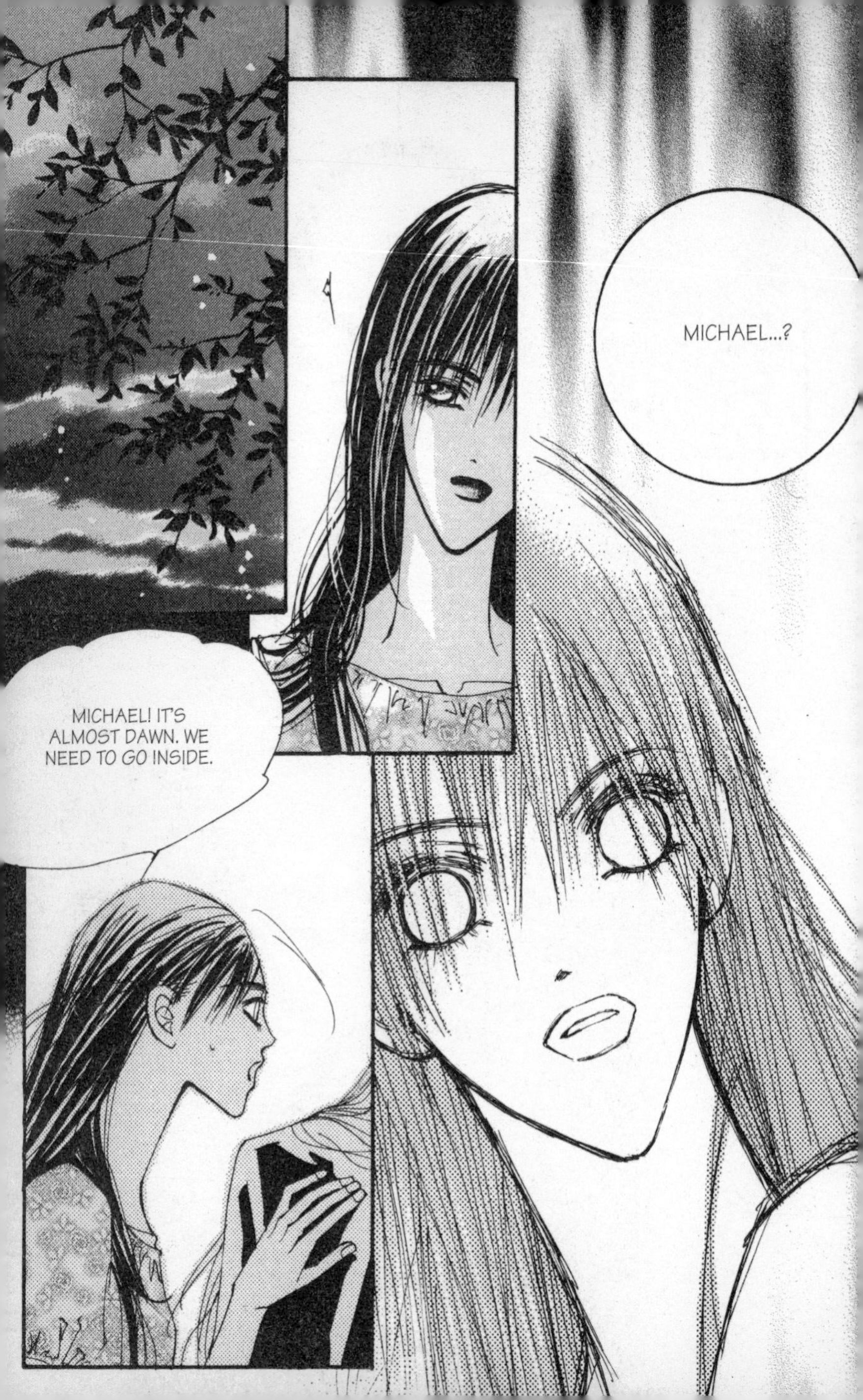
MICHAEL...?
MICHAEL! IT'S ALMOST DAWN. WE NEED TO GO INSIDE.

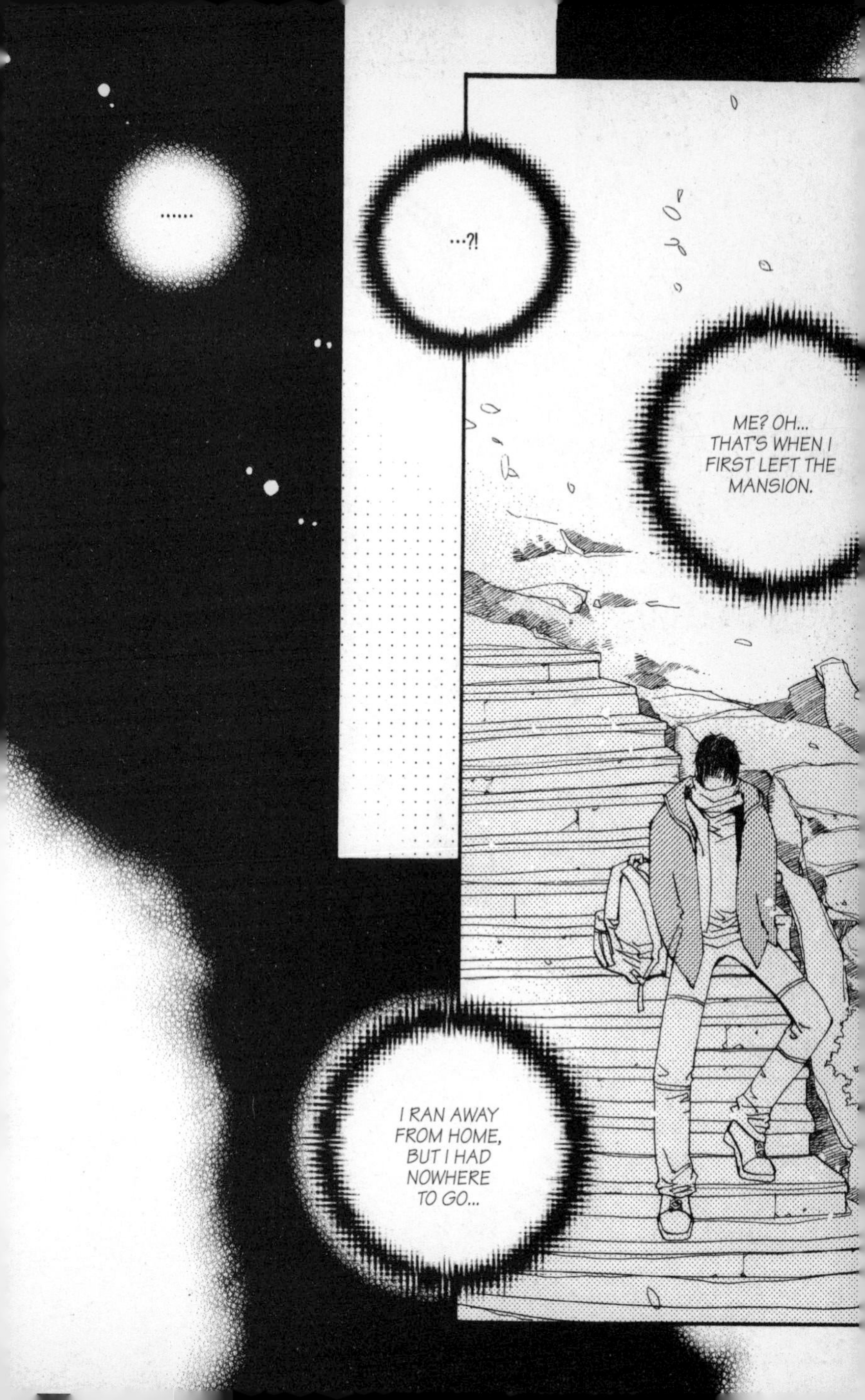
......
...?!
ME? OH... THAT'S WHEN I FIRST LEFT THE MANSION.
I RAN AWAY FROM HOME, BUT I HAD NOWHERE TO GO...

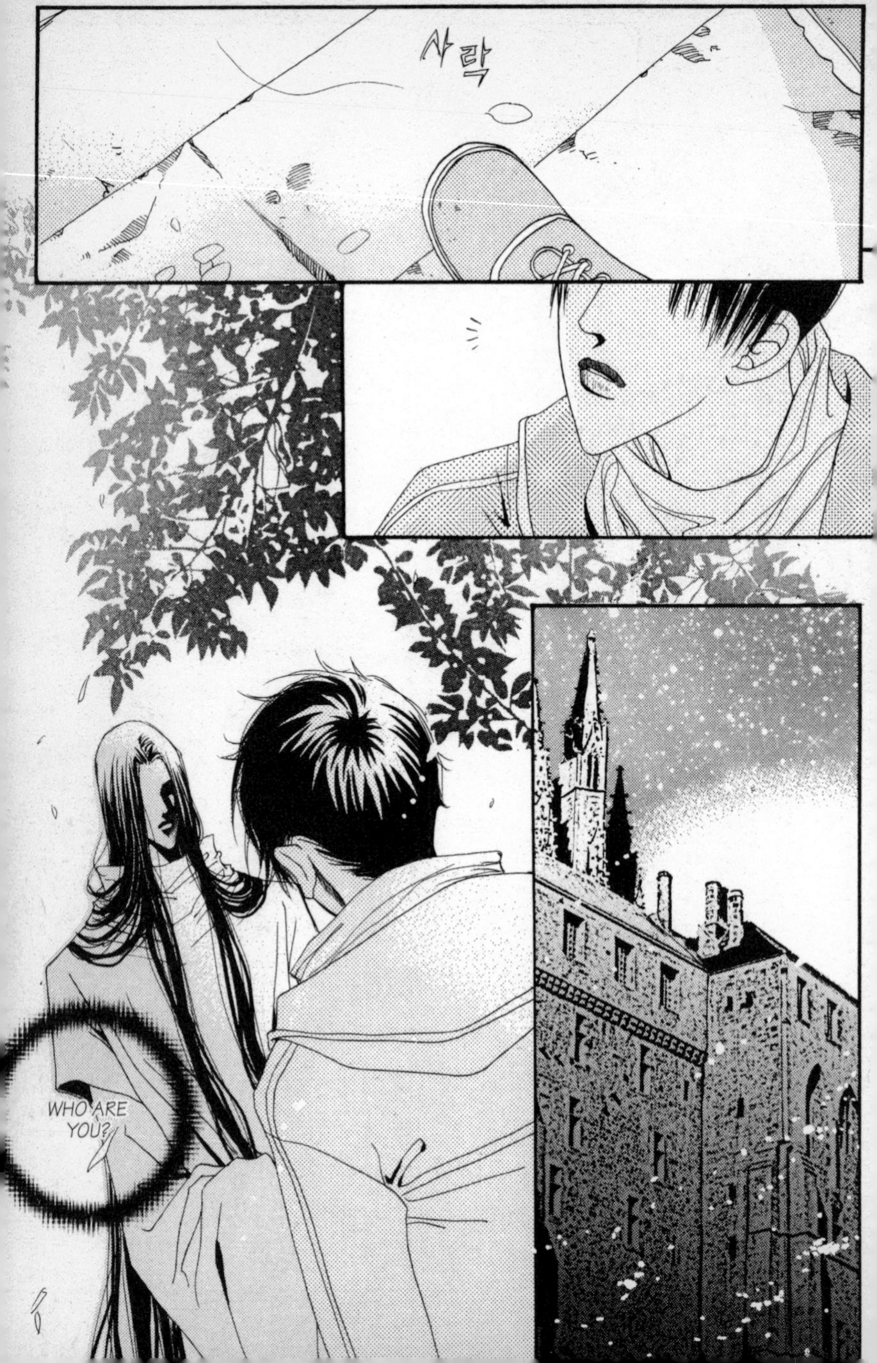
사락
WHO ARE YOU?

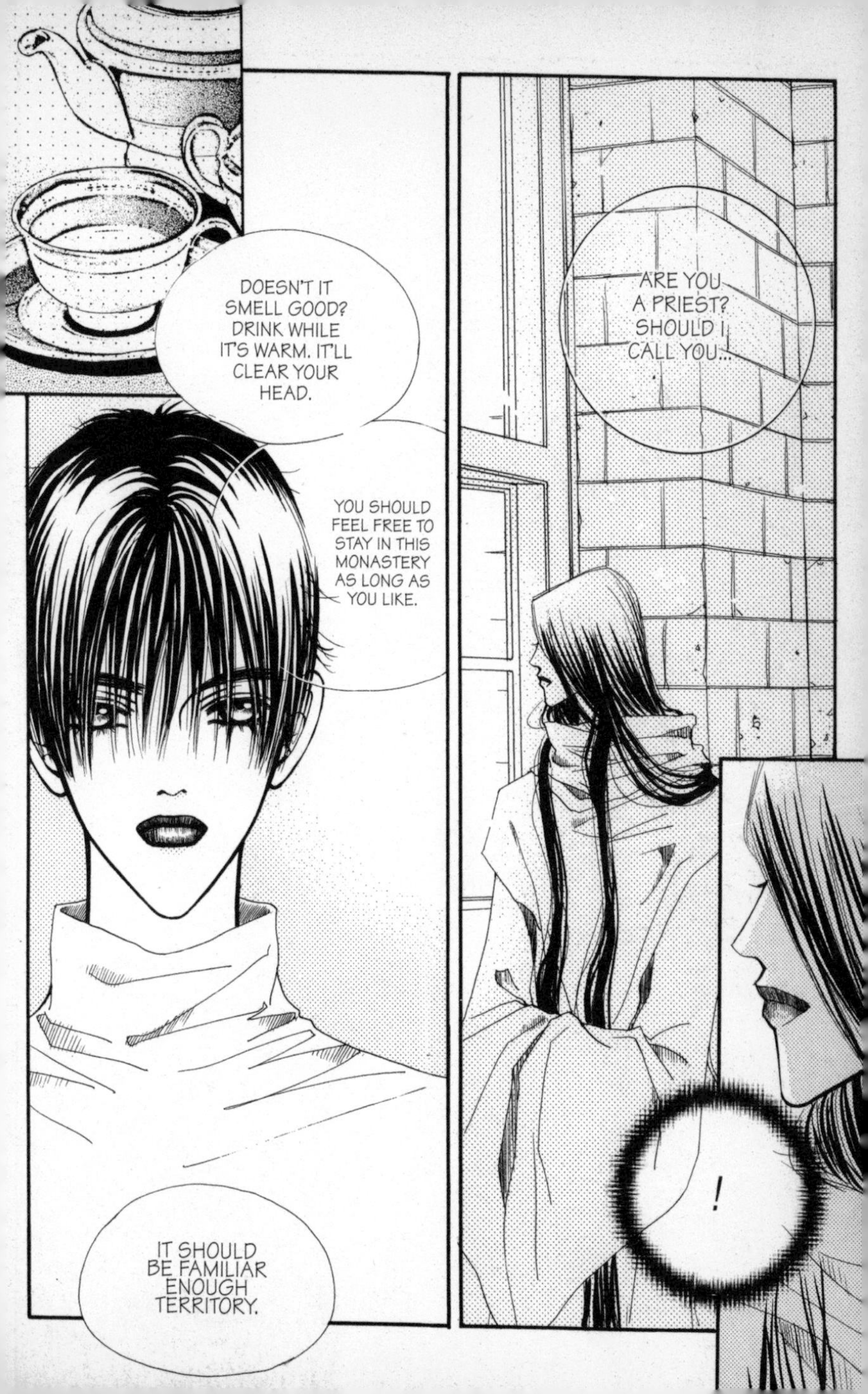
DOESN'T IT SMELL GOOD? DRINK WHILE IT'S WARM. IT'LL CLEAR YOUR HEAD.
YOU SHOULD FEEL FREE TO STAY IN THIS MONASTERY AS LONG AS YOU LIKE.
IT SHOULD BE FAMILIAR ENOUGH TERRITORY.
ARE YOU A PRIEST? SHOULD I CALL YOU...
!

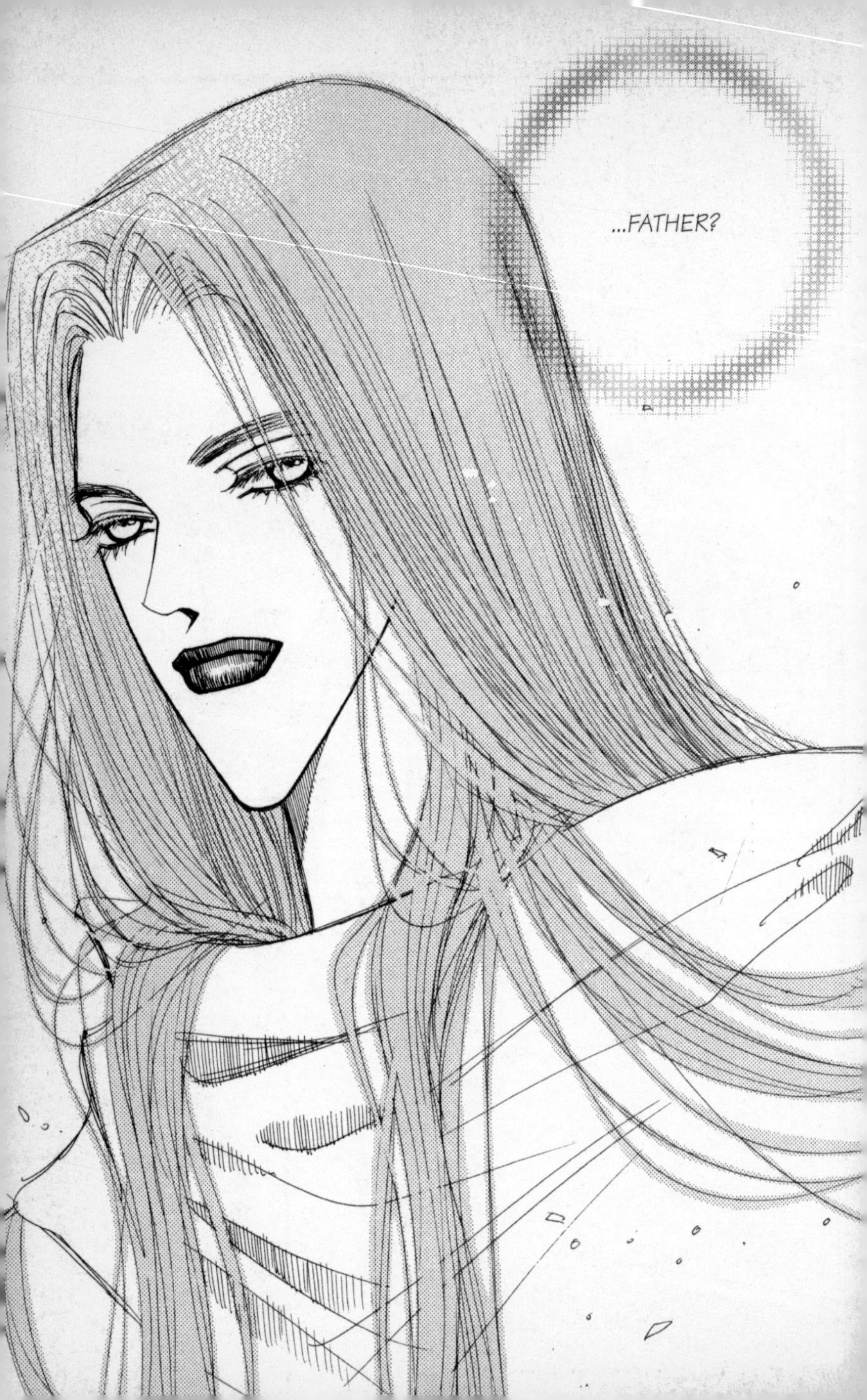
...FATHER?

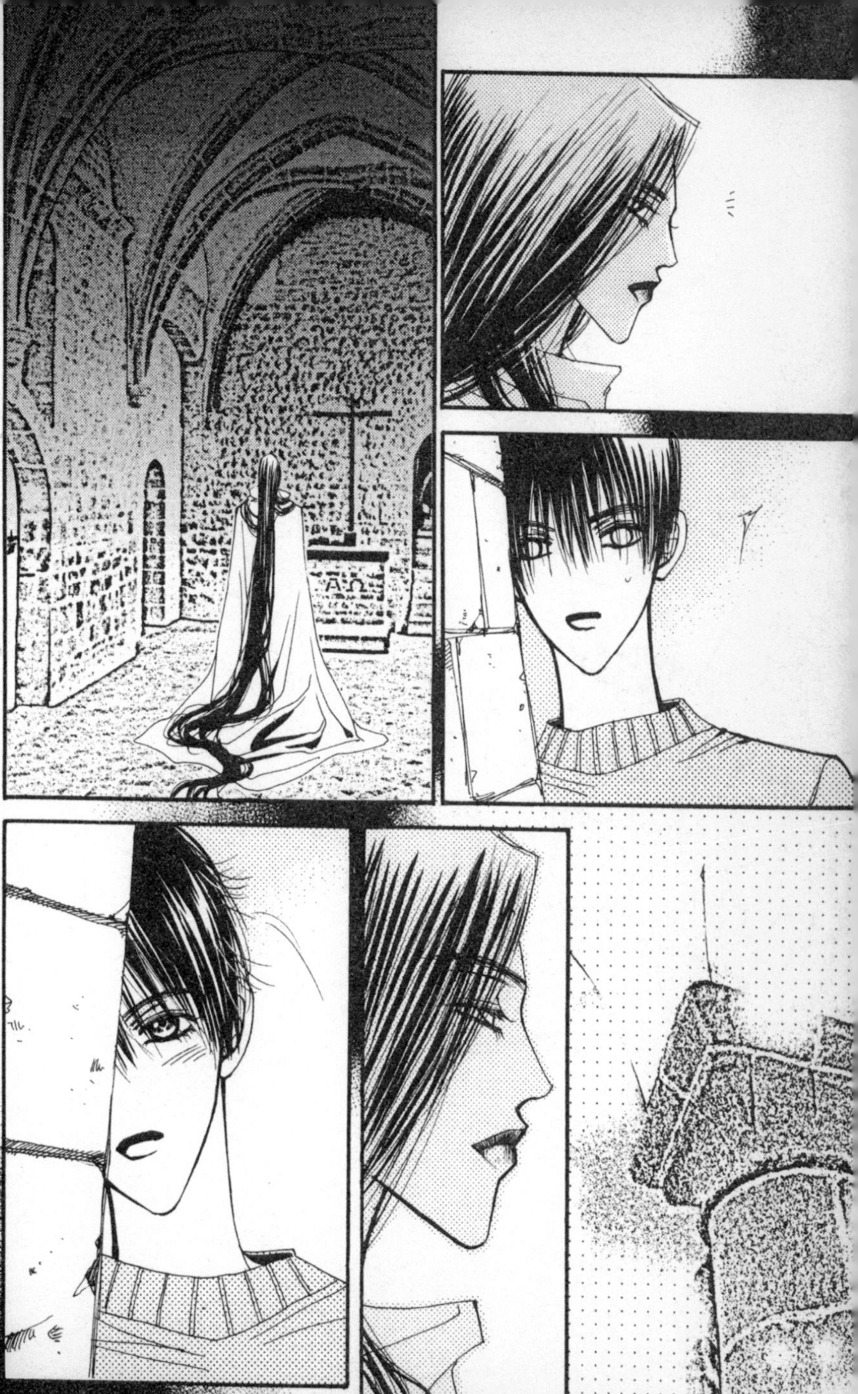
AΩ

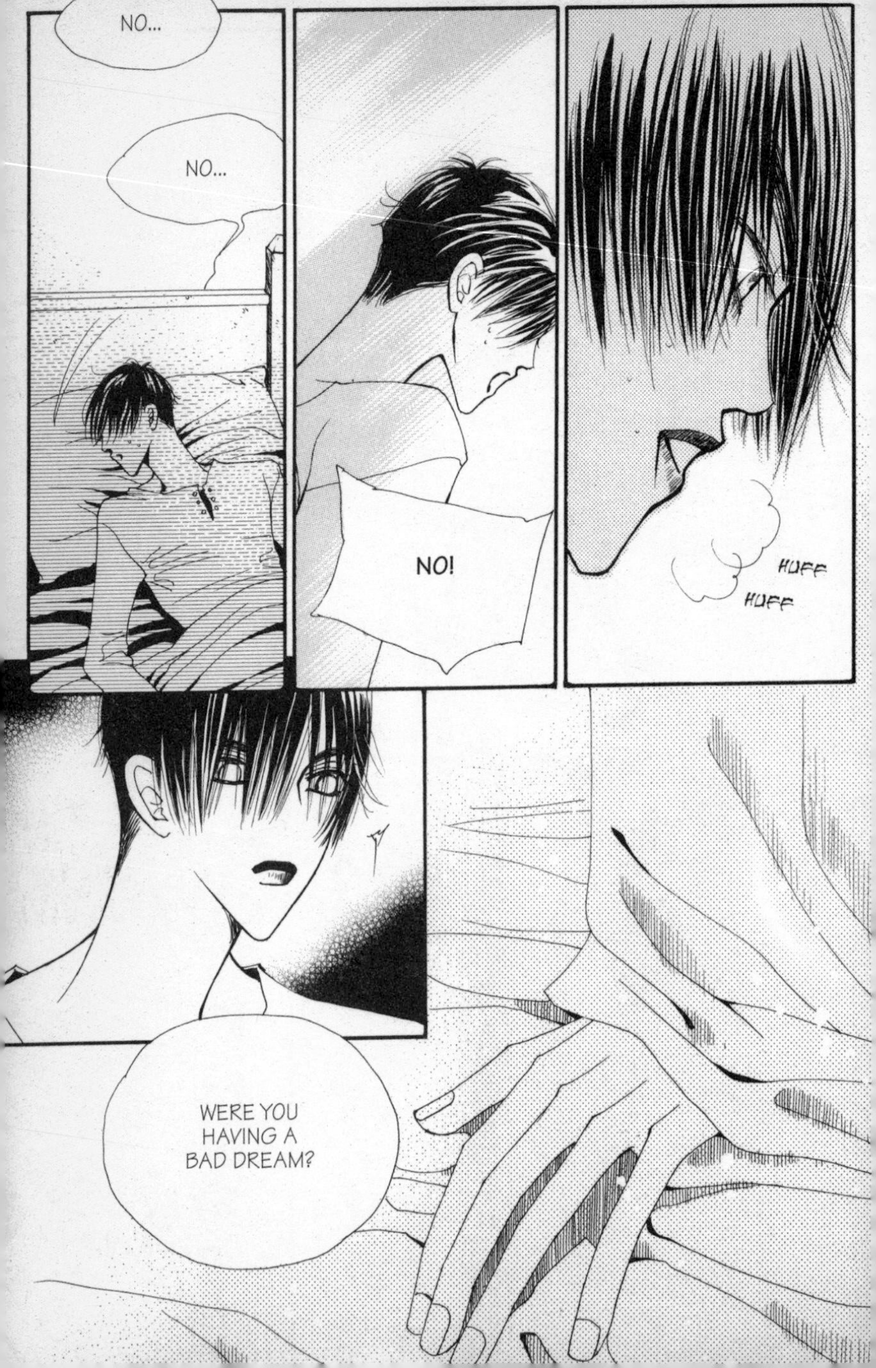
NO...
NO...
NO!
HUFF
HUFF
WERE YOU HAVING A BAD DREAM?

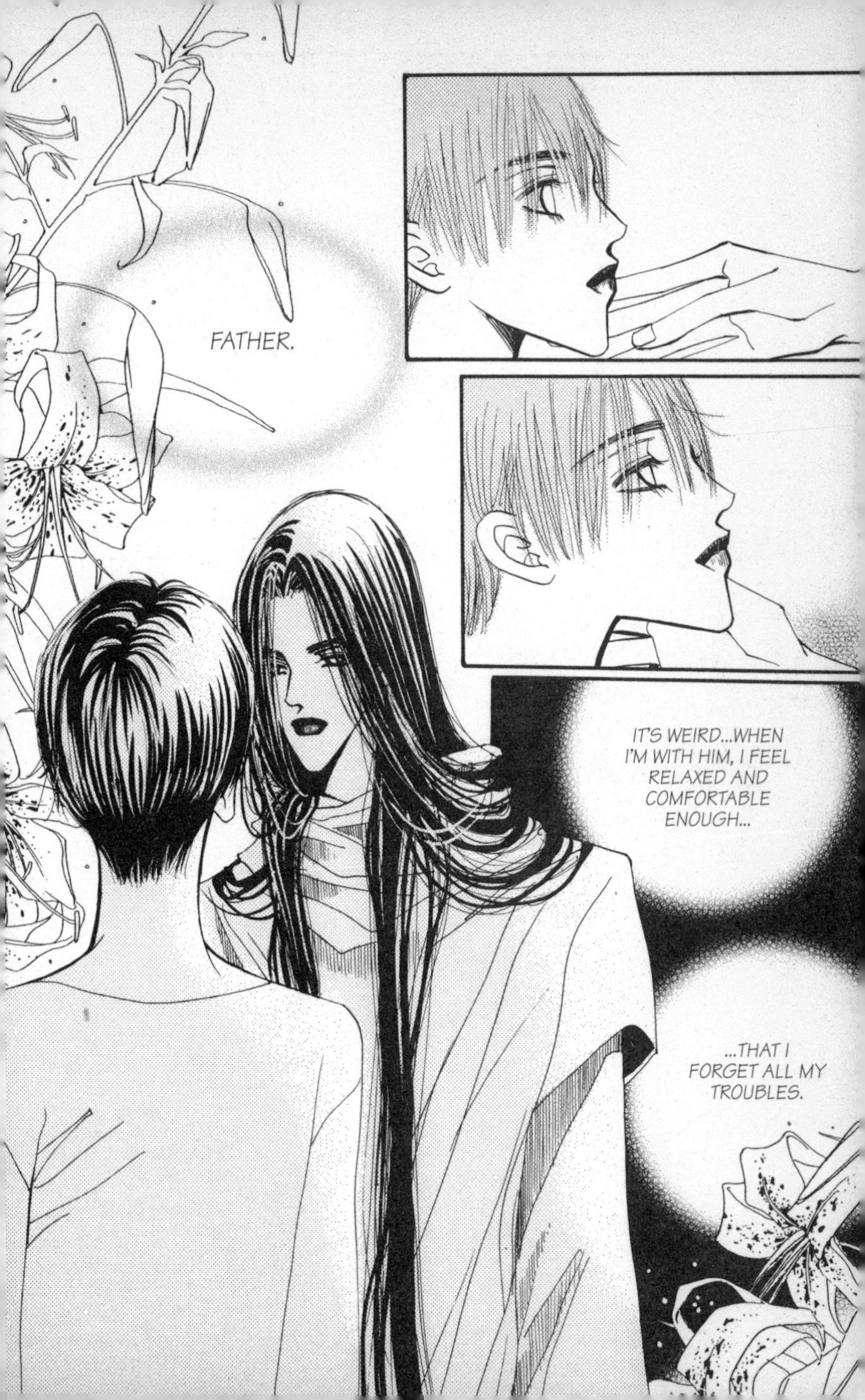
IT'S WEIRD...WHEN I'M WITH HIM, I FEEL RELAXED AND COMFORTABLE ENOUGH...
...THAT I FORGET ALL MY TROUBLES.
FATHER.

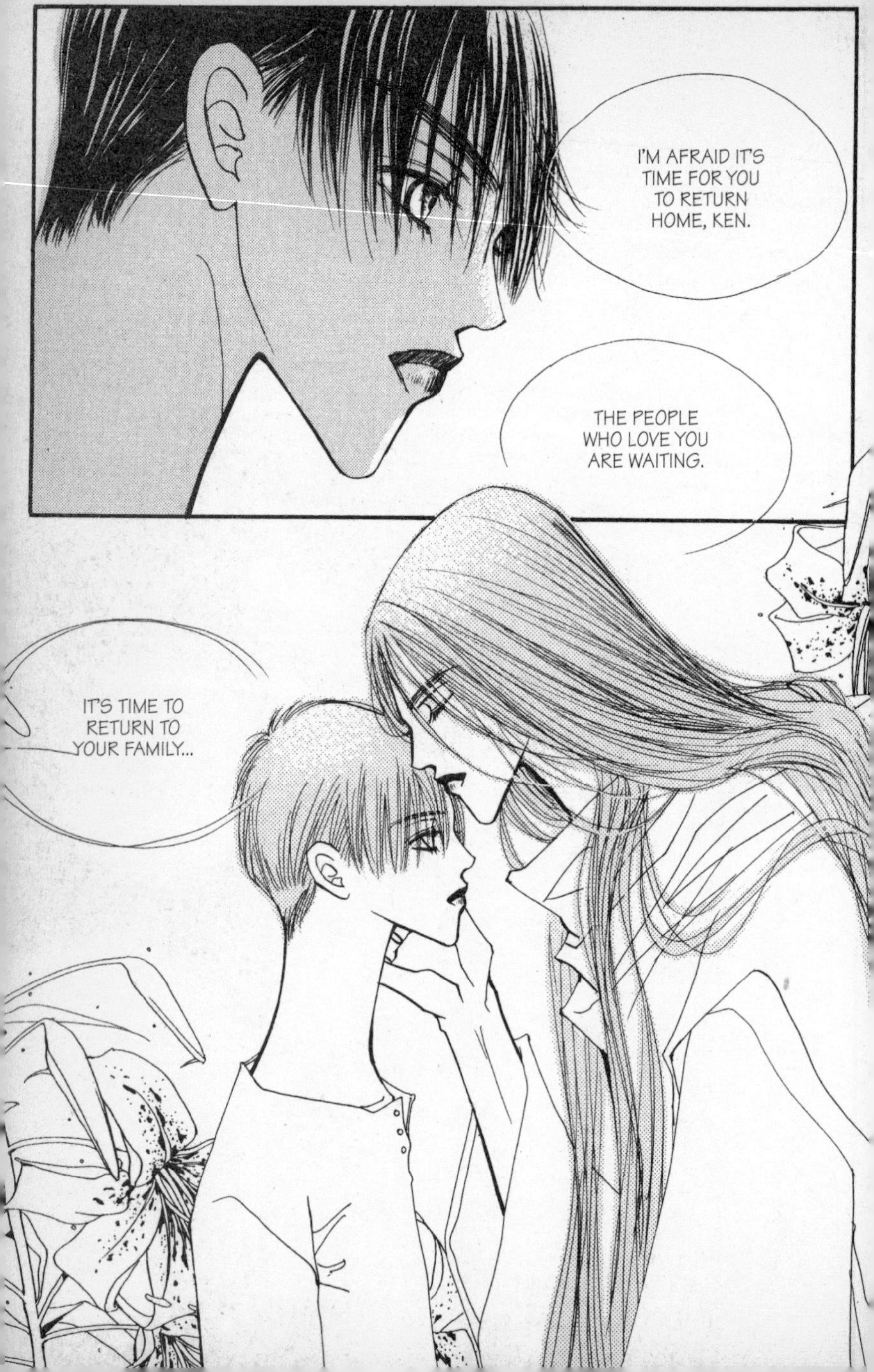
I'M AFRAID IT'S TIME FOR YOU TO RETURN HOME, KEN.
THE PEOPLE WHO LOVE YOU ARE WAITING.
IT'S TIME TO RETURN TO YOUR FAMILY...

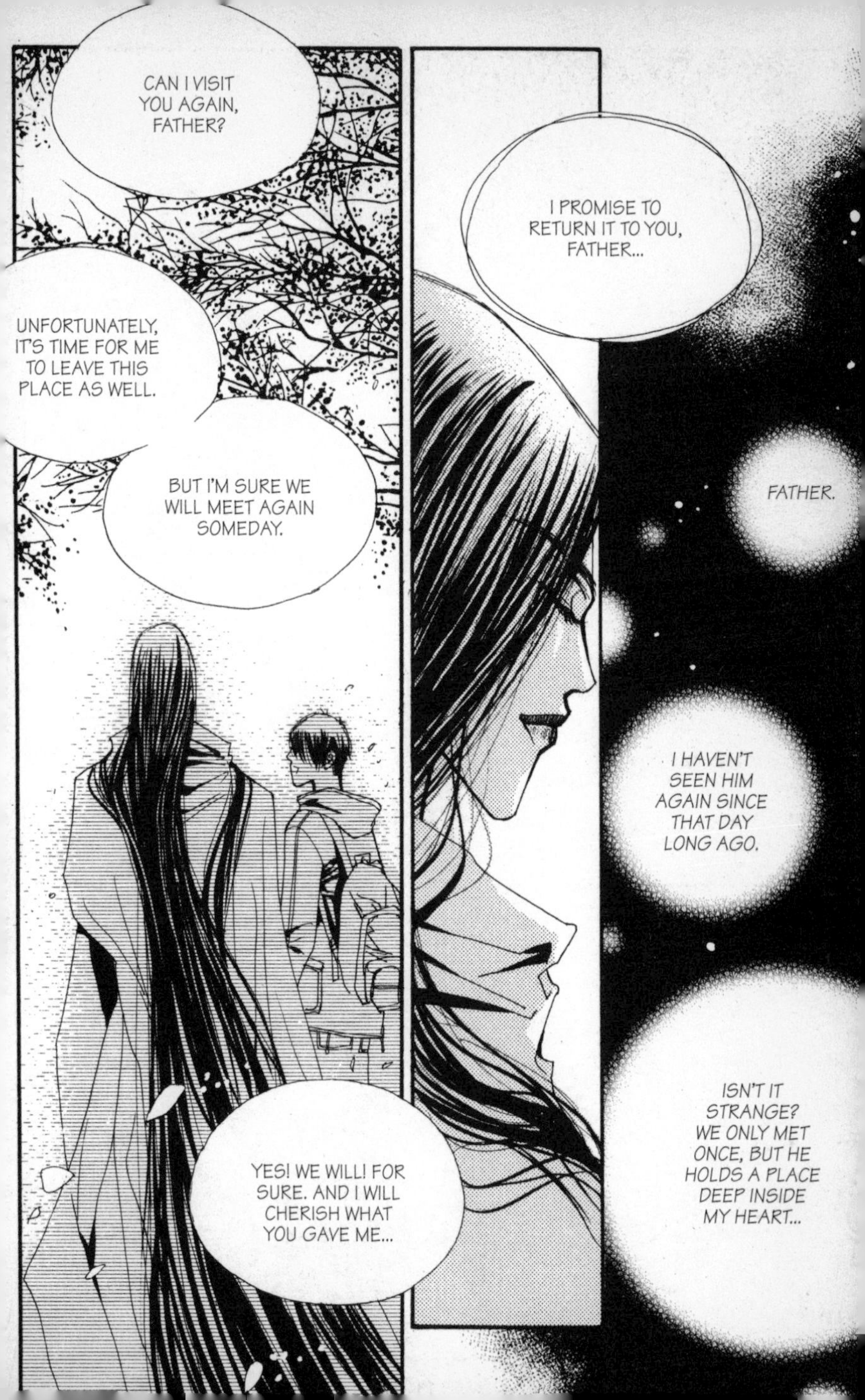
CAN I VISIT YOU AGAIN, FATHER?
UNFORTUNATELY, IT'S TIME FOR ME TO LEAVE THIS PLACE AS WELL.
BUT I'M SURE WE WILL MEET AGAIN SOMEDAY.
YES! WE WILL! FOR SURE. AND I WILL CHERISH WHAT YOU GAVE ME...
I PROMISE TO RETURN IT TO YOU, FATHER...
FATHER.
I HAVEN'T SEEN HIM AGAIN SINCE THAT DAY LONG AGO.
ISN'T IT STRANGE? WE ONLY MET ONCE, BUT HE HOLDS A PLACE DEEP INSIDE MY HEART...

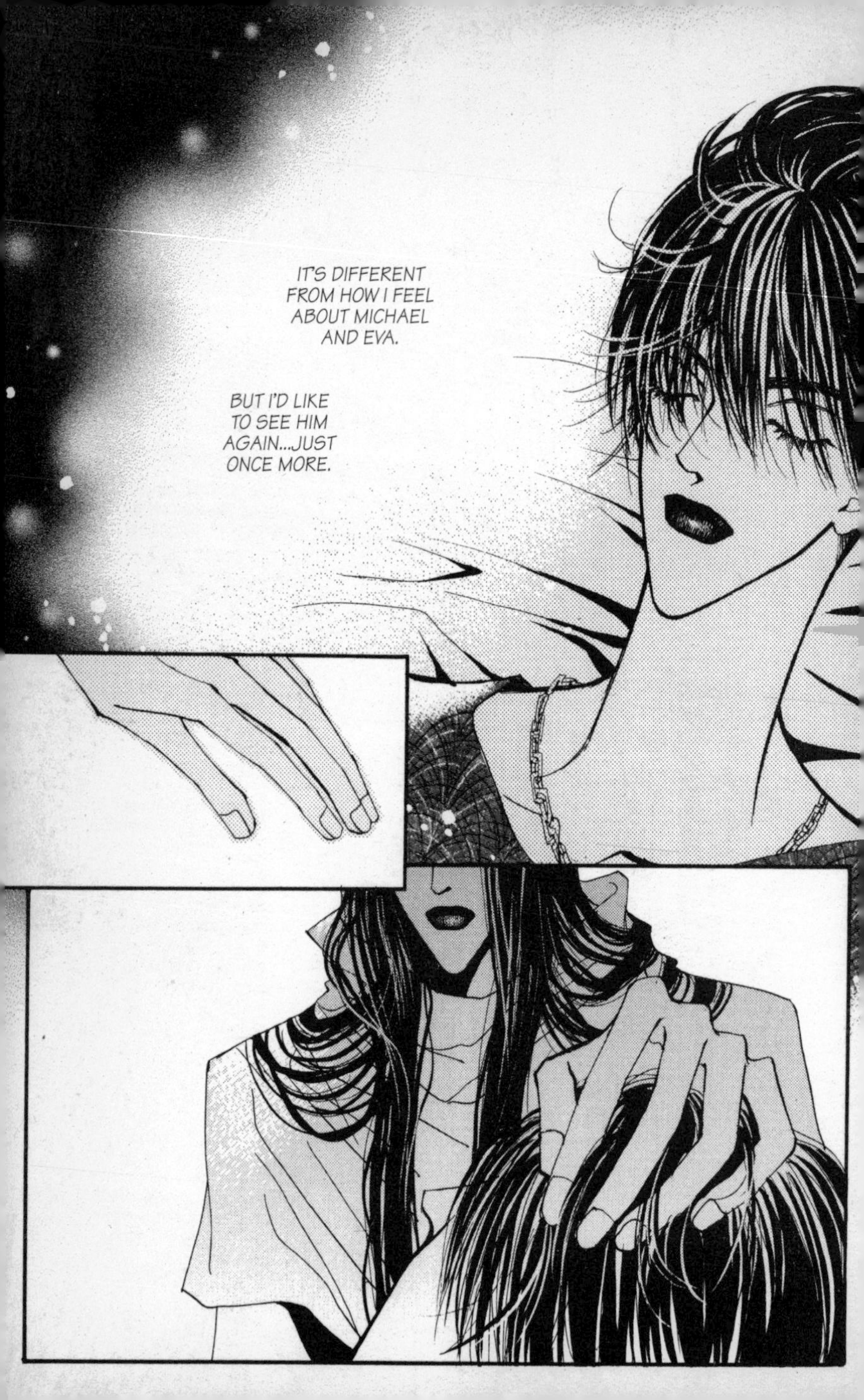
IT'S DIFFERENT FROM HOW I FEEL ABOUT MICHAEL AND EVA.
BUT I'D LIKE TO SEE HIM AGAIN...JUST ONCE MORE.

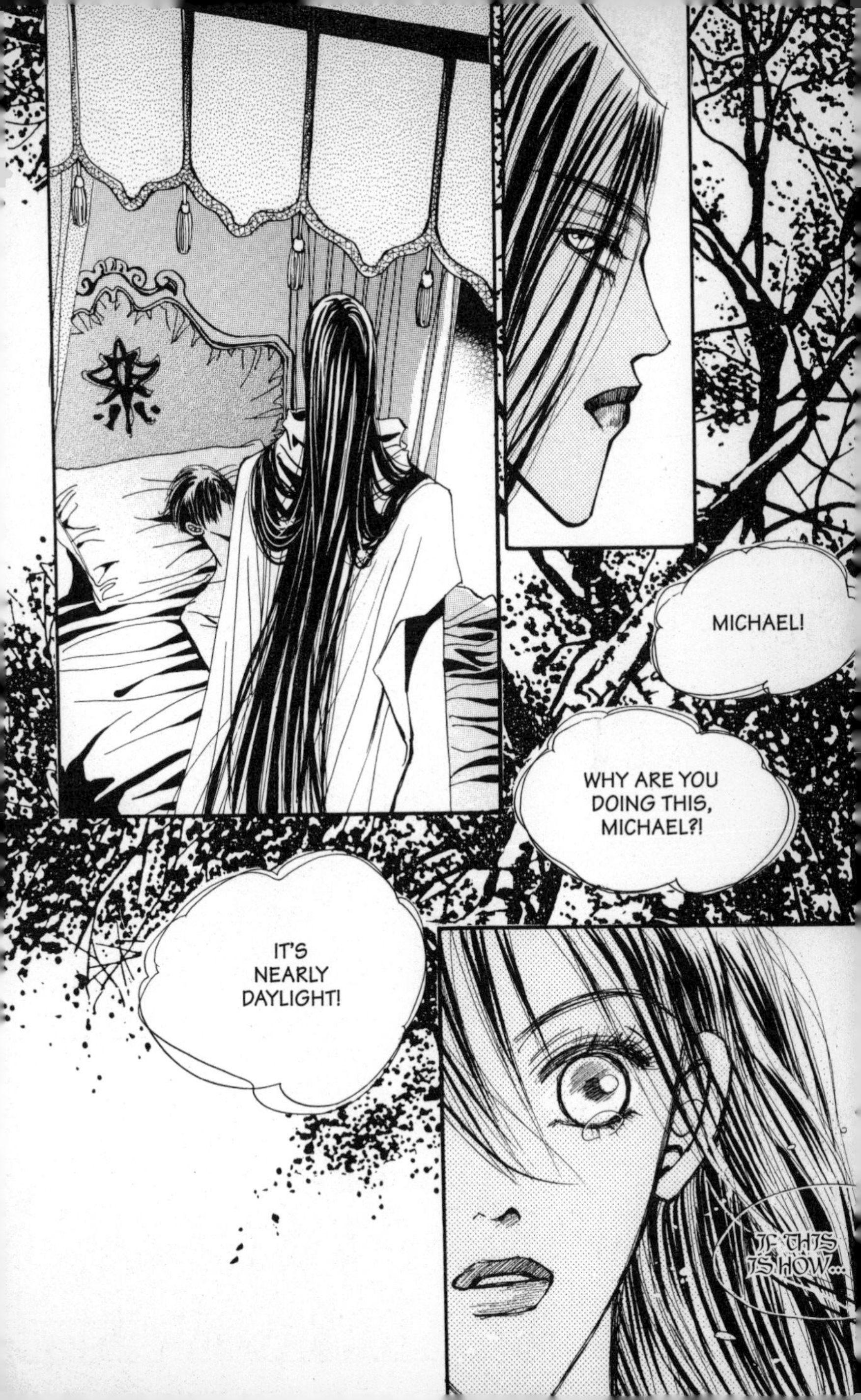
MICHAEL!
WHY ARE YOU DOING THIS, MICHAEL?!
IT'S NEARLY DAYLIGHT!
IF THIS IS HOW...

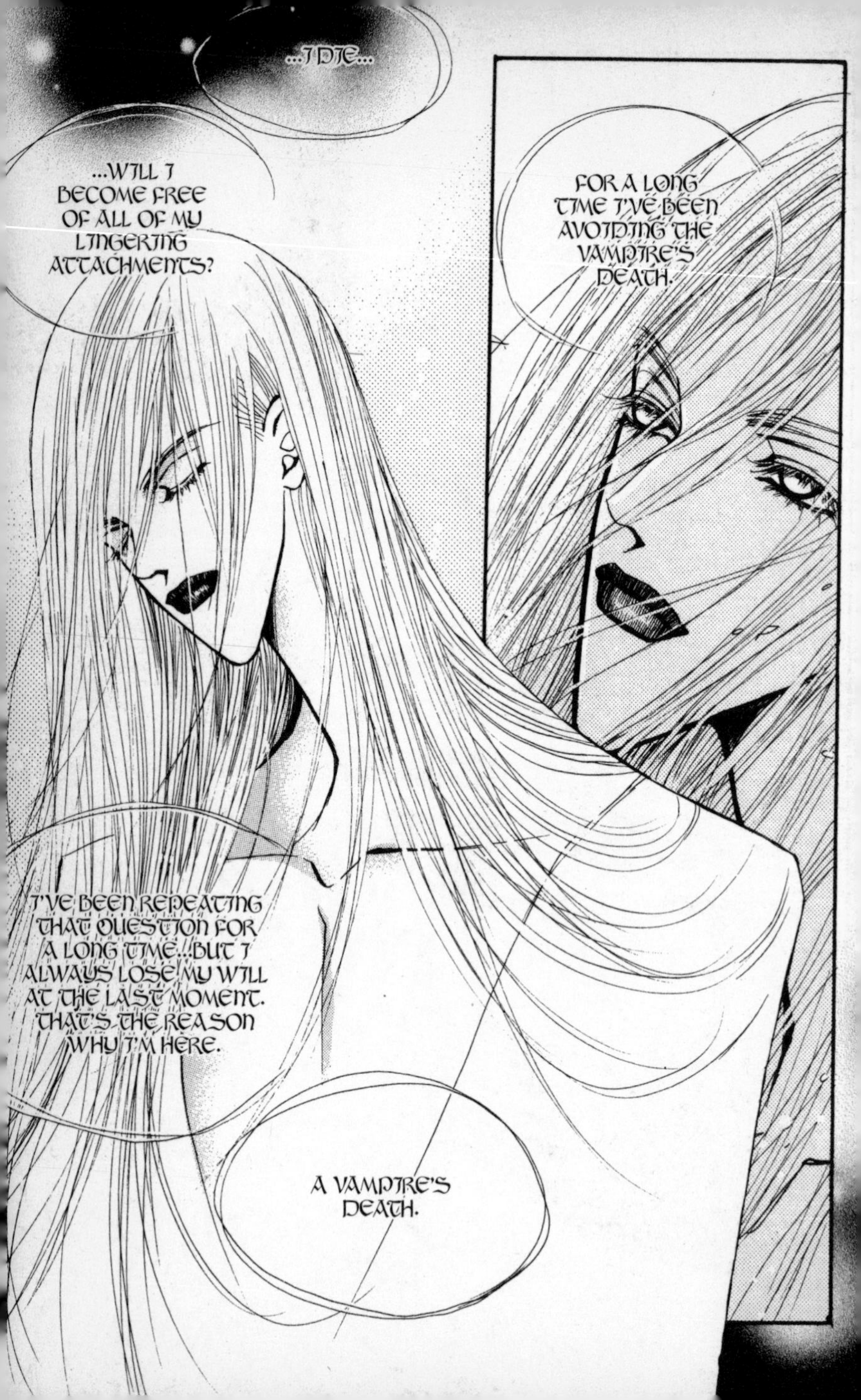
...I DIE...
...WILL I BECOME FREE OF ALL OF MY LINGERING ATTACHMENTS?
I'VE BEEN REPEATING THAT QUESTION FOR A LONG TIME...BUT I ALWAYS LOSE MY WILL AT THE LAST MOMENT. THAT'S THE REASON WHY I'M HERE.
FOR A LONG TIME I'VE BEEN AVOIDING THE VAMPIRE'S DEATH.
A VAMPIRE'S DEATH.

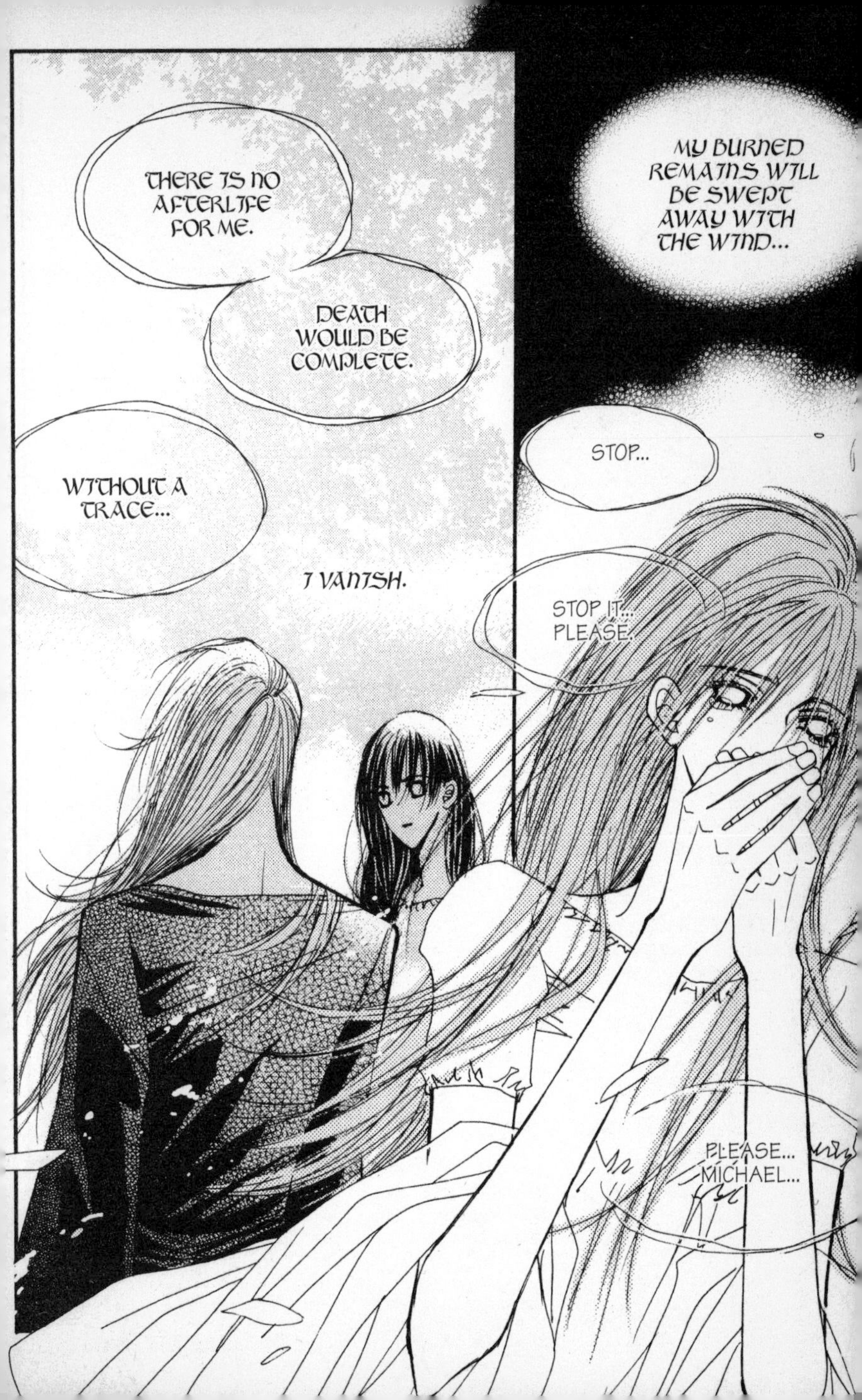
THERE IS NO AFTERLIFE FOR ME.
DEATH WOULD BE COMPLETE.
WITHOUT A TRACE...
I VANISH.
MY BURNED REMAINS WILL BE SWEPT AWAY WITH THE WIND...
STOP...
STOP IT... PLEASE.
PLEASE... MICHAEL...

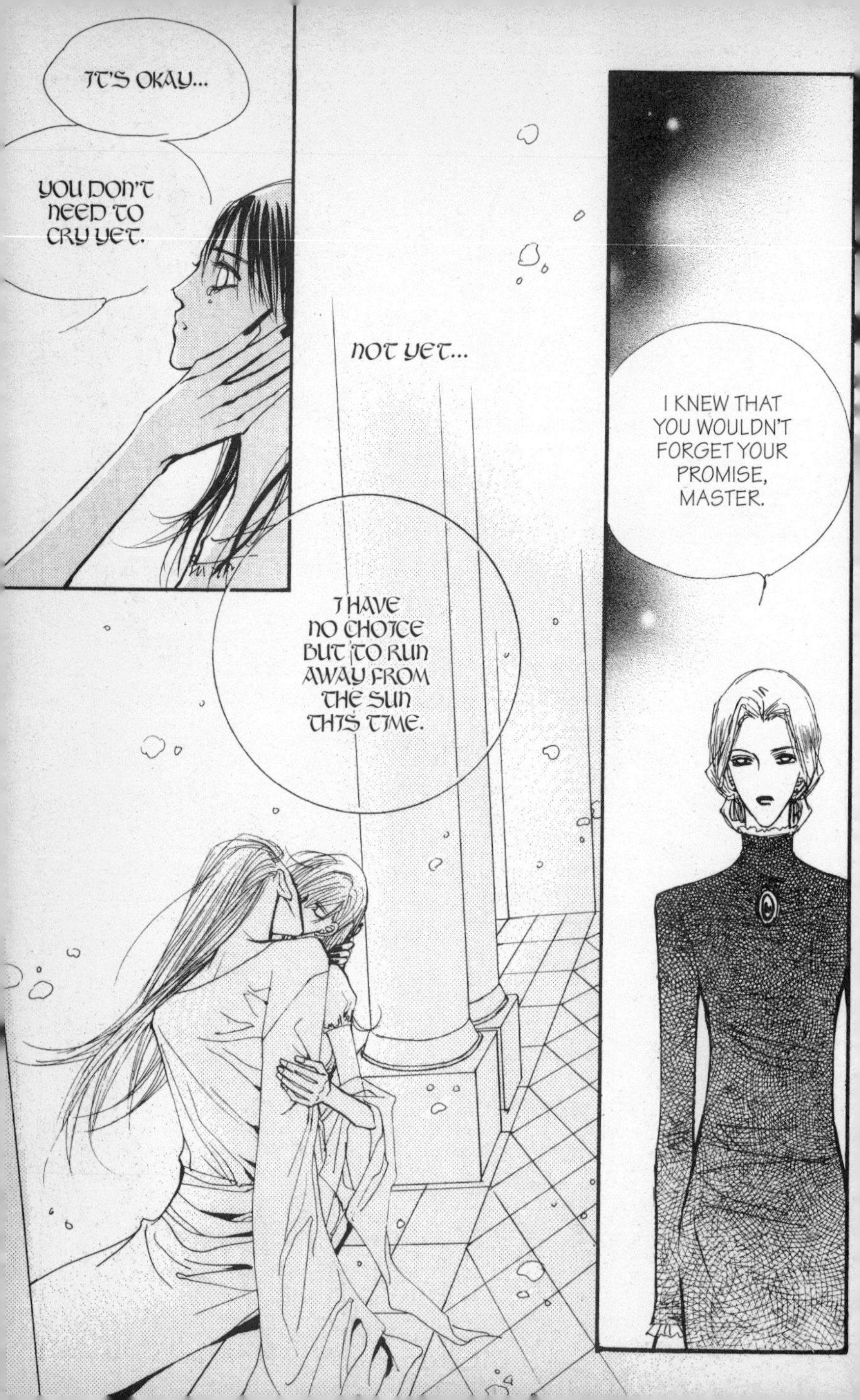
IT'S OKAY...
YOU DON'T NEED TO CRY YET.
NOT YET...
I HAVE NO CHOICE BUT TO RUN AWAY FROM THE SUN THIS TIME.
I KNEW THAT YOU WOULDN'T FORGET YOUR PROMISE, MASTER.

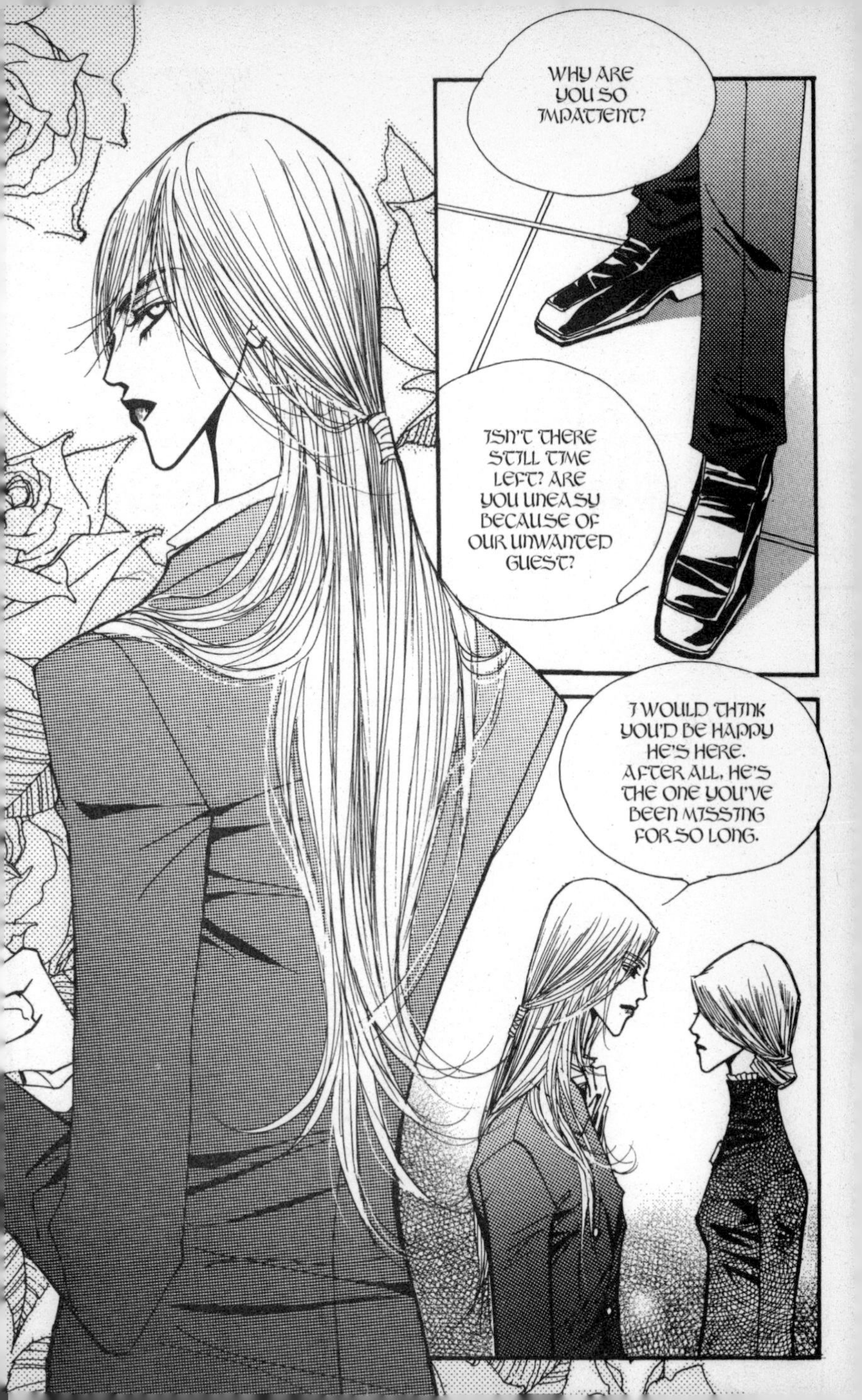
WHY ARE YOU SO IMPATIENT?
ISN'T THERE STILL TIME LEFT? ARE YOU UNEASY BECAUSE OF OUR UNWANTED GUEST?
I WOULD THINK YOU'D BE HAPPY HE'S HERE. AFTER ALL, HE'S THE ONE YOU'VE BEEN MISSING FOR SO LONG.

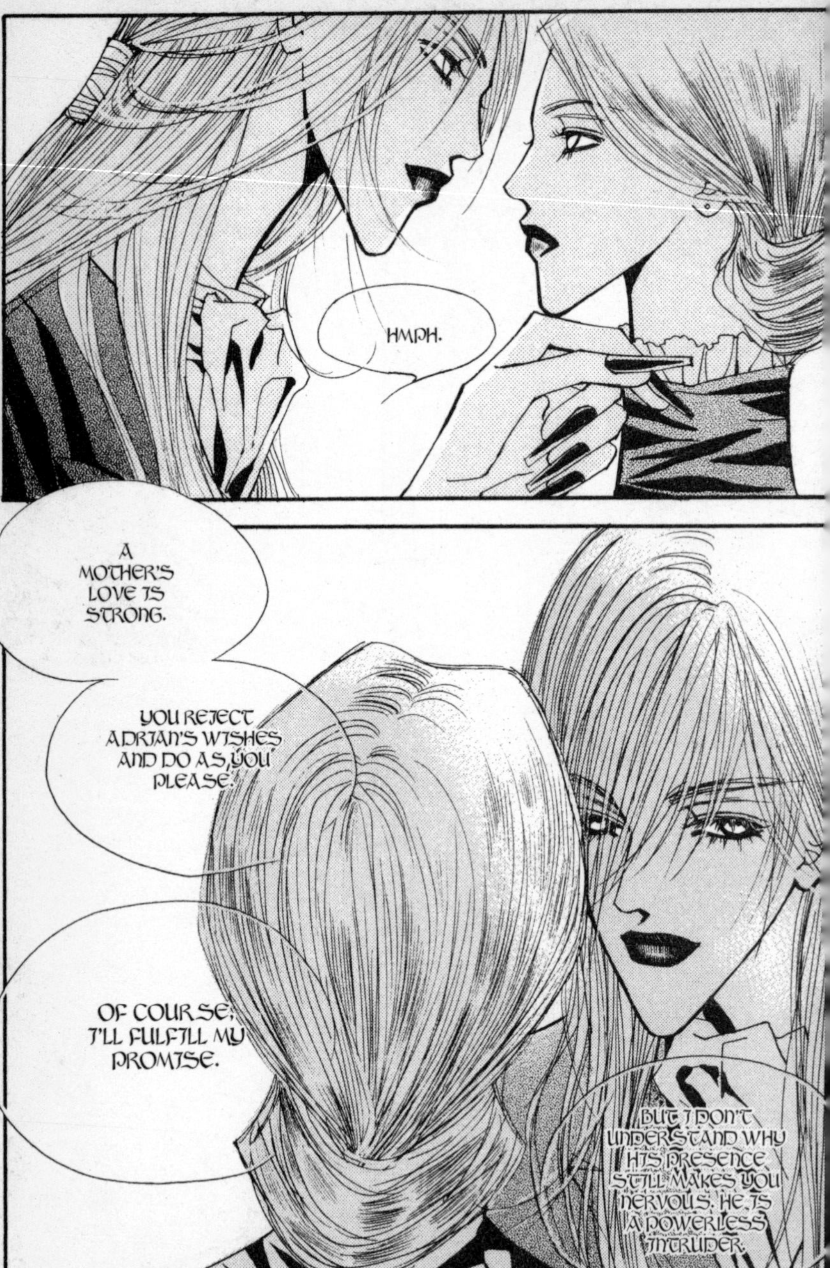
HMPH.
A MOTHER'S LOVE IS STRONG.
YOU REJECT ADRIAN'S WISHES AND DO AS YOU PLEASE.
OF COURSE, I'LL FULFILL MY PROMISE.
BUT I DON'T UNDERSTAND WHY HIS PRESENCE STILL MAKES YOU NERVOUS. HE IS A POWERLESS INTRUDER.

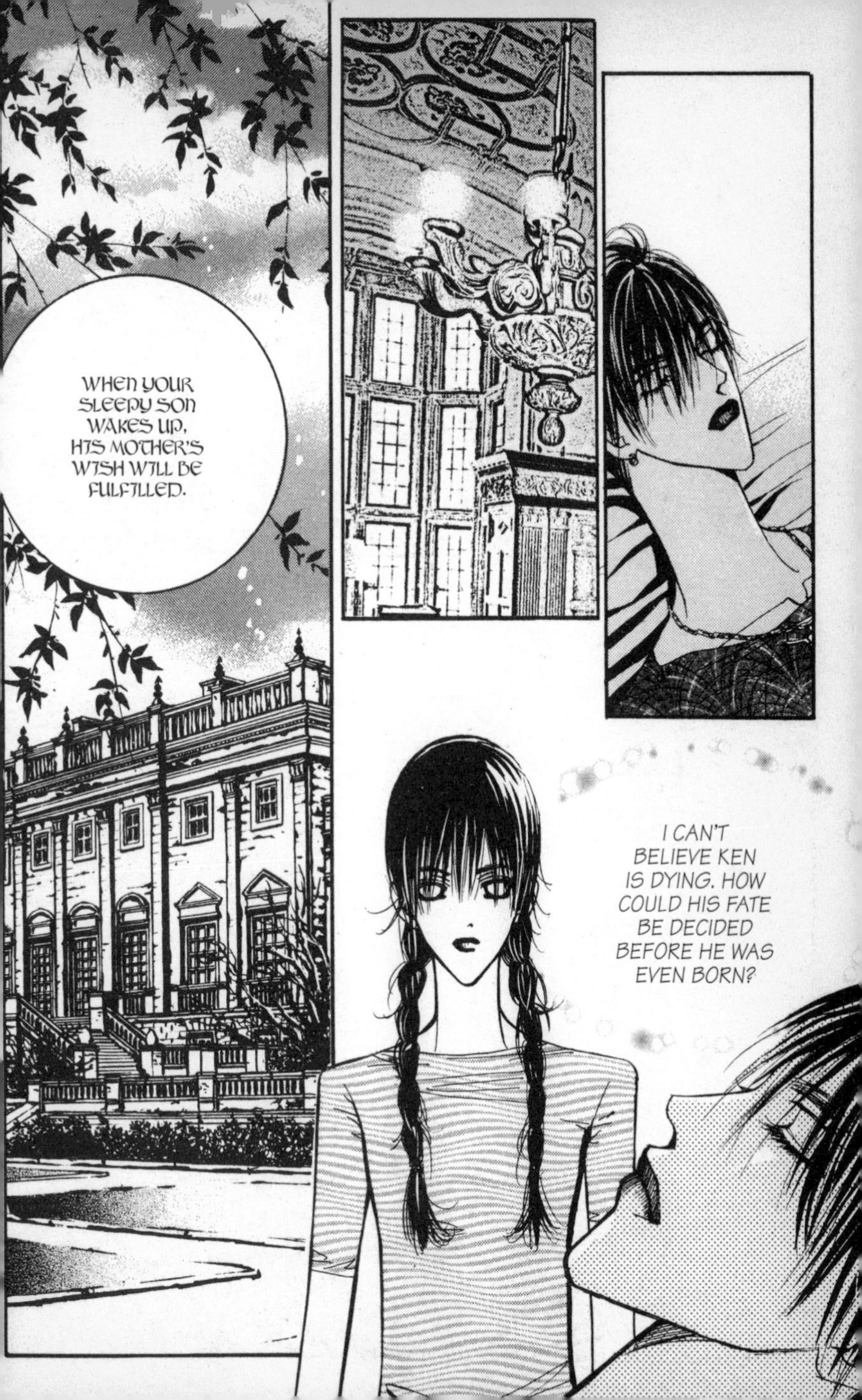
I CAN'T BELIEVE KEN IS DYING. HOW COULD HIS FATE BE DECIDED BEFORE HE WAS EVEN BORN?
WHEN YOUR SLEEPY SON WAKES UP, HIS MOTHER'S WISH WILL BE FULFILLED.

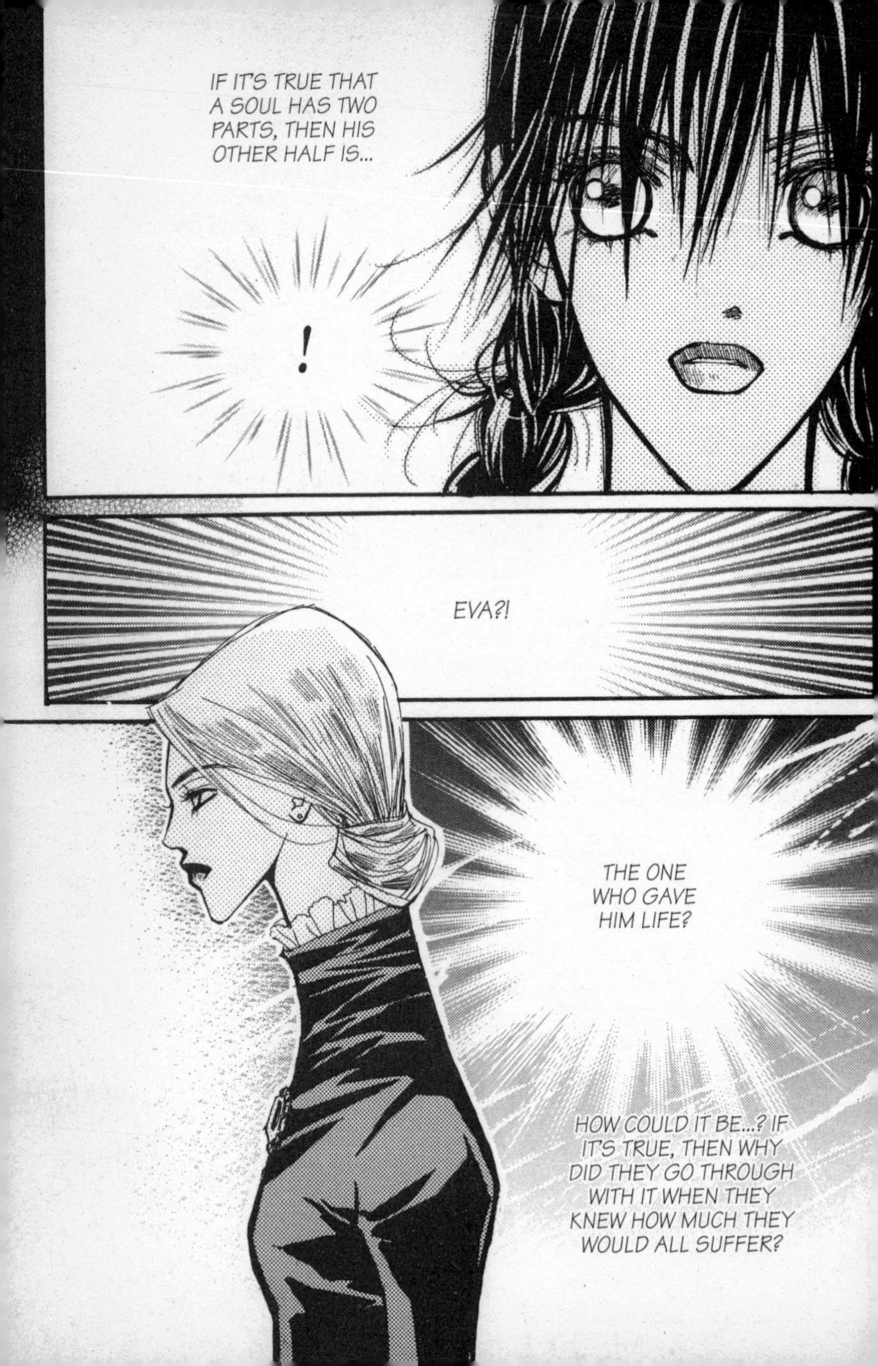
IF IT'S TRUE THAT A SOUL HAS TWO PARTS, THEN HIS OTHER HALF IS...
!
EVA?!
THE ONE WHO GAVE HIM LIFE?
HOW COULD IT BE...? IF IT'S TRUE, THEN WHY DID THEY GO THROUGH WITH IT WHEN THEY KNEW HOW MUCH THEY WOULD ALL SUFFER?

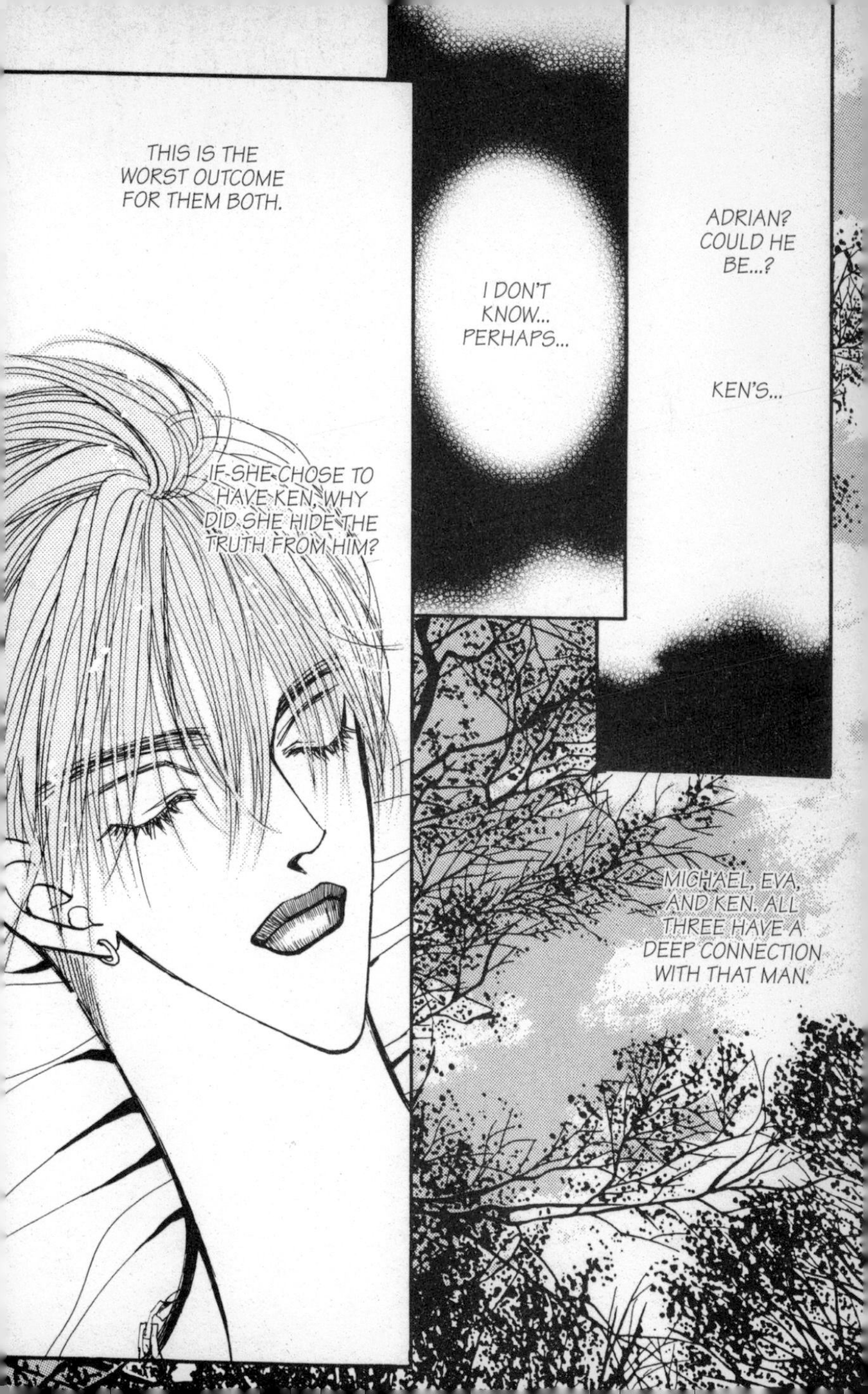
ADRIAN? COULD HE BE...?
KEN'S...
I DON'T KNOW... PERHAPS...
THIS IS THE WORST OUTCOME FOR THEM BOTH.
IF SHE CHOSE TO HAVE KEN, WHY DID SHE HIDE THE TRUTH FROM HIM?
MICHAEL, EVA, AND KEN. ALL THREE HAVE A DEEP CONNECTION WITH THAT MAN.

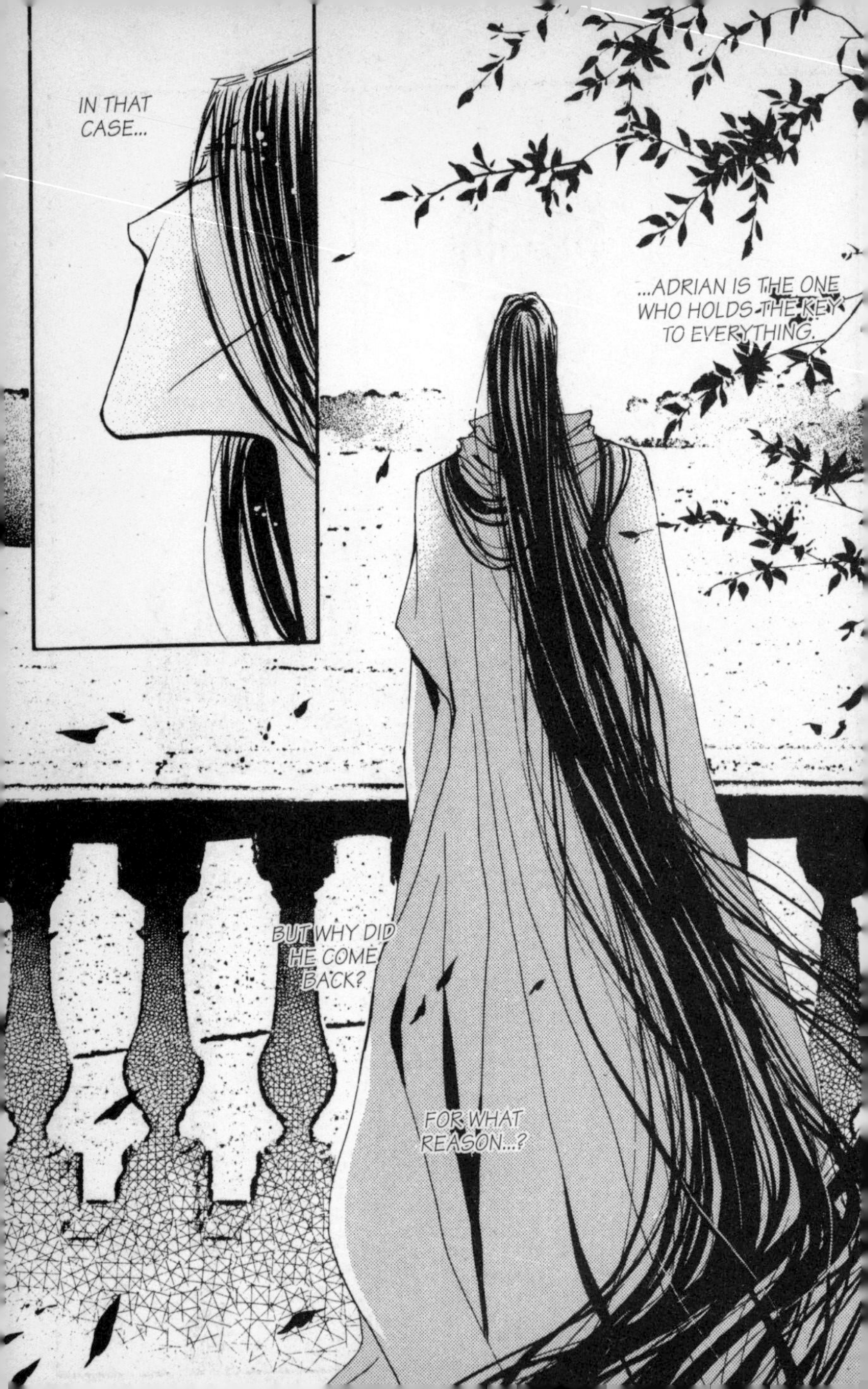
IN THAT CASE...
...ADRIAN IS THE ONE WHO HOLDS THE KEY TO EVERYTHING.
BUT WHY DID HE COME BACK?
FOR WHAT REASON...?

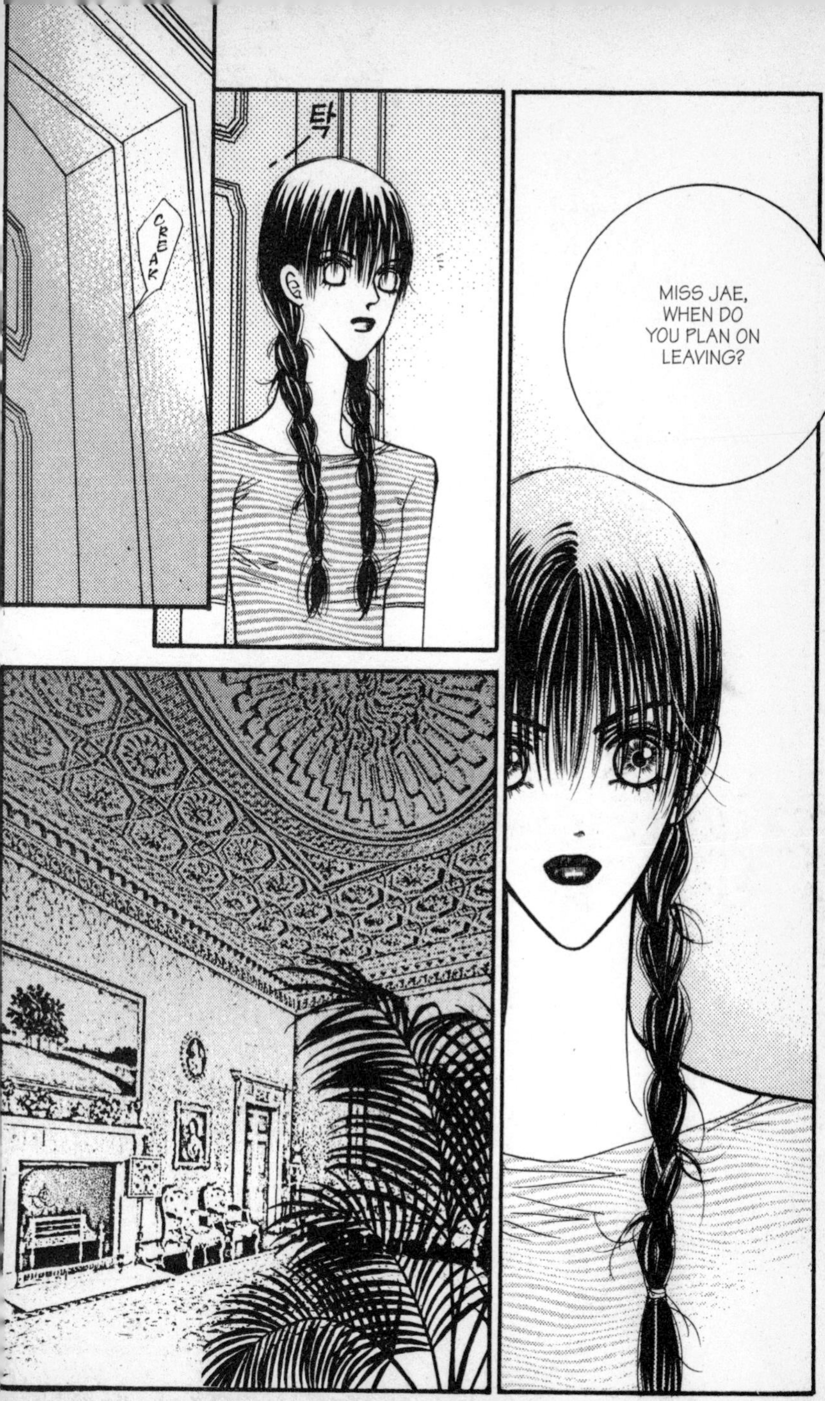
CREAK
탁
MISS JAE,
WHEN DO
YOU PLAN ON
LEAVING?

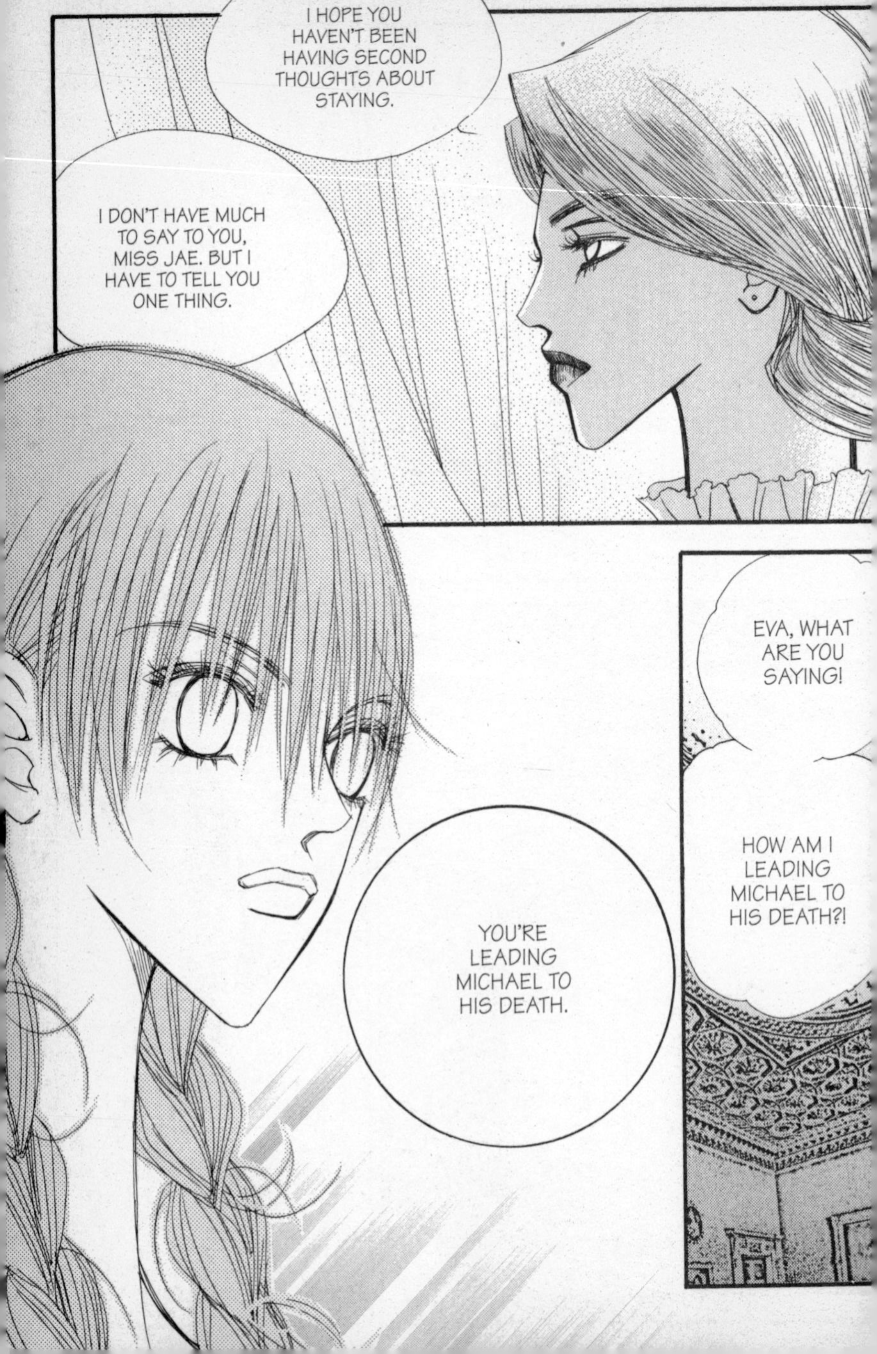
I HOPE YOU HAVEN'T BEEN HAVING SECOND THOUGHTS ABOUT STAYING.
I DON'T HAVE MUCH TO SAY TO YOU, MISS JAE. BUT I HAVE TO TELL YOU ONE THING.
YOU'RE LEADING MICHAEL TO HIS DEATH.
EVA, WHAT ARE YOU SAYING!
HOW AM I LEADING MICHAEL TO HIS DEATH?!

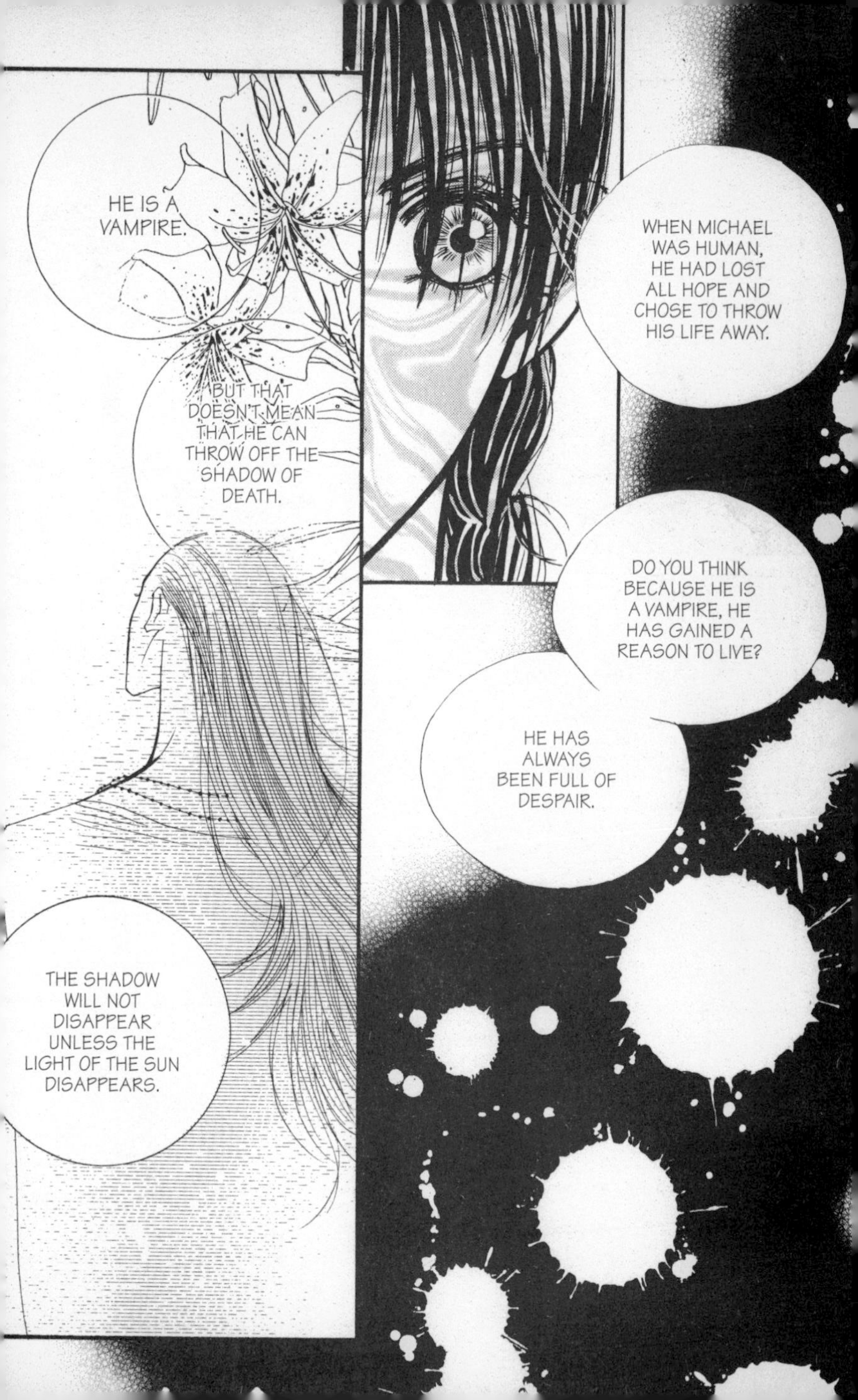
WHEN MICHAEL WAS HUMAN, HE HAD LOST ALL HOPE AND CHOSE TO THROW HIS LIFE AWAY.
DO YOU THINK BECAUSE HE IS A VAMPIRE, HE HAS GAINED A REASON TO LIVE?
HE HAS ALWAYS BEEN FULL OF DESPAIR.
HE IS A VAMPIRE.
BUT THAT DOESN'T MEAN THAT HE CAN THROW OFF THE SHADOW OF DEATH.
THE SHADOW WILL NOT DISAPPEAR UNLESS THE LIGHT OF THE SUN DISAPPEARS.

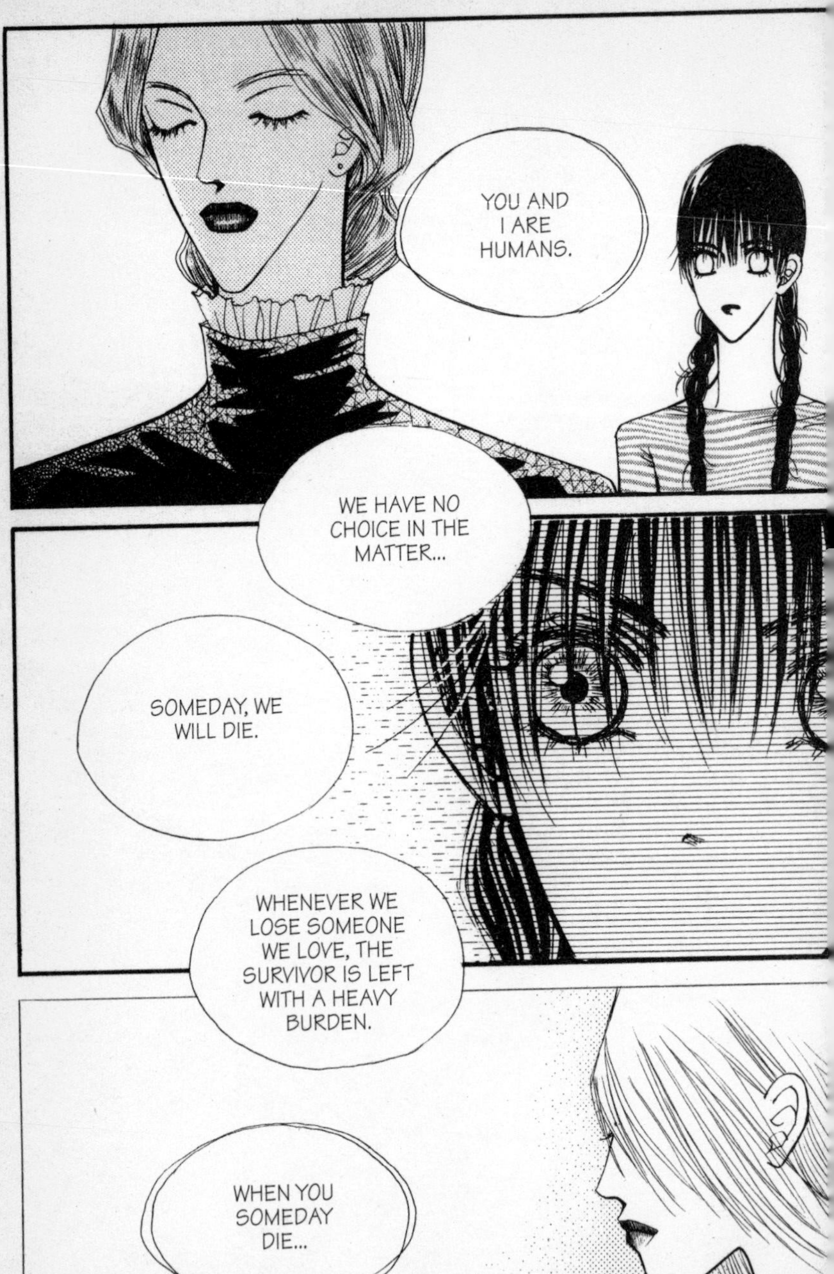
YOU AND I ARE HUMANS.
WE HAVE NO CHOICE IN THE MATTER...
SOMEDAY, WE WILL DIE.
WHENEVER WE LOSE SOMEONE WE LOVE, THE SURVIVOR IS LEFT WITH A HEAVY BURDEN.
WHEN YOU SOMEDAY DIE...

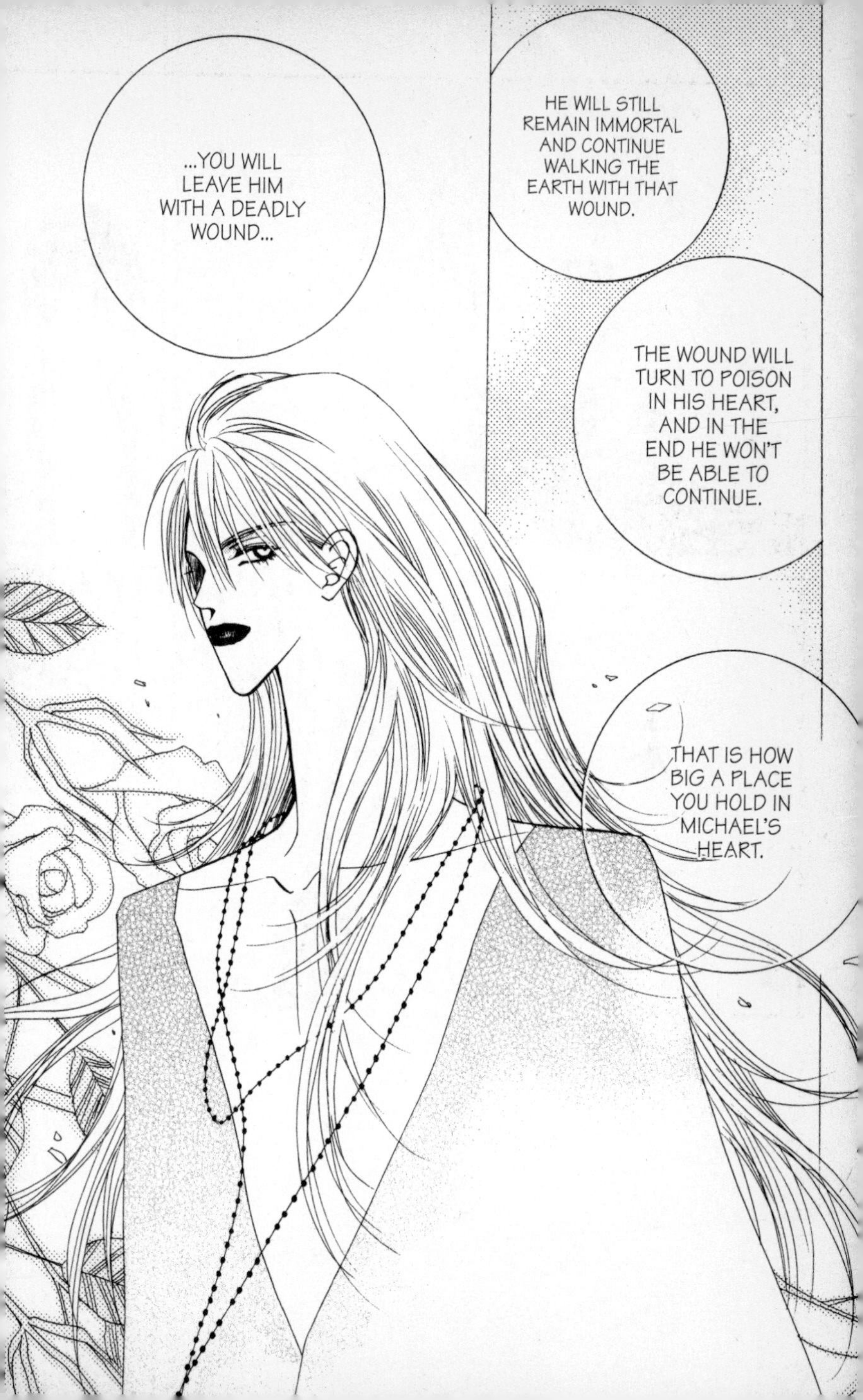
...YOU WILL LEAVE HIM WITH A DEADLY WOUND...
HE WILL STILL REMAIN IMMORTAL AND CONTINUE WALKING THE EARTH WITH THAT WOUND.
THE WOUND WILL TURN TO POISON IN HIS HEART, AND IN THE END HE WON'T BE ABLE TO CONTINUE.
THAT IS HOW BIG A PLACE YOU HOLD IN MICHAEL'S HEART.

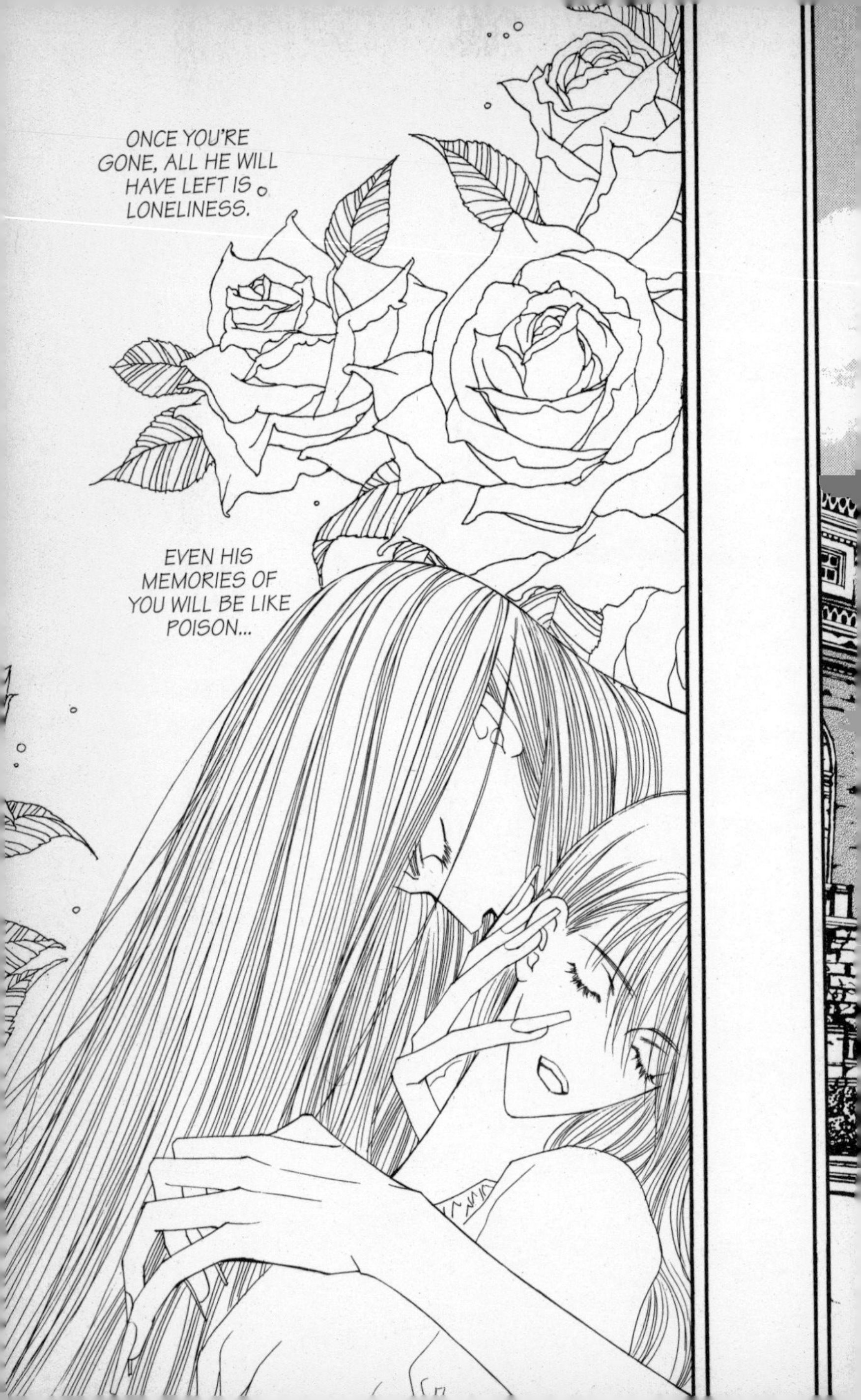
ONCE YOU'RE GONE, ALL HE WILL HAVE LEFT IS LONELINESS.
EVEN HIS MEMORIES OF YOU WILL BE LIKE POISON...

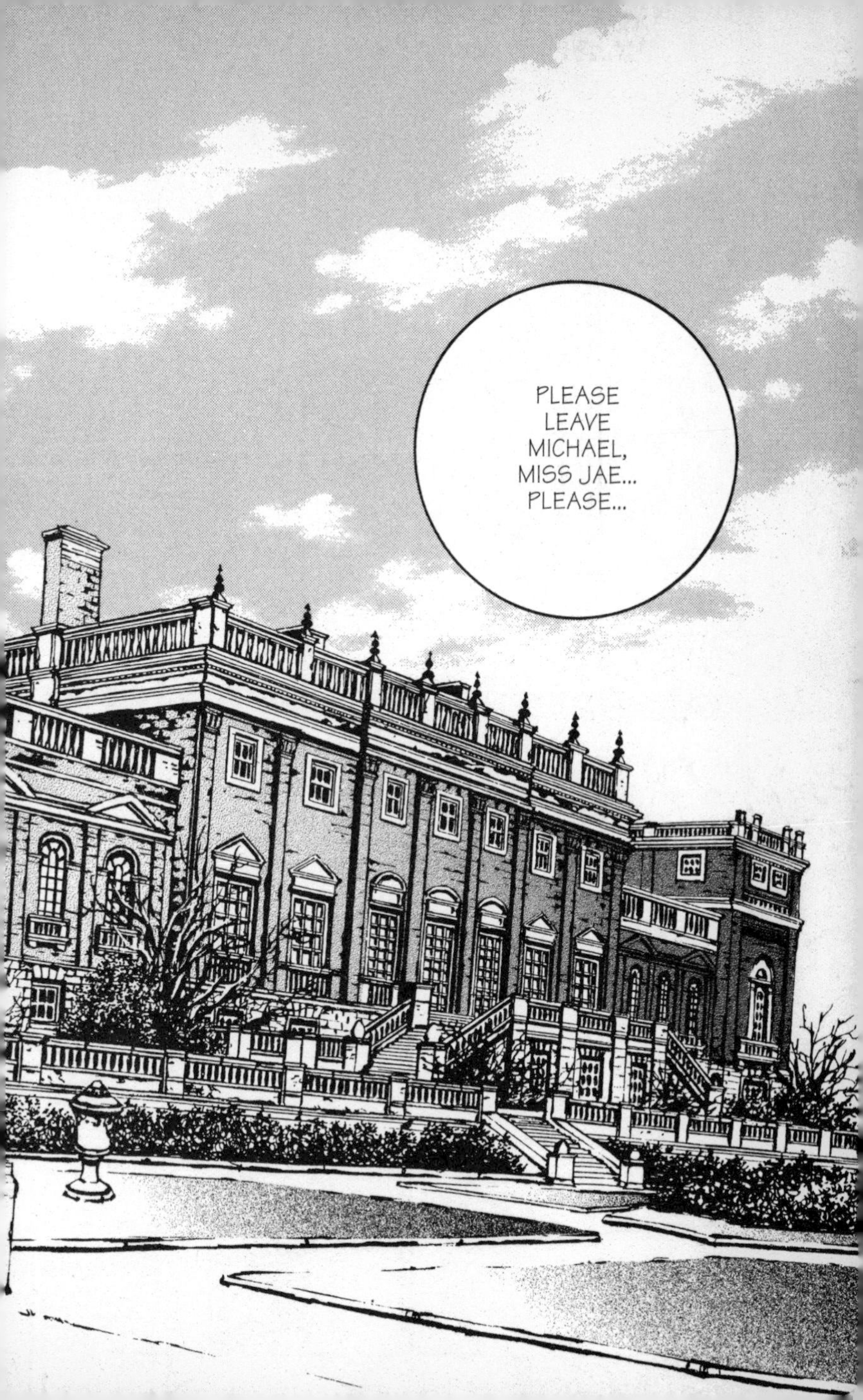
PLEASE LEAVE MICHAEL, MISS JAE... PLEASE...

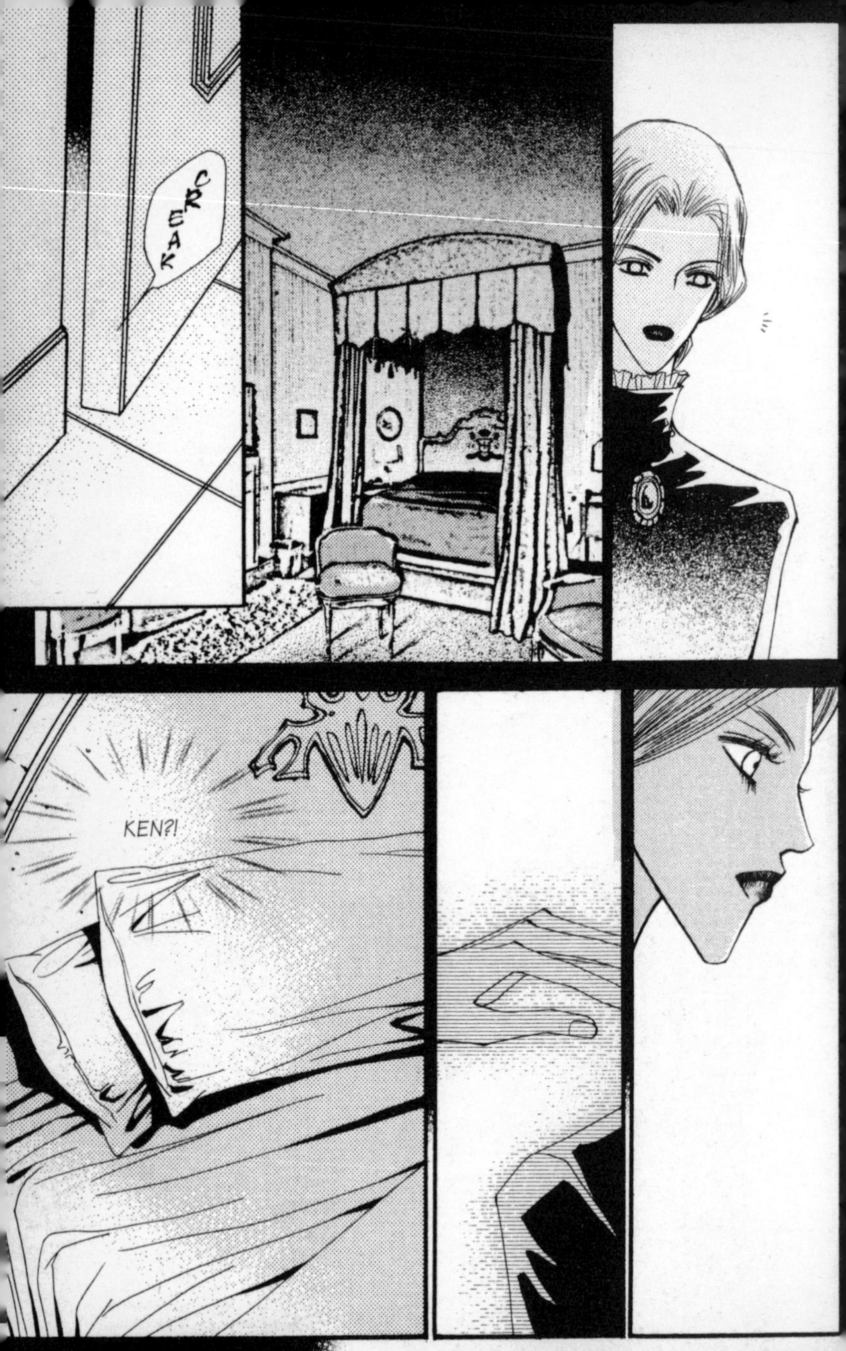
CREAK
KEN?!

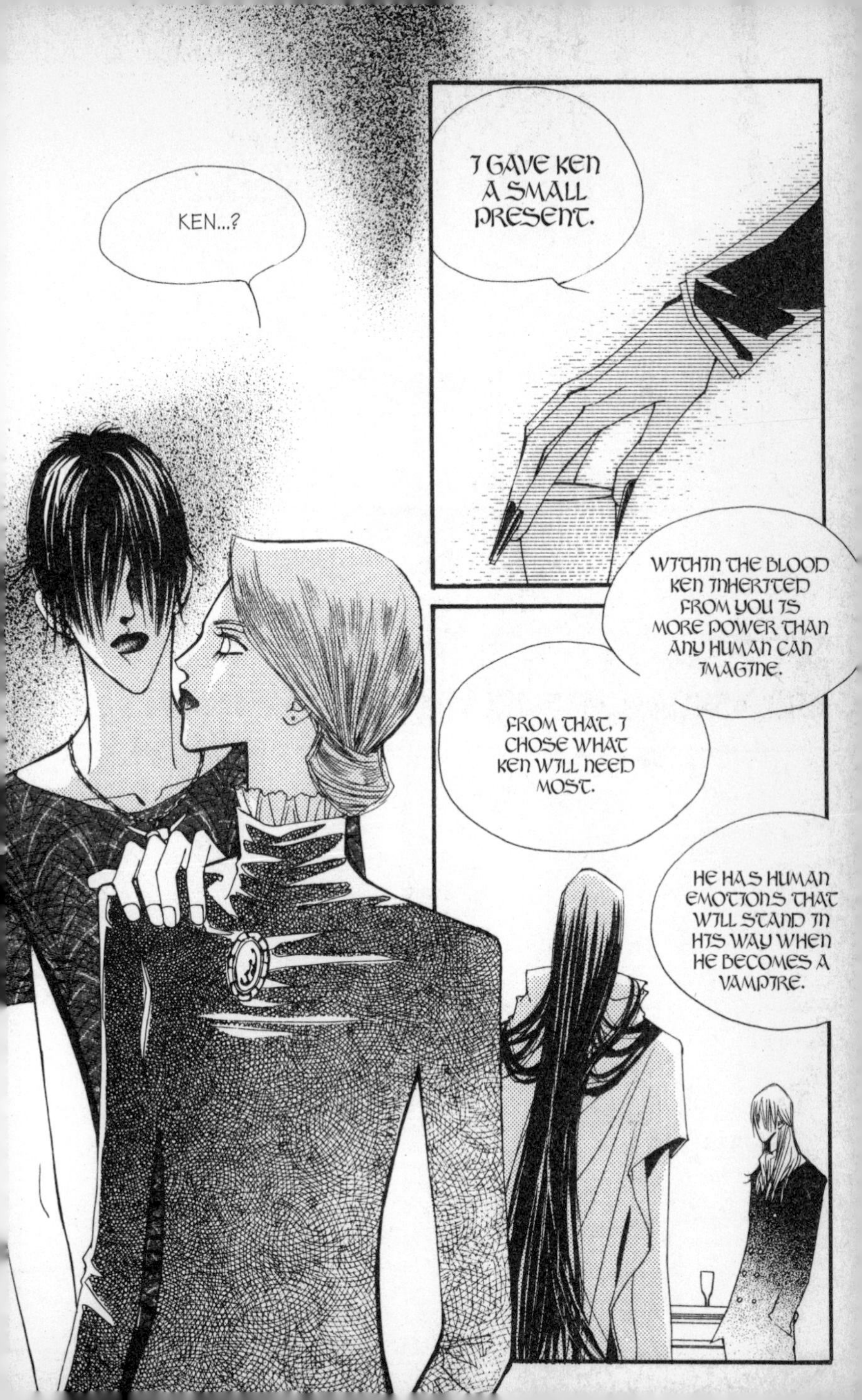
KEN...?
I GAVE KEN A SMALL PRESENT.
WITHIN THE BLOOD KEN INHERITED FROM YOU IS MORE POWER THAN ANY HUMAN CAN IMAGINE.
FROM THAT, I CHOSE WHAT KEN WILL NEED MOST.
HE HAS HUMAN EMOTIONS THAT WILL STAND IN HIS WAY WHEN HE BECOMES A VAMPIRE.

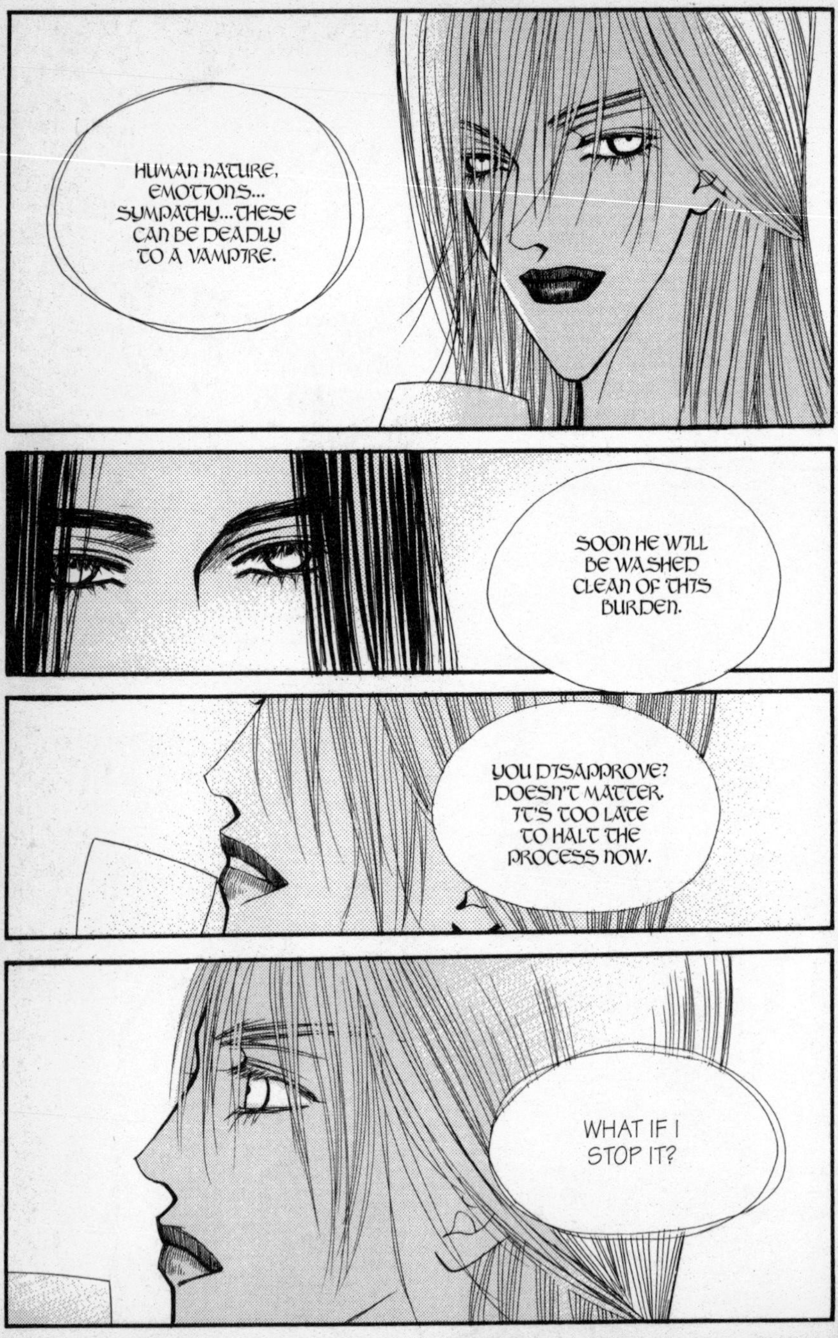
HUMAN NATURE, EMOTIONS... SYMPATHY...THESE CAN BE DEADLY TO A VAMPIRE.
SOON HE WILL BE WASHED CLEAN OF THIS BURDEN.
YOU DISAPPROVE? DOESN'T MATTER. IT'S TOO LATE TO HALT THE PROCESS NOW.
WHAT IF I STOP IT?

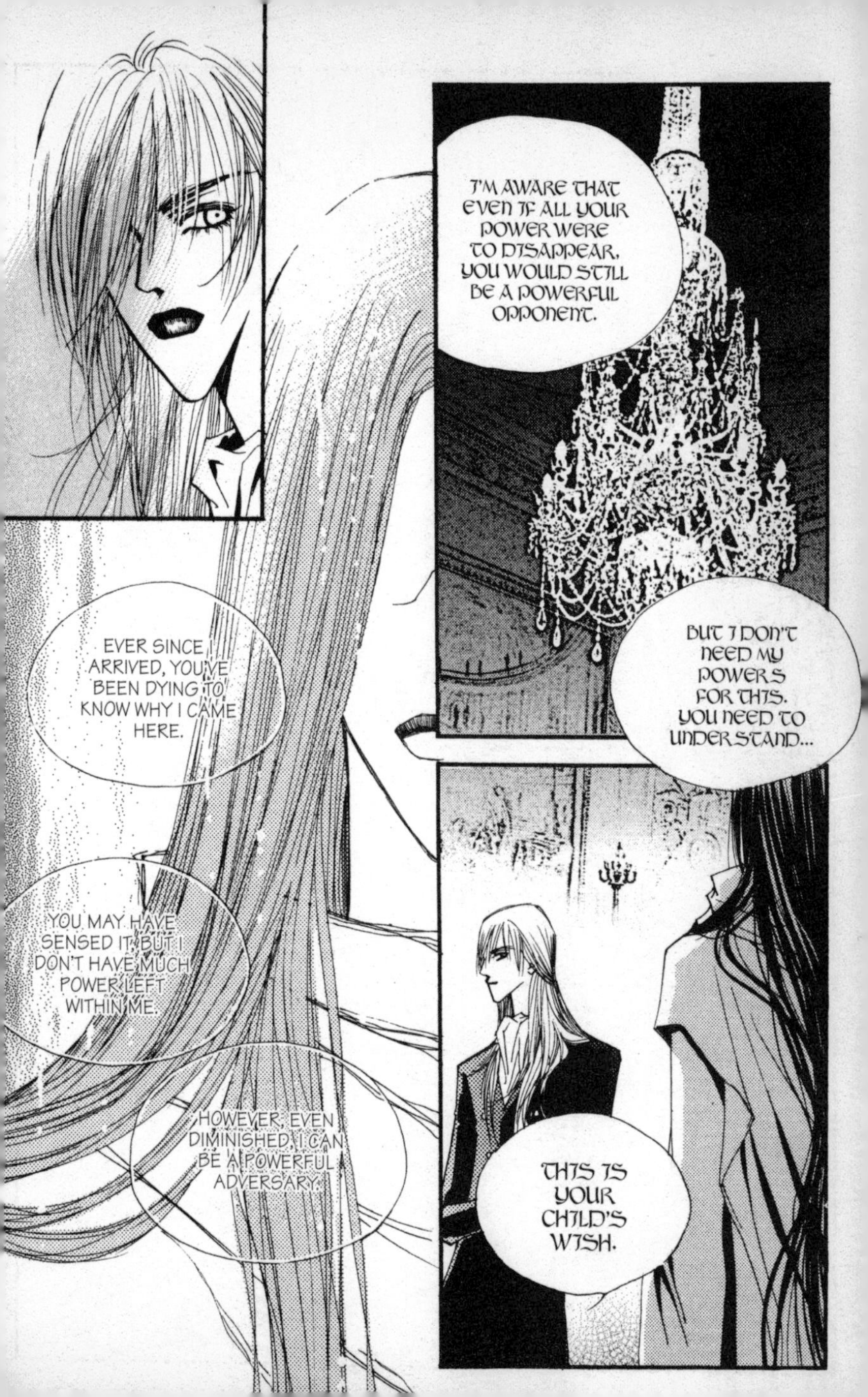
EVER SINCE I ARRIVED, YOU'VE BEEN DYING TO KNOW WHY I CAME HERE.
YOU MAY HAVE SENSED IT, BUT I DON'T HAVE MUCH POWER LEFT WITHIN ME.
HOWEVER, EVEN DIMINISHED, I CAN BE A POWERFUL ADVERSARY.
I'M AWARE THAT EVEN IF ALL YOUR POWER WERE TO DISAPPEAR, YOU WOULD STILL BE A POWERFUL OPPONENT.
BUT I DON'T NEED MY POWERS FOR THIS. YOU NEED TO UNDERSTAND...
THIS IS YOUR CHILD'S WISH.

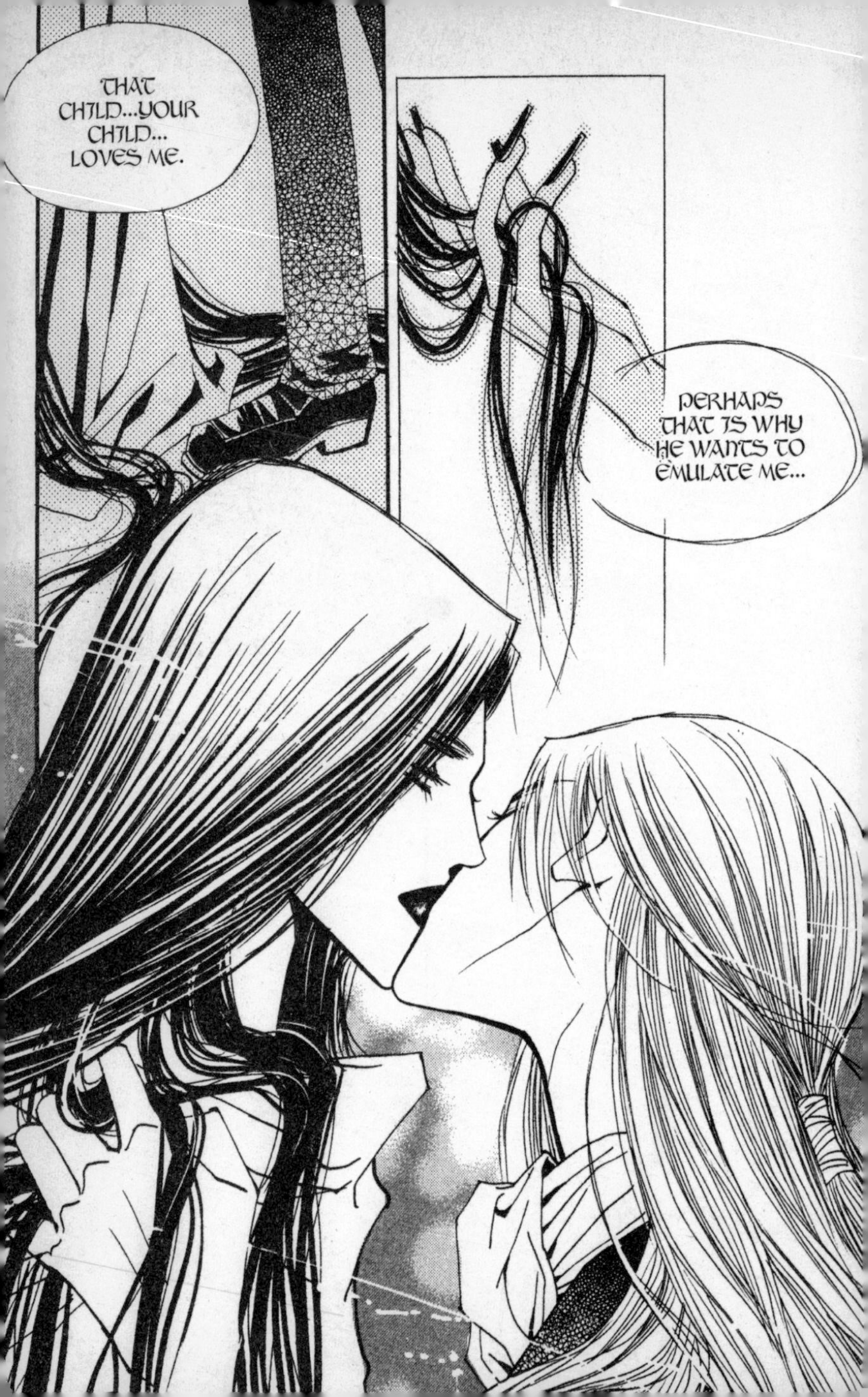
PERHAPS THAT IS WHY HE WANTS TO EMULATE ME...
THAT CHILD...YOUR CHILD... LOVES ME.

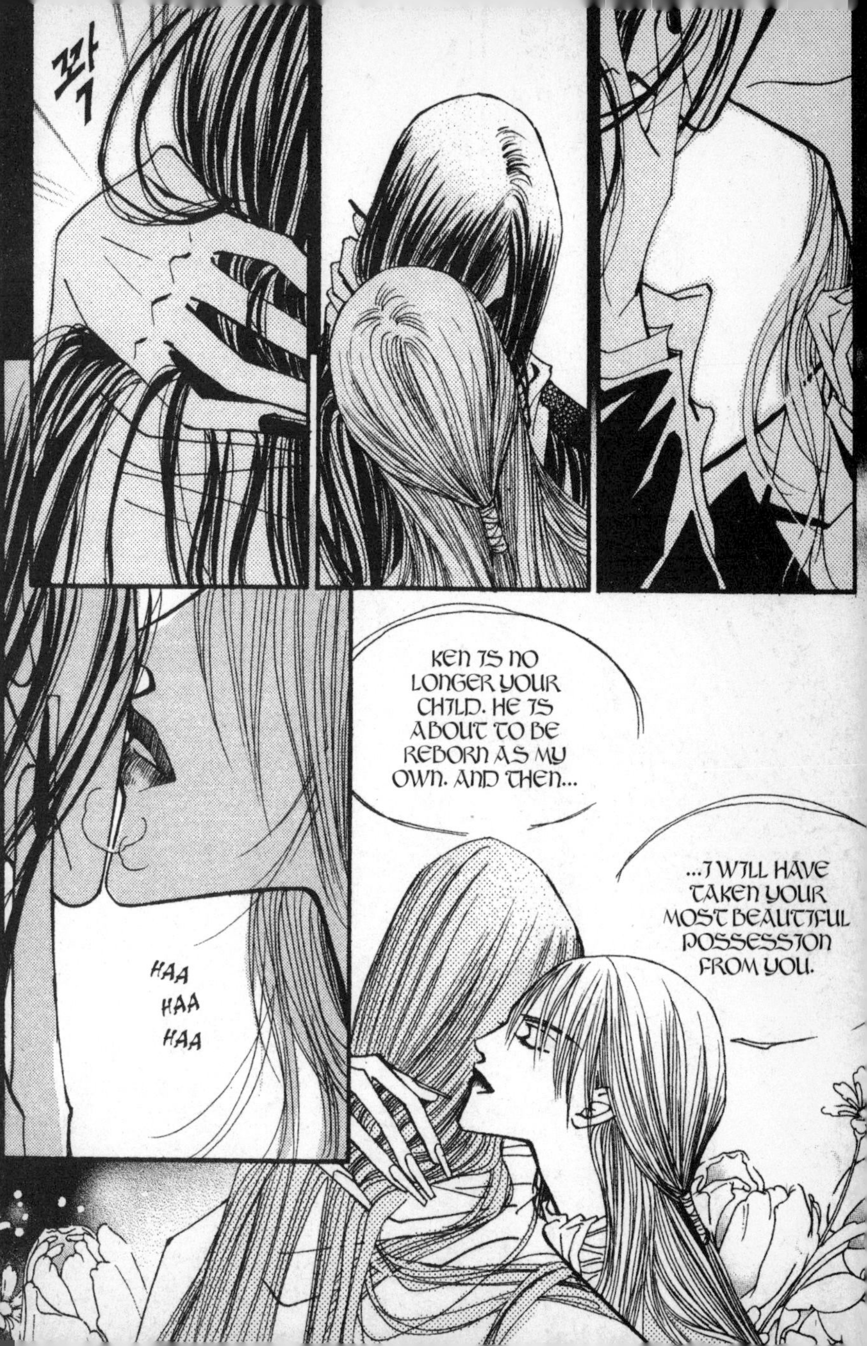
꽉
HAA
HAA
HAA
KEN IS NO LONGER YOUR CHILD. HE IS ABOUT TO BE REBORN AS MY OWN. AND THEN...
...I WILL HAVE TAKEN YOUR MOST BEAUTIFUL POSSESSION FROM YOU.

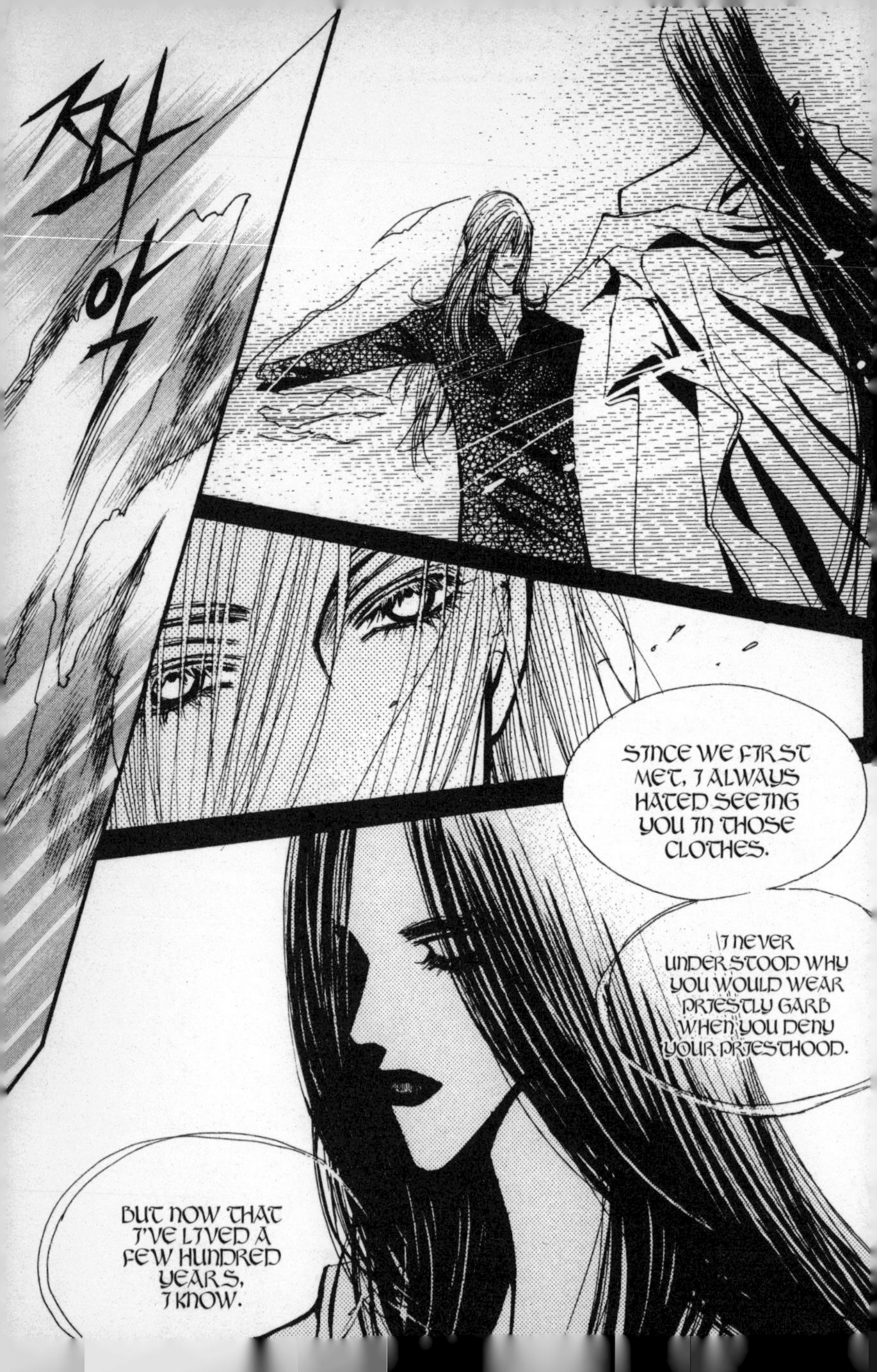
SINCE WE FIRST MET, I ALWAYS HATED SEEING YOU IN THOSE CLOTHES.
I NEVER UNDERSTOOD WHY YOU WOULD WEAR PRIESTLY GARB WHEN YOU DENY YOUR PRIESTHOOD.
BUT NOW THAT I'VE LIVED A FEW HUNDRED YEARS, I KNOW.

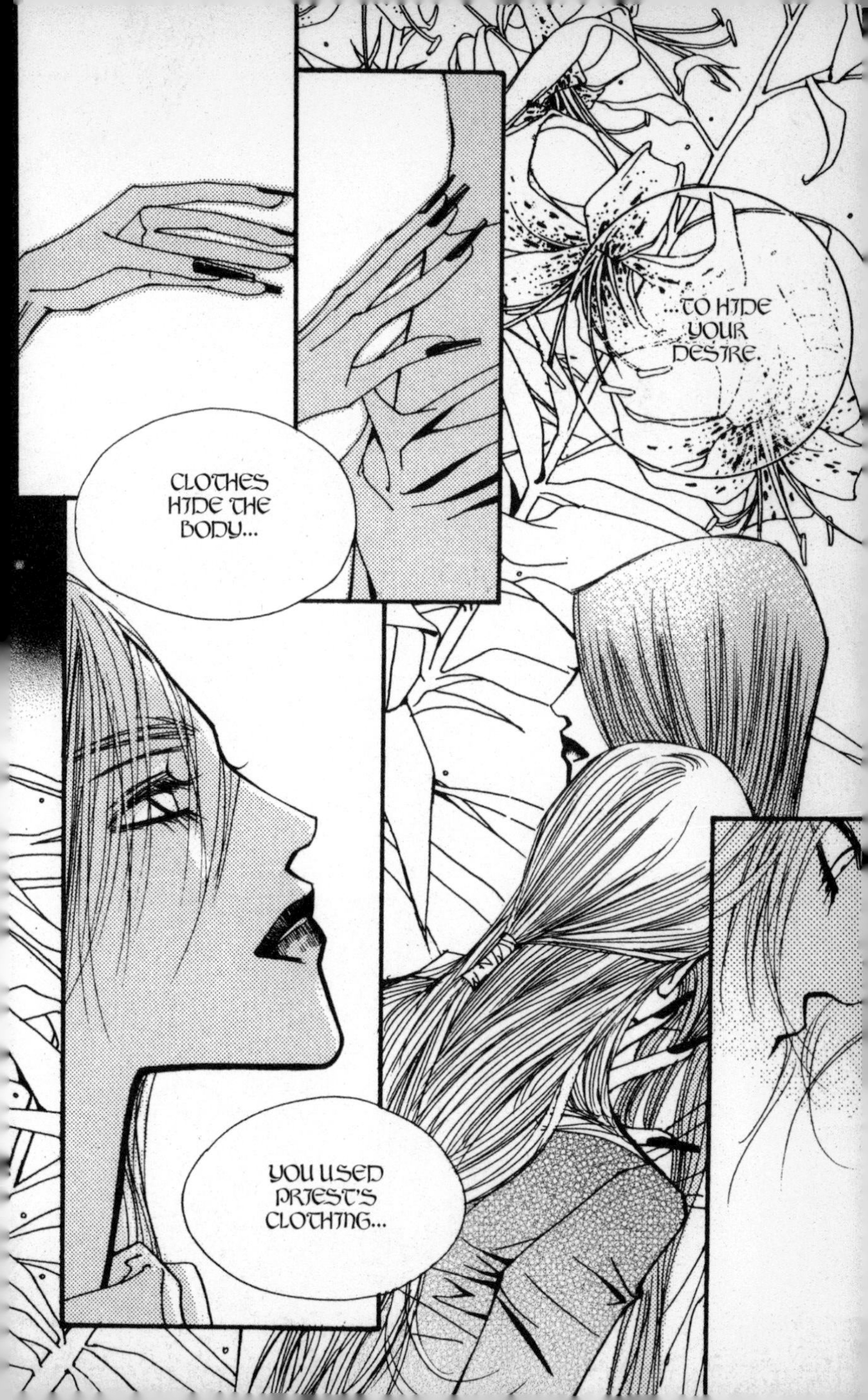
CLOTHES HIDE THE BODY...
YOU USED PRIEST'S CLOTHING...
...TO HIDE YOUR DESIRE.

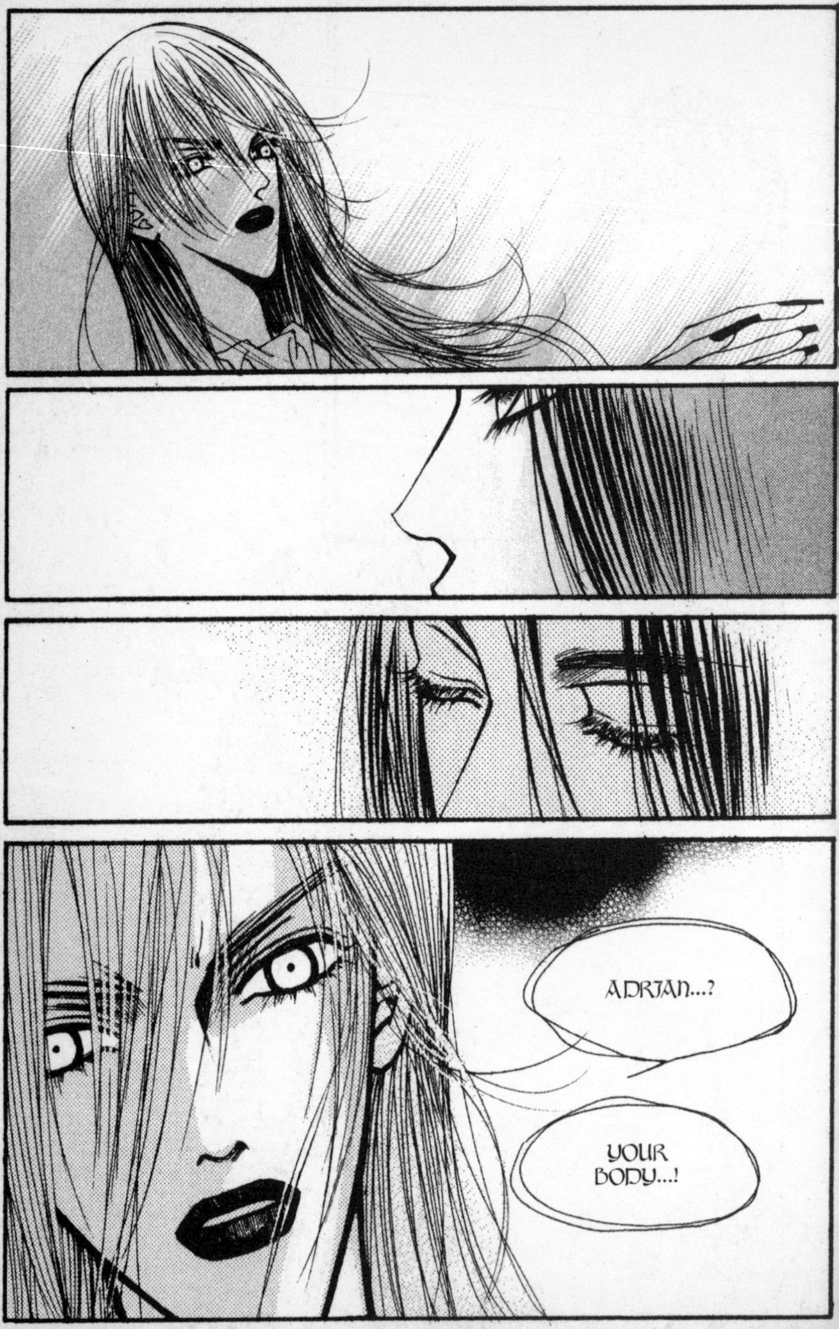
ADRIAN...?
YOUR BODY...!

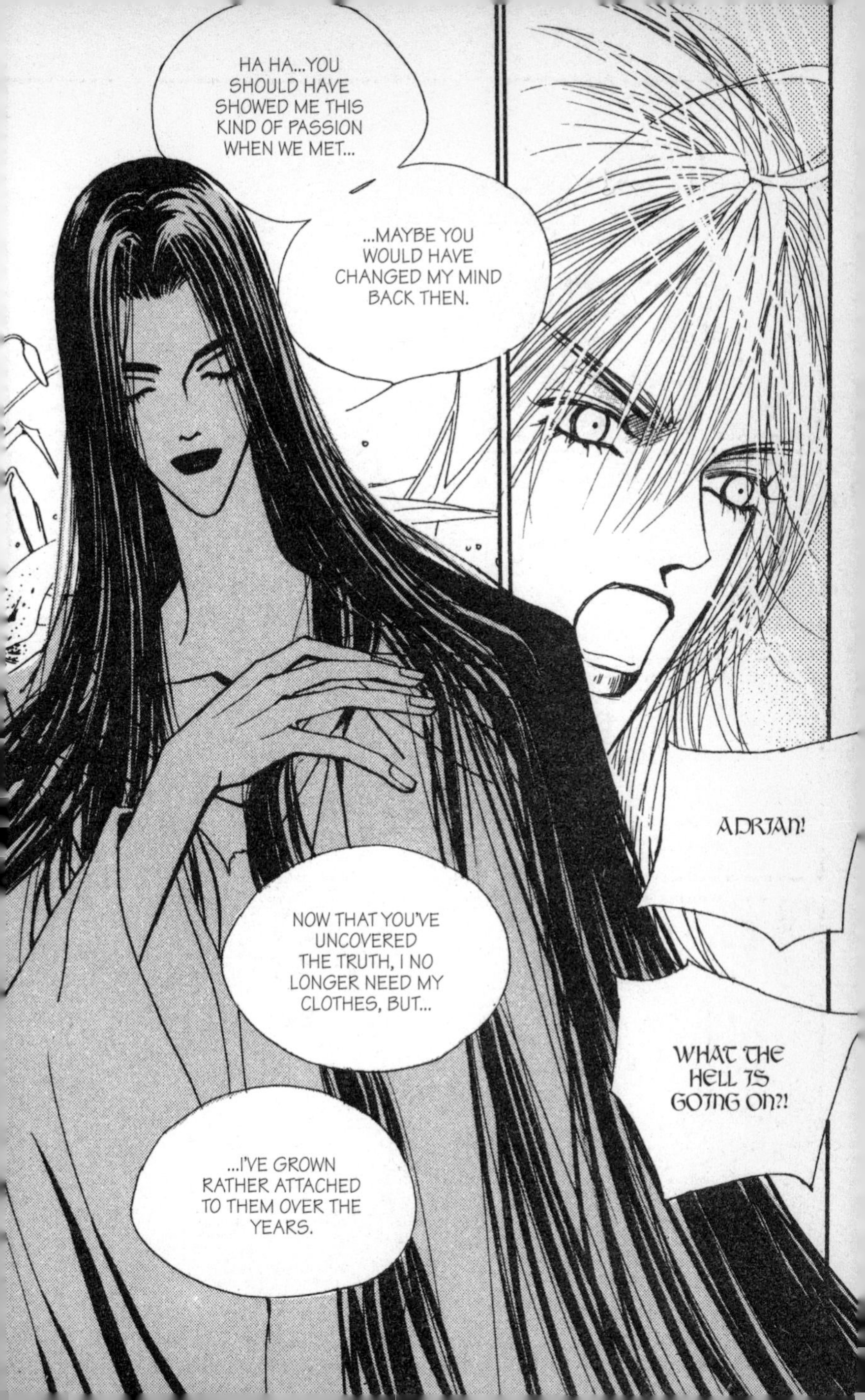
HA HA...YOU SHOULD HAVE SHOWED ME THIS KIND OF PASSION WHEN WE MET...
...MAYBE YOU WOULD HAVE CHANGED MY MIND BACK THEN.
NOW THAT YOU'VE UNCOVERED THE TRUTH, I NO LONGER NEED MY CLOTHES, BUT...
...I'VE GROWN RATHER ATTACHED TO THEM OVER THE YEARS.
ADRIAN!
WHAT THE HELL IS GOING ON?!

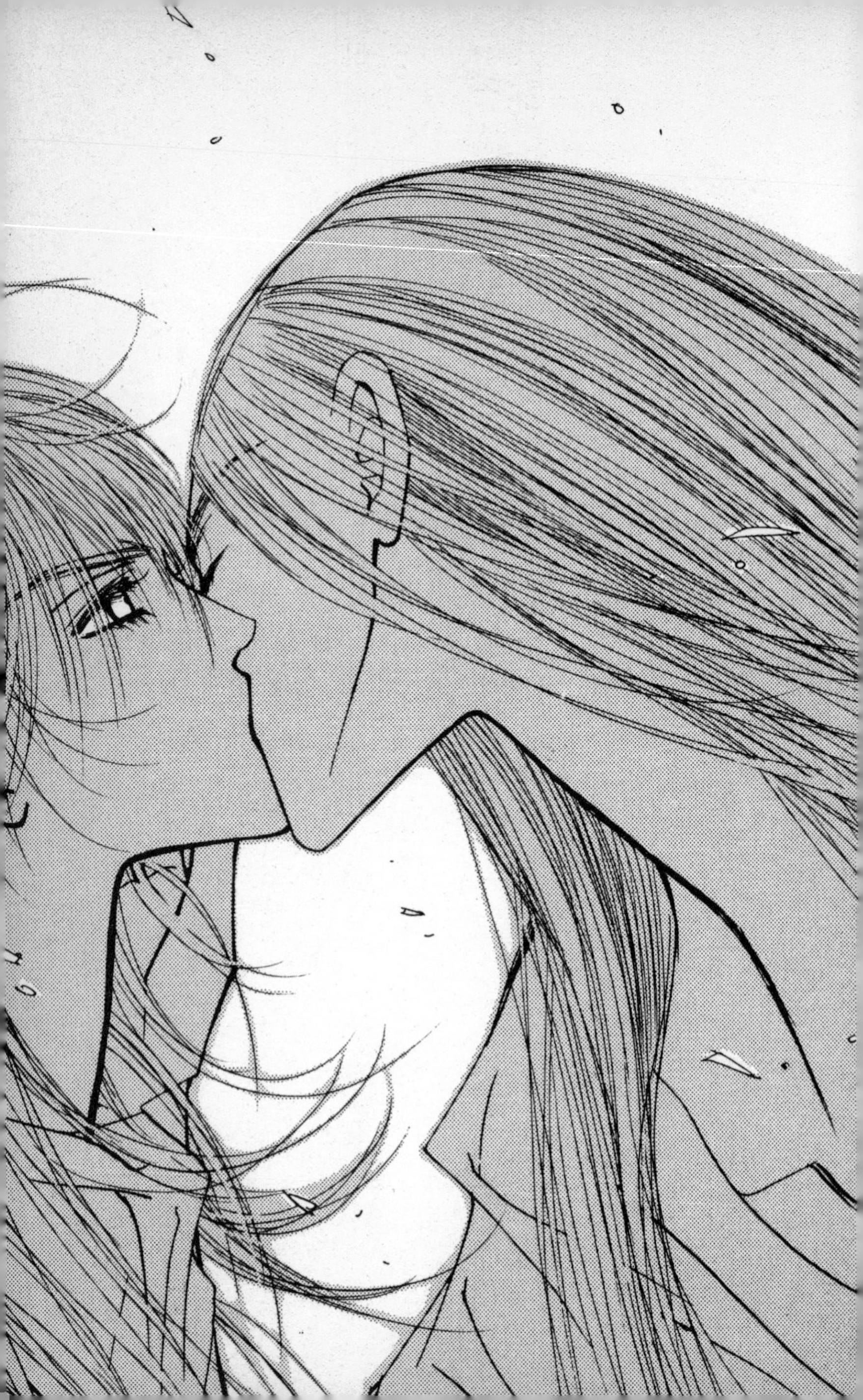

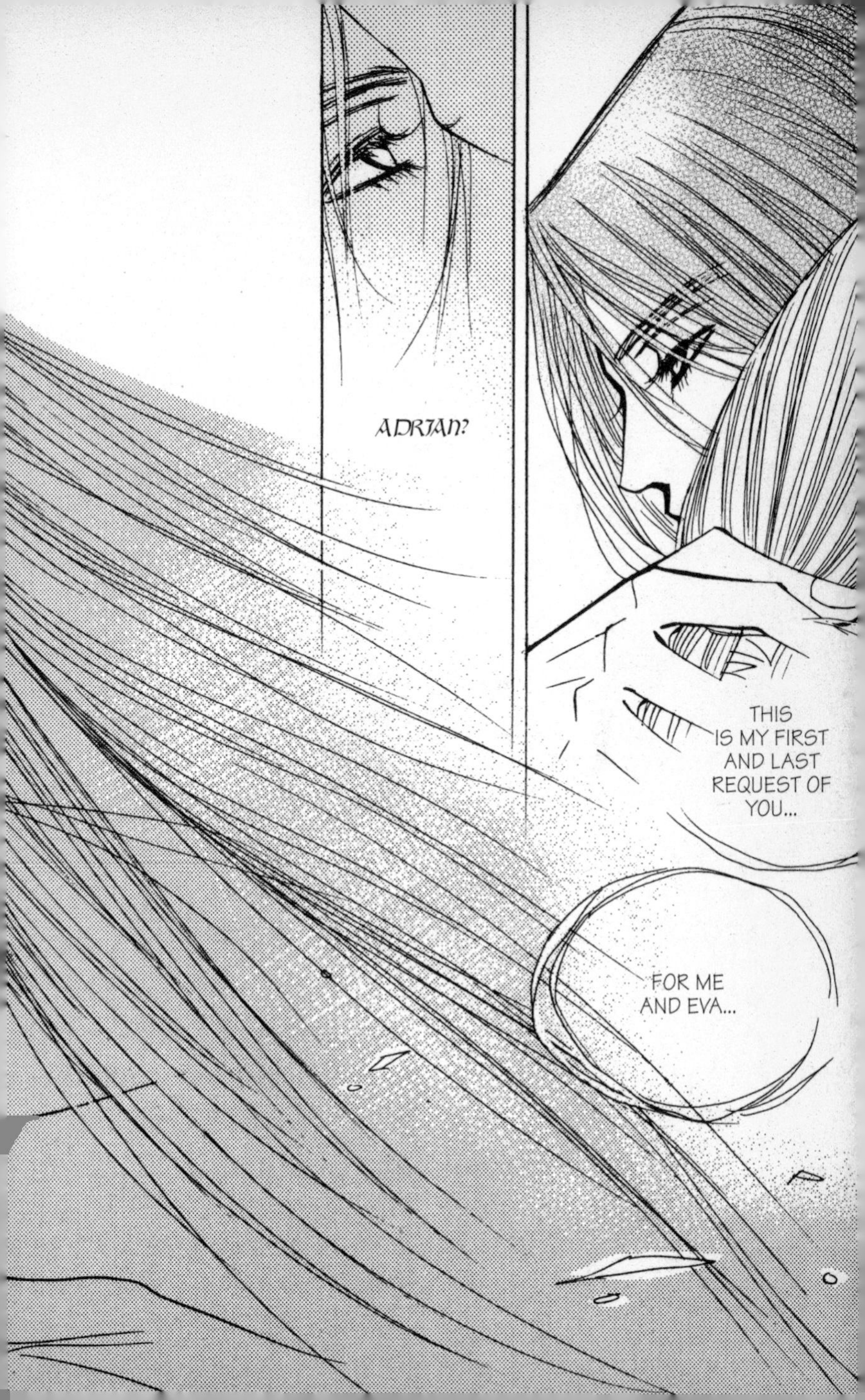
ADRIAN?
THIS IS MY FIRST AND LAST REQUEST OF YOU...
FOR ME AND EVA...

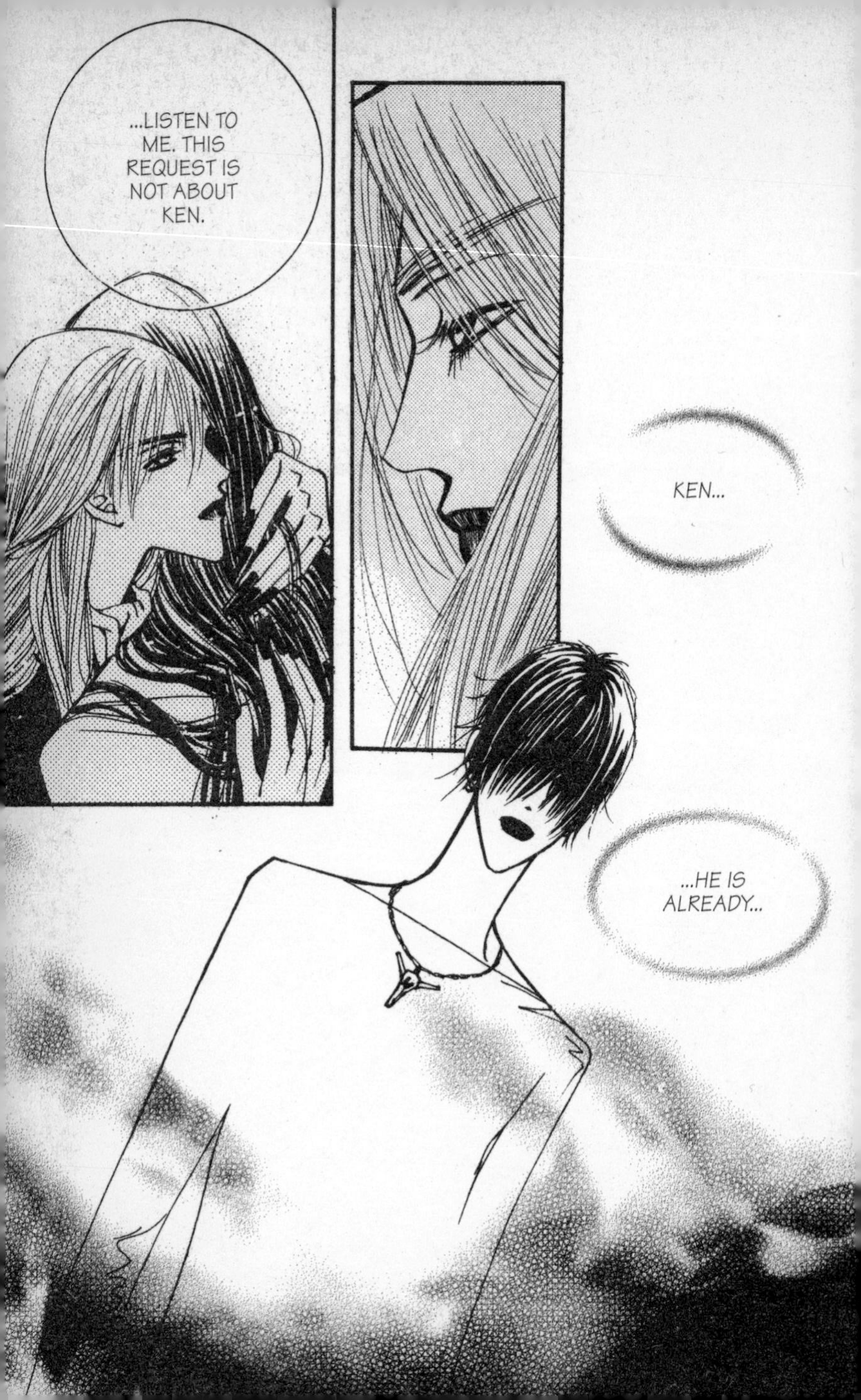
...LISTEN TO ME. THIS REQUEST IS NOT ABOUT KEN.
KEN...
...HE IS ALREADY...

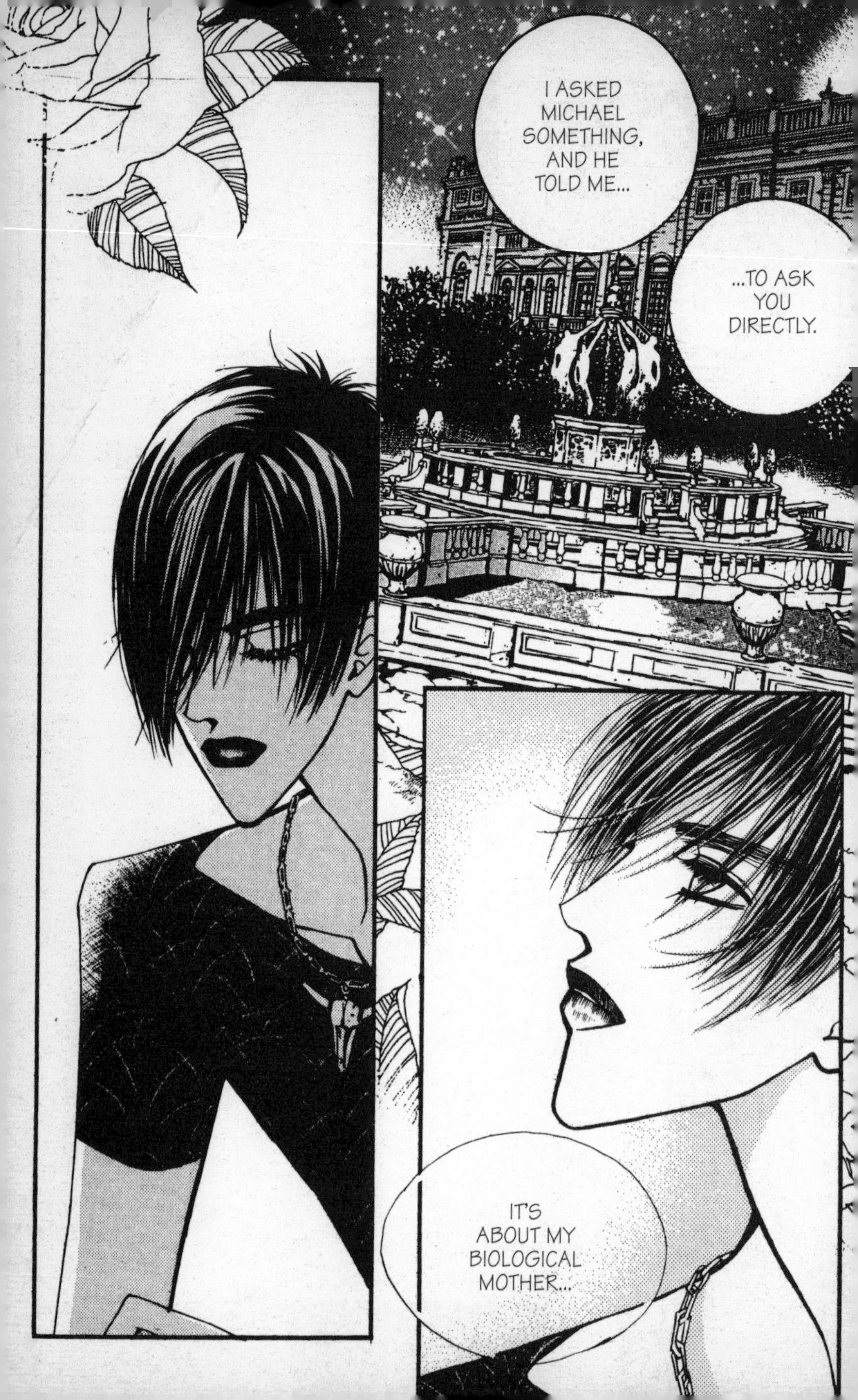
I ASKED MICHAEL SOMETHING, AND HE TOLD ME...
...TO ASK YOU DIRECTLY.
IT'S ABOUT MY BIOLOGICAL MOTHER...

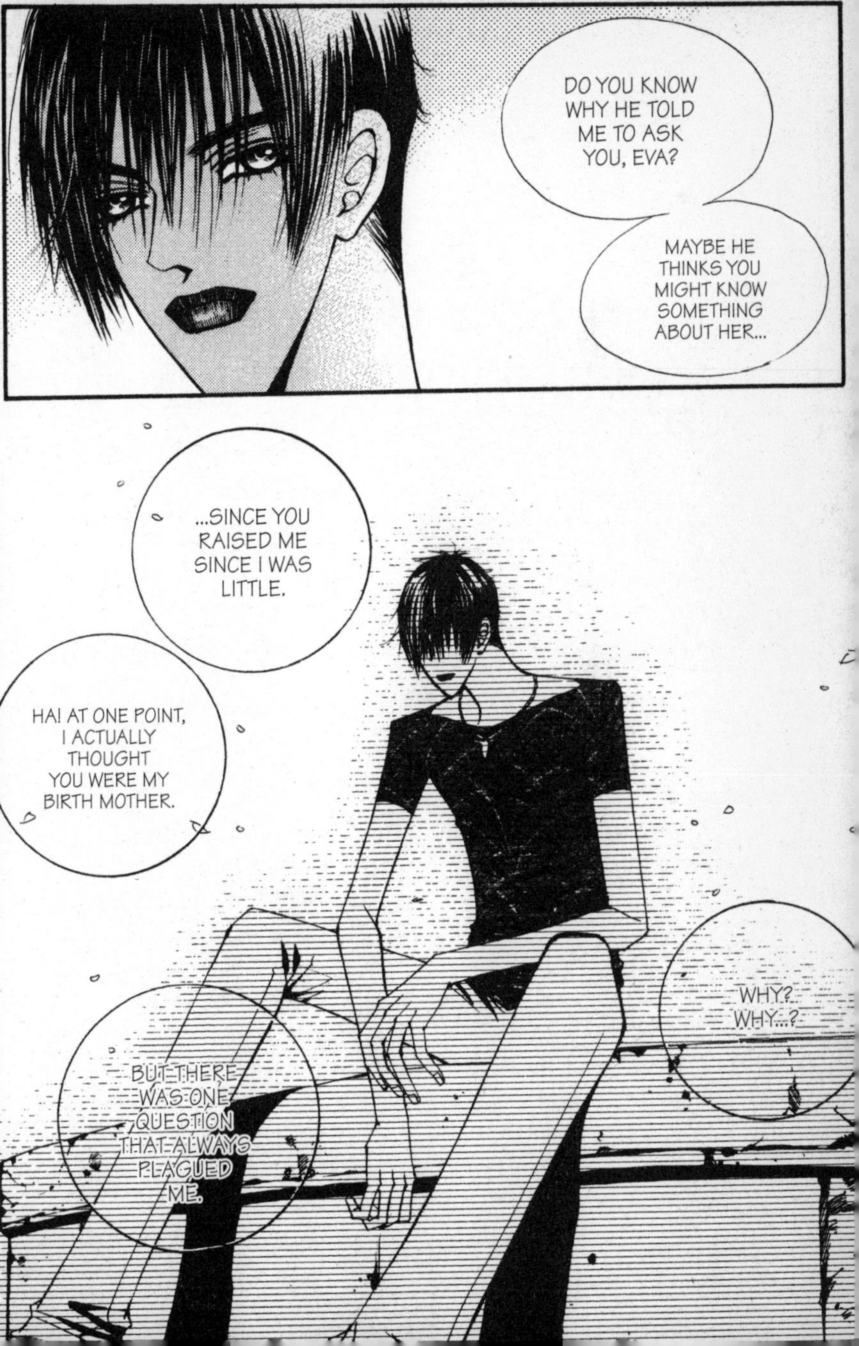
DO YOU KNOW WHY HE TOLD ME TO ASK YOU, EVA?
MAYBE HE THINKS YOU MIGHT KNOW SOMETHING ABOUT HER...
...SINCE YOU RAISED ME SINCE I WAS LITTLE.
HA! AT ONE POINT, I ACTUALLY THOUGHT YOU WERE MY BIRTH MOTHER.
WHY? WHY...?
BUT THERE WAS ONE QUESTION THAT ALWAYS PLAGUED ME.

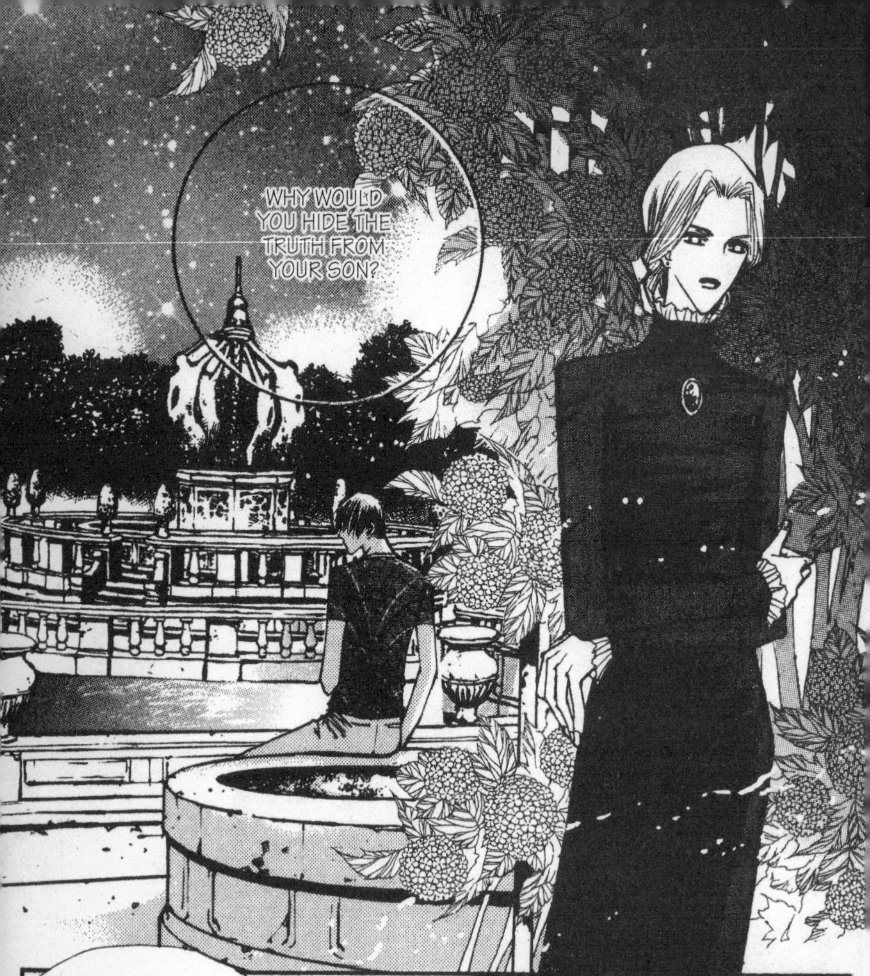
WHY WOULD YOU HIDE THE TRUTH FROM YOUR SON?
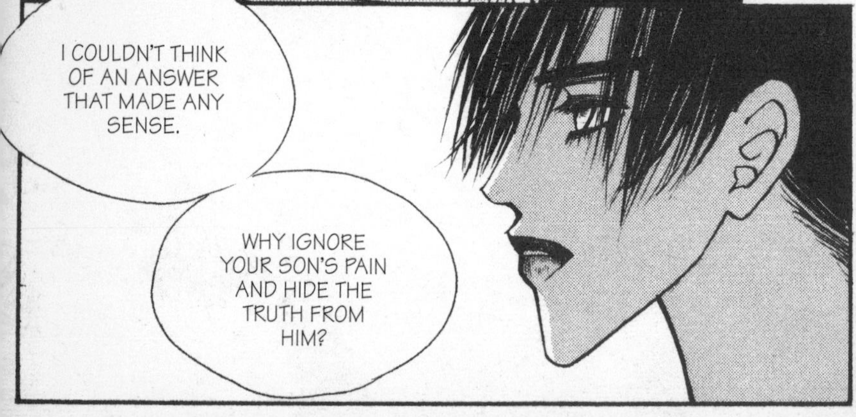
I COULDN'T THINK OF AN ANSWER THAT MADE ANY SENSE.
WHY IGNORE YOUR SON'S PAIN AND HIDE THE TRUTH FROM HIM?

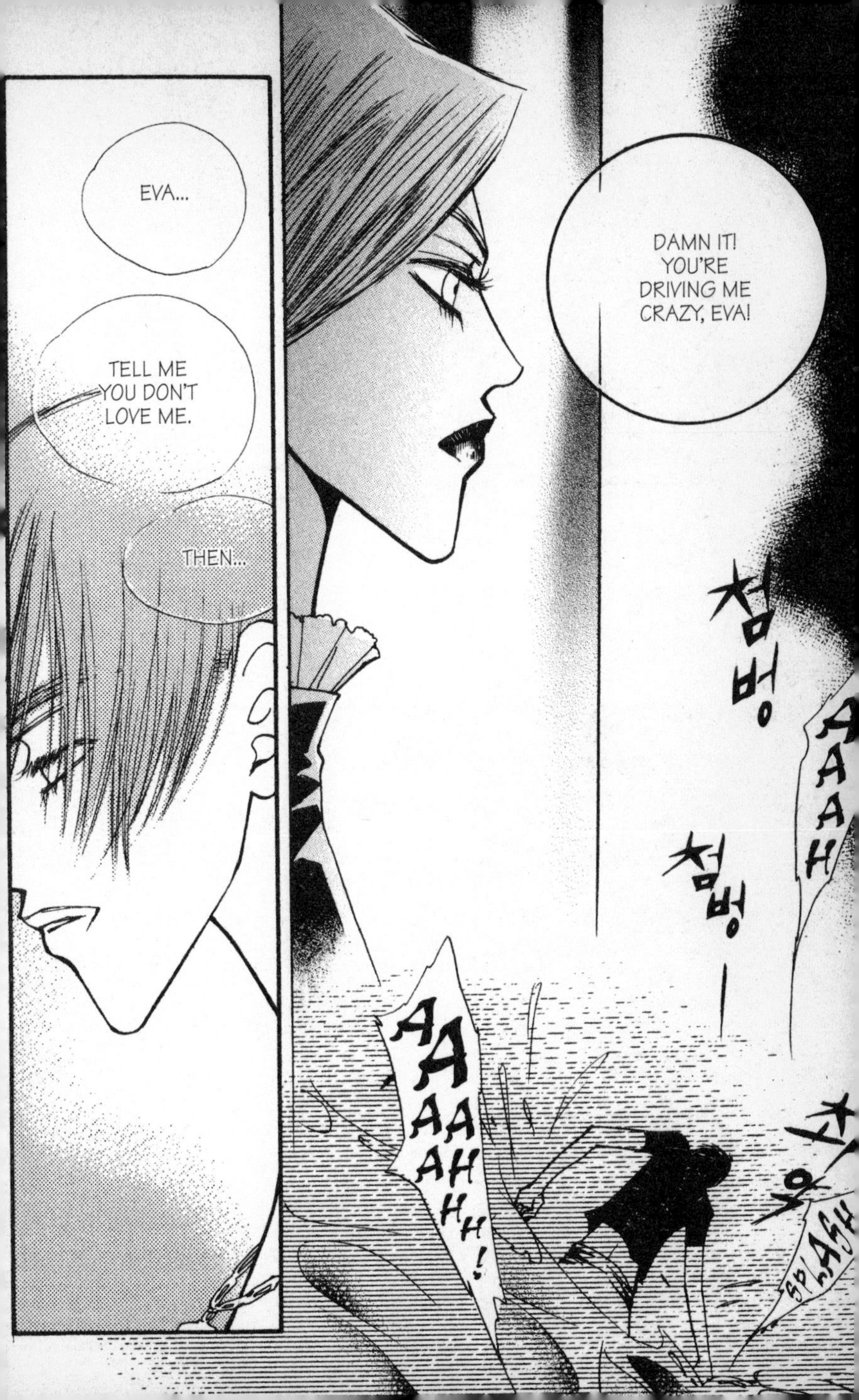
EVA...
TELL ME YOU DON'T LOVE ME.
THEN...
DAMN IT! YOU'RE DRIVING ME CRAZY, EVA!
첨벙
AAAAH
첨벙
AAAAAHHH!
촤악
SPLASH

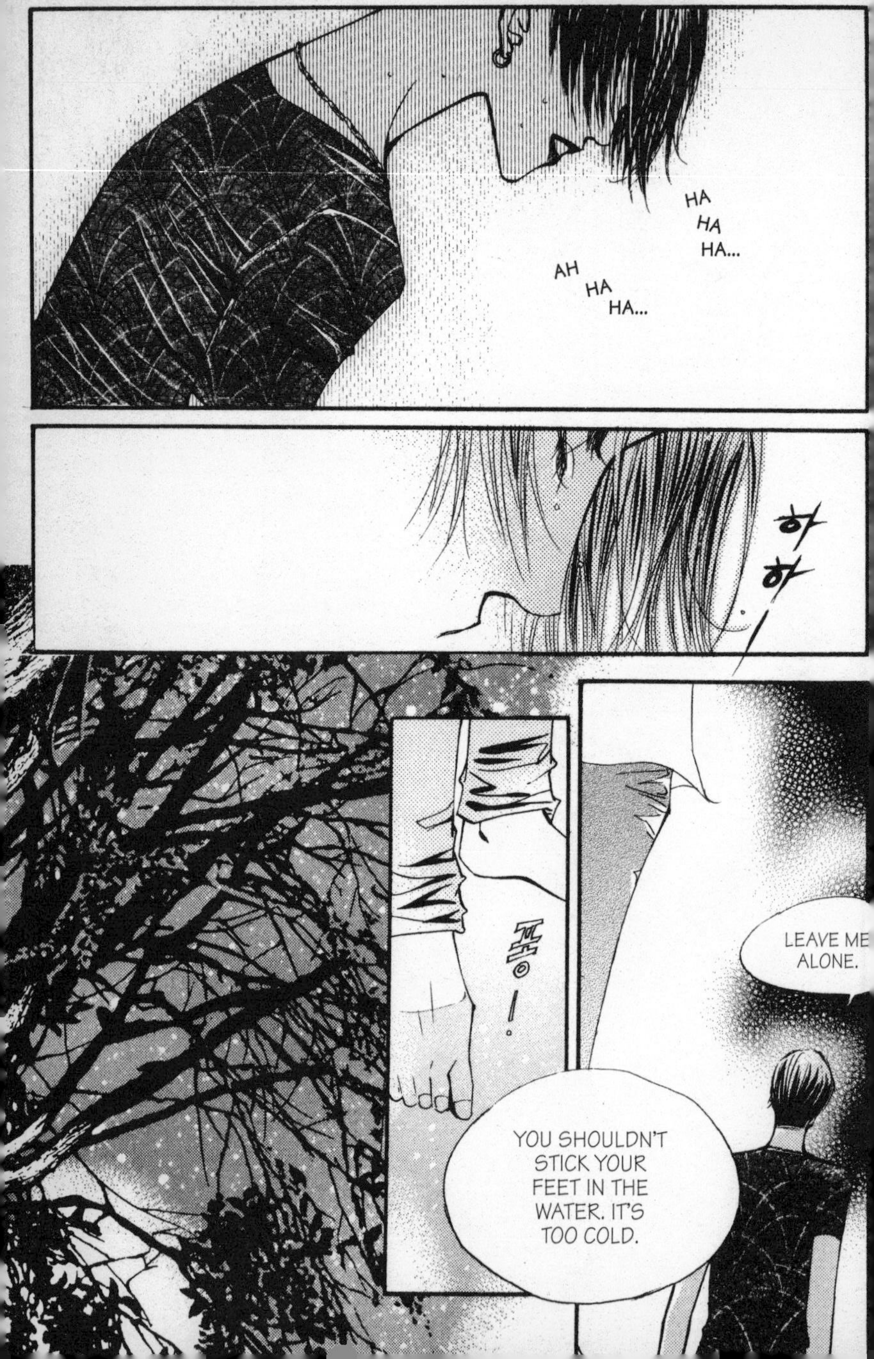
HA HA HA...
AH HA HA...
하 하
LEAVE ME ALONE.
YOU SHOULDN'T STICK YOUR FEET IN THE WATER. IT'S TOO COLD.

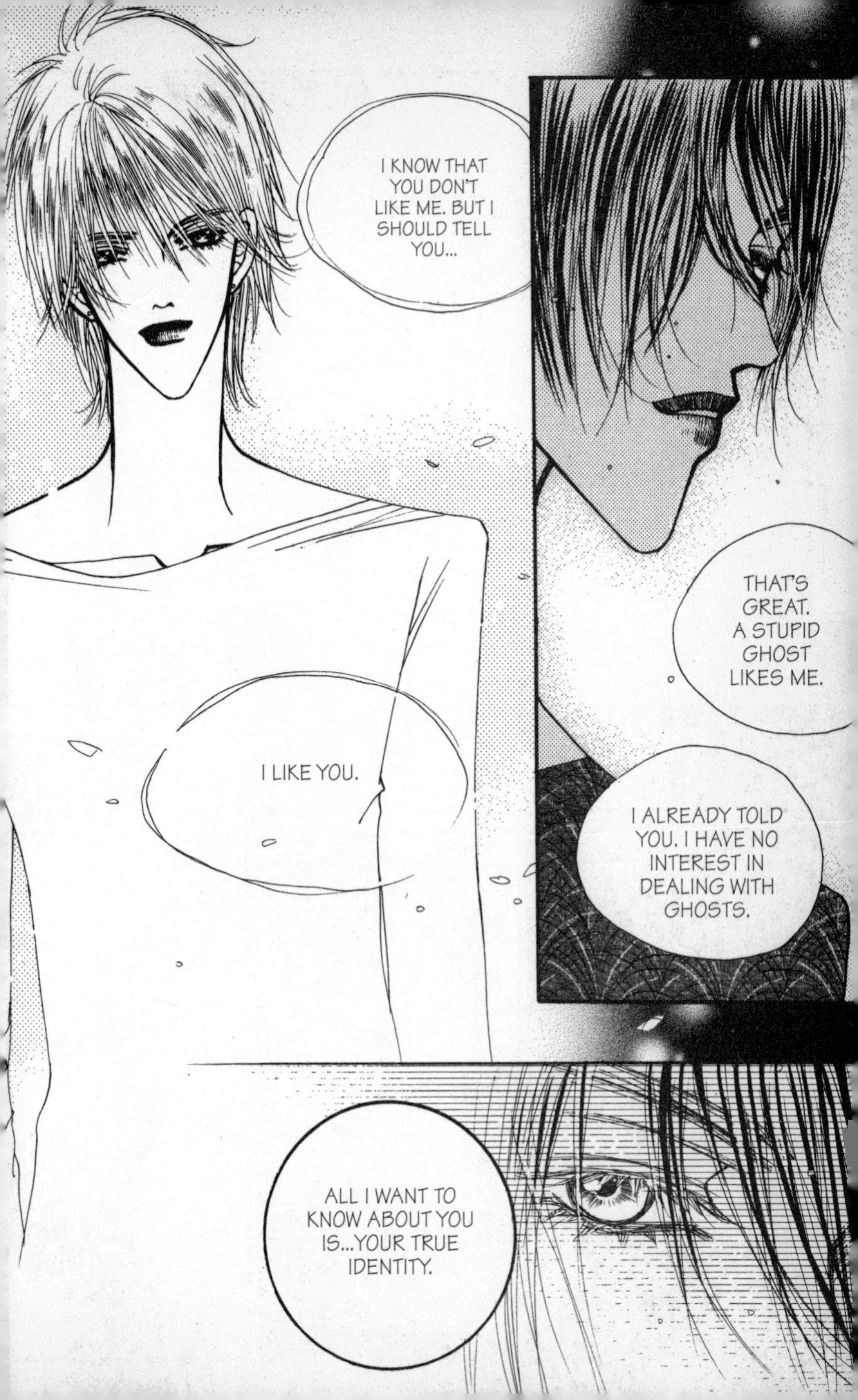
I KNOW THAT YOU DON'T LIKE ME. BUT I SHOULD TELL YOU...
I LIKE YOU.
THAT'S GREAT. A STUPID GHOST LIKES ME.
I ALREADY TOLD YOU. I HAVE NO INTEREST IN DEALING WITH GHOSTS.
ALL I WANT TO KNOW ABOUT YOU IS...YOUR TRUE IDENTITY.

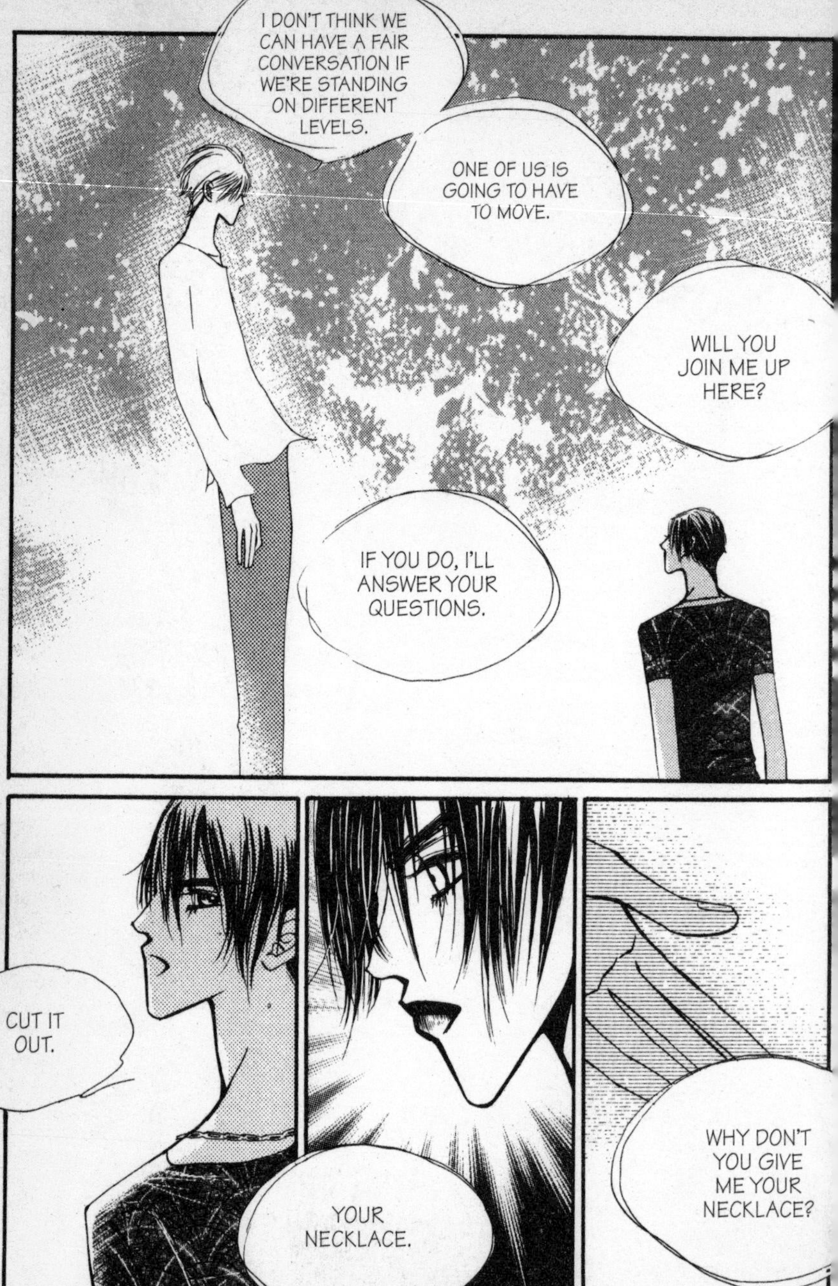
I DON'T THINK WE CAN HAVE A FAIR CONVERSATION IF WE'RE STANDING ON DIFFERENT LEVELS.
ONE OF US IS GOING TO HAVE TO MOVE.
WILL YOU JOIN ME UP HERE?
IF YOU DO, I'LL ANSWER YOUR QUESTIONS.
WHY DON'T YOU GIVE ME YOUR NECKLACE?
YOUR NECKLACE.
CUT IT OUT.

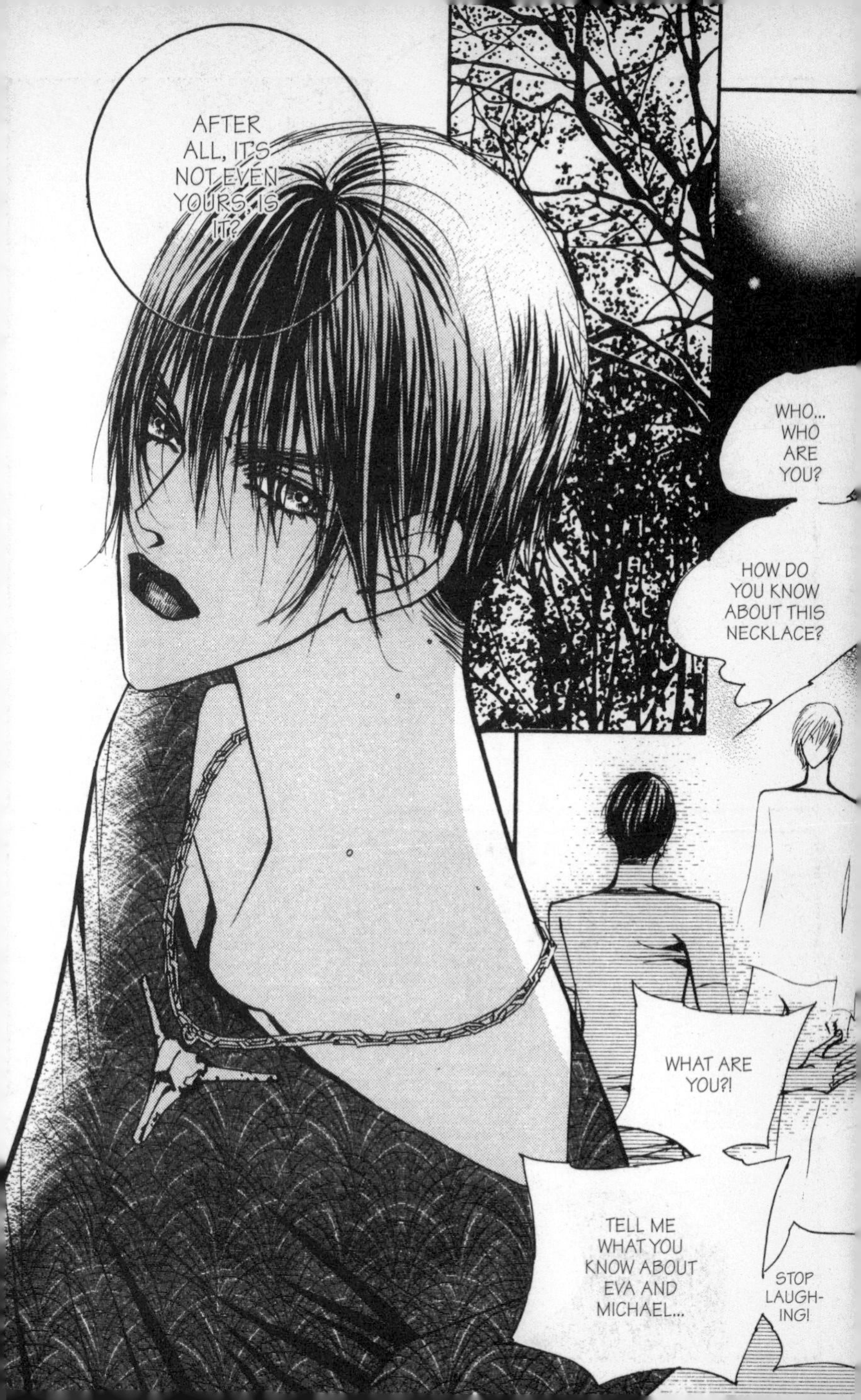
AFTER ALL, IT'S NOT EVEN YOURS, IS IT?
WHO... WHO ARE YOU?
HOW DO YOU KNOW ABOUT THIS NECKLACE?
WHAT ARE YOU?!
TELL ME WHAT YOU KNOW ABOUT EVA AND MICHAEL...
STOP LAUGHING!

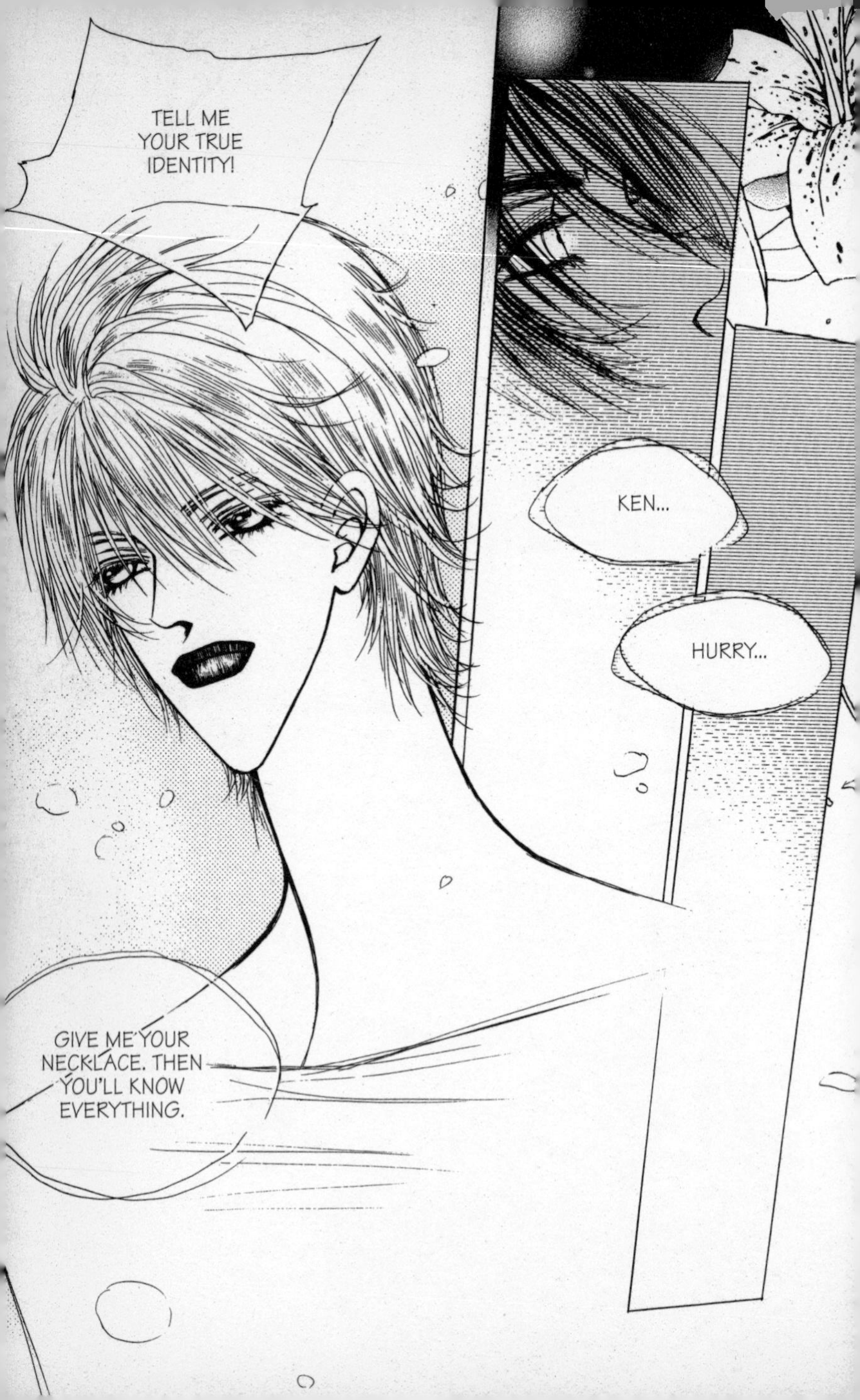
KEN...
HURRY...
TELL ME YOUR TRUE IDENTITY!
GIVE ME YOUR NECKLACE. THEN YOU'LL KNOW EVERYTHING.

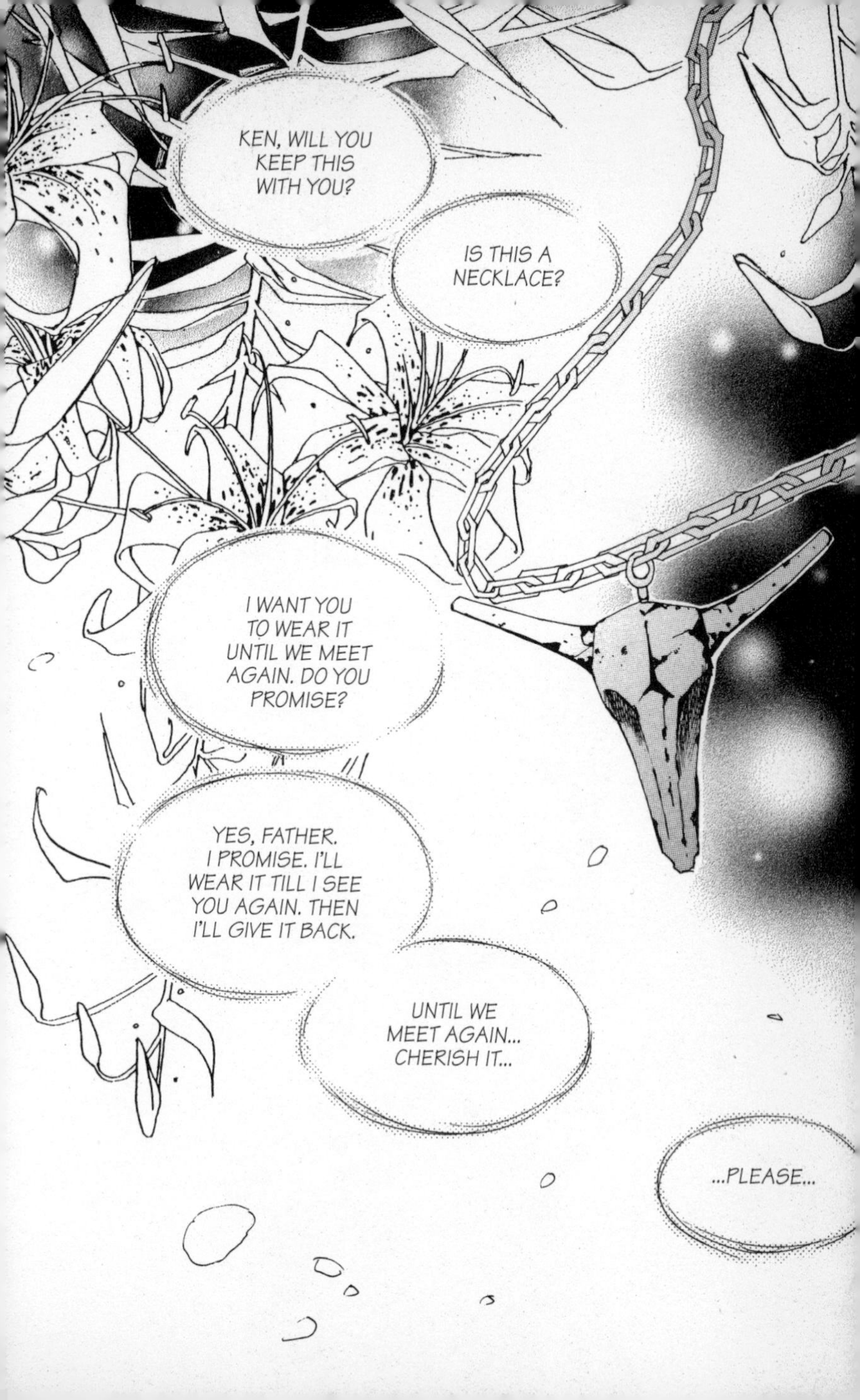
KEN, WILL YOU KEEP THIS WITH YOU?
IS THIS A NECKLACE?
I WANT YOU TO WEAR IT UNTIL WE MEET AGAIN. DO YOU PROMISE?
YES, FATHER. I PROMISE. I'LL WEAR IT TILL I SEE YOU AGAIN. THEN I'LL GIVE IT BACK.
UNTIL WE MEET AGAIN... CHERISH IT...
...PLEASE...

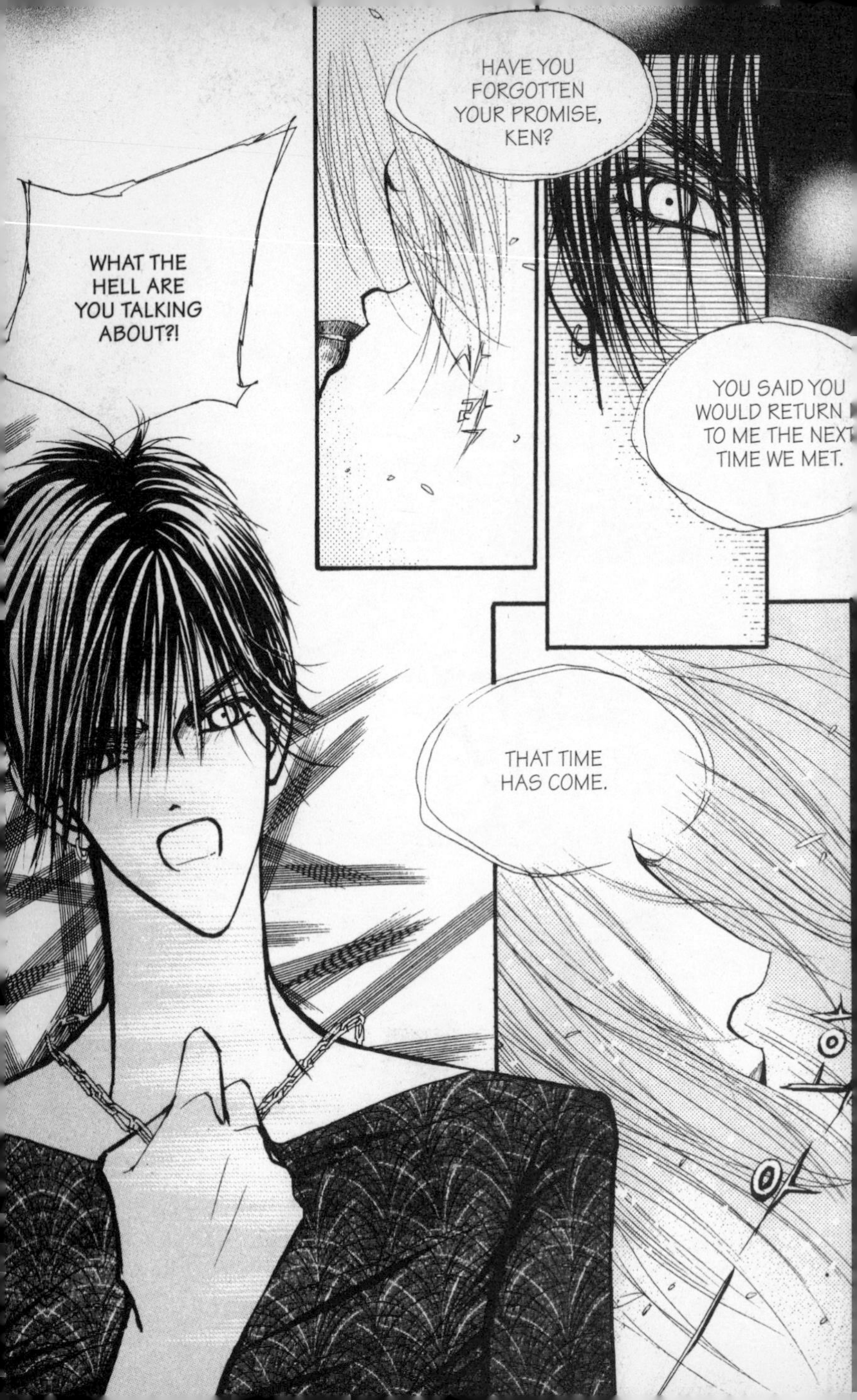
HAVE YOU FORGOTTEN YOUR PROMISE, KEN?
YOU SAID YOU WOULD RETURN TO ME THE NEXT TIME WE MET.
THAT TIME HAS COME.
WHAT THE HELL ARE YOU TALKING ABOUT?!

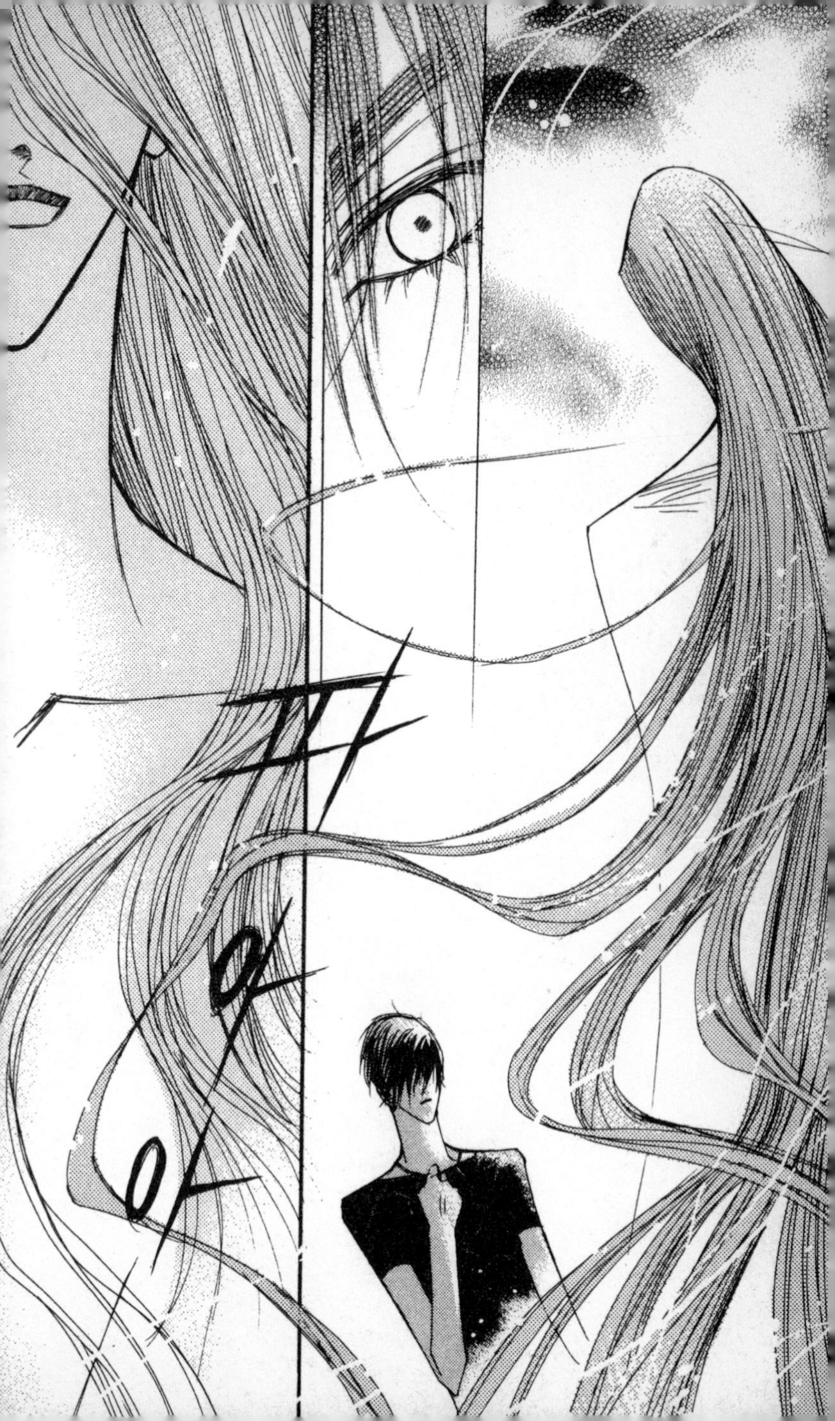
끼아아

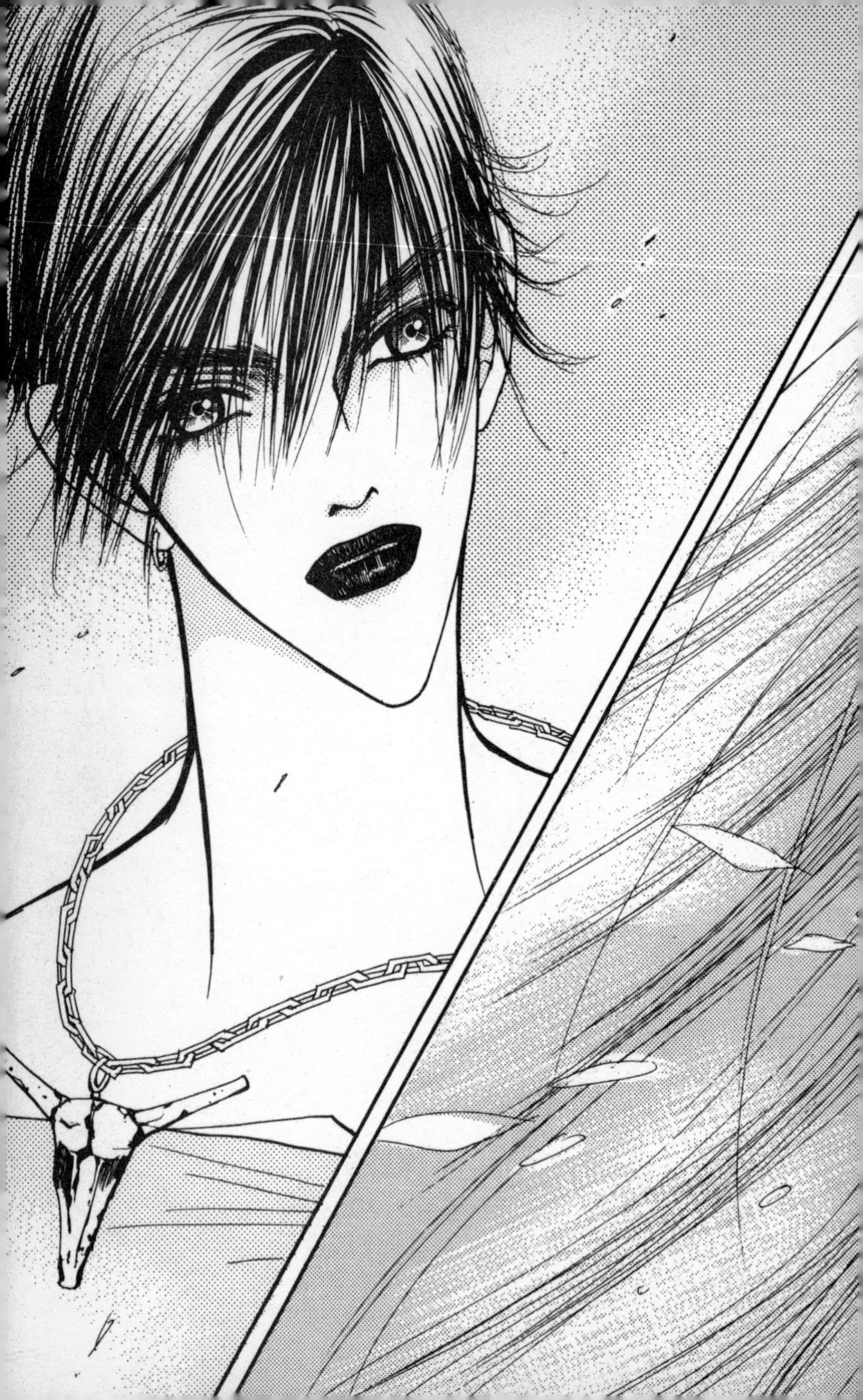

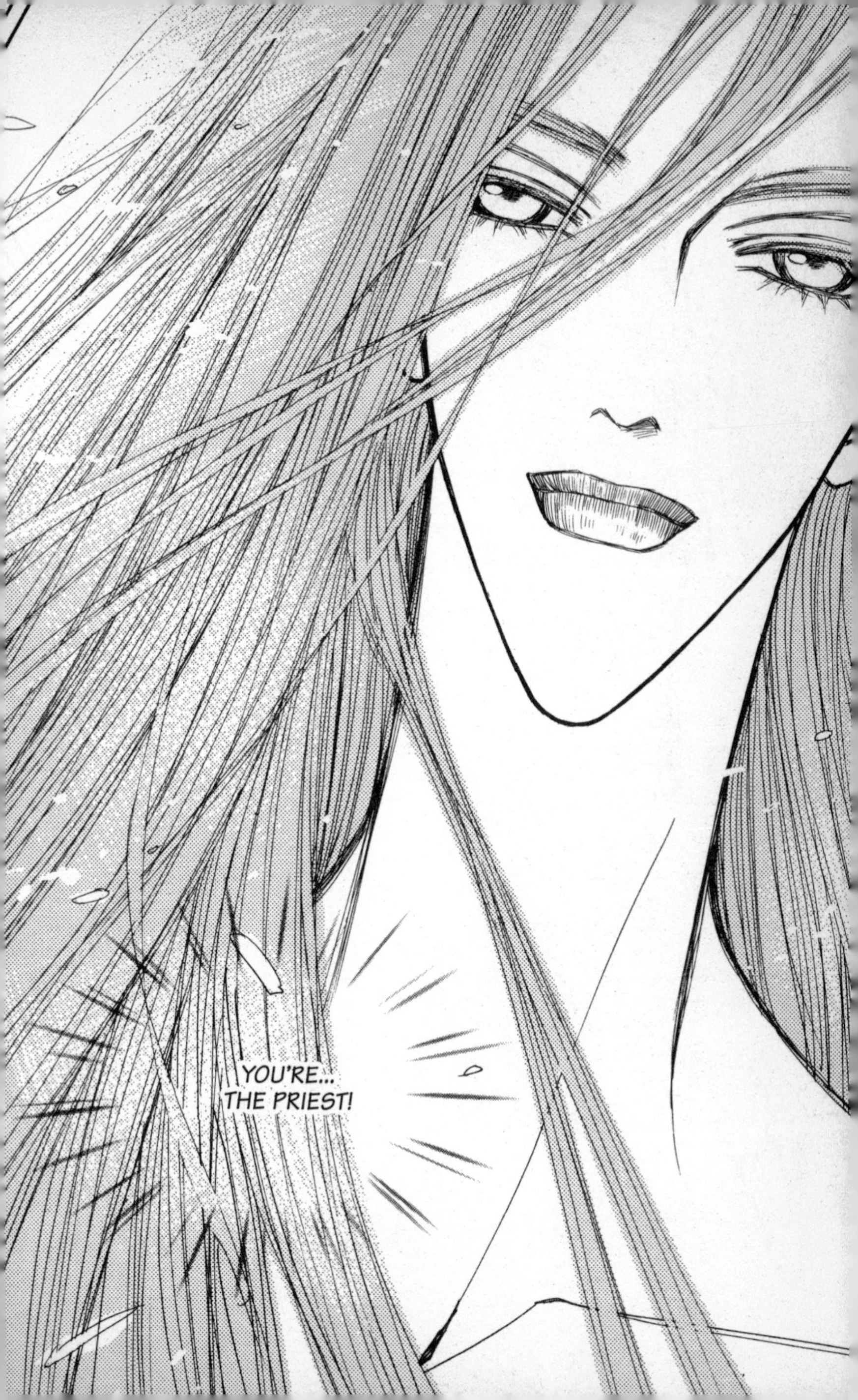
YOU'RE... THE PRIEST!

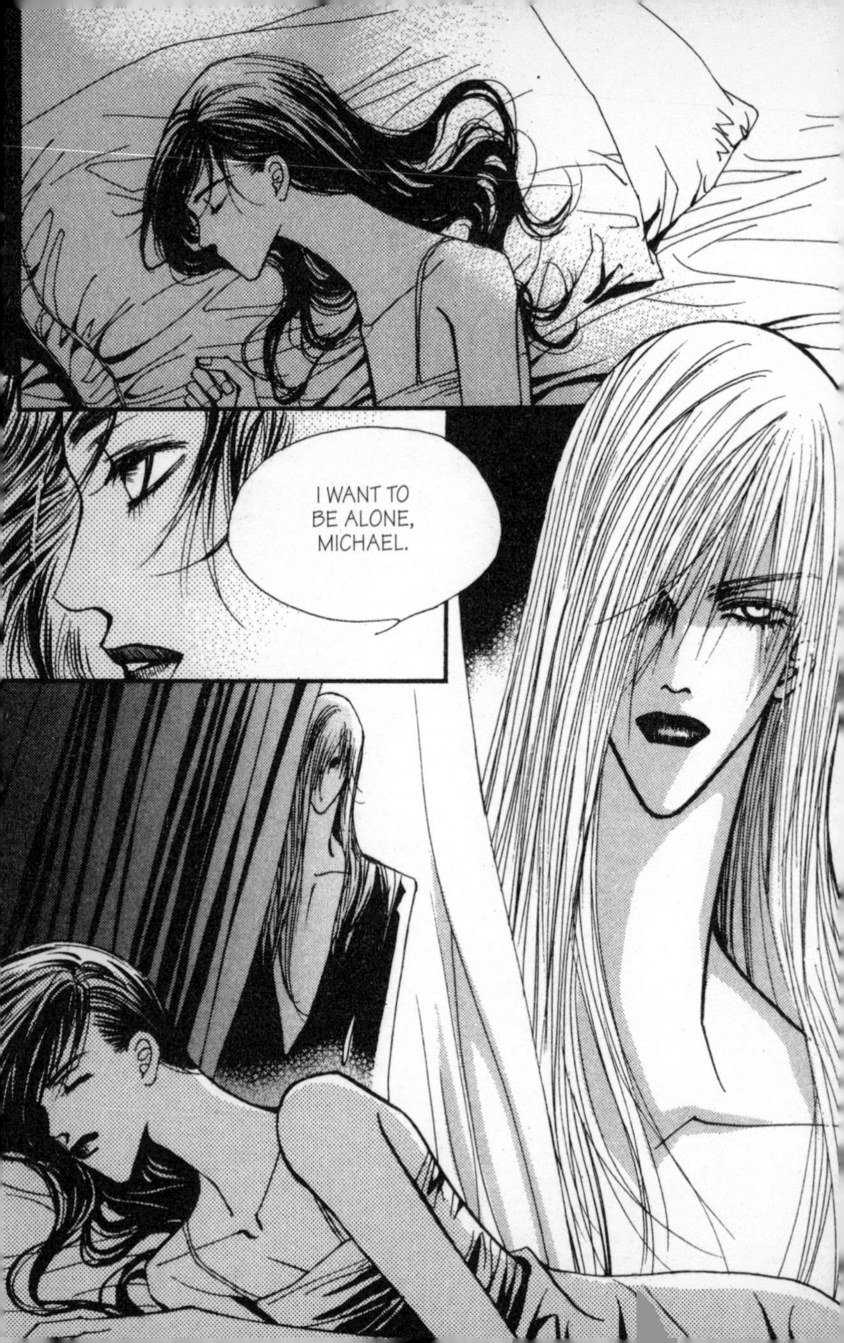
I WANT TO BE ALONE, MICHAEL.

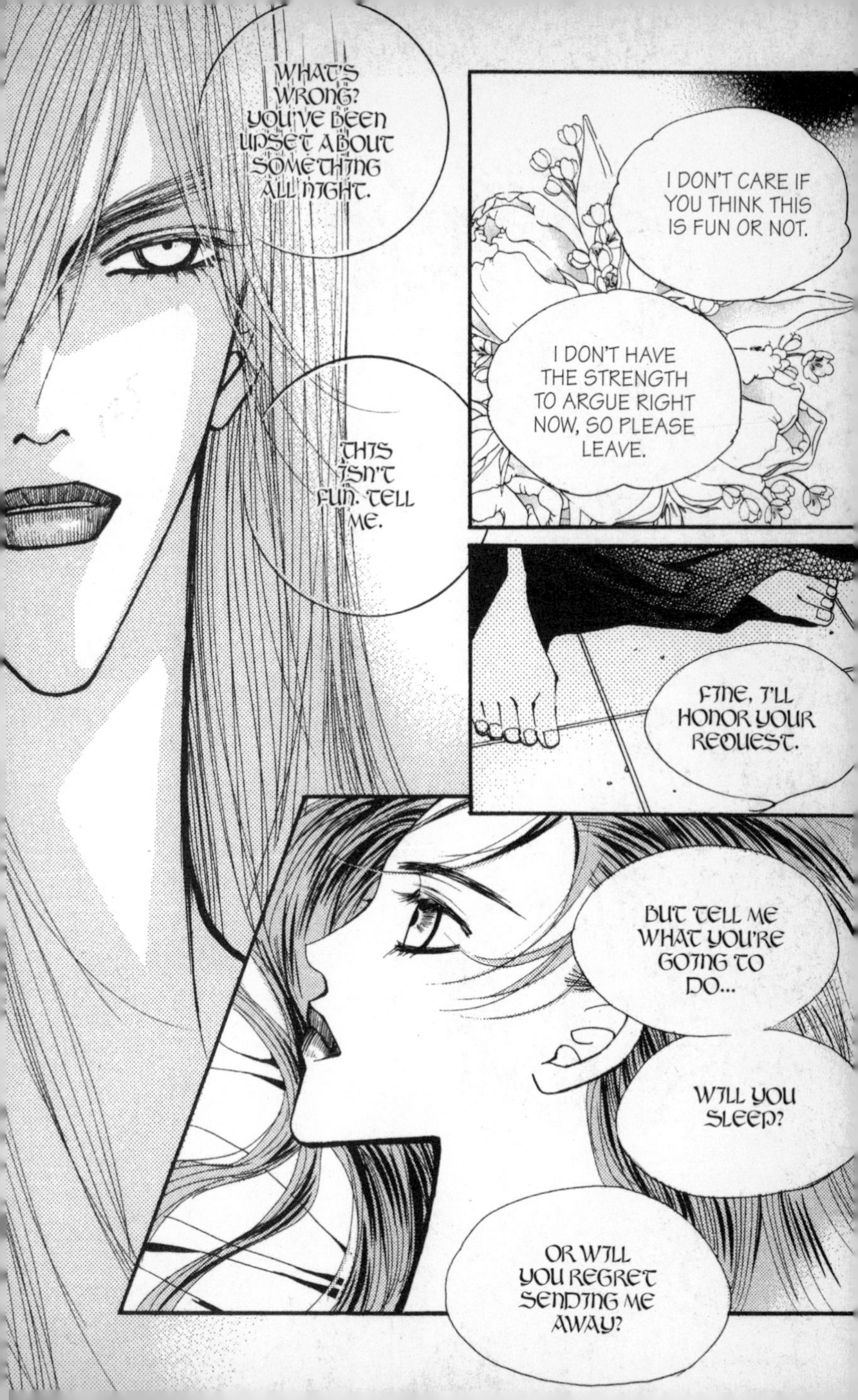
WHAT'S WRONG? YOU'VE BEEN UPSET ABOUT SOMETHING ALL NIGHT.
THIS ISN'T FUN. TELL ME.
I DON'T CARE IF YOU THINK THIS IS FUN OR NOT.
I DON'T HAVE THE STRENGTH TO ARGUE RIGHT NOW, SO PLEASE LEAVE.
FINE, I'LL HONOR YOUR REQUEST.
BUT TELL ME WHAT YOU'RE GOING TO DO...
WILL YOU SLEEP?
OR WILL YOU REGRET SENDING ME AWAY?

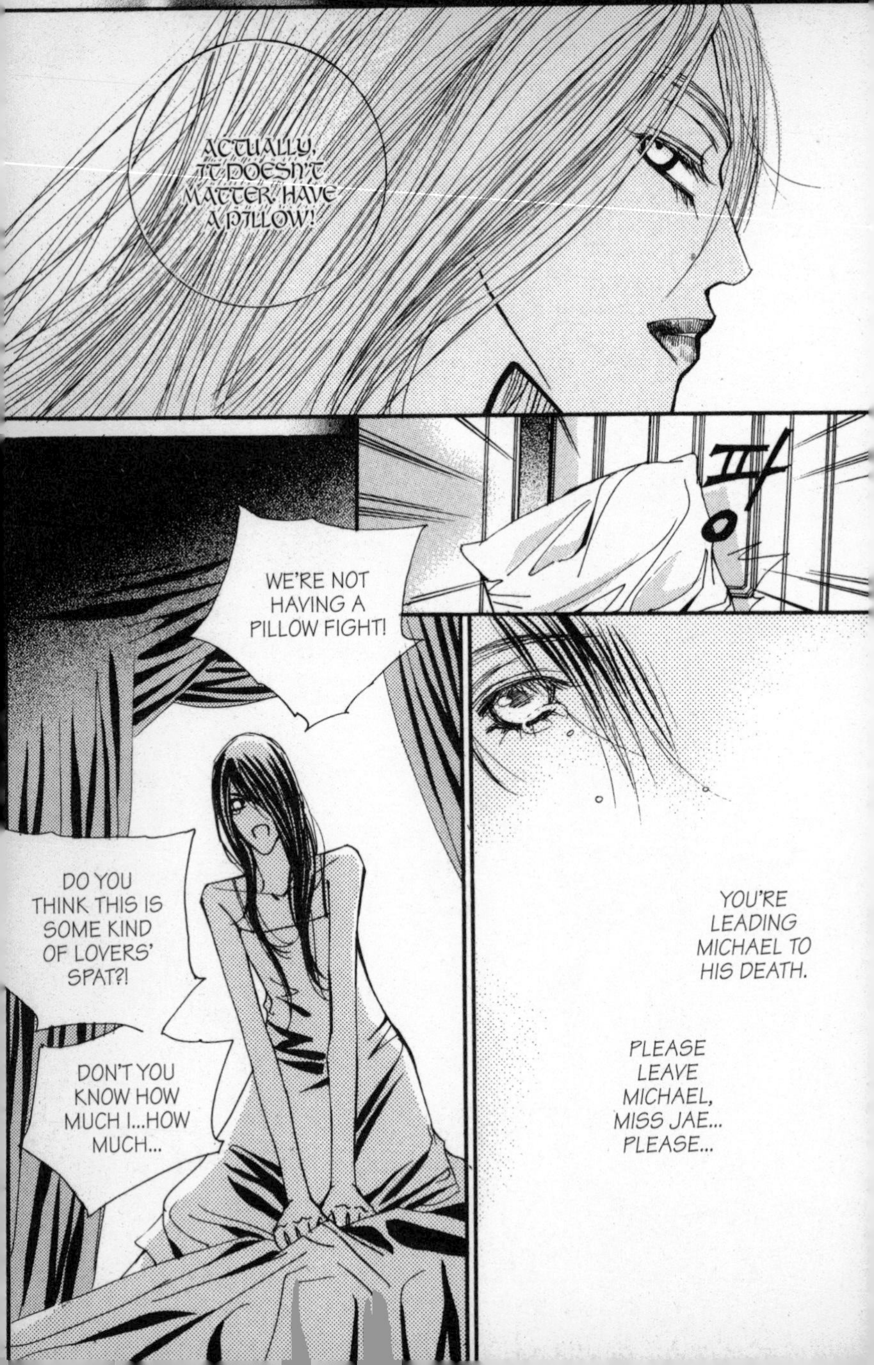
ACTUALLY, IT DOESN'T MATTER. HAVE A PILLOW!
WE'RE NOT HAVING A PILLOW FIGHT!
DO YOU THINK THIS IS SOME KIND OF LOVERS' SPAT?!
DON'T YOU KNOW HOW MUCH I...HOW MUCH...
YOU'RE LEADING MICHAEL TO HIS DEATH.
PLEASE LEAVE MICHAEL, MISS JAE... PLEASE...

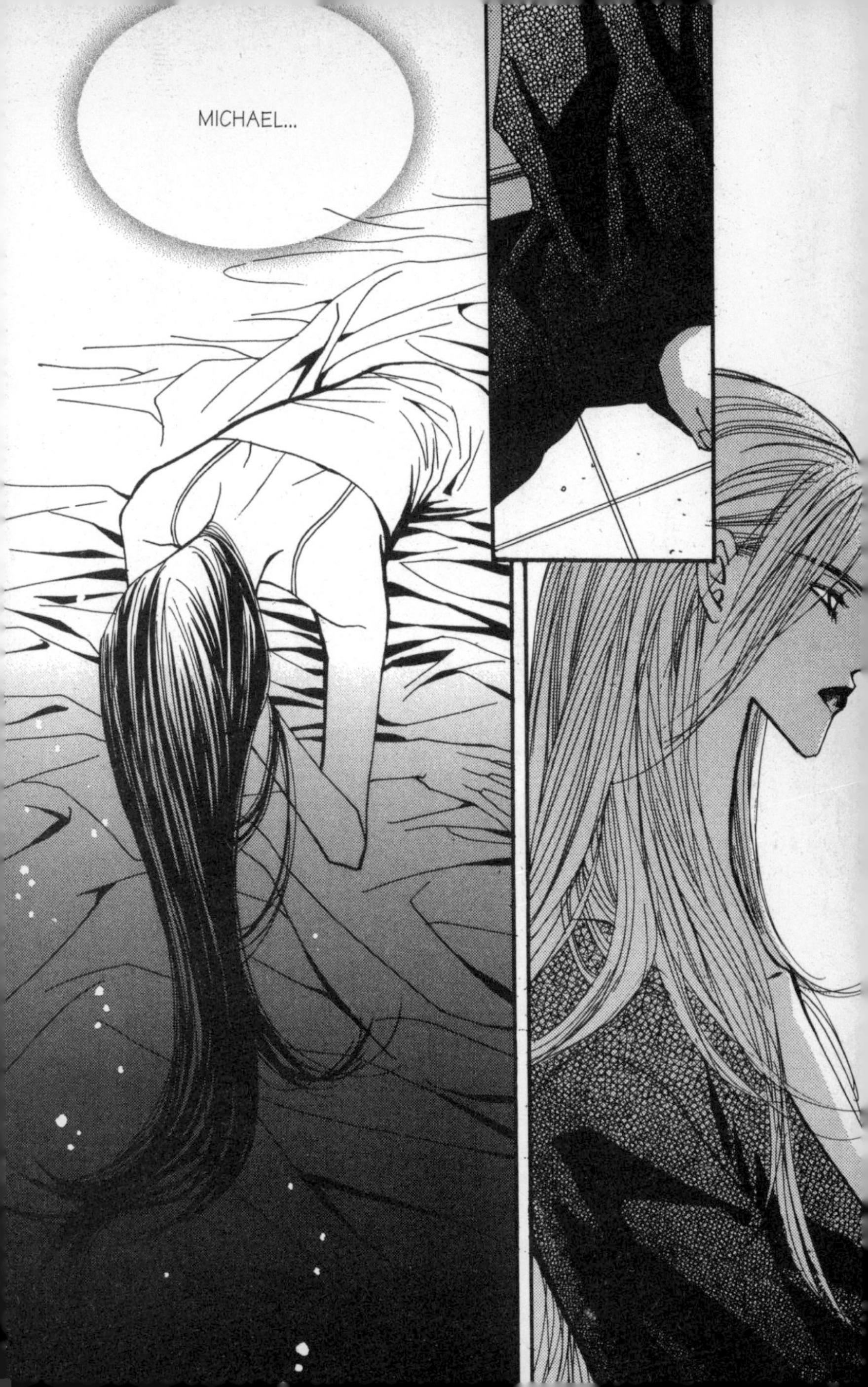
MICHAEL...

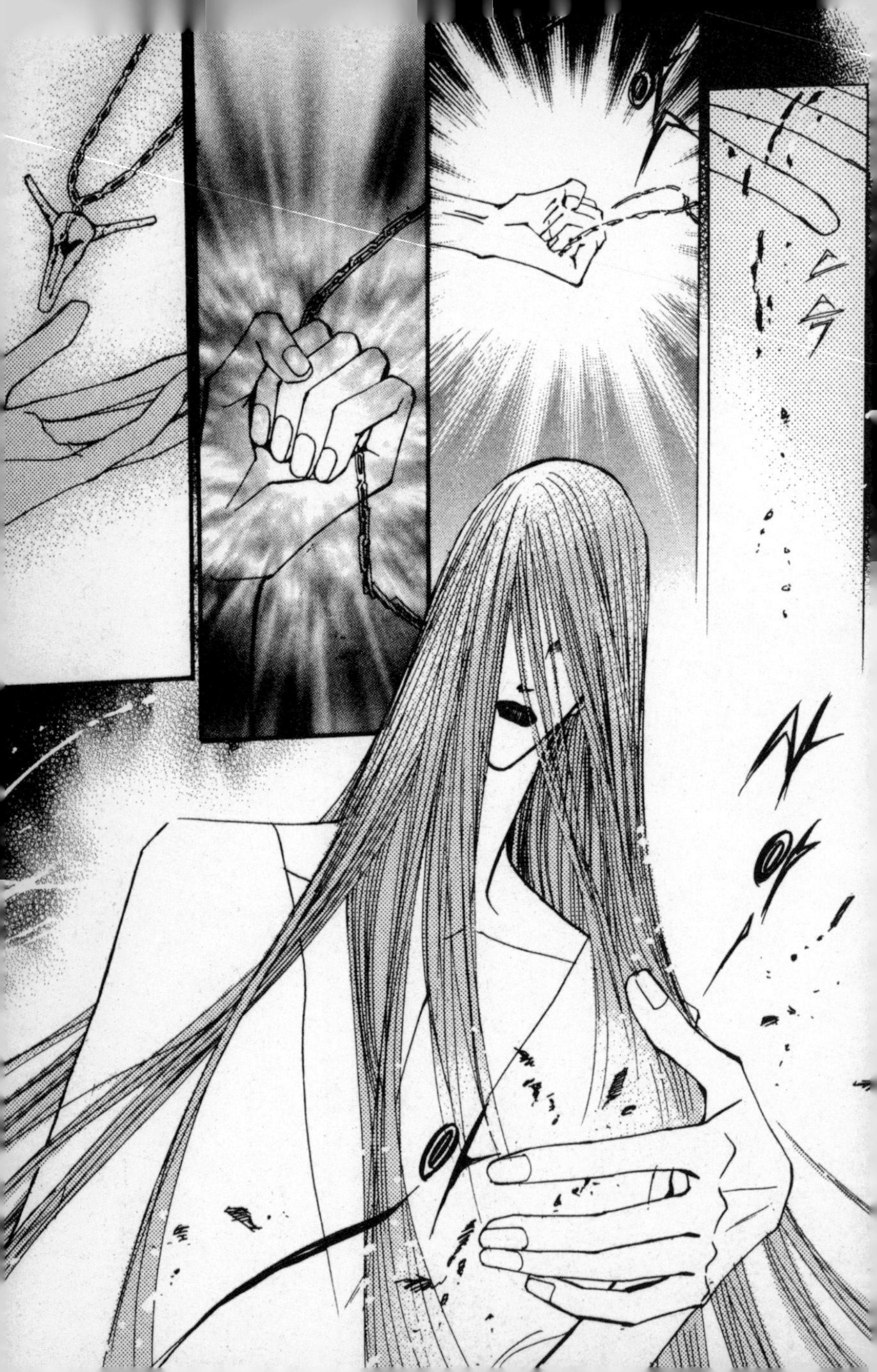

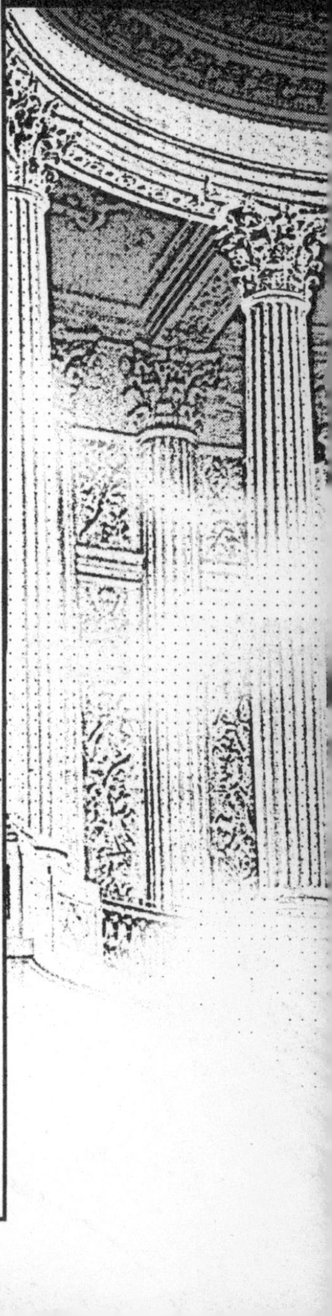
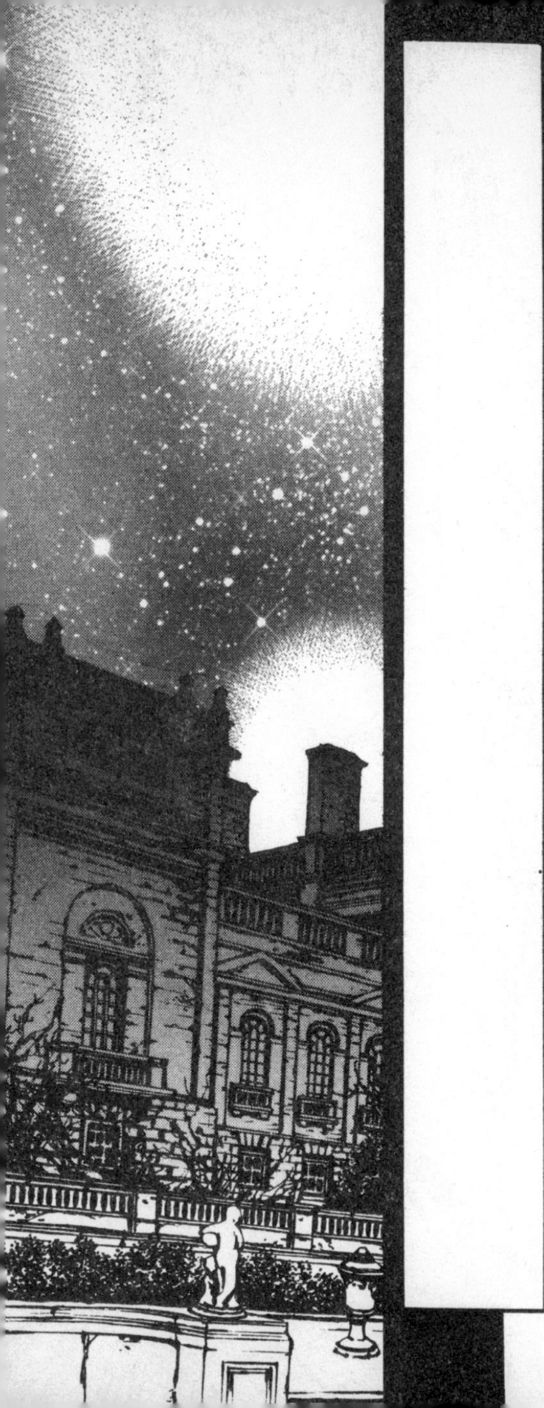

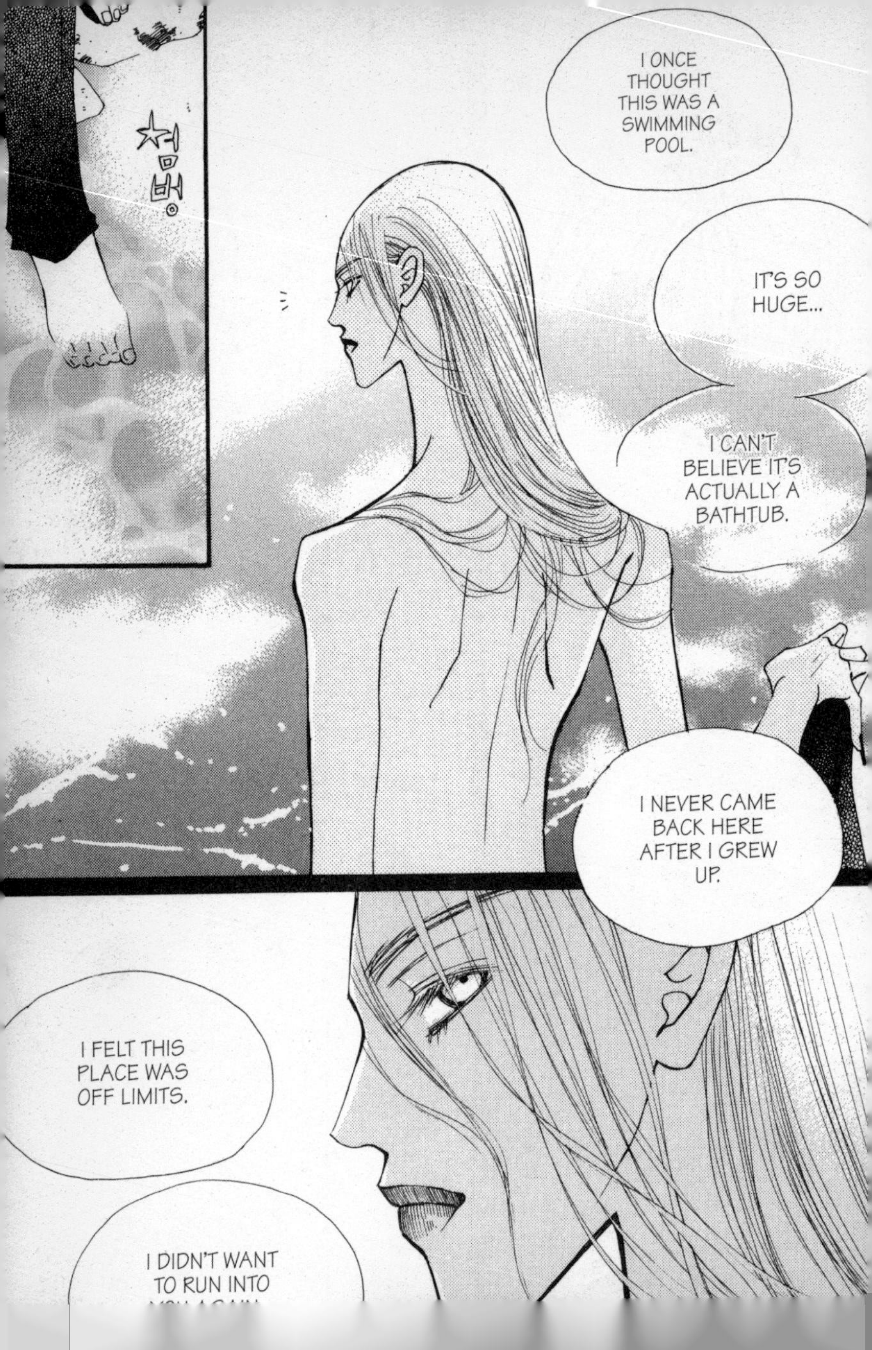
I ONCE THOUGHT THIS WAS A SWIMMING POOL.
IT'S SO HUGE...
I CAN'T BELIEVE IT'S ACTUALLY A BATHTUB.
I NEVER CAME BACK HERE AFTER I GREW UP.
I FELT THIS PLACE WAS OFF LIMITS.
I DIDN'T WANT TO RUN INTO

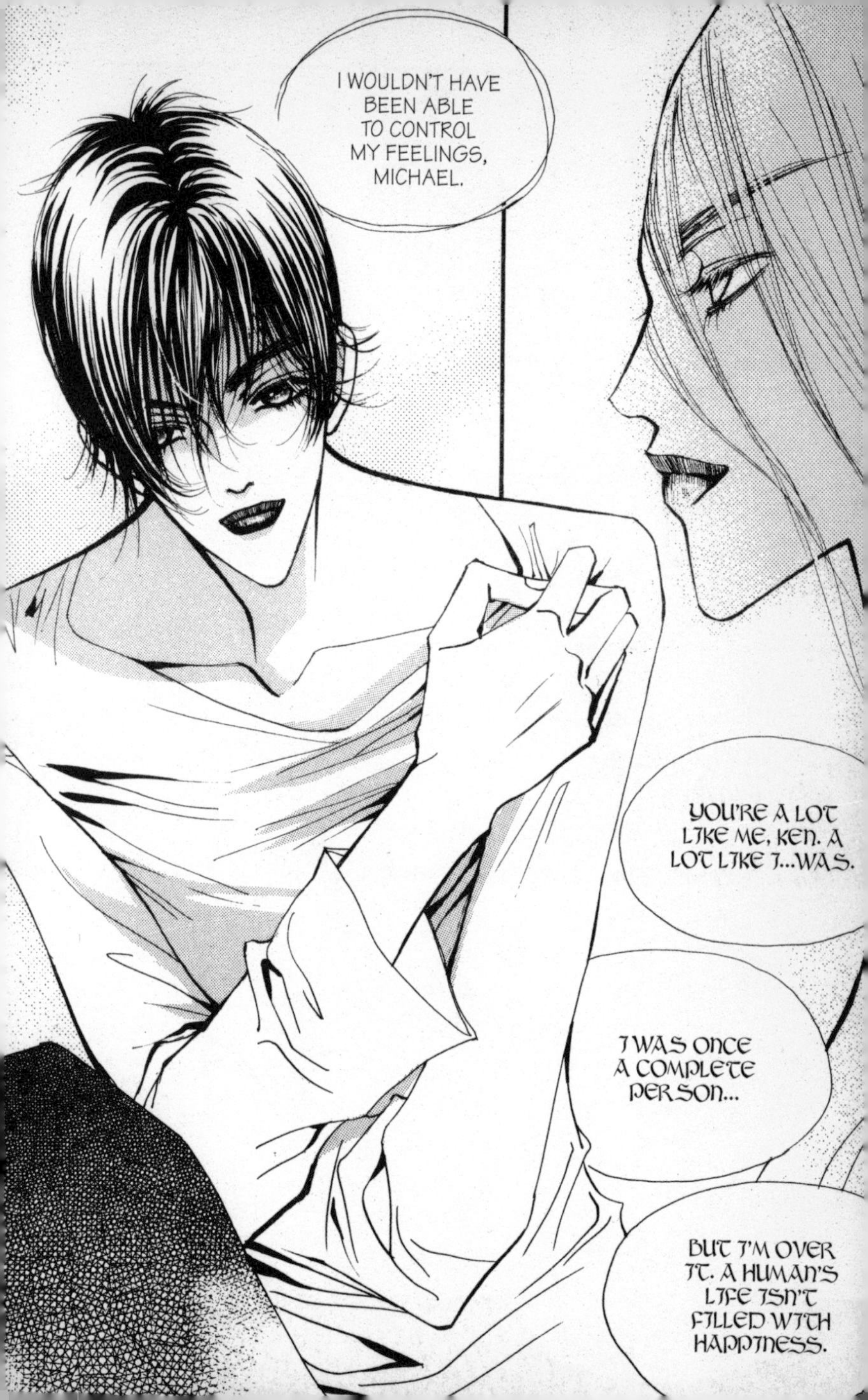
I WOULDN'T HAVE BEEN ABLE TO CONTROL MY FEELINGS, MICHAEL.
YOU'RE A LOT LIKE ME, KEN. A LOT LIKE I...WAS.
I WAS ONCE A COMPLETE PERSON...
BUT I'M OVER IT. A HUMAN'S LIFE ISN'T FILLED WITH HAPPINESS.

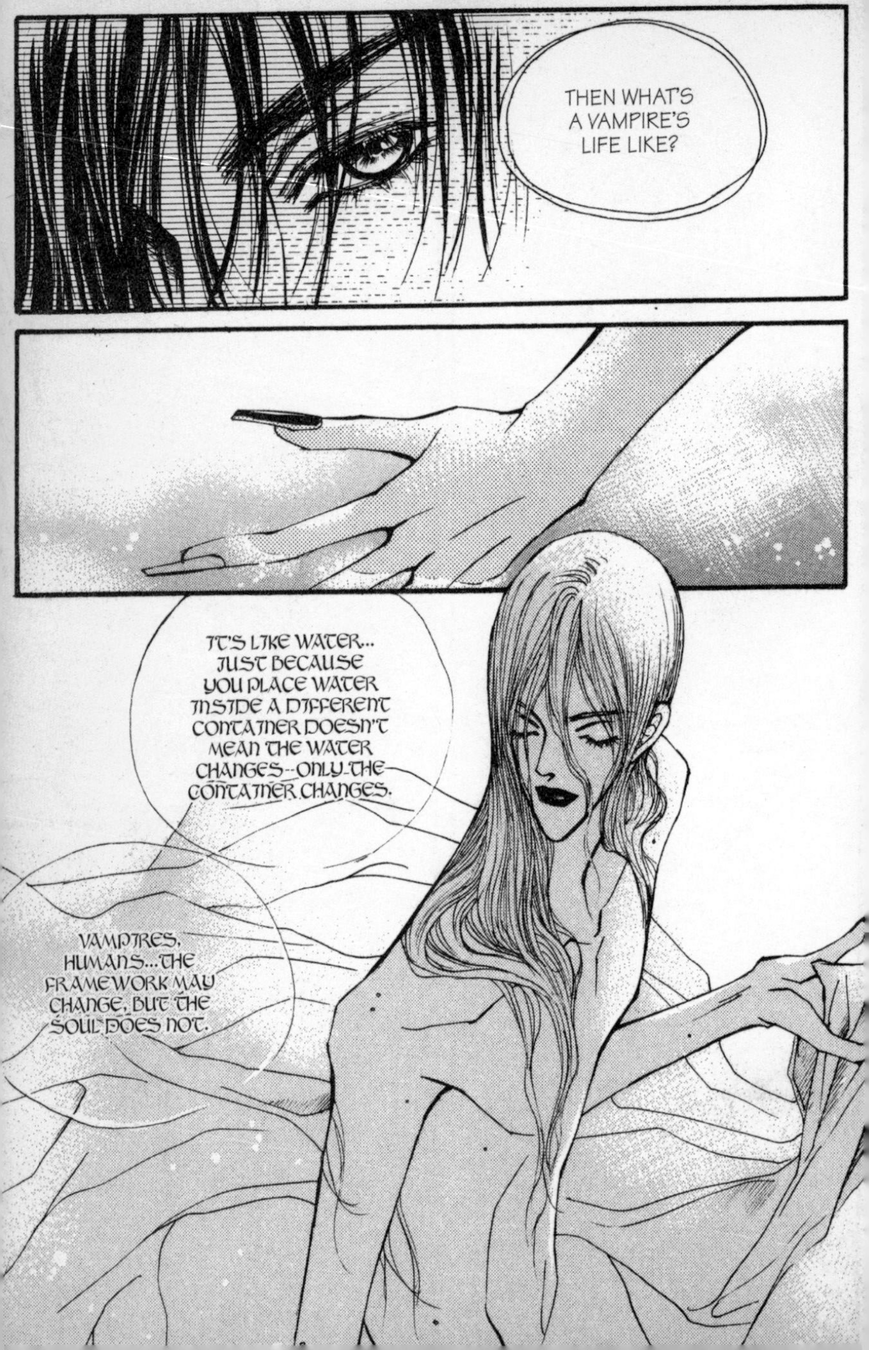
THEN WHAT'S A VAMPIRE'S LIFE LIKE?
IT'S LIKE WATER... JUST BECAUSE YOU PLACE WATER INSIDE A DIFFERENT CONTAINER DOESN'T MEAN THE WATER CHANGES--ONLY THE CONTAINER CHANGES.
VAMPIRES, HUMANS...THE FRAMEWORK MAY CHANGE, BUT THE SOUL DOES NOT.

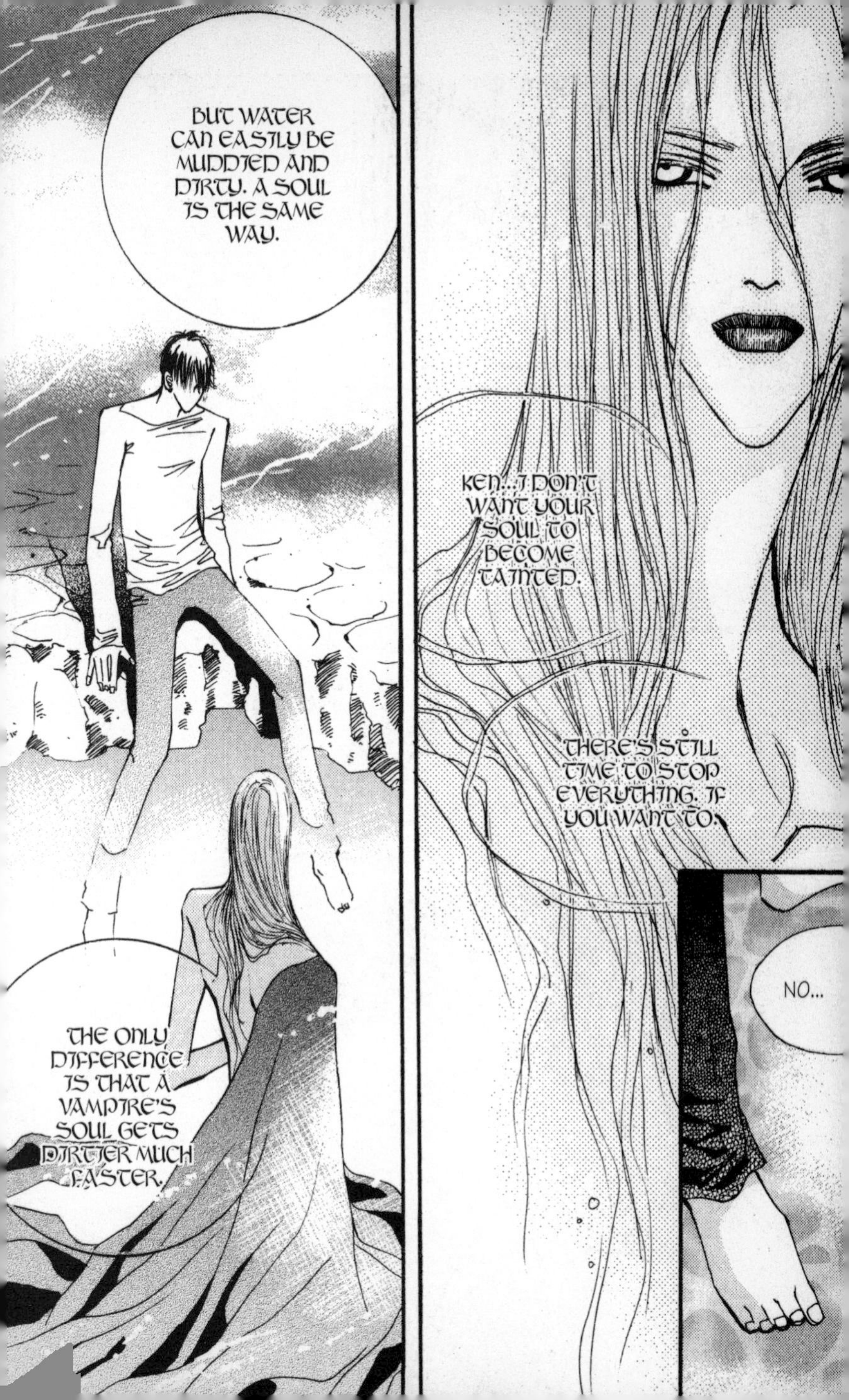
KEN... I DON'T WANT YOUR SOUL TO BECOME TAINTED.
THERE'S STILL TIME TO STOP EVERYTHING. IF YOU WANT TO.
NO...
BUT WATER CAN EASILY BE MUDDIED AND DIRTY. A SOUL IS THE SAME WAY.
THE ONLY DIFFERENCE IS THAT A VAMPIRE'S SOUL GETS DIRTIER MUCH FASTER.

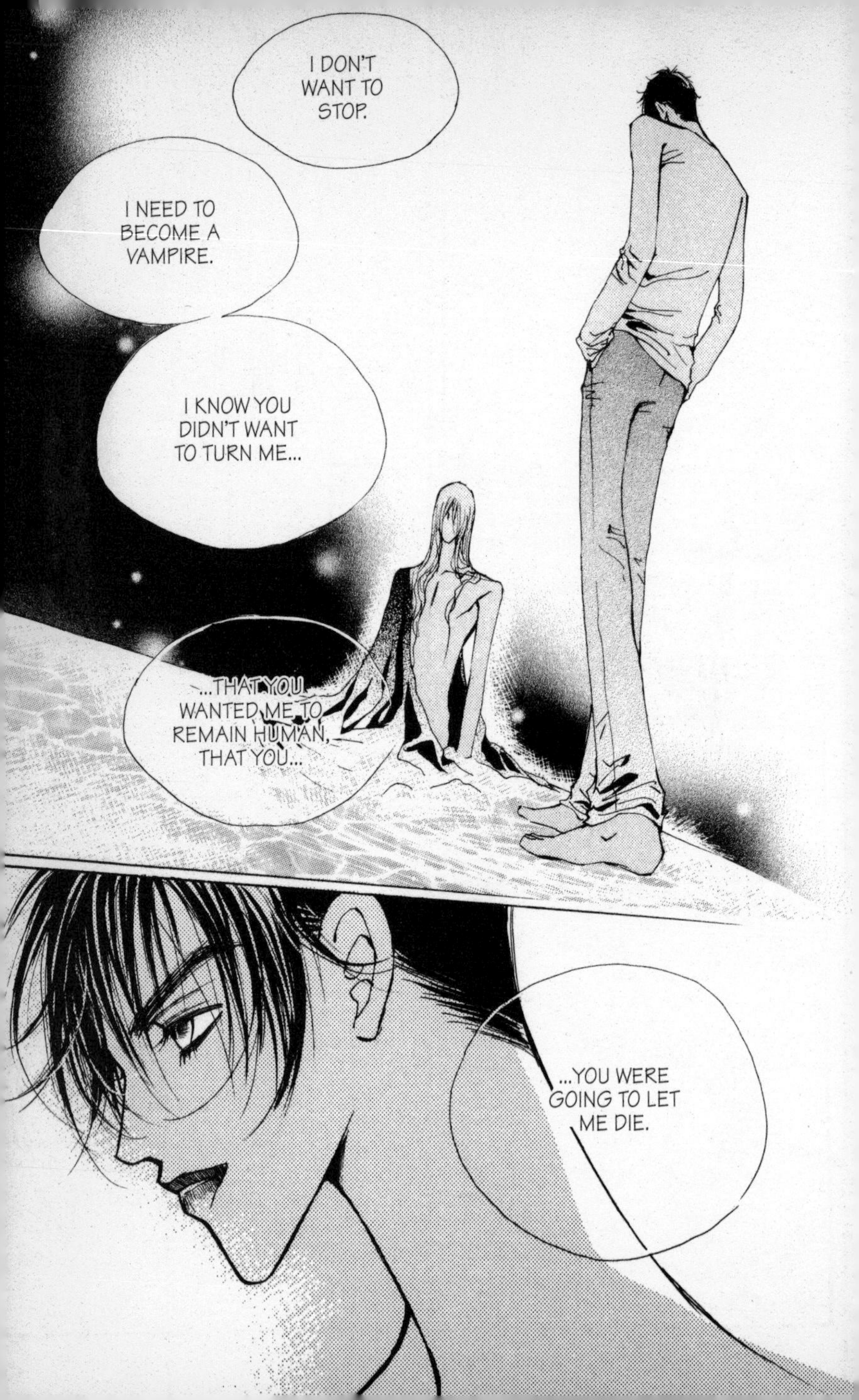
I DON'T WANT TO STOP.
I NEED TO BECOME A VAMPIRE.
I KNOW YOU DIDN'T WANT TO TURN ME...
...THAT YOU WANTED ME TO REMAIN HUMAN, THAT YOU...
...YOU WERE GOING TO LET ME DIE.

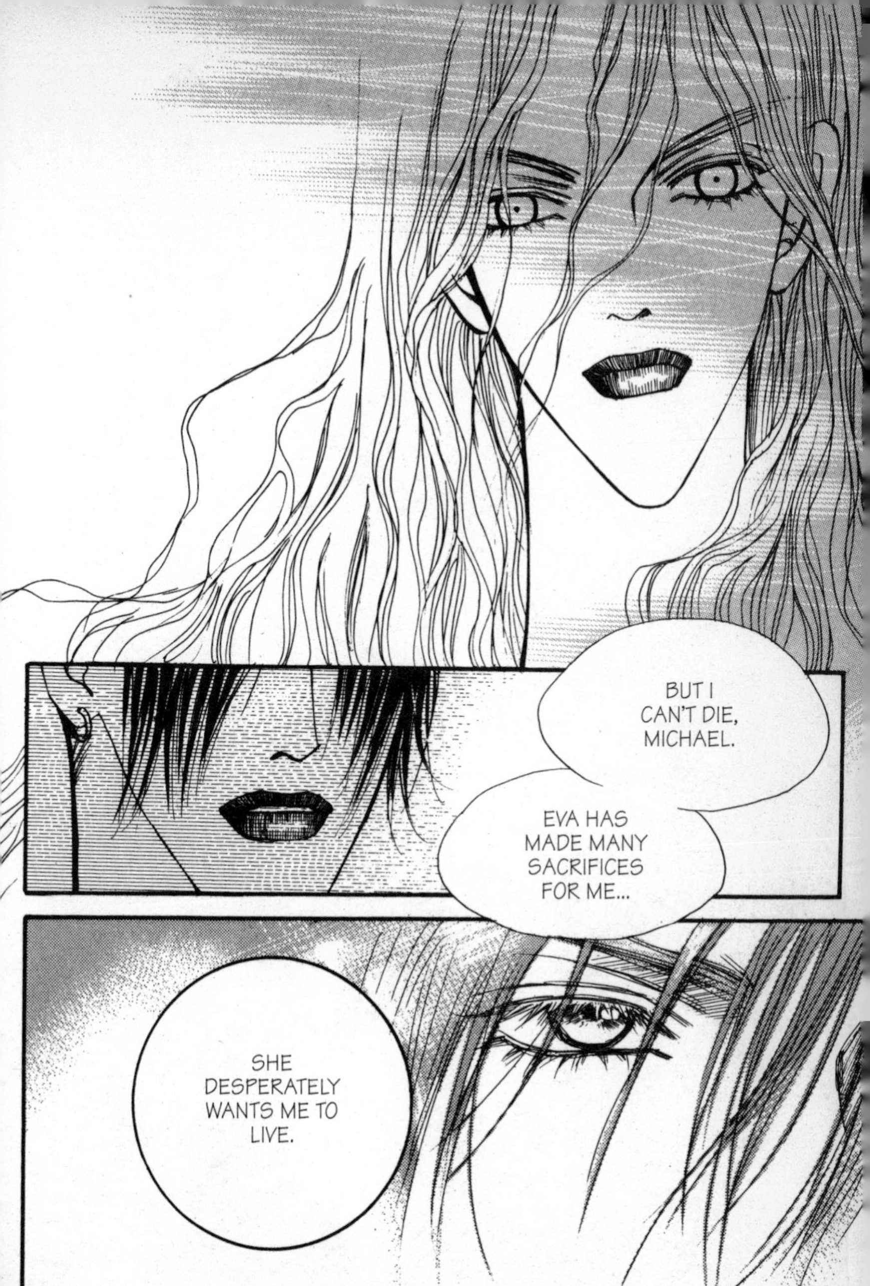
BUT I CAN'T DIE, MICHAEL.
EVA HAS MADE MANY SACRIFICES FOR ME...
SHE DESPERATELY WANTS ME TO LIVE.

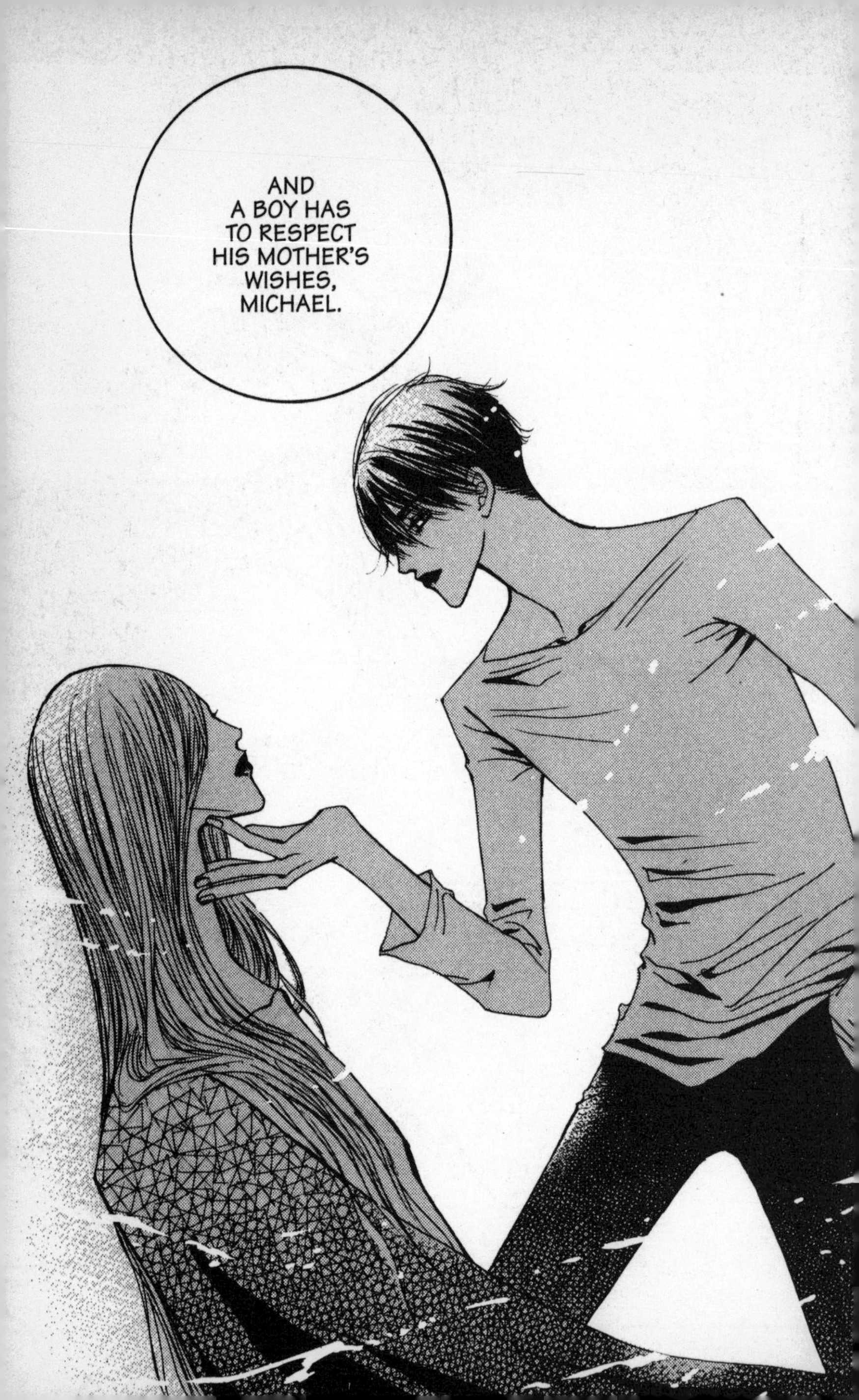
AND A BOY HAS TO RESPECT HIS MOTHER'S WISHES, MICHAEL.

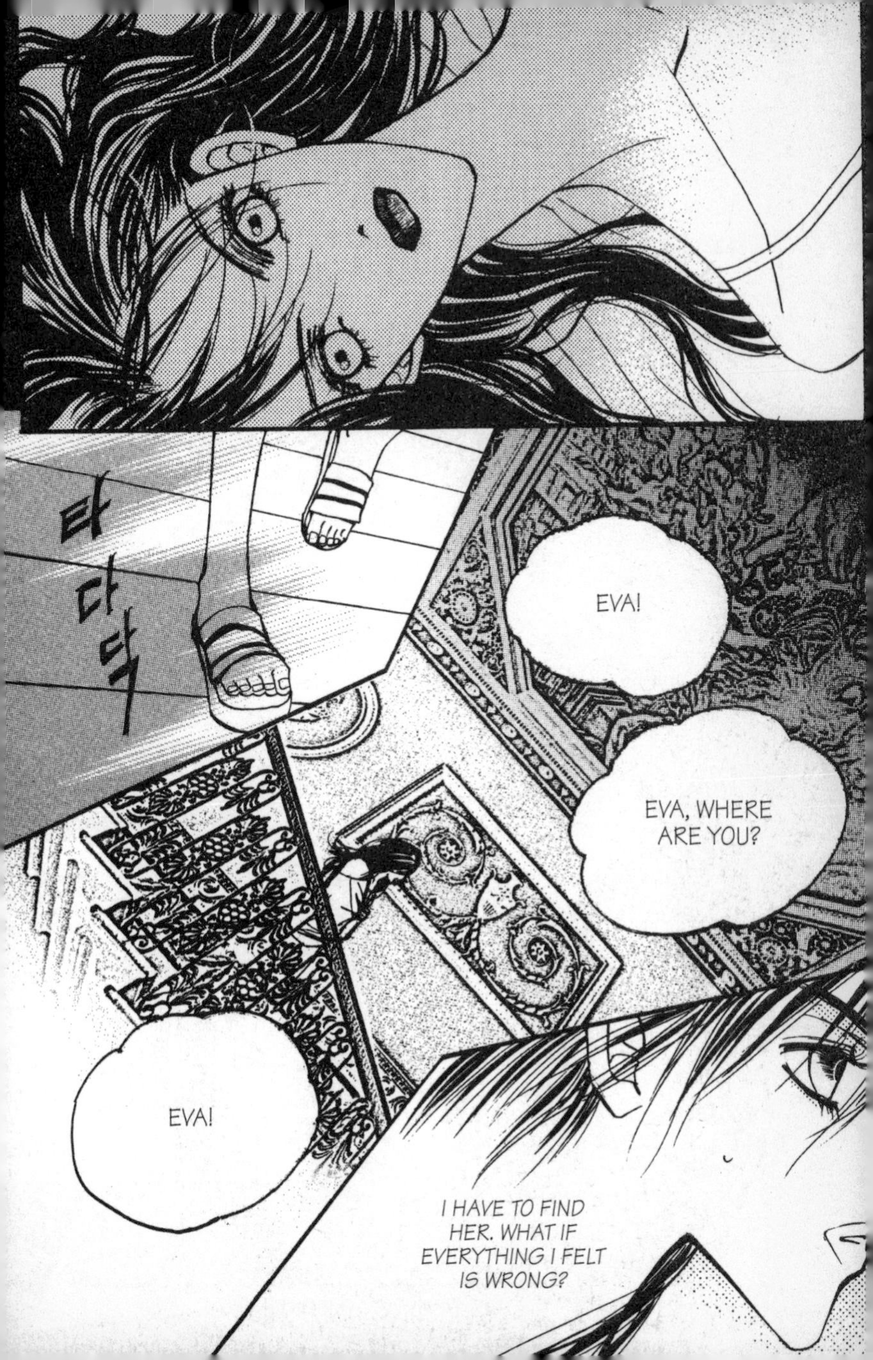
타다닥
EVA!
EVA, WHERE ARE YOU?
EVA!
I HAVE TO FIND HER. WHAT IF EVERYTHING I FELT IS WRONG?

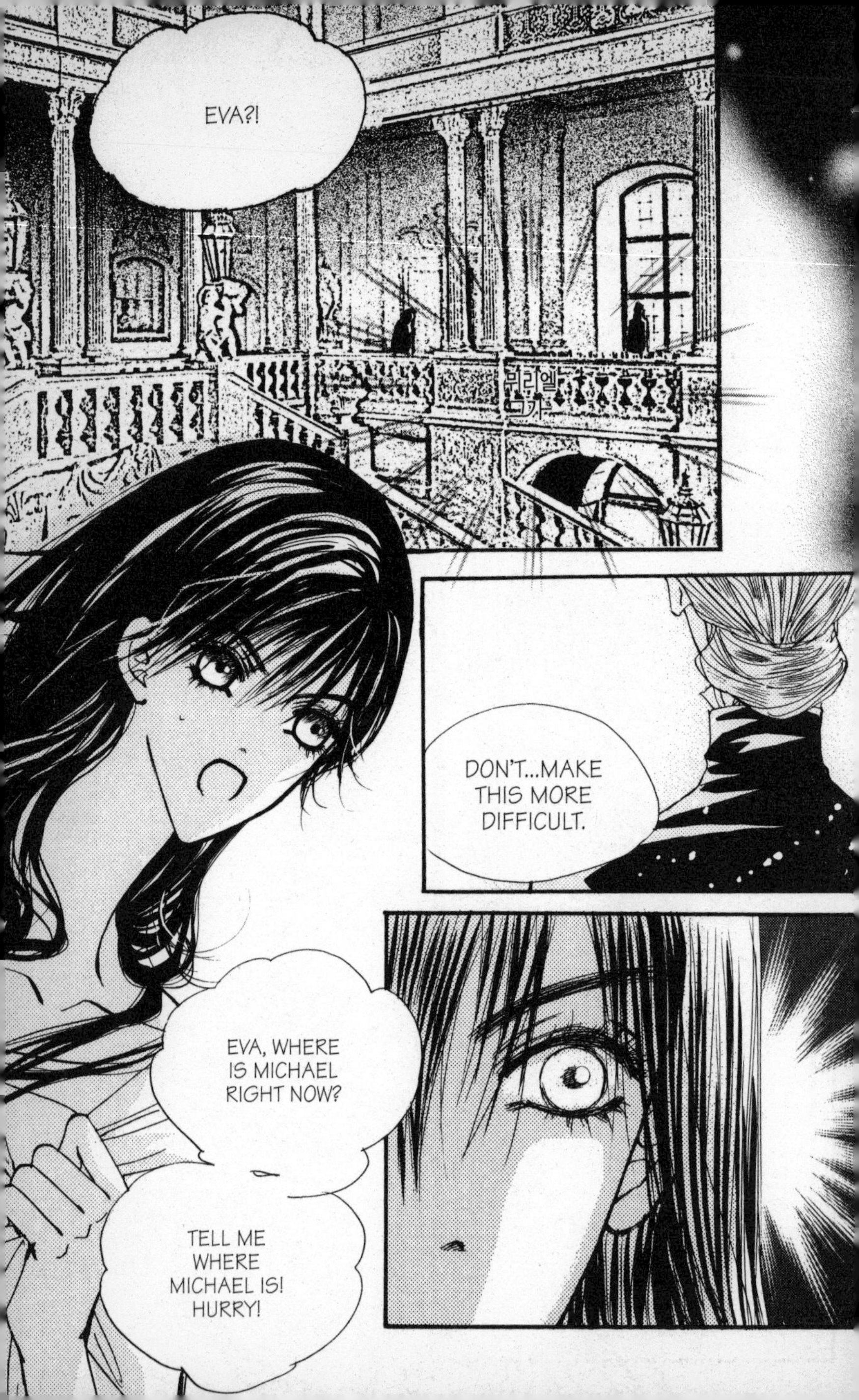
EVA?!
뮤리엘 가
DON'T...MAKE THIS MORE DIFFICULT.
EVA, WHERE IS MICHAEL RIGHT NOW?
TELL ME WHERE MICHAEL IS! HURRY!

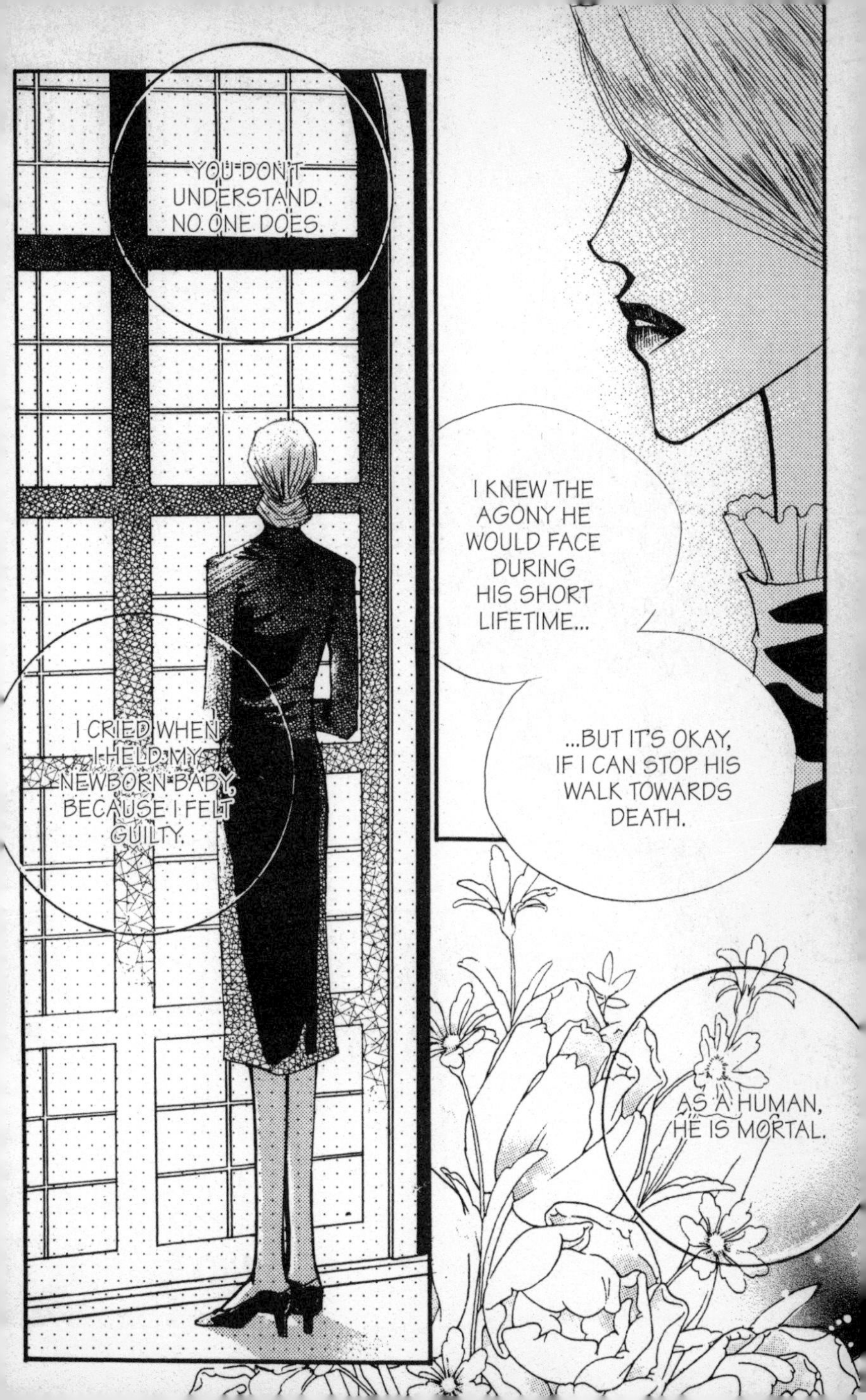
I KNEW THE AGONY HE WOULD FACE DURING HIS SHORT LIFETIME...
...BUT IT'S OKAY, IF I CAN STOP HIS WALK TOWARDS DEATH.
AS A HUMAN, HE IS MORTAL.
YOU DON'T UNDERSTAND. NO ONE DOES.
I CRIED WHEN I HELD MY NEWBORN BABY, BECAUSE I FELT GUILTY.

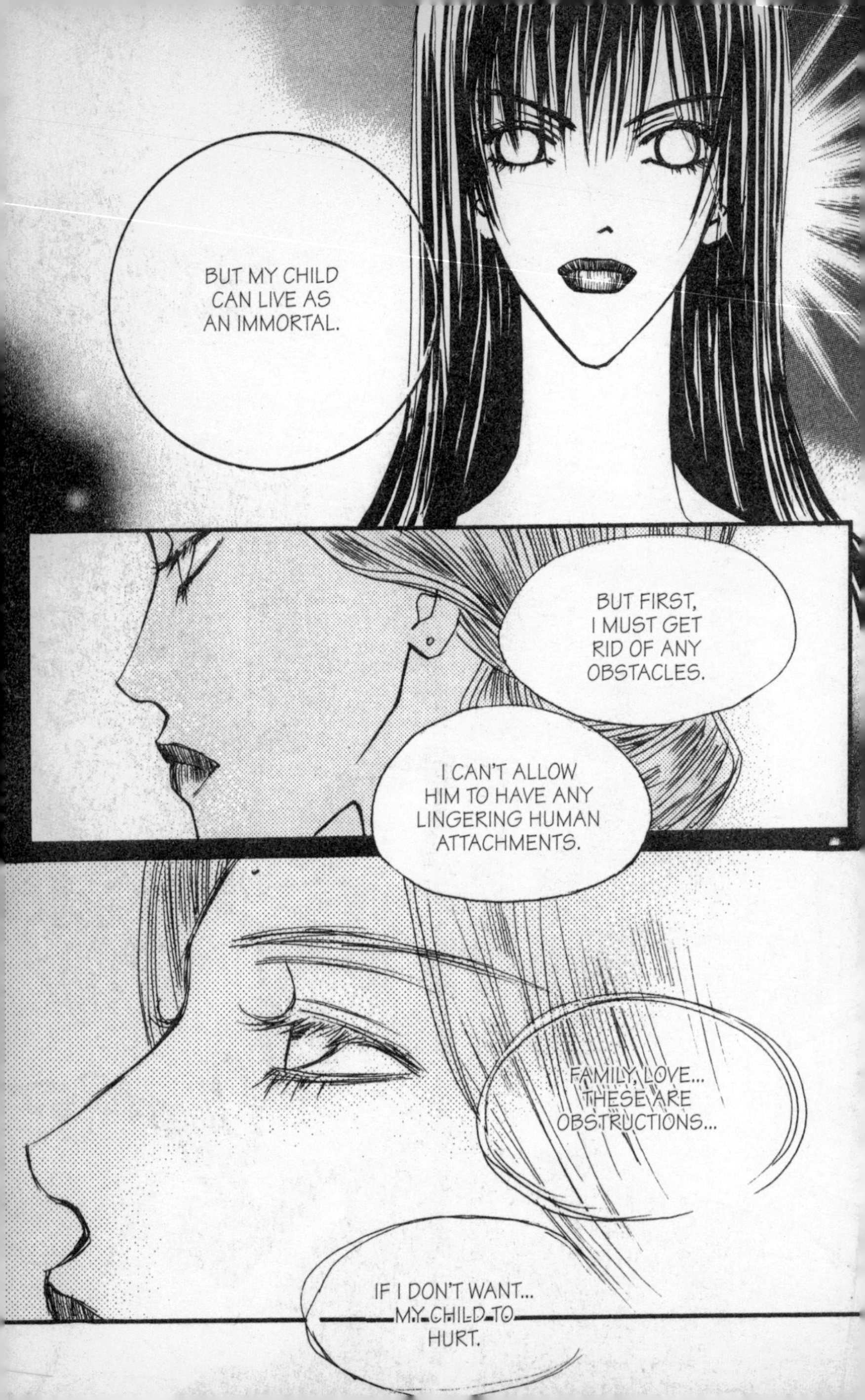
BUT MY CHILD CAN LIVE AS AN IMMORTAL.
BUT FIRST, I MUST GET RID OF ANY OBSTACLES.
I CAN'T ALLOW HIM TO HAVE ANY LINGERING HUMAN ATTACHMENTS.
FAMILY, LOVE... THESE ARE OBSTRUCTIONS...
IF I DON'T WANT... MY CHILD TO HURT.

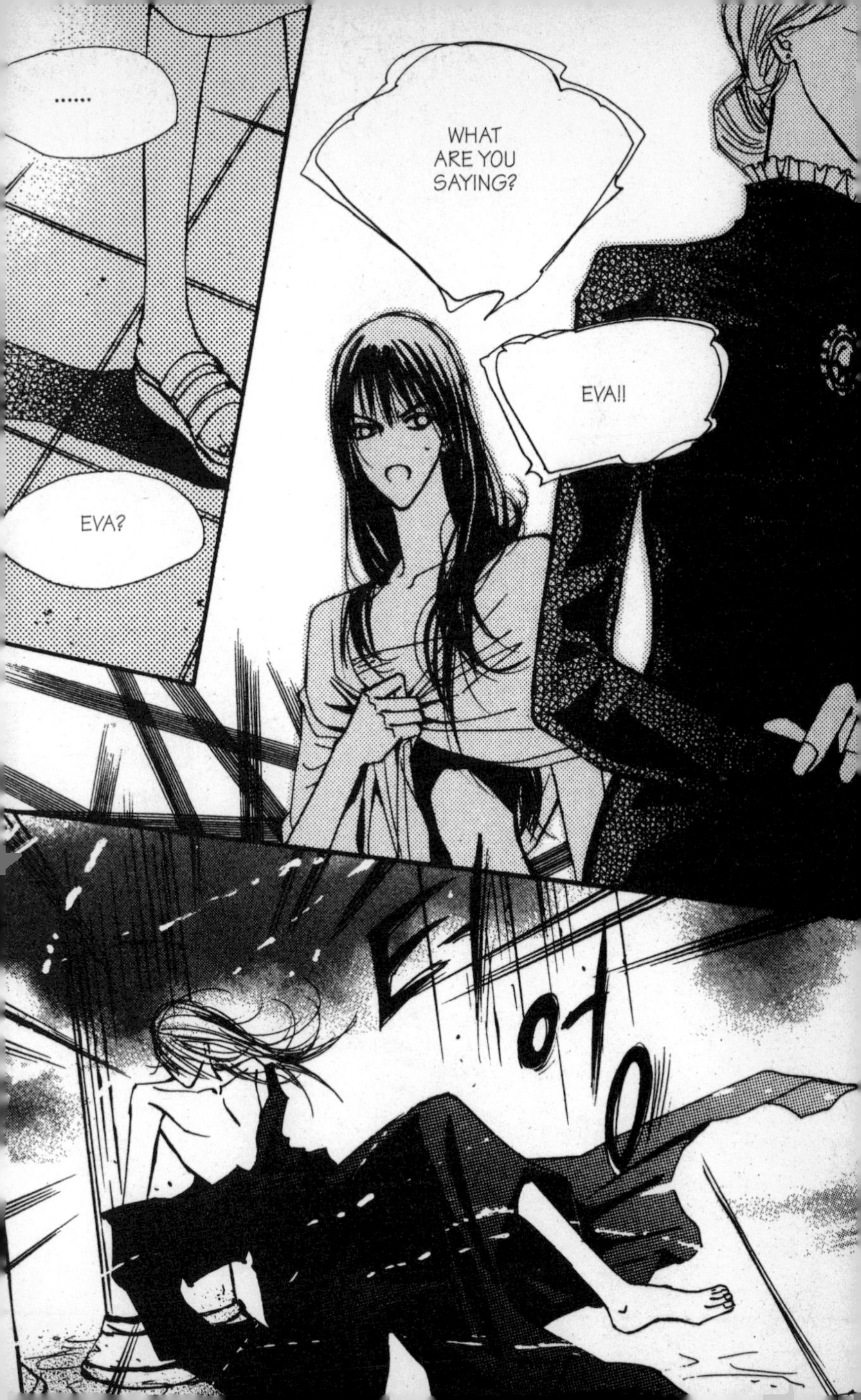
......
EVA?
WHAT ARE YOU SAYING?
EVA!!

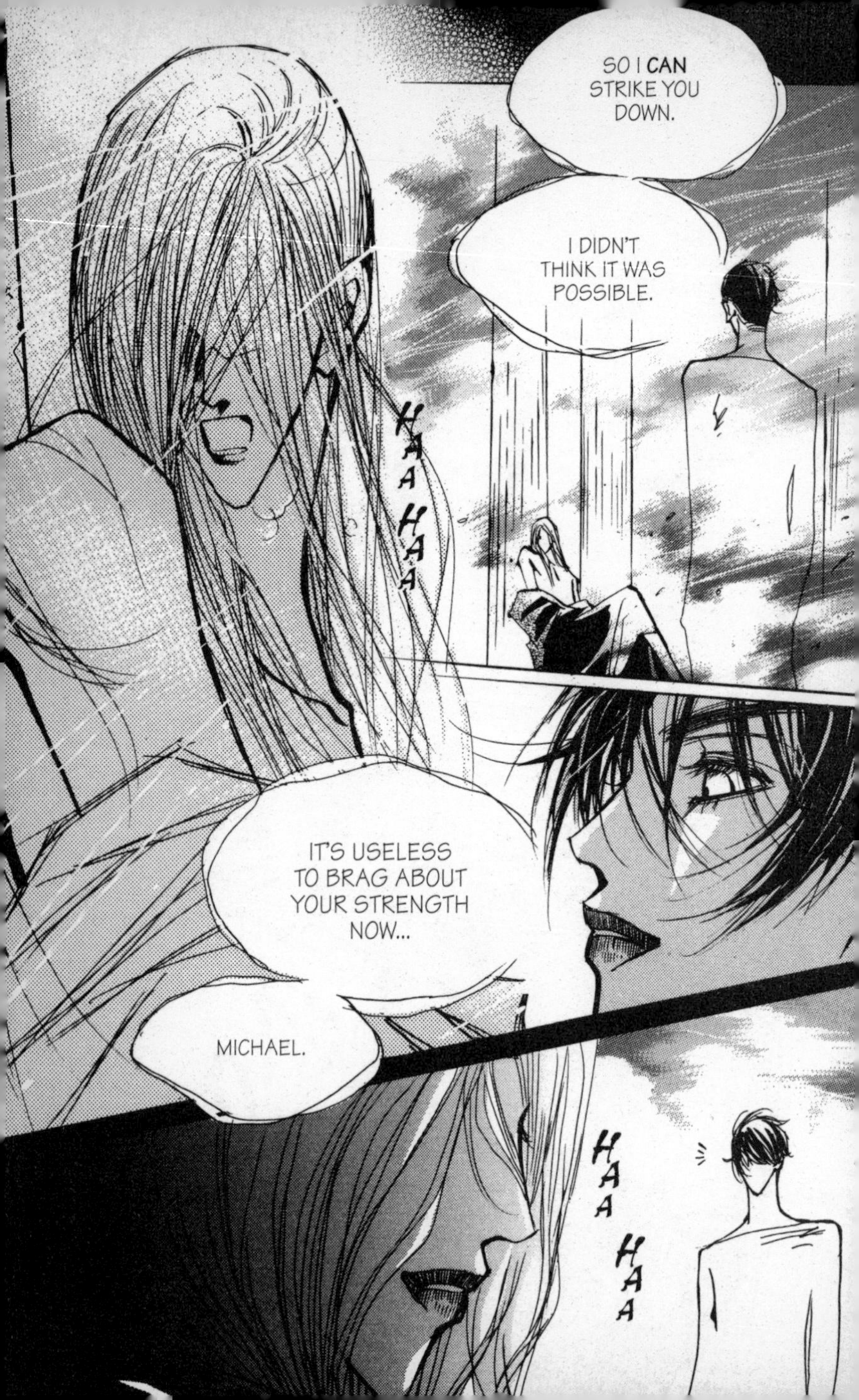
SO I CAN STRIKE YOU DOWN.
I DIDN'T THINK IT WAS POSSIBLE.
HA HA HA HA
IT'S USELESS TO BRAG ABOUT YOUR STRENGTH NOW...
MICHAEL.
HA HA HA HA

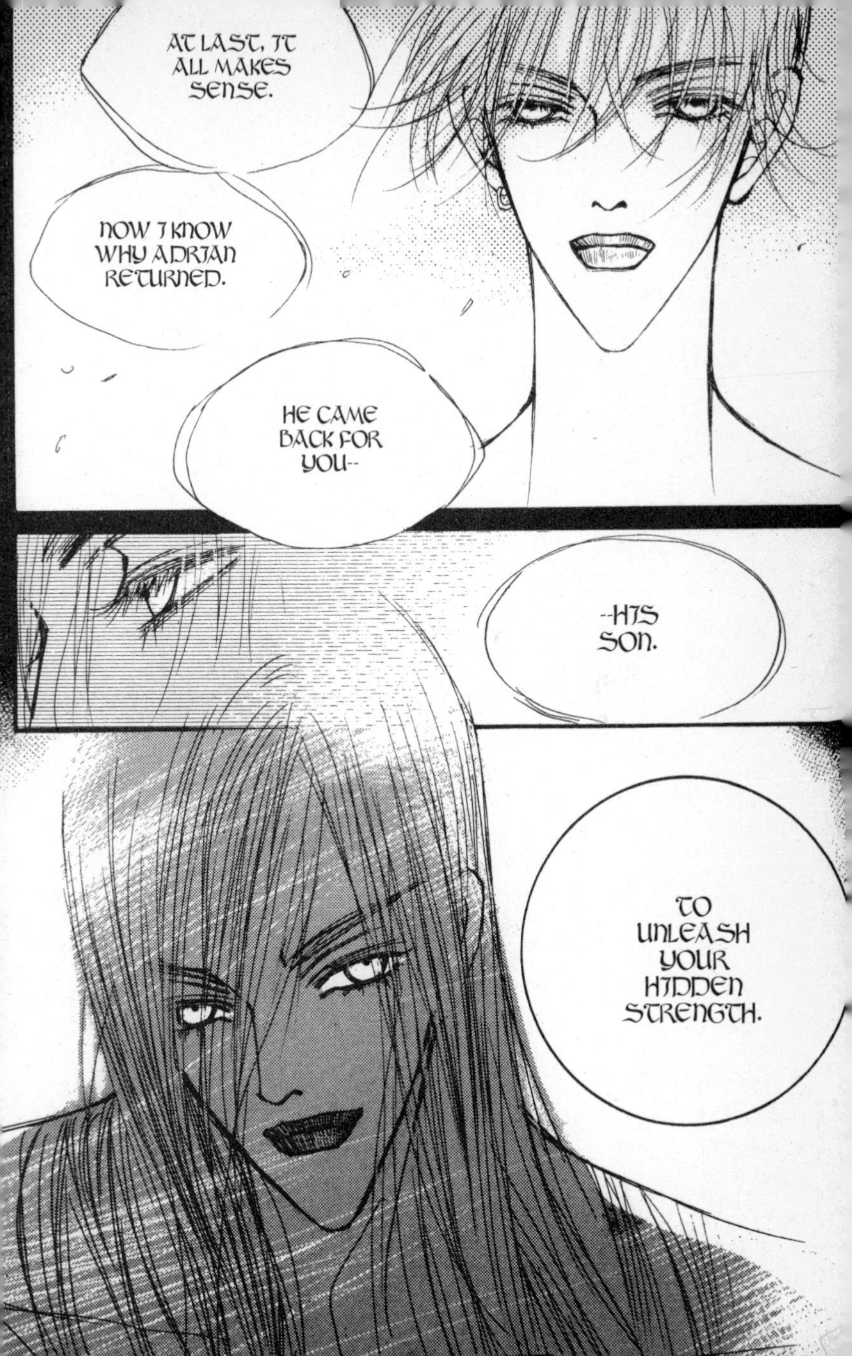
AT LAST, IT ALL MAKES SENSE.
NOW I KNOW WHY ADRIAN RETURNED.
HE CAME BACK FOR YOU--
--HIS SON.
TO UNLEASH YOUR HIDDEN STRENGTH.

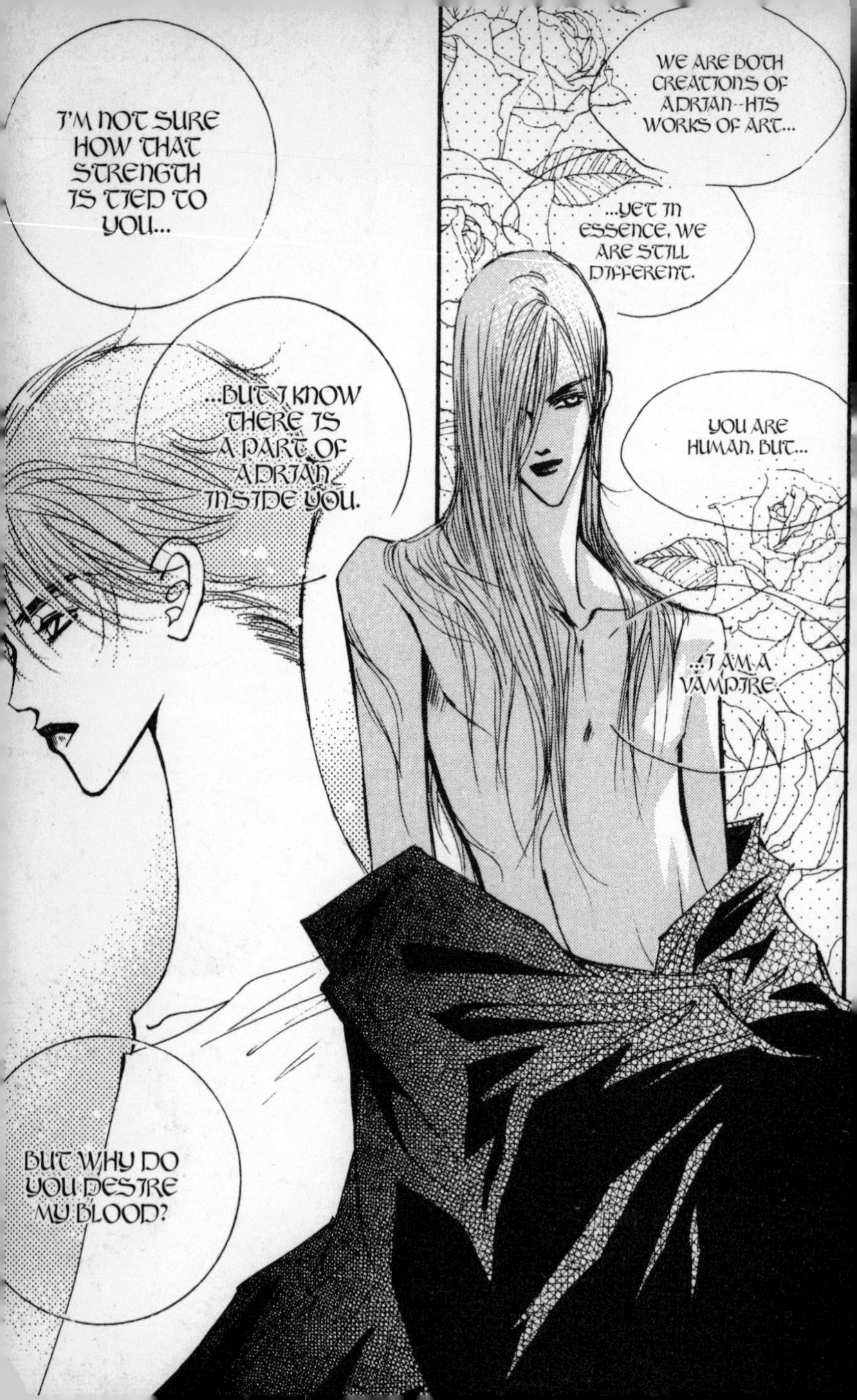
WE ARE BOTH CREATIONS OF ADRIAN--HIS WORKS OF ART...
...YET IN ESSENCE, WE ARE STILL DIFFERENT.
YOU ARE HUMAN, BUT...
...I AM A VAMPIRE.
I'M NOT SURE HOW THAT STRENGTH IS TIED TO YOU...
...BUT I KNOW THERE IS A PART OF ADRIAN INSIDE YOU.
BUT WHY DO YOU DESIRE MY BLOOD?

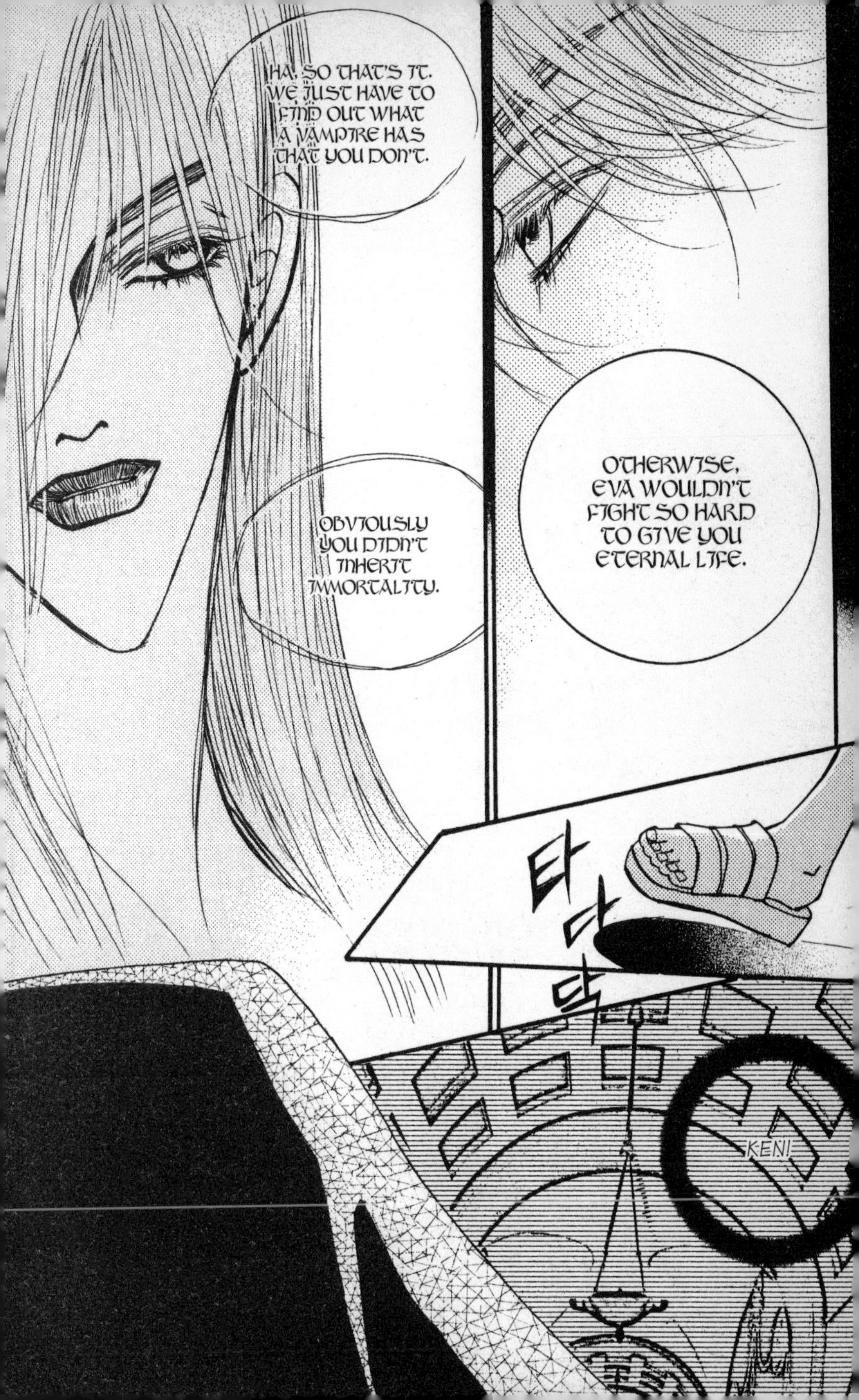
HA! SO THAT'S IT. WE JUST HAVE TO FIND OUT WHAT A VAMPIRE HAS THAT YOU DON'T.
OBVIOUSLY YOU DIDN'T INHERIT IMMORTALITY.
OTHERWISE, EVA WOULDN'T FIGHT SO HARD TO GIVE YOU ETERNAL LIFE.
타다닥
KEN!

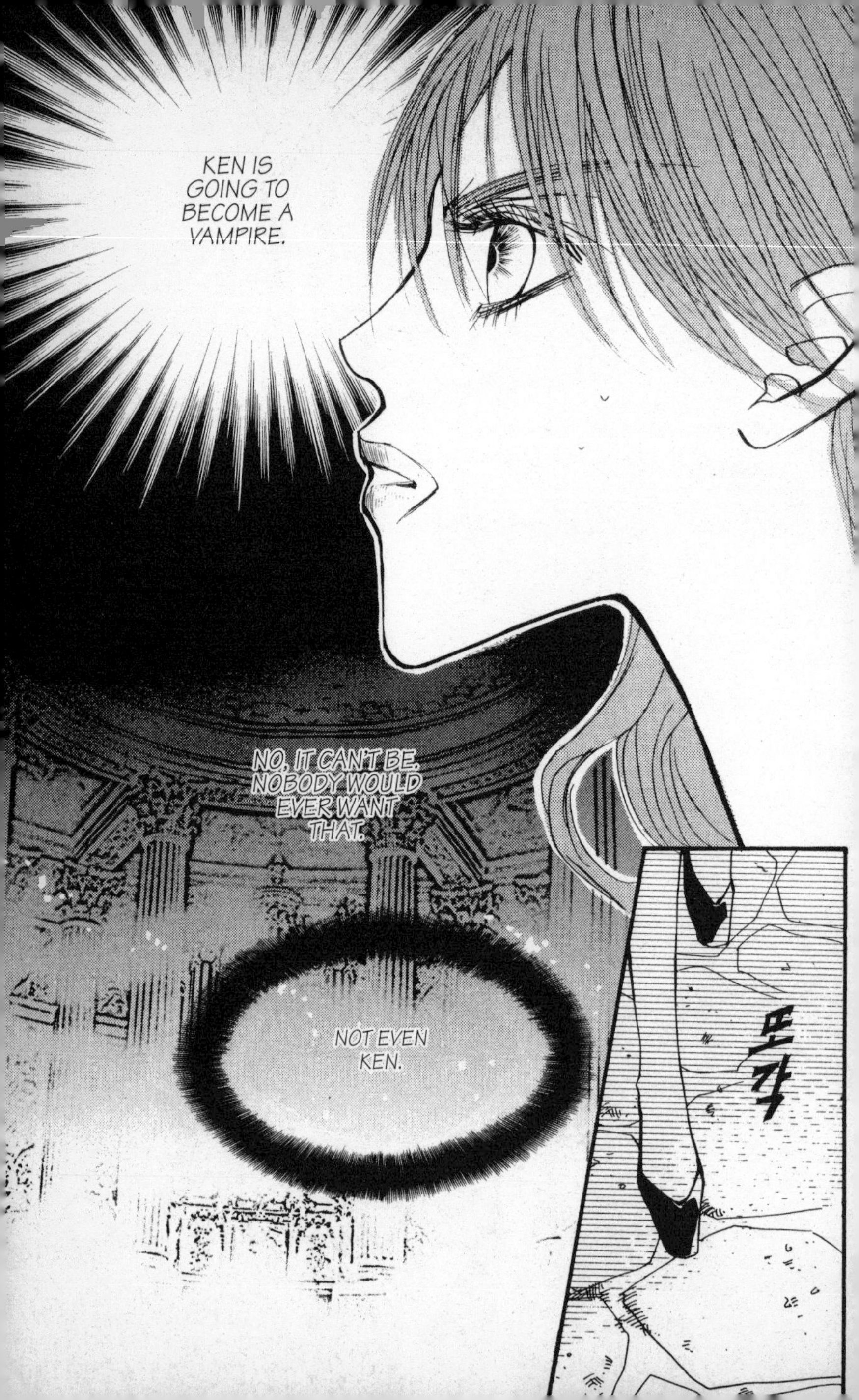
KEN IS GOING TO BECOME A VAMPIRE.
NO, IT CAN'T BE. NOBODY WOULD EVER WANT THAT.
NOT EVEN KEN.
또각

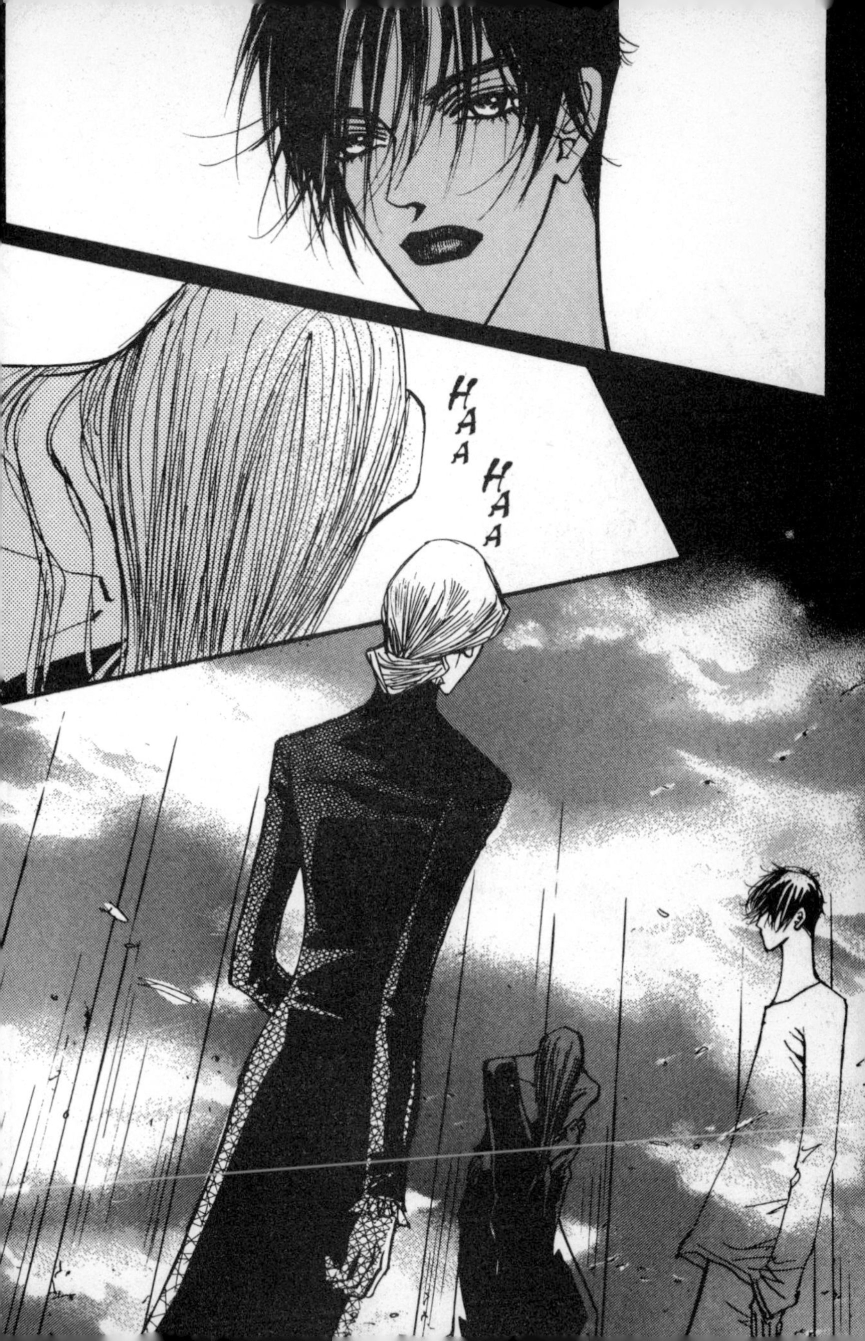
HAA
HAA

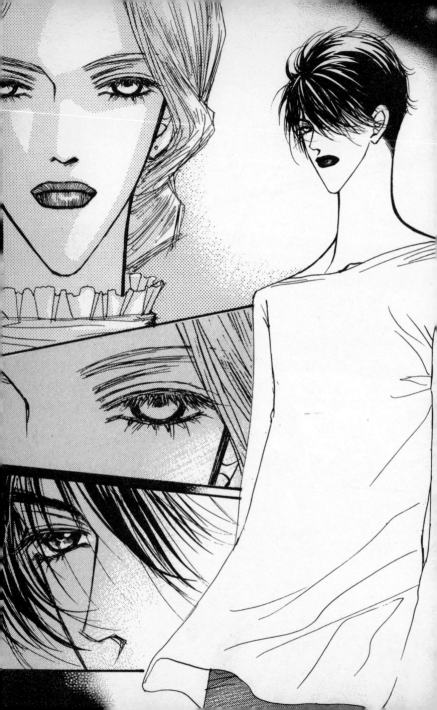

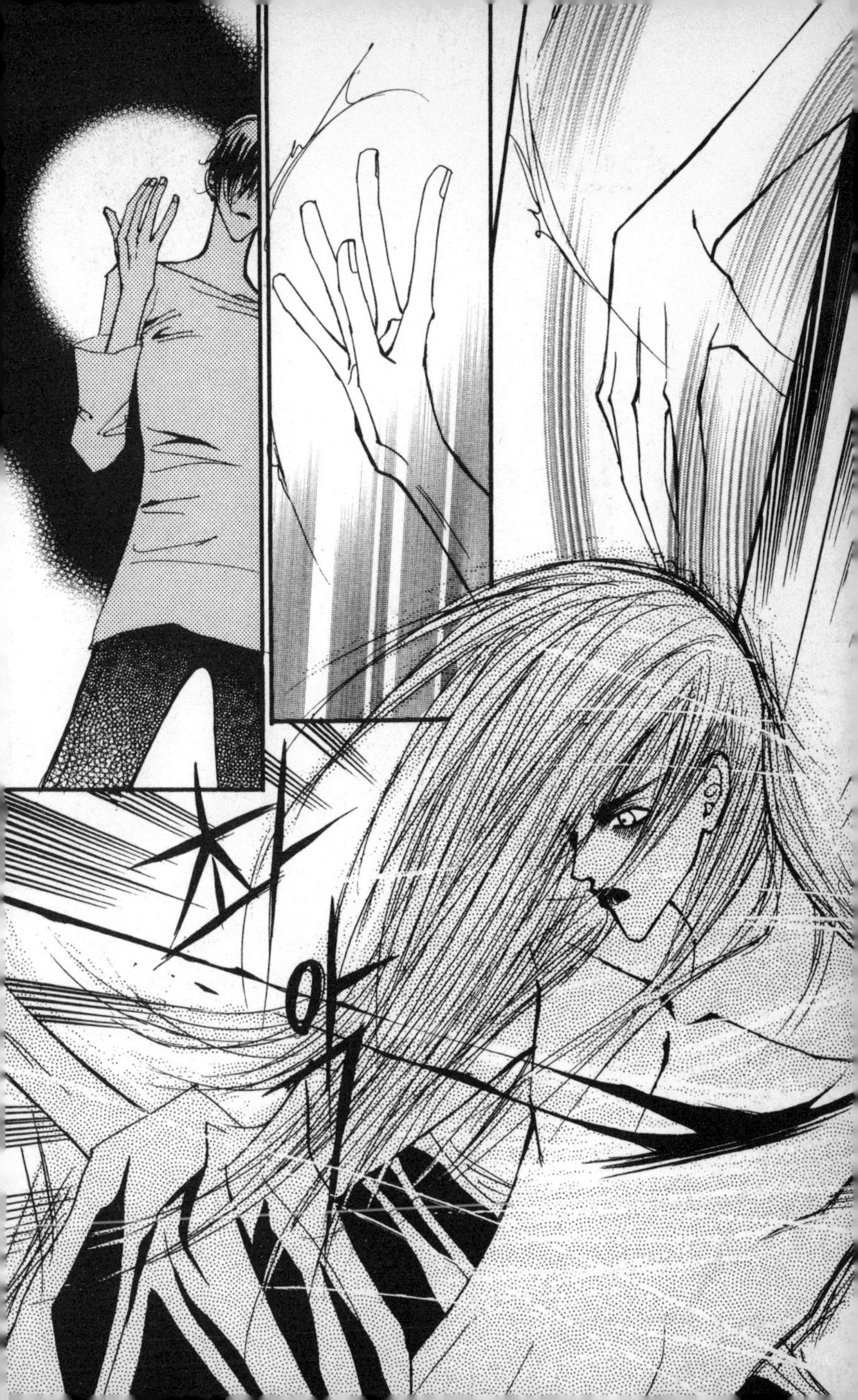

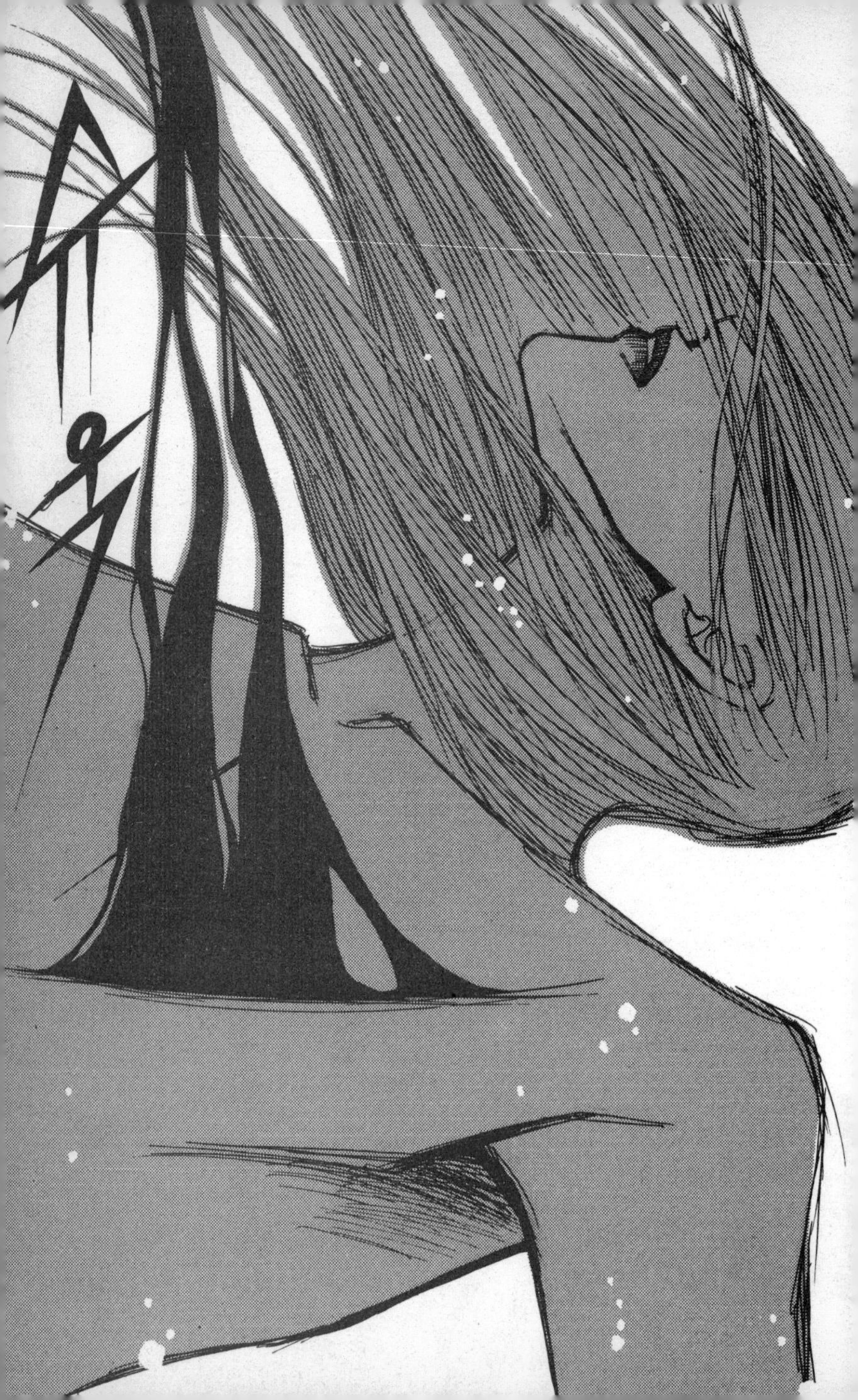

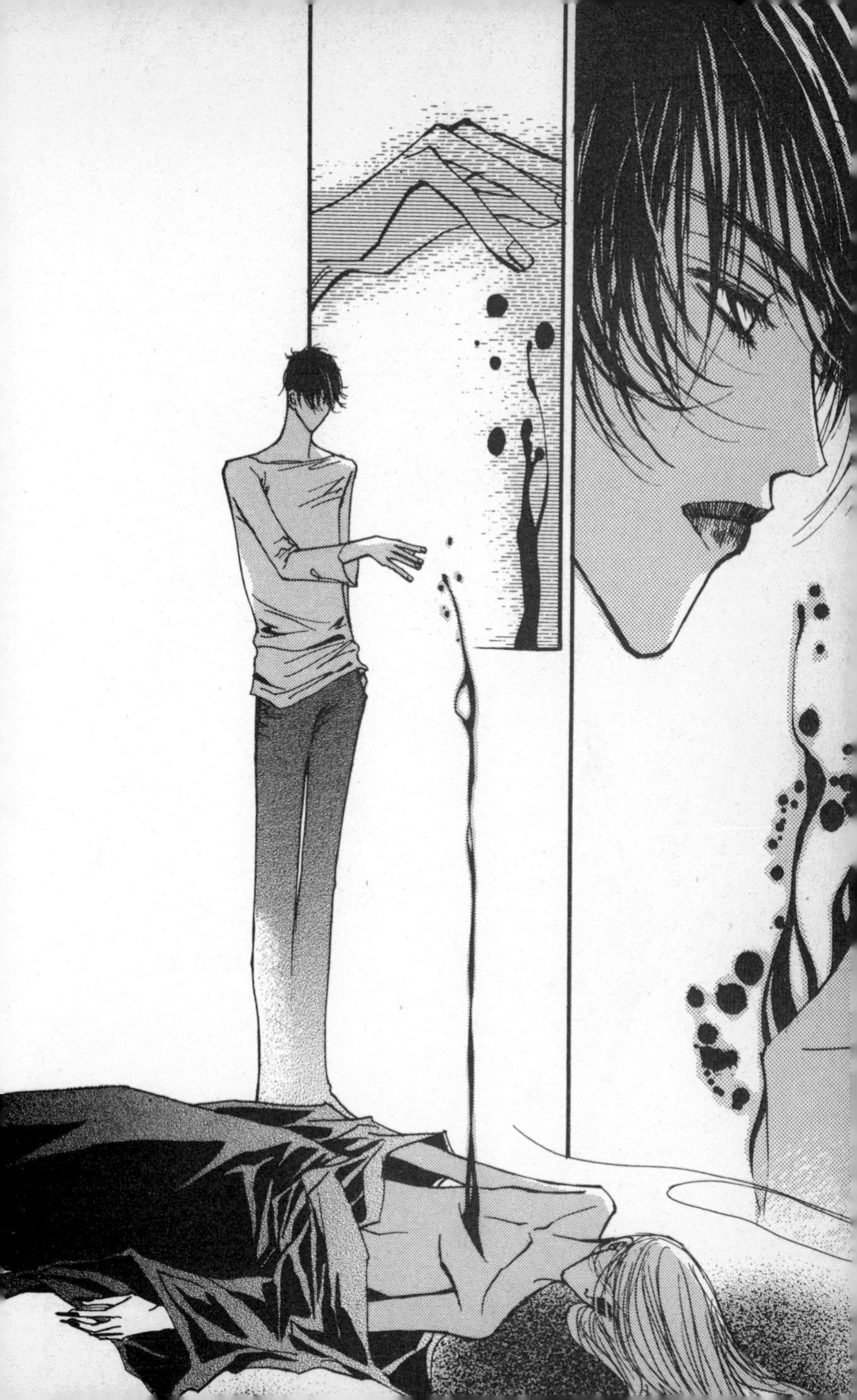

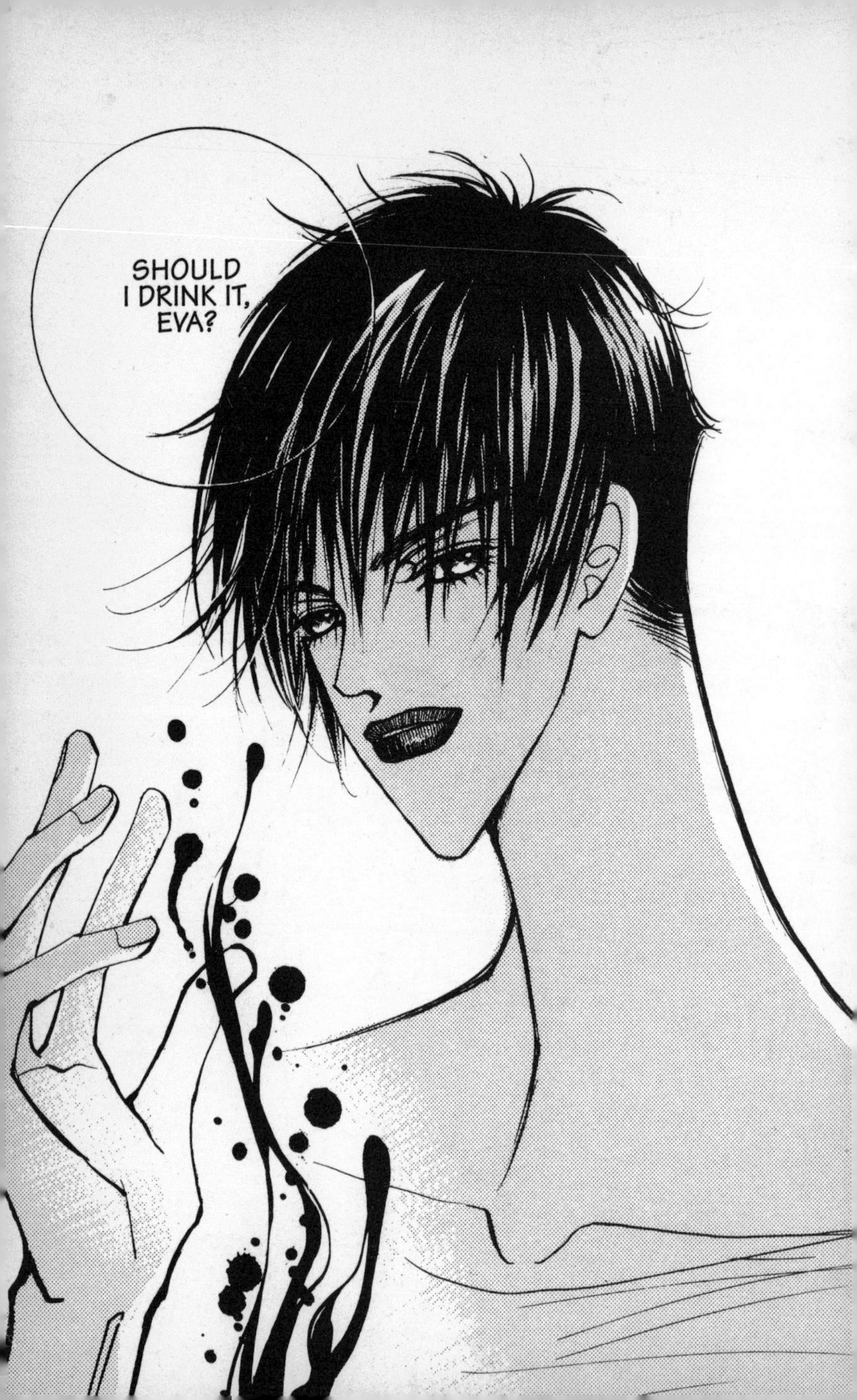
SHOULD I DRINK IT, EVA?

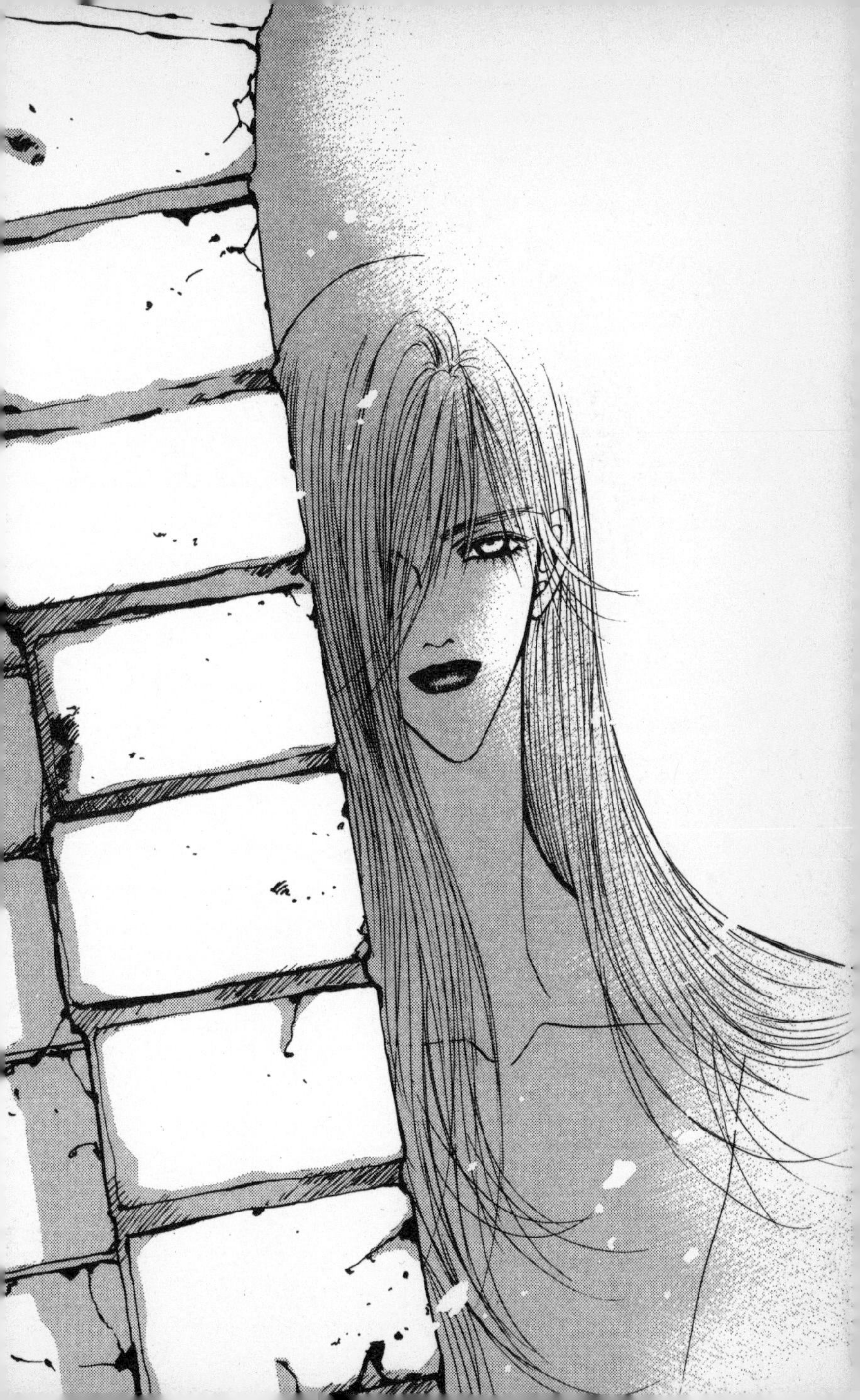

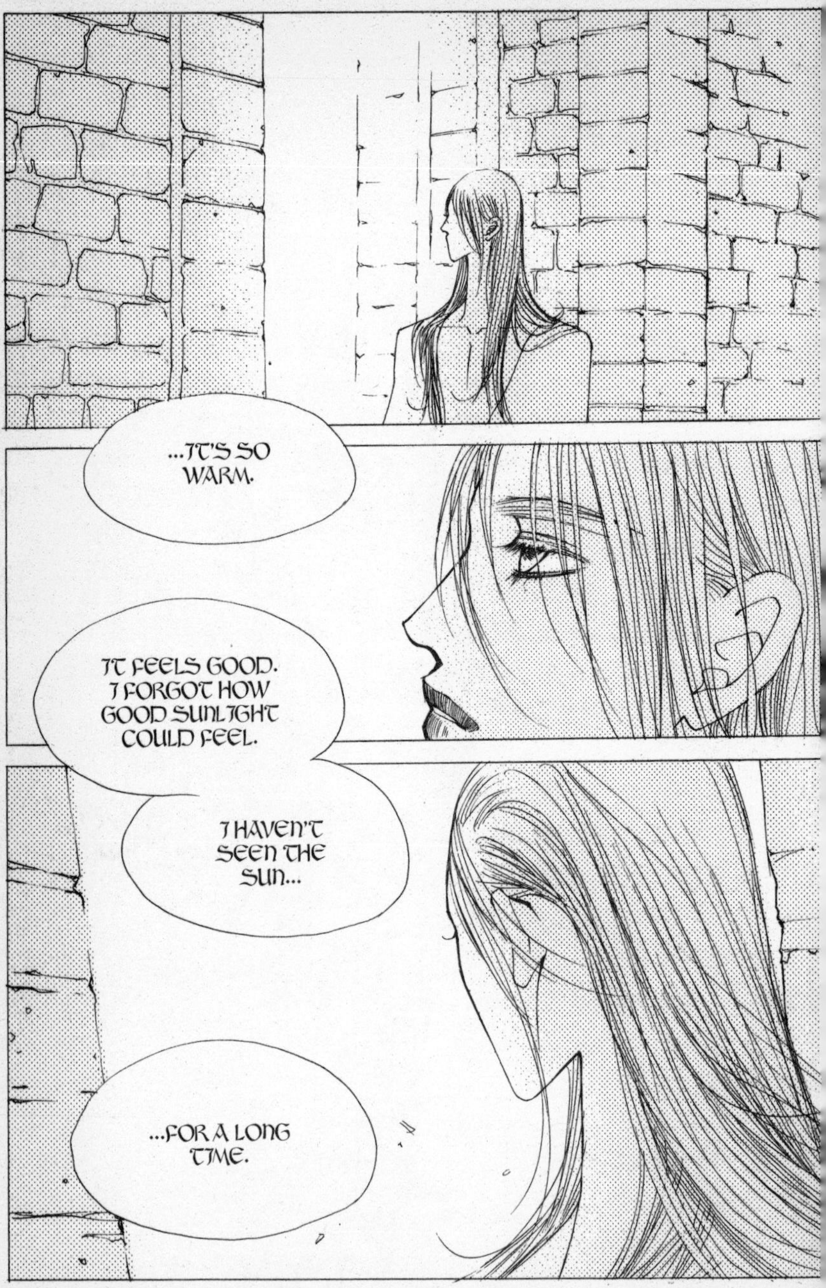
...IT'S SO WARM.
IT FEELS GOOD. I FORGOT HOW GOOD SUNLIGHT COULD FEEL.
I HAVEN'T SEEN THE SUN...
...FOR A LONG TIME.

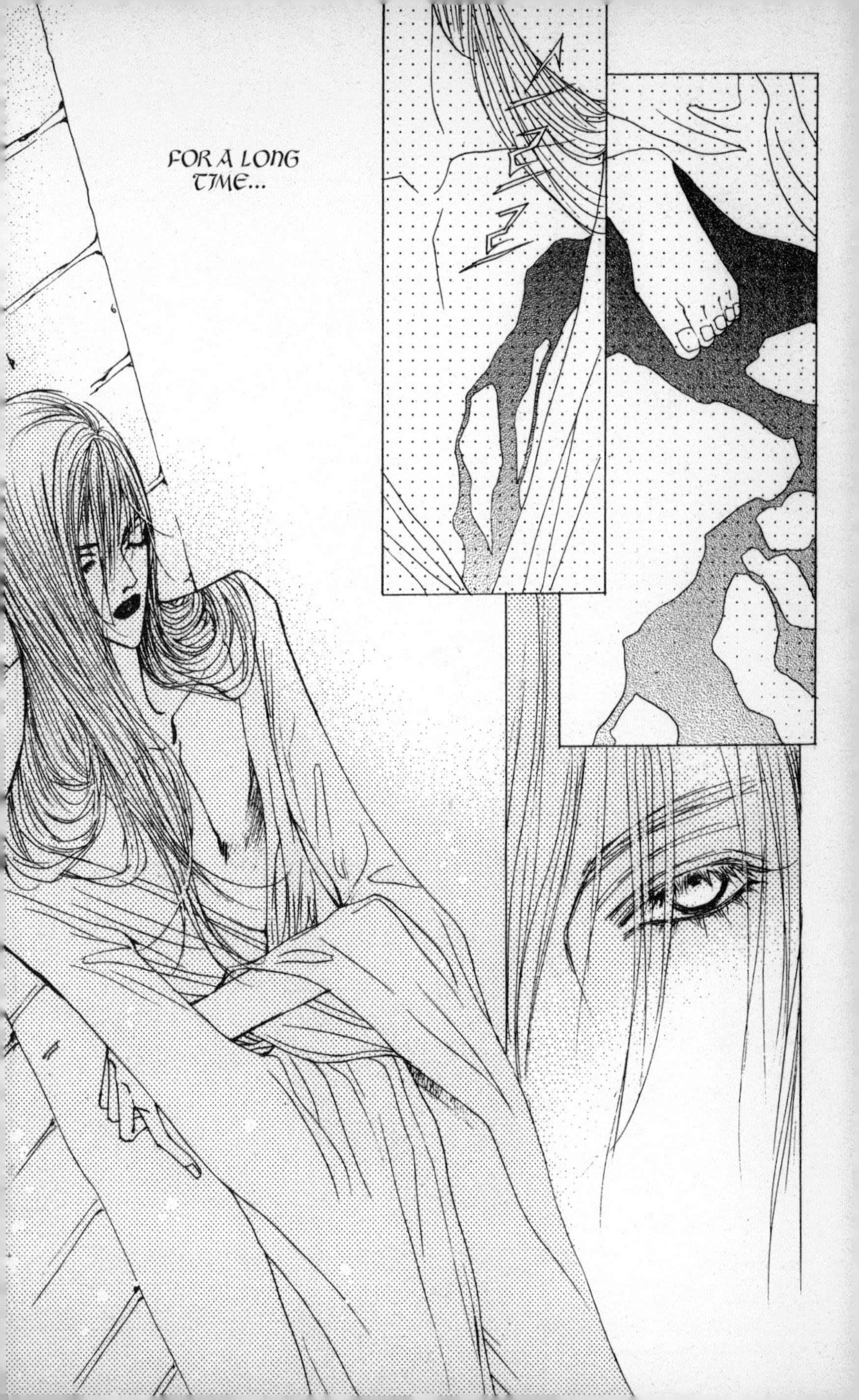
FOR A LONG TIME...

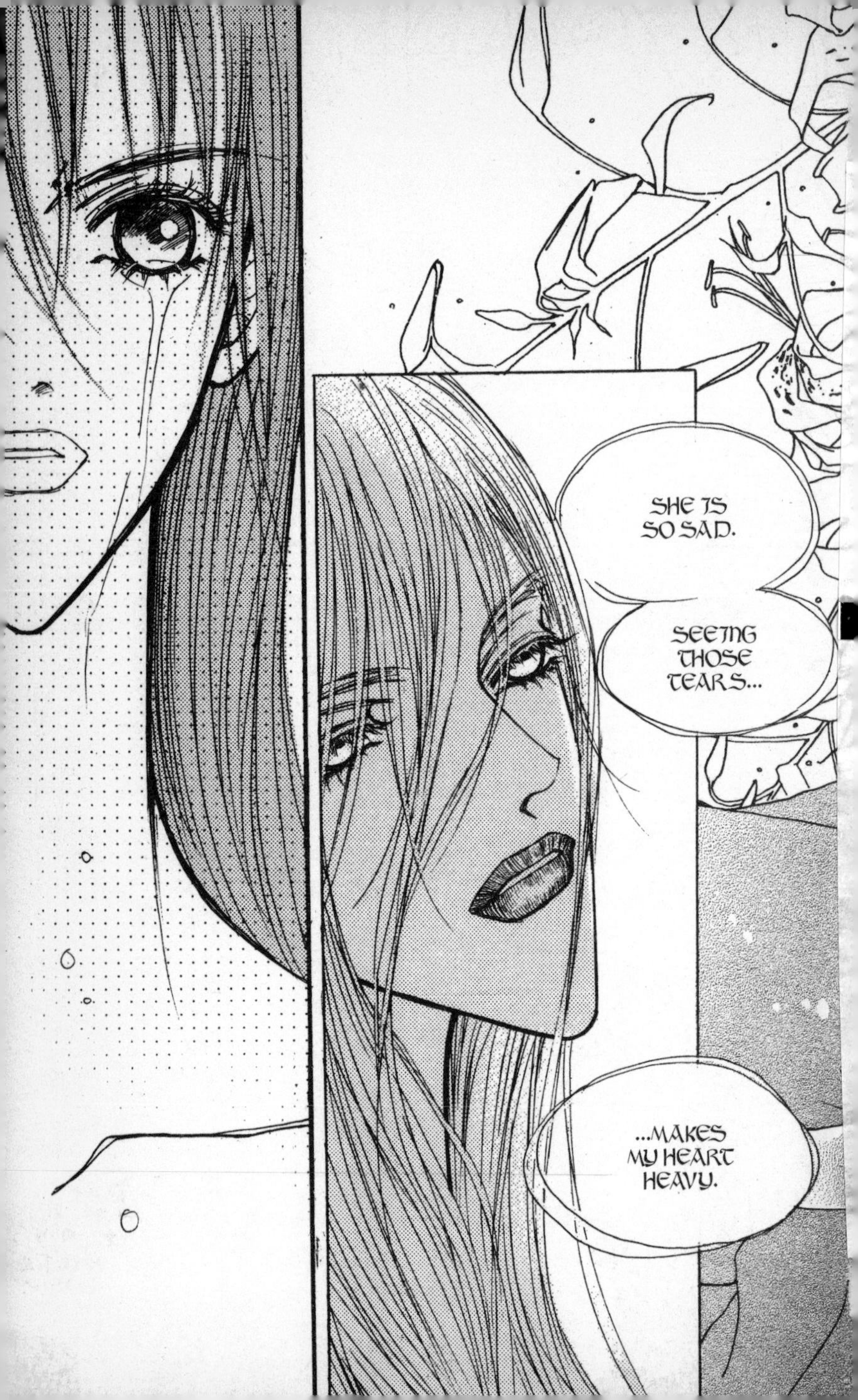
SHE IS SO SAD.
SEEING THOSE TEARS...
...MAKES MY HEART HEAVY.

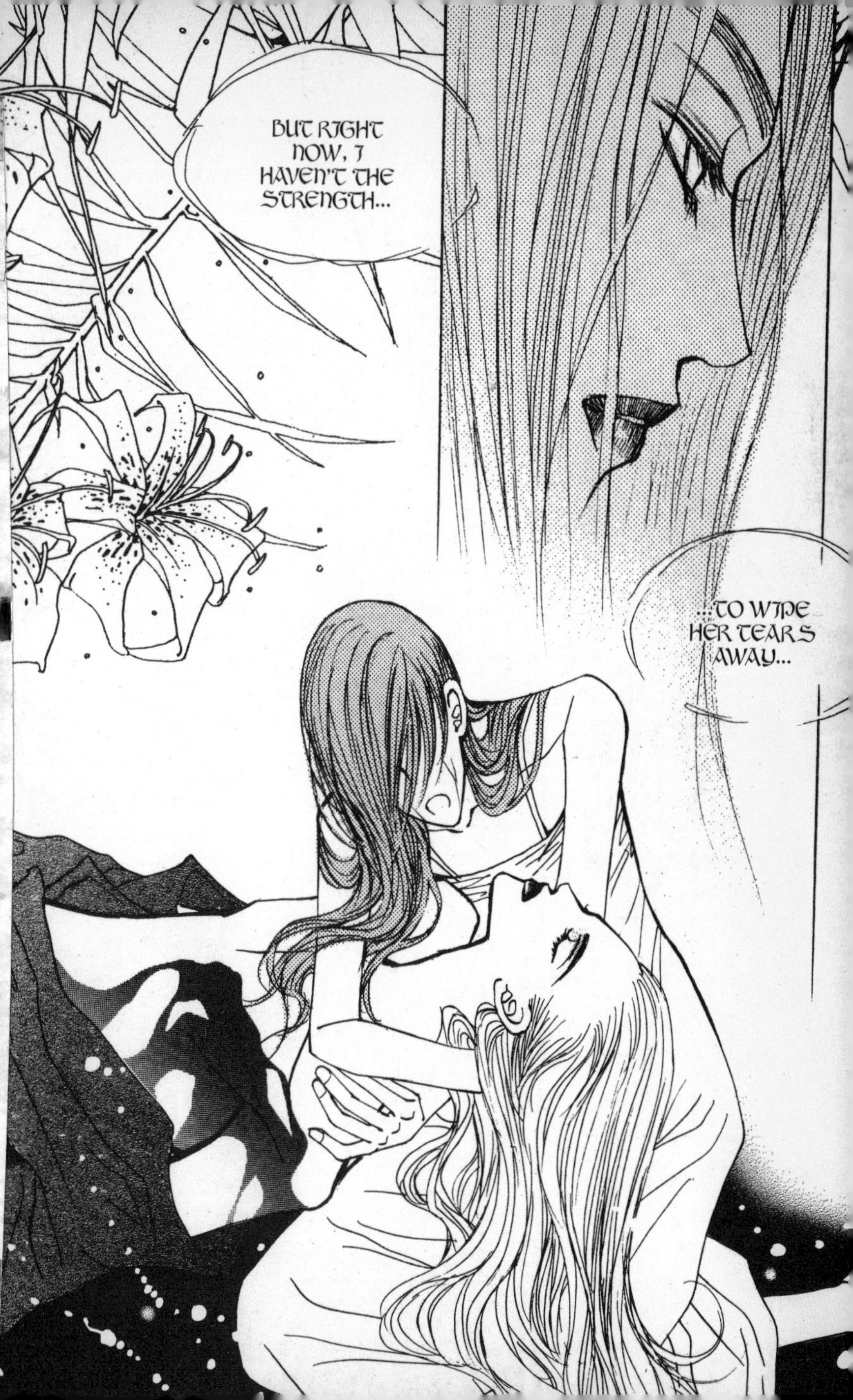
BUT RIGHT NOW, I HAVEN'T THE STRENGTH...
...TO WIPE HER TEARS AWAY...

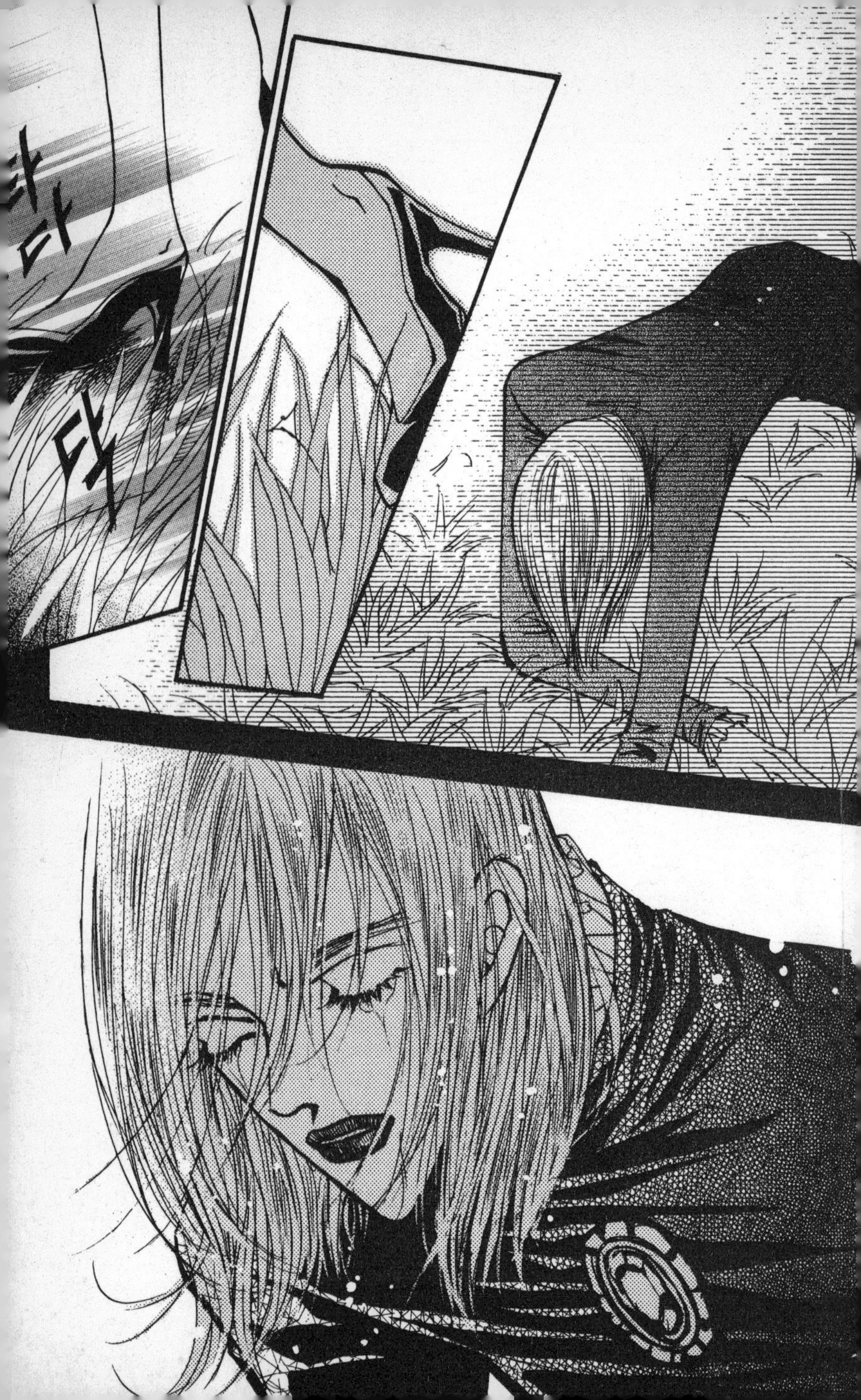
다닥

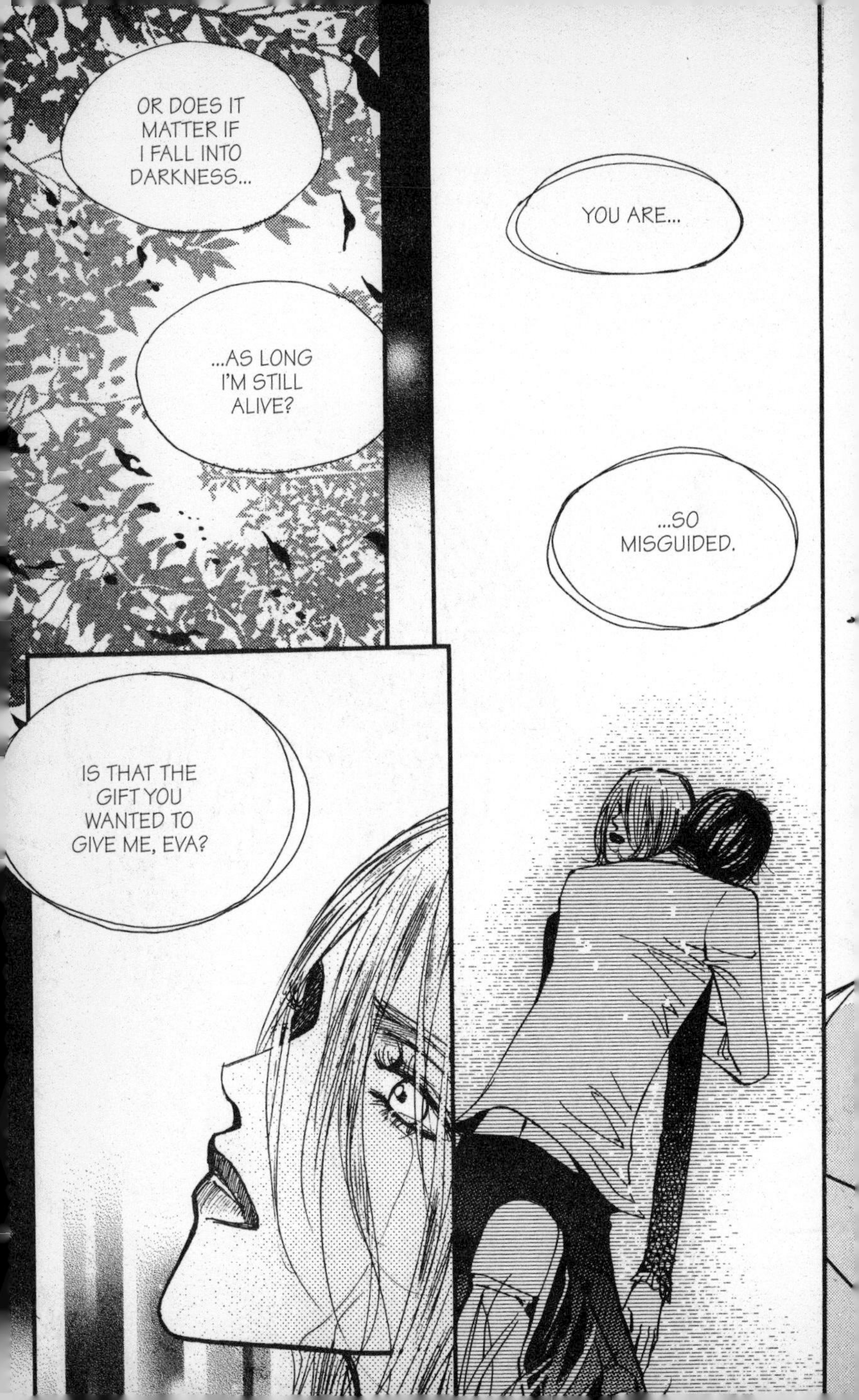
OR DOES IT MATTER IF I FALL INTO DARKNESS...
...AS LONG I'M STILL ALIVE?
YOU ARE...
...SO MISGUIDED.
IS THAT THE GIFT YOU WANTED TO GIVE ME, EVA?

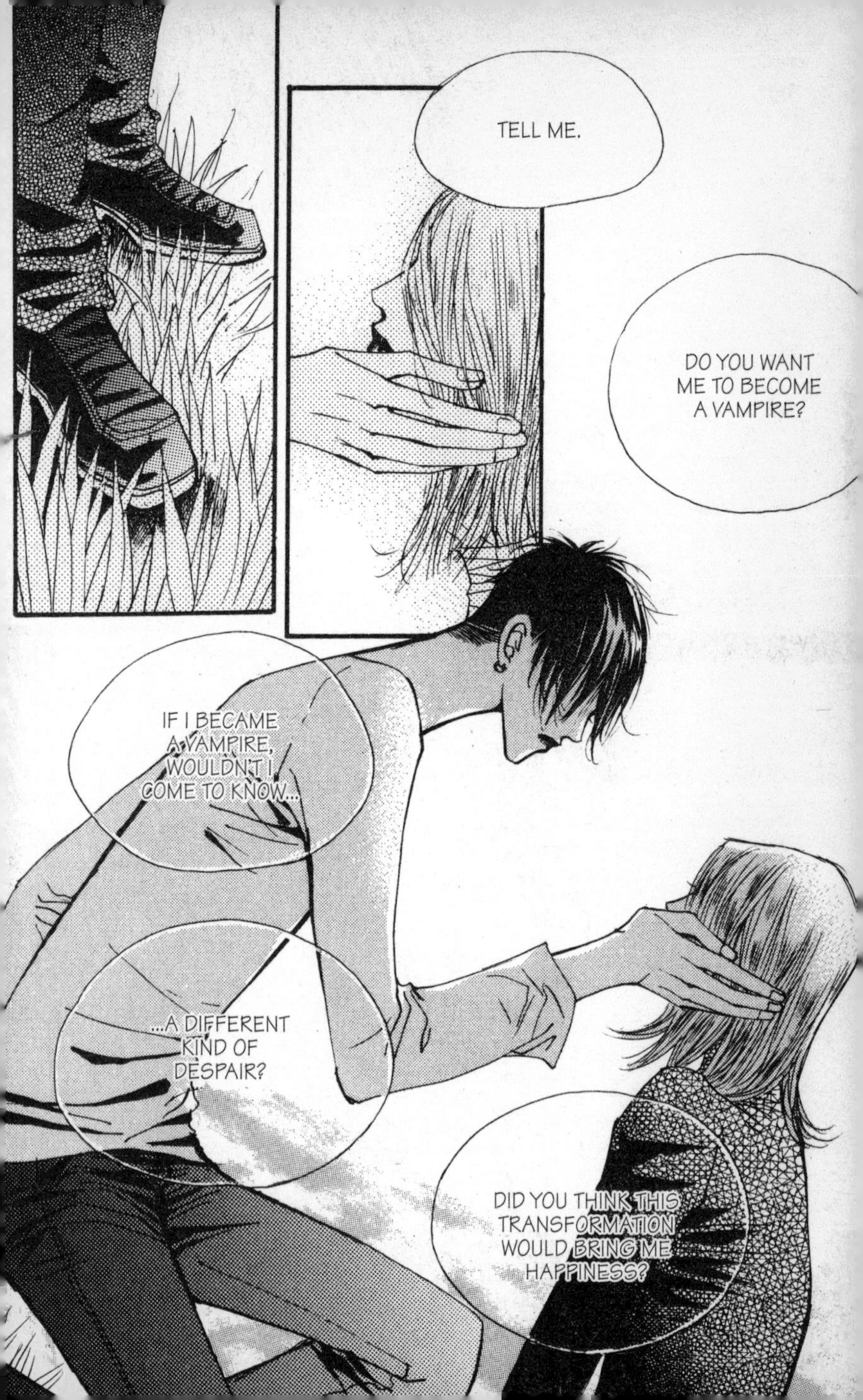
TELL ME.
DO YOU WANT ME TO BECOME A VAMPIRE?
IF I BECAME A VAMPIRE, WOULDN'T I COME TO KNOW...
...A DIFFERENT KIND OF DESPAIR?
DID YOU THINK THIS TRANSFORMATION WOULD BRING ME HAPPINESS?

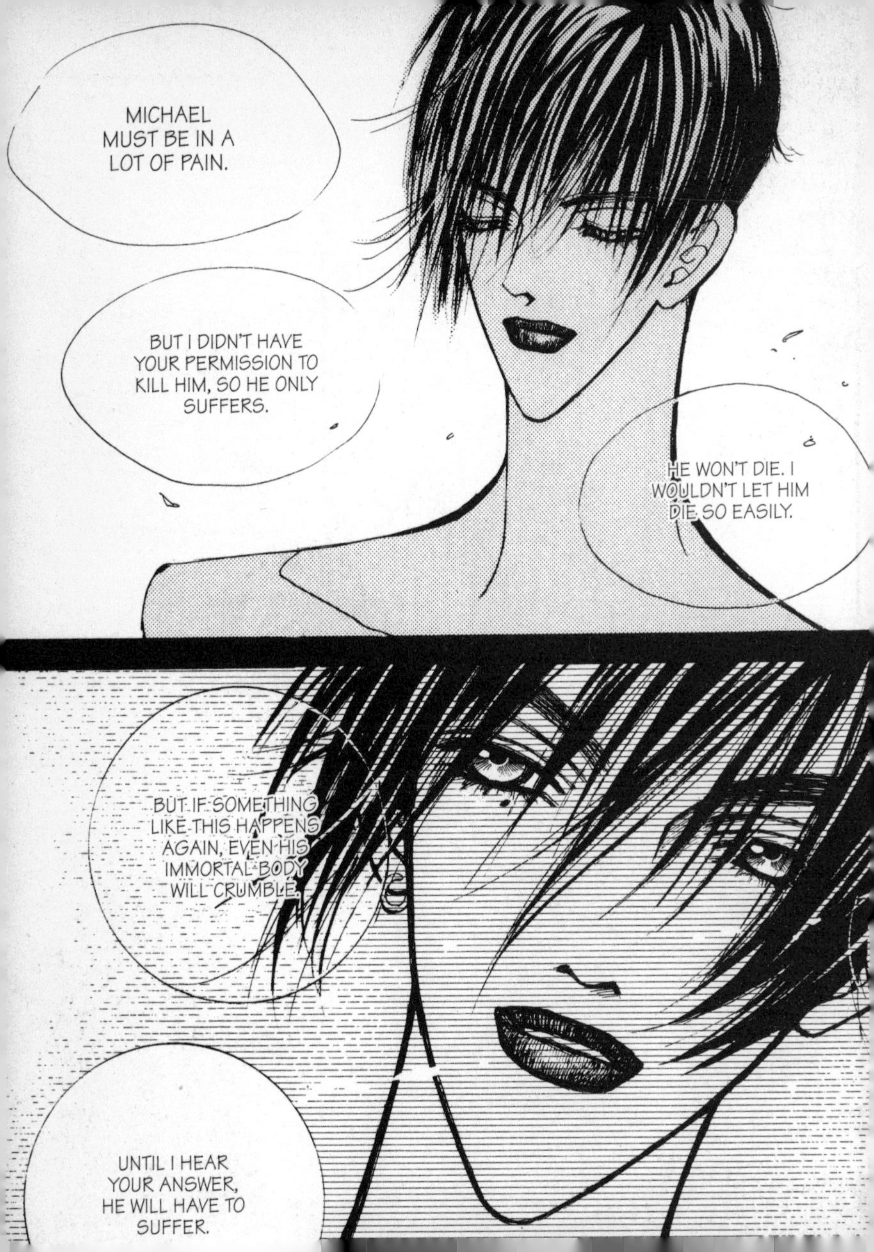
MICHAEL MUST BE IN A LOT OF PAIN.
BUT I DIDN'T HAVE YOUR PERMISSION TO KILL HIM, SO HE ONLY SUFFERS.
HE WON'T DIE. I WOULDN'T LET HIM DIE SO EASILY.
BUT IF SOMETHING LIKE THIS HAPPENS AGAIN, EVEN HIS IMMORTAL BODY WILL CRUMBLE.
UNTIL I HEAR YOUR ANSWER, HE WILL HAVE TO SUFFER.

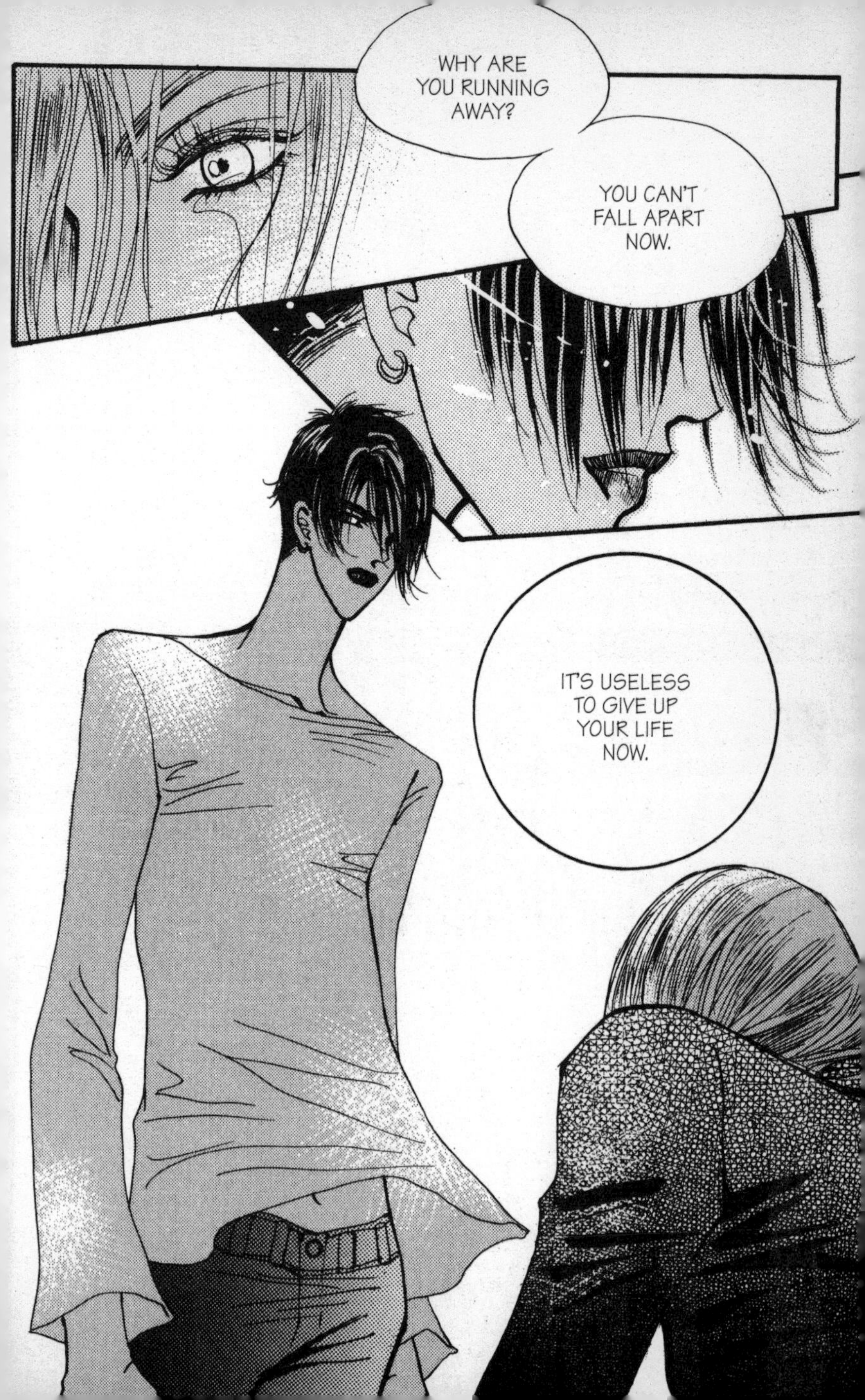
WHY ARE YOU RUNNING AWAY?
YOU CAN'T FALL APART NOW.
IT'S USELESS TO GIVE UP YOUR LIFE NOW.

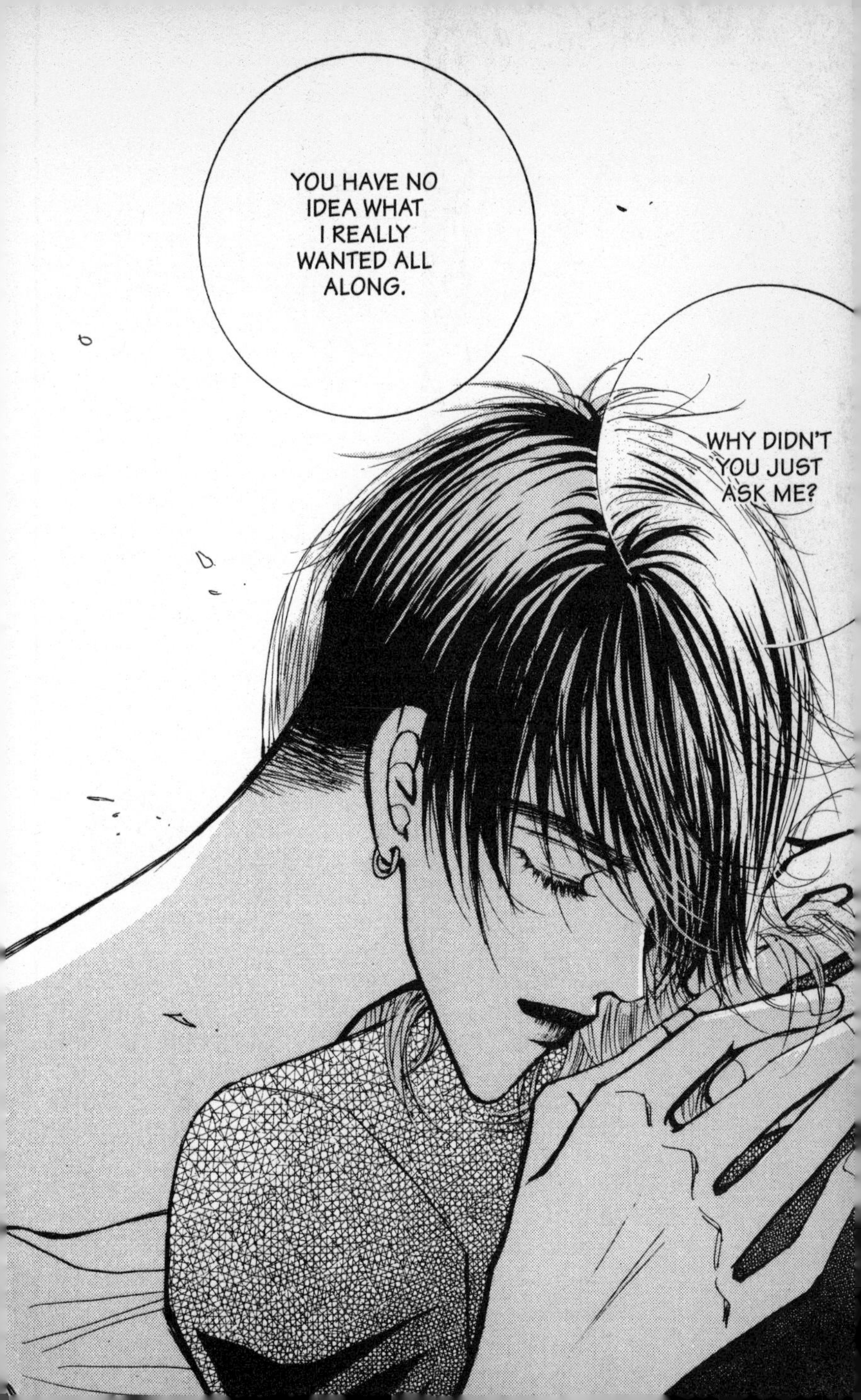
YOU HAVE NO IDEA WHAT I REALLY WANTED ALL ALONG.
WHY DIDN'T YOU JUST ASK ME?

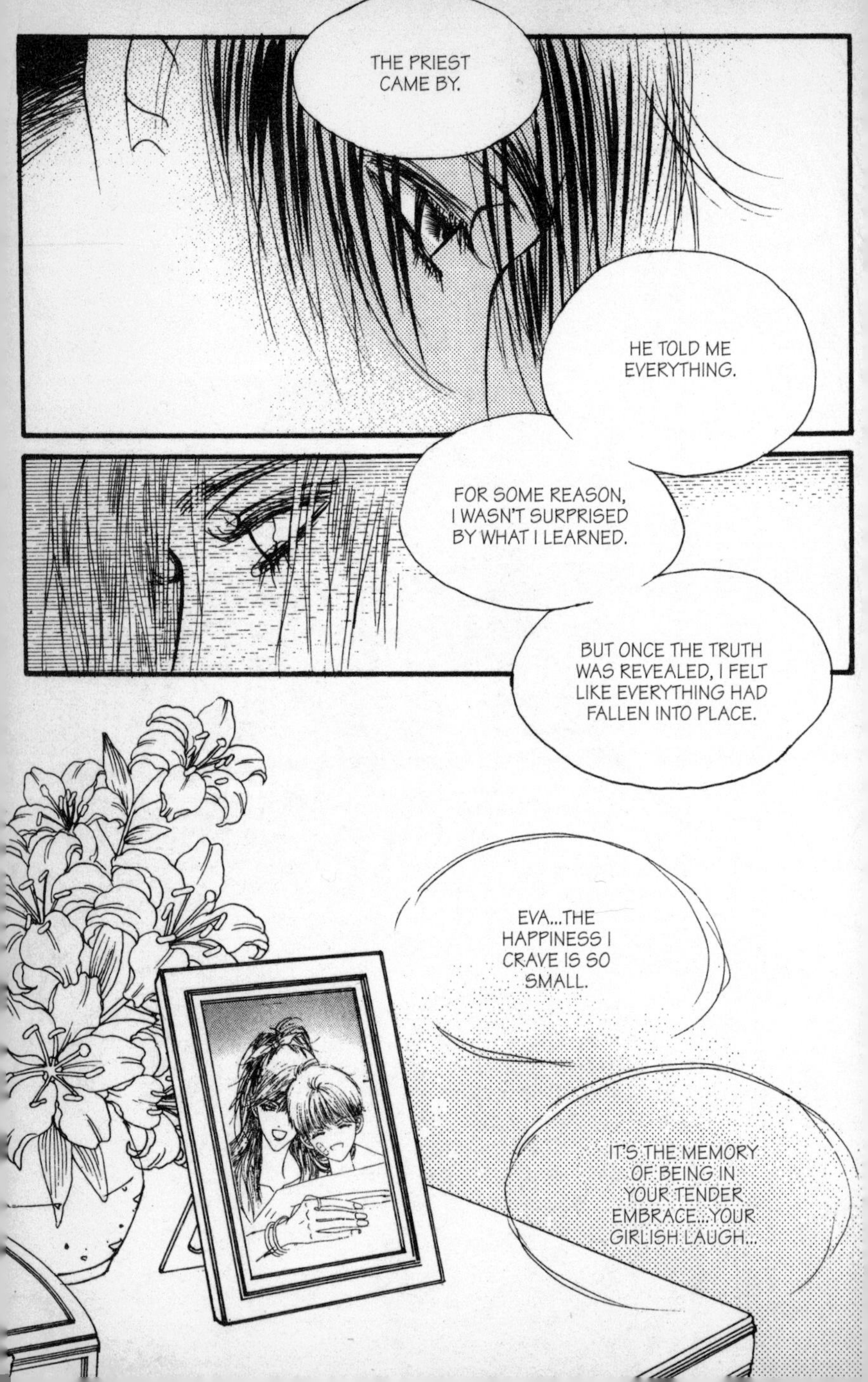
THE PRIEST CAME BY.
HE TOLD ME EVERYTHING.
FOR SOME REASON, I WASN'T SURPRISED BY WHAT I LEARNED.
BUT ONCE THE TRUTH WAS REVEALED, I FELT LIKE EVERYTHING HAD FALLEN INTO PLACE.
EVA...THE HAPPINESS I CRAVE IS SO SMALL.
IT'S THE MEMORY OF BEING IN YOUR TENDER EMBRACE...YOUR GIRLISH LAUGH...

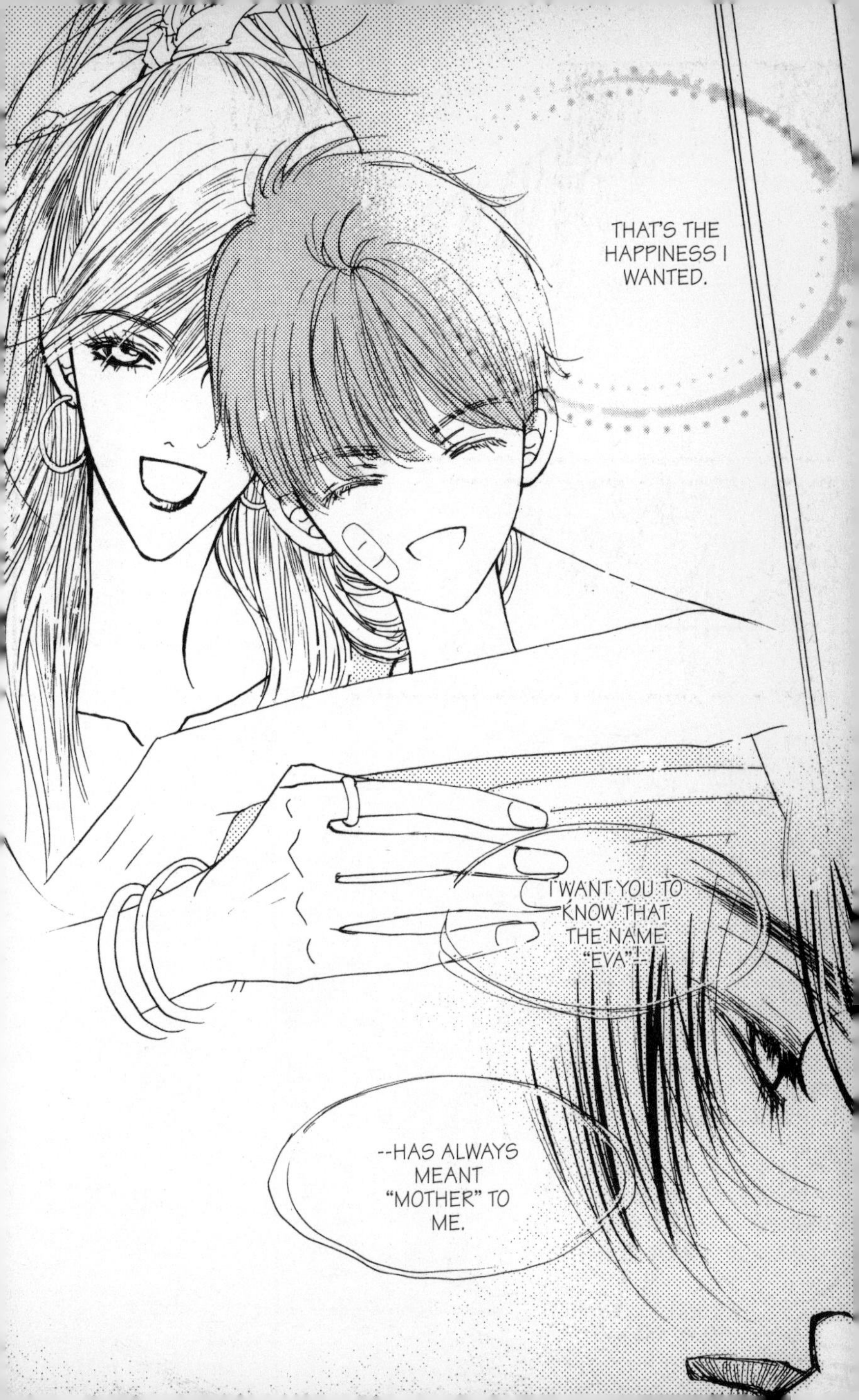
THAT'S THE HAPPINESS I WANTED.
I WANT YOU TO KNOW THAT THE NAME "EVA"--
--HAS ALWAYS MEANT "MOTHER" TO ME.

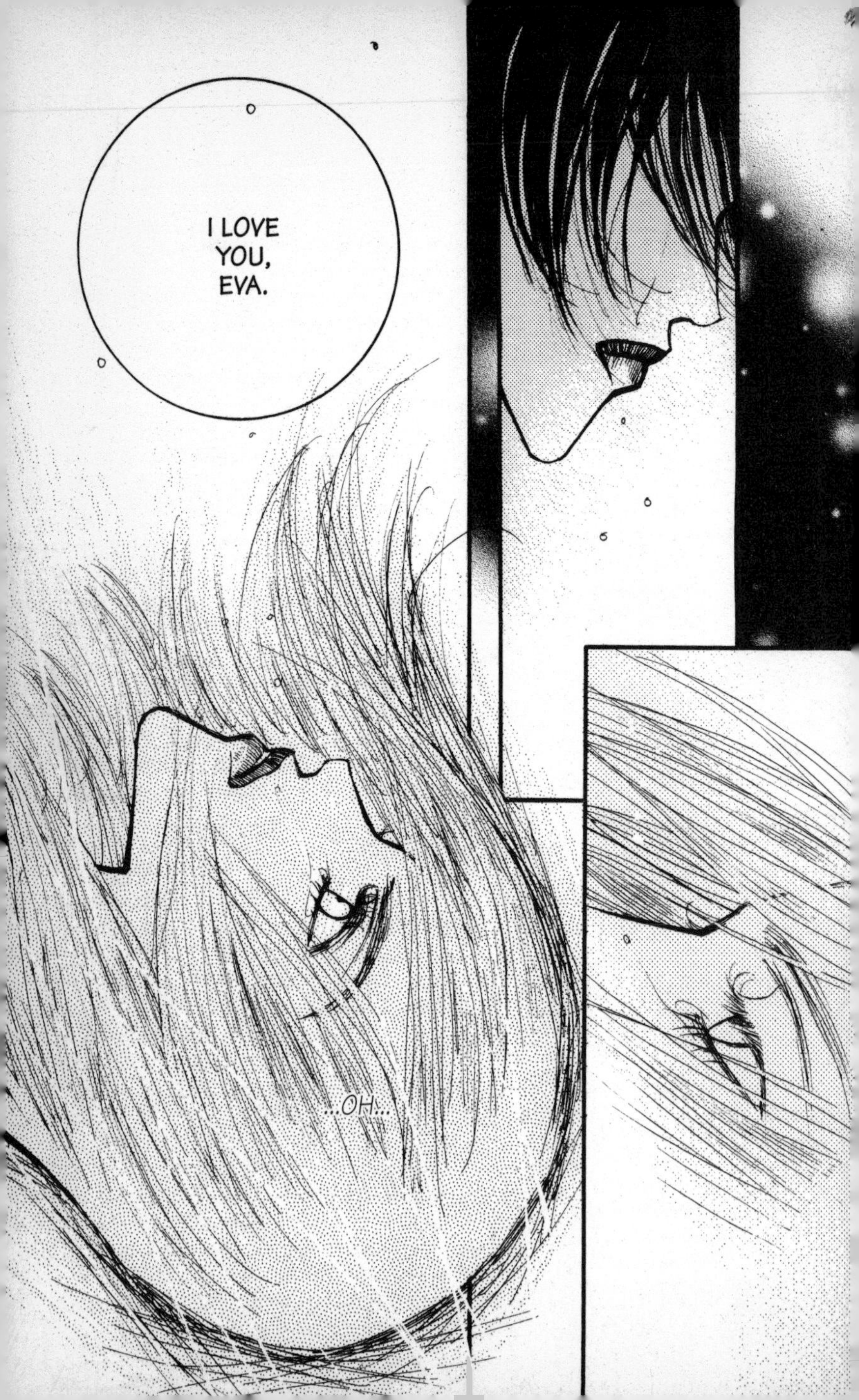
I LOVE YOU, EVA.
...OH...

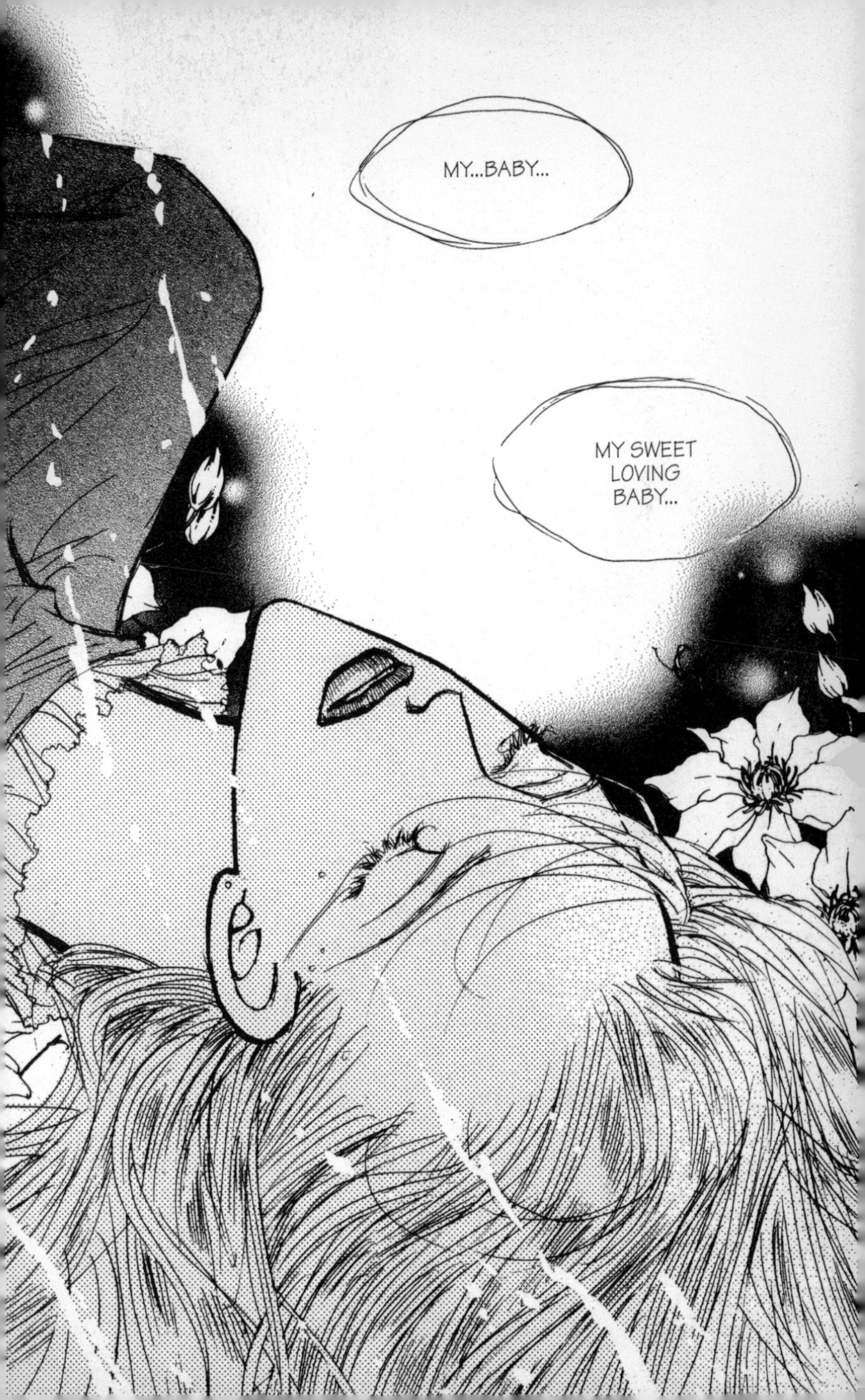
MY...BABY...
MY SWEET LOVING BABY...

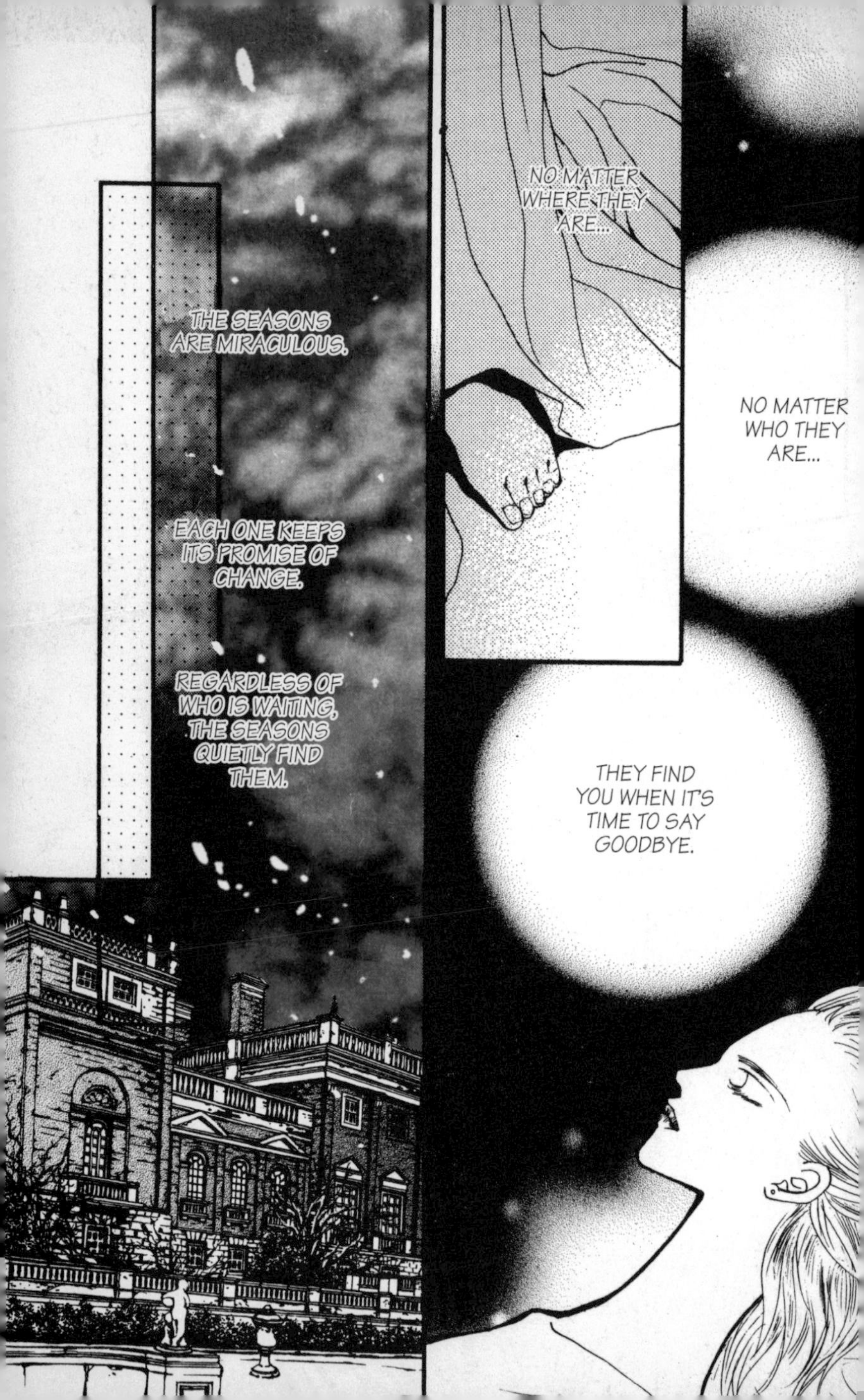
THE SEASONS ARE MIRACULOUS.
EACH ONE KEEPS ITS PROMISE OF CHANGE.
REGARDLESS OF WHO IS WAITING, THE SEASONS QUIETLY FIND THEM.
NO MATTER WHERE THEY ARE...
NO MATTER WHO THEY ARE...
THEY FIND YOU WHEN IT'S TIME TO SAY GOODBYE.

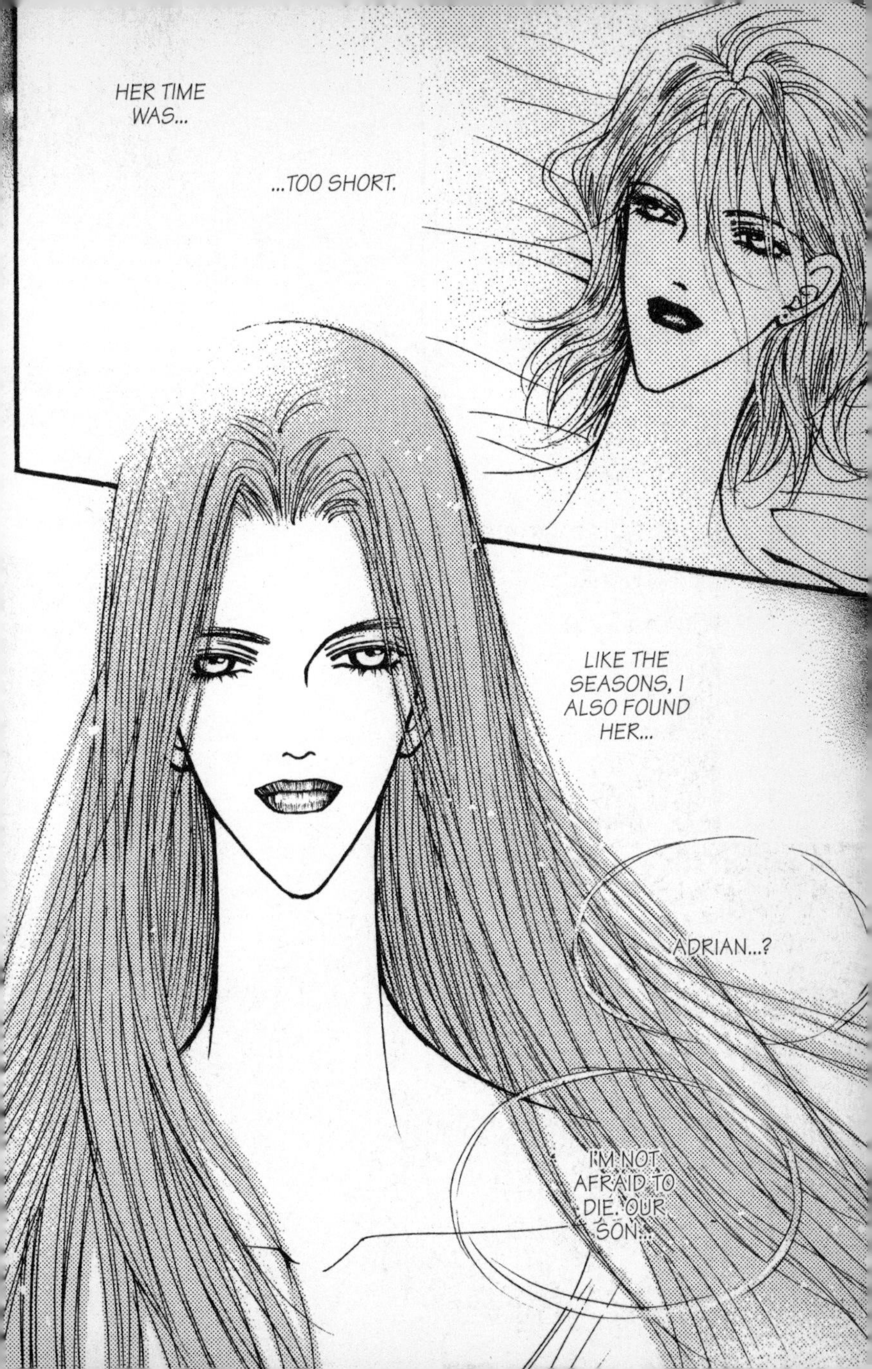
HER TIME WAS...
...TOO SHORT.
LIKE THE SEASONS, I ALSO FOUND HER...
ADRIAN...?
I'M NOT AFRAID TO DIE. OUR SON...

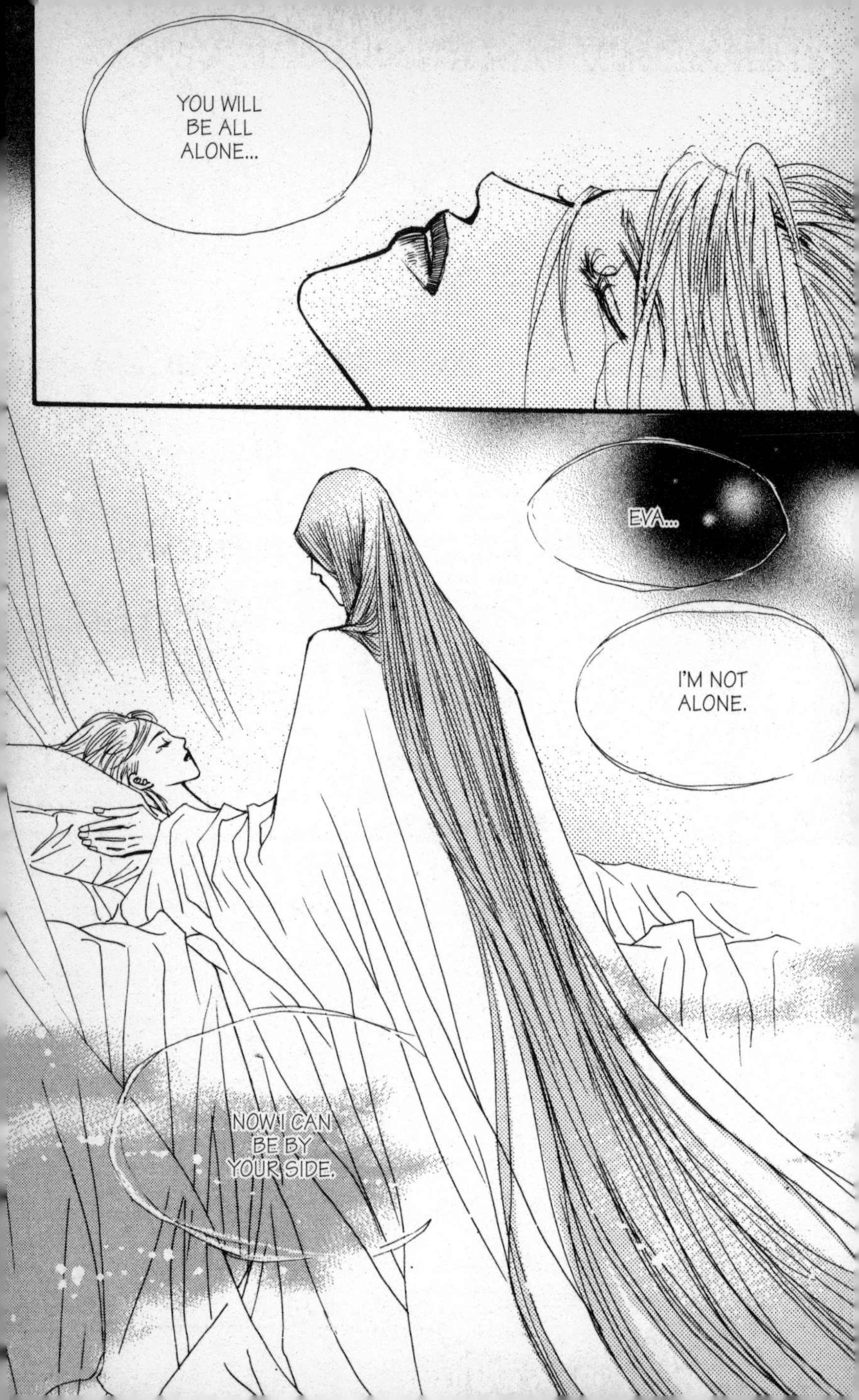
YOU WILL BE ALL ALONE...
EVA...
I'M NOT ALONE.
NOW I CAN BE BY YOUR SIDE.

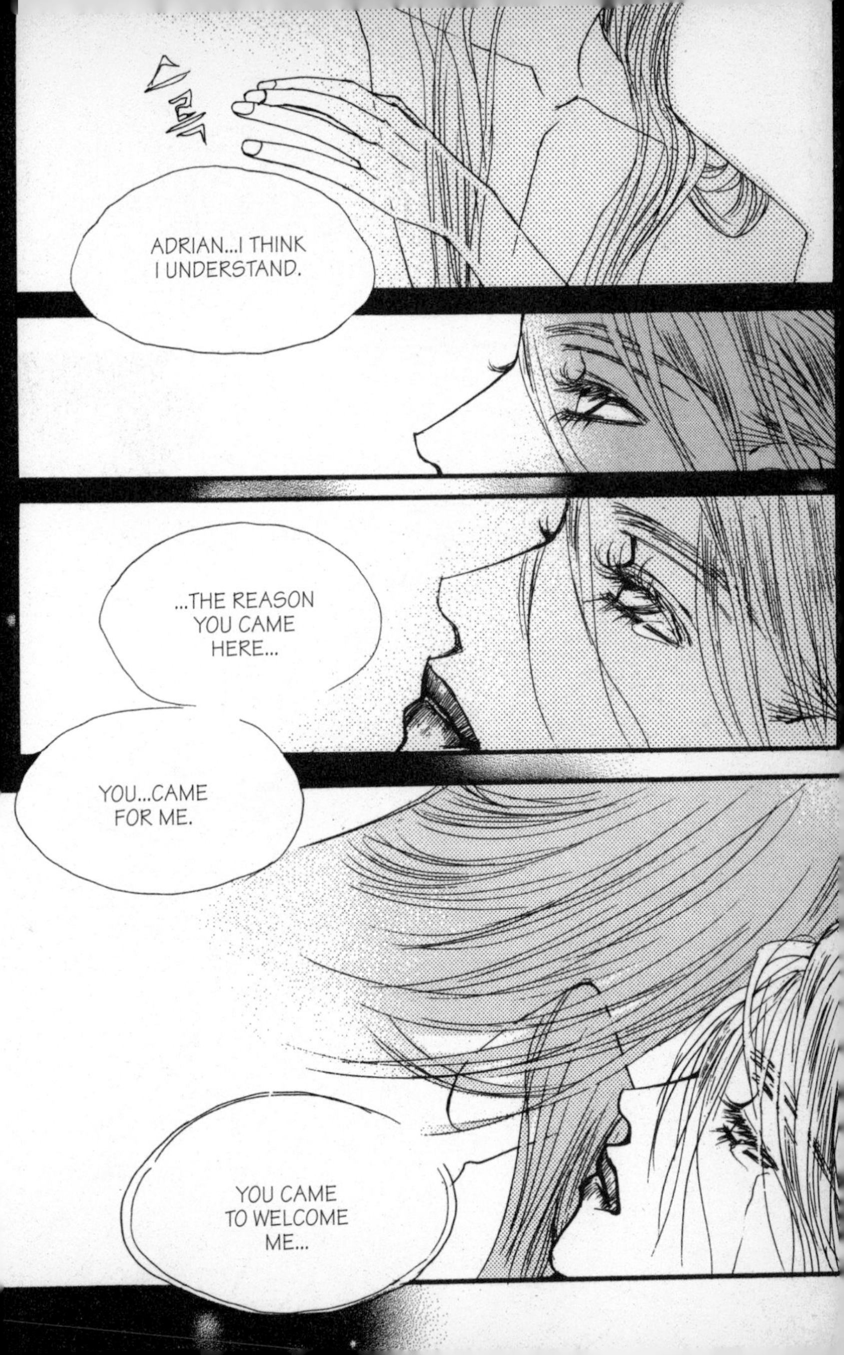
스르륵
ADRIAN...I THINK I UNDERSTAND.
...THE REASON YOU CAME HERE...
YOU...CAME FOR ME.
YOU CAME TO WELCOME ME...

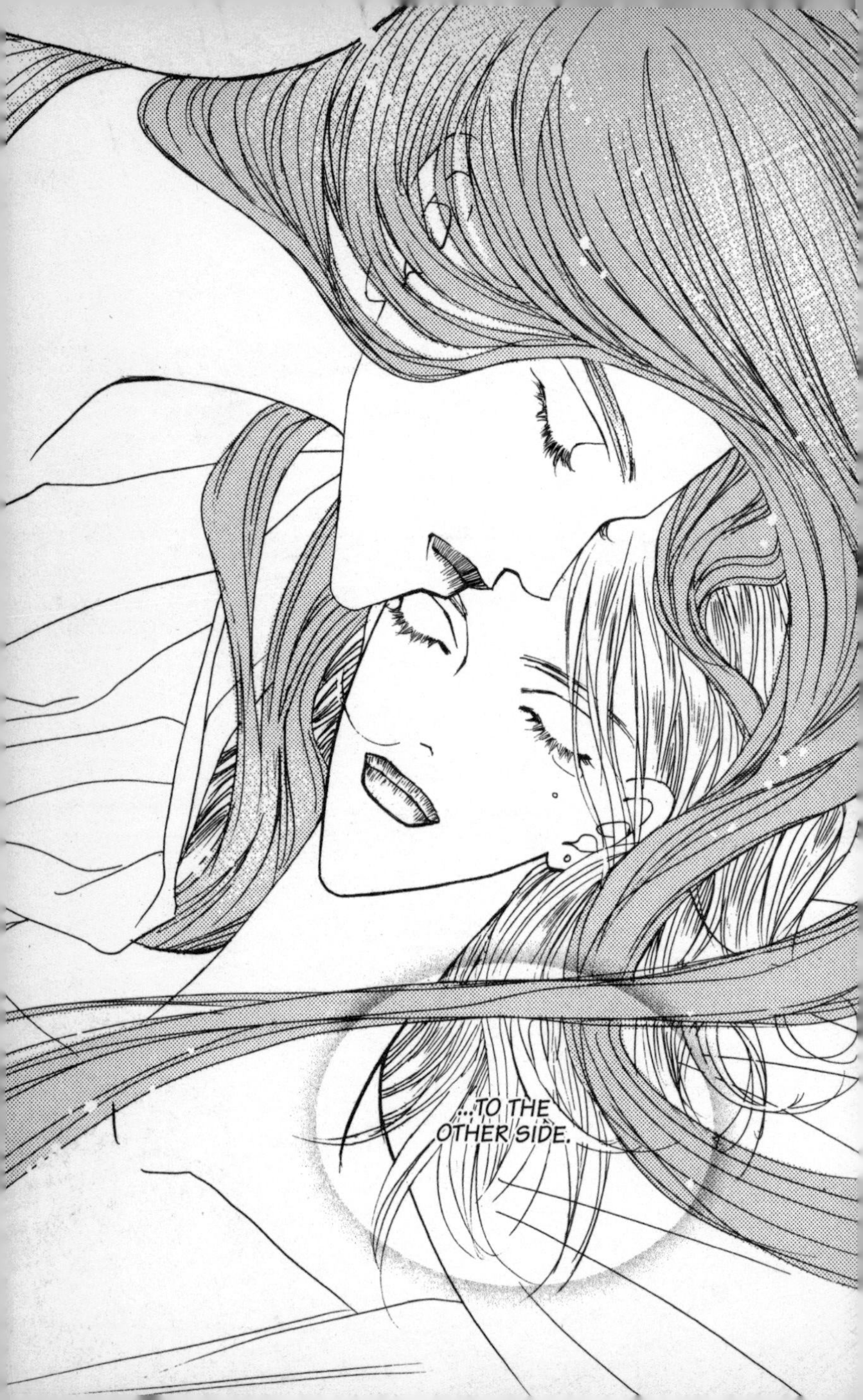
...TO THE OTHER SIDE.

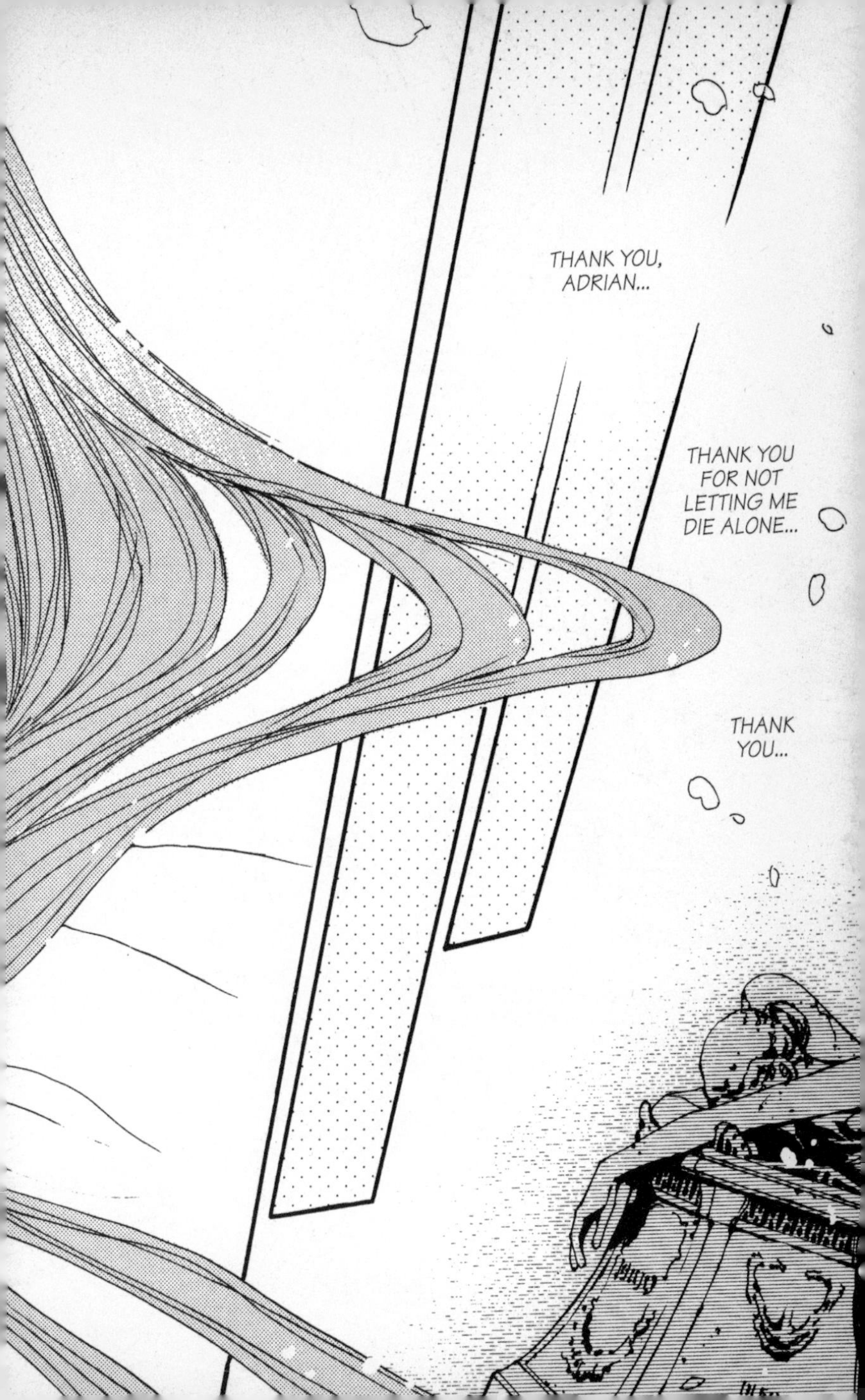
THANK YOU, ADRIAN...
THANK YOU FOR NOT LETTING ME DIE ALONE...
THANK YOU...

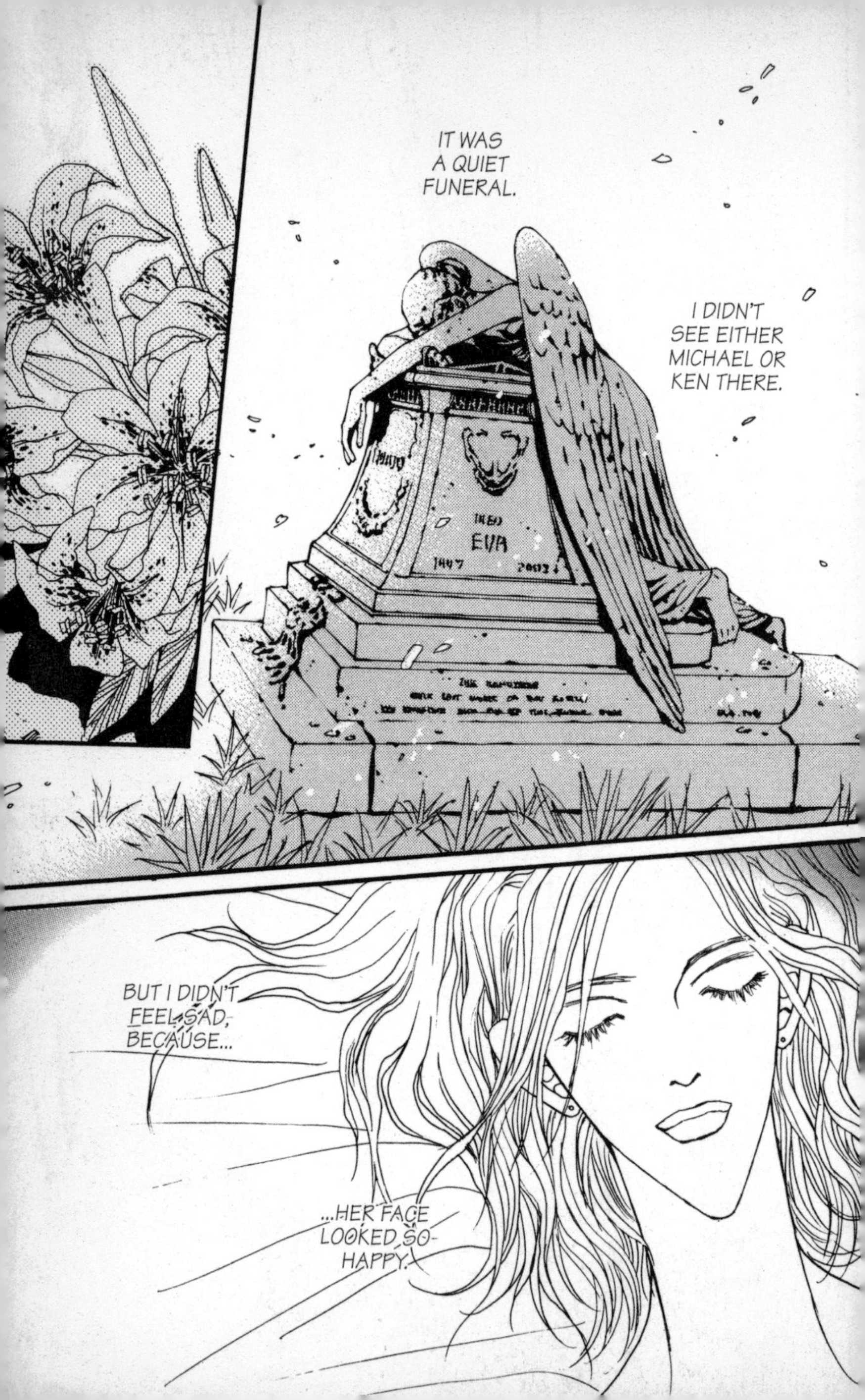
IT WAS A QUIET FUNERAL.
I DIDN'T SEE EITHER MICHAEL OR KEN THERE.
BUT I DIDN'T FEEL SAD, BECAUSE...
...HER FACE LOOKED SO HAPPY.

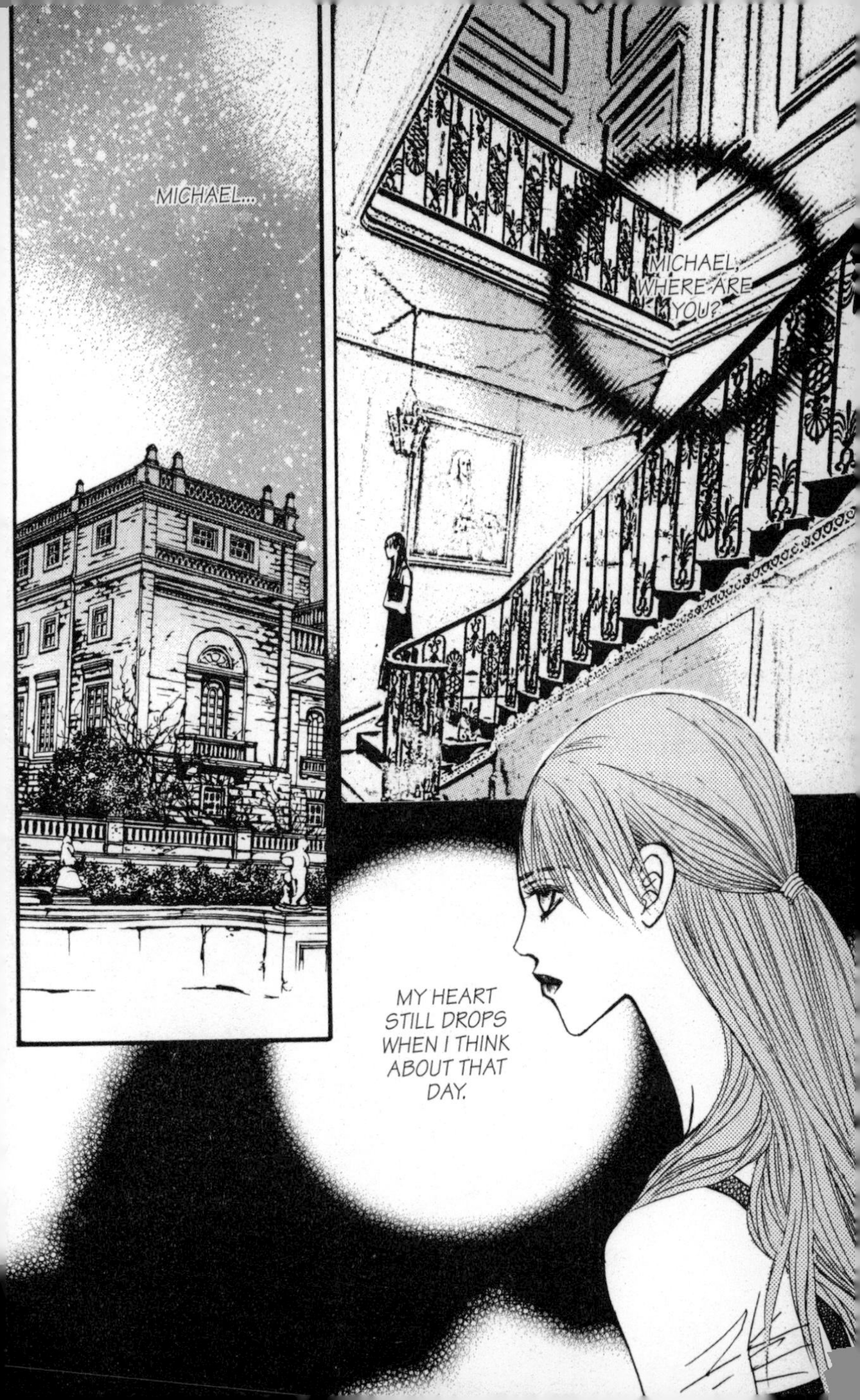
MICHAEL, WHERE ARE YOU?
MY HEART STILL DROPS WHEN I THINK ABOUT THAT DAY.
MICHAEL...

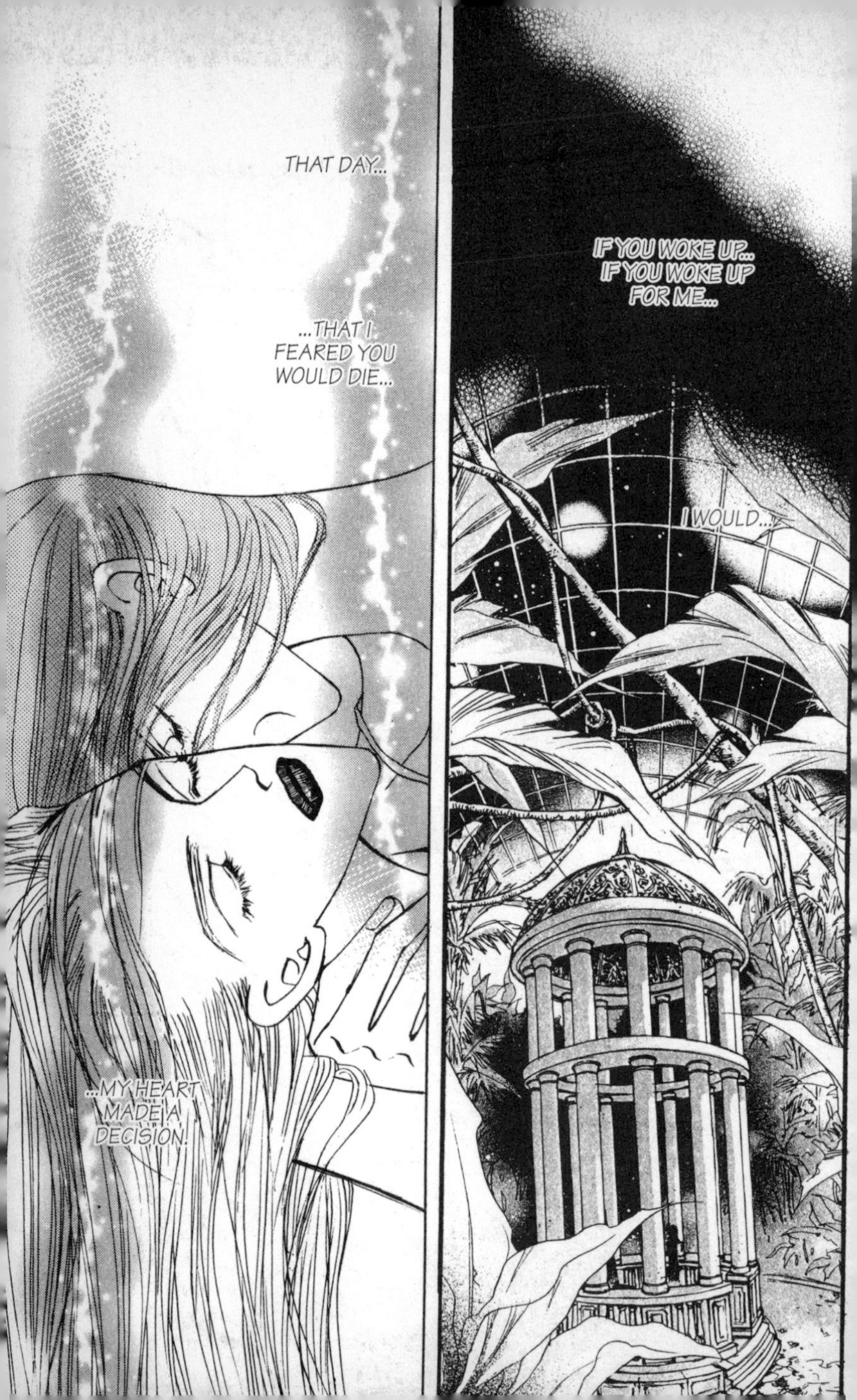
THAT DAY...
...THAT I FEARED YOU WOULD DIE...
...MY HEART MADE A DECISION.
IF YOU WOKE UP... IF YOU WOKE UP FOR ME...
I WOULD...

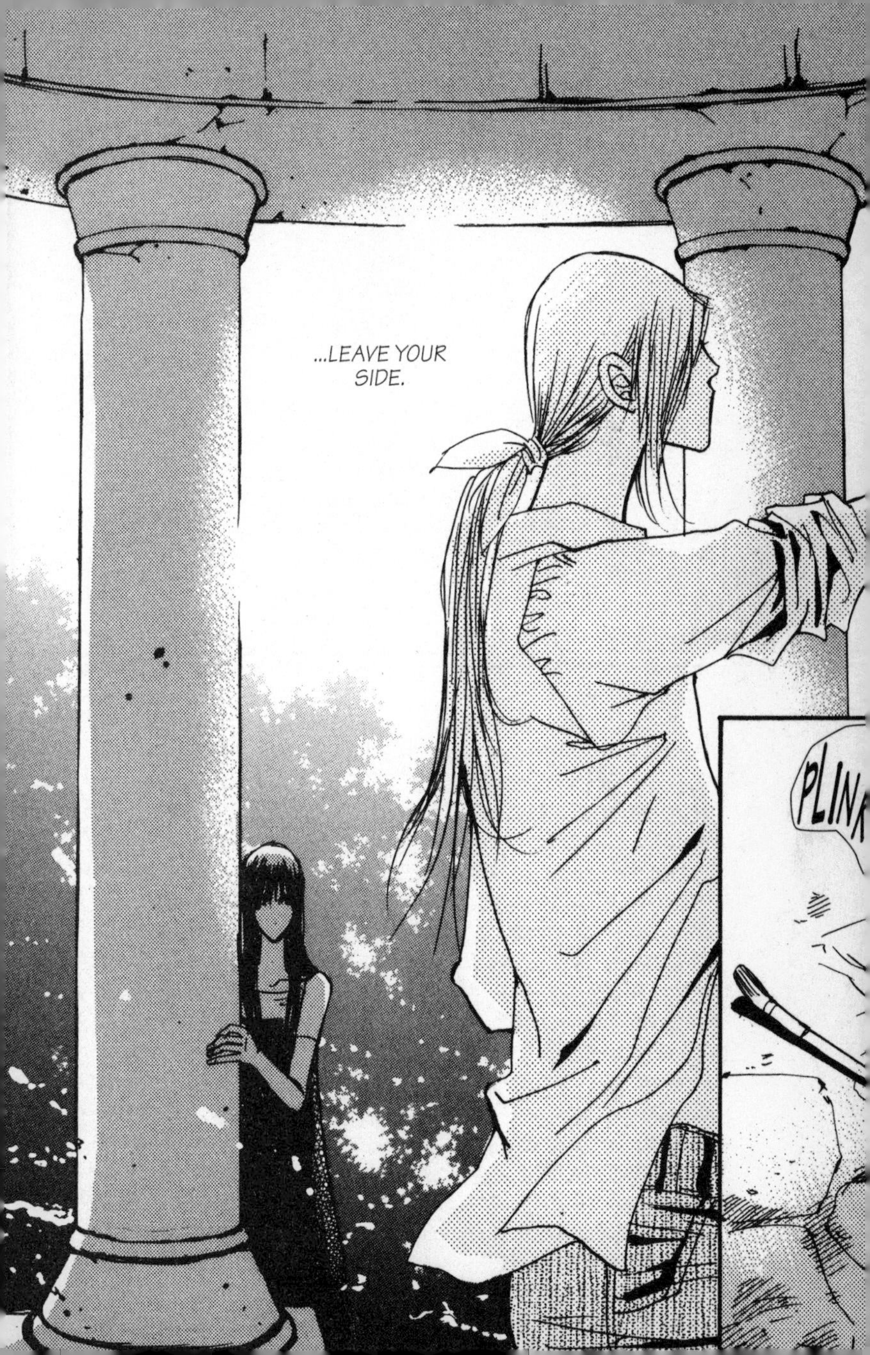
...LEAVE YOUR SIDE.
PLIN

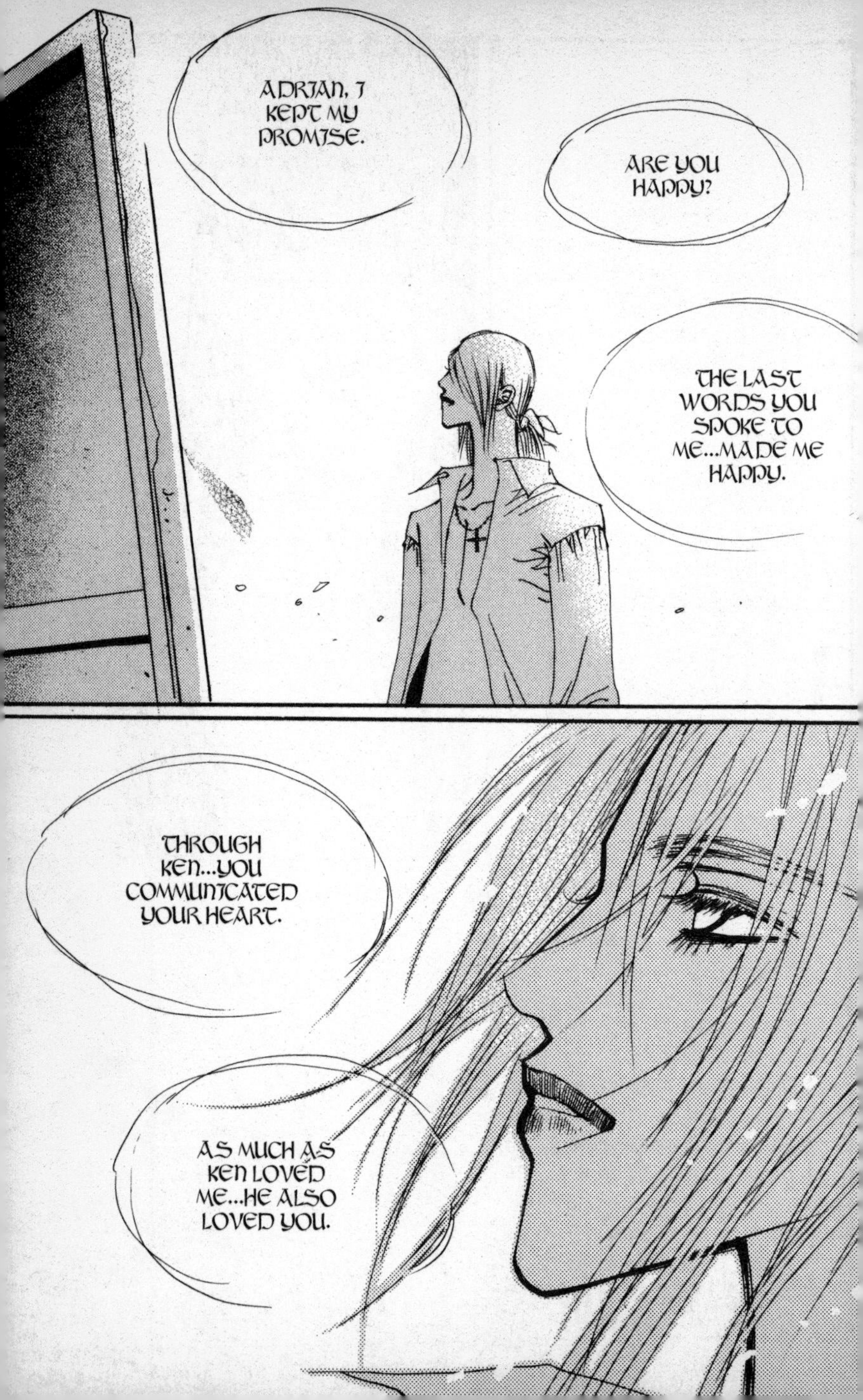
ADRIAN, I KEPT MY PROMISE.
ARE YOU HAPPY?
THE LAST WORDS YOU SPOKE TO ME...MADE ME HAPPY.
THROUGH KEN...YOU COMMUNICATED YOUR HEART.
AS MUCH AS KEN LOVED ME...HE ALSO LOVED YOU.

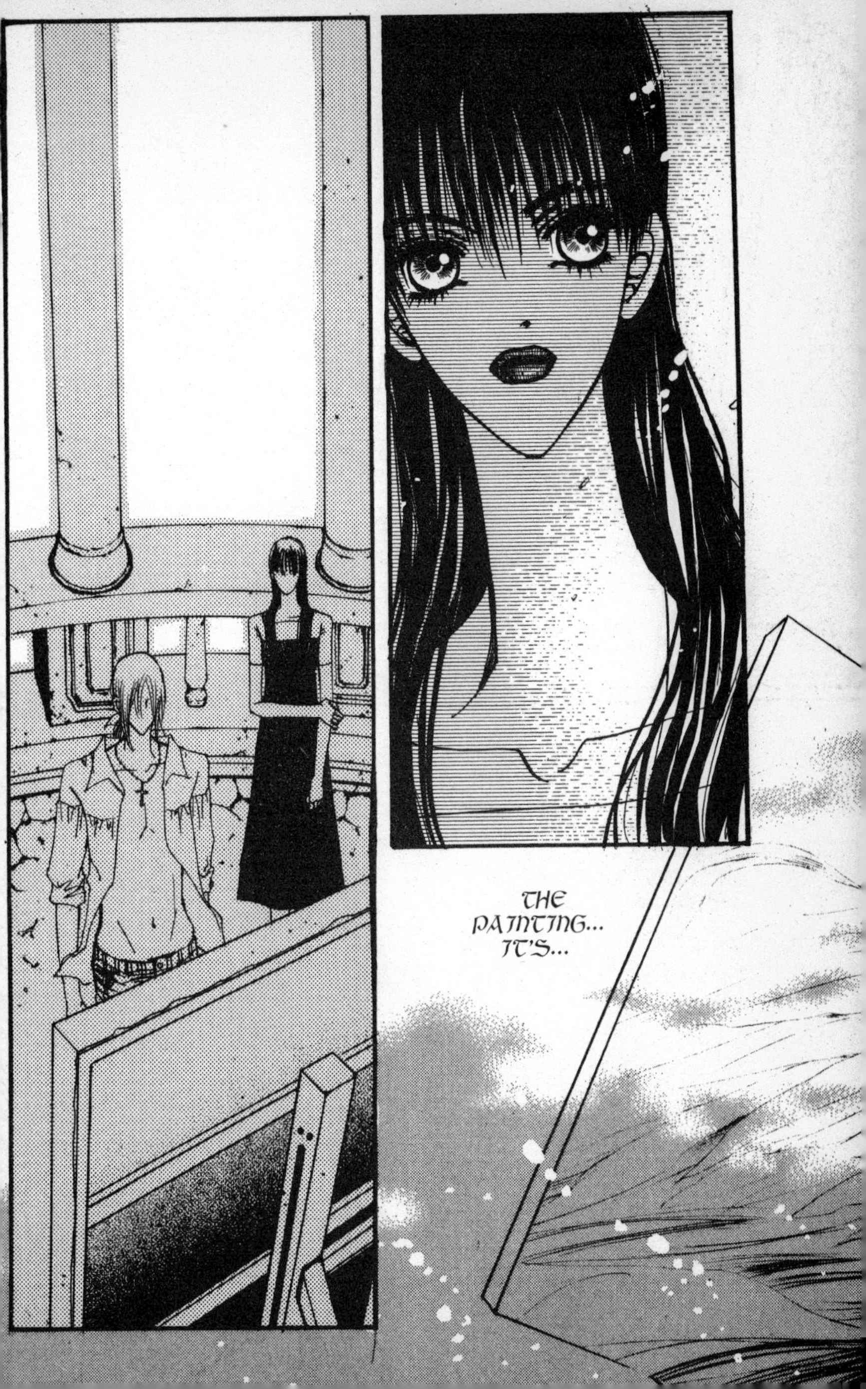
THE PAINTING... IT'S...

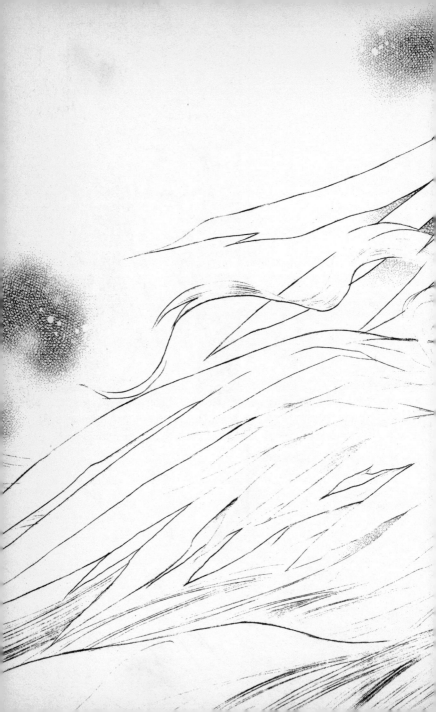

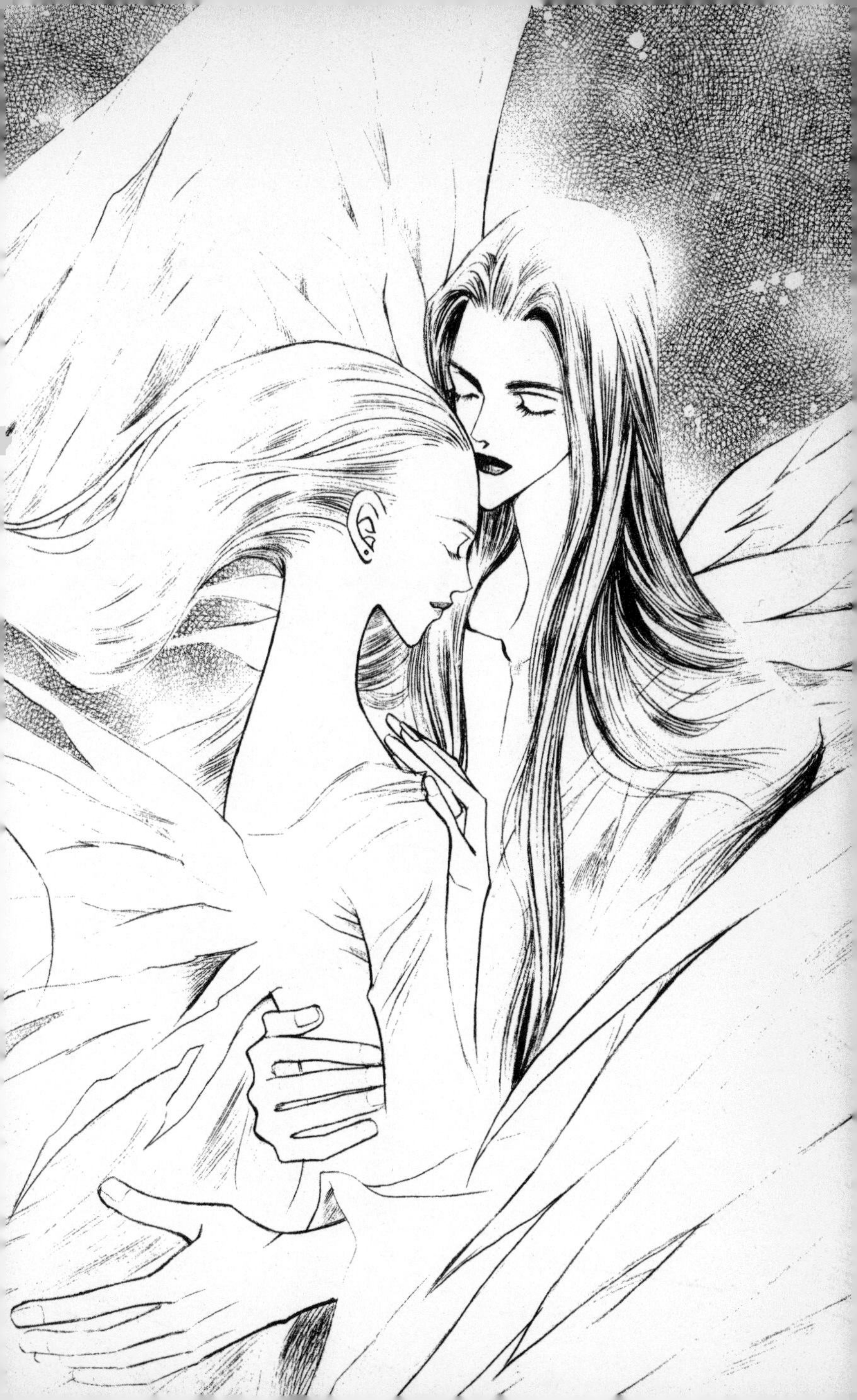

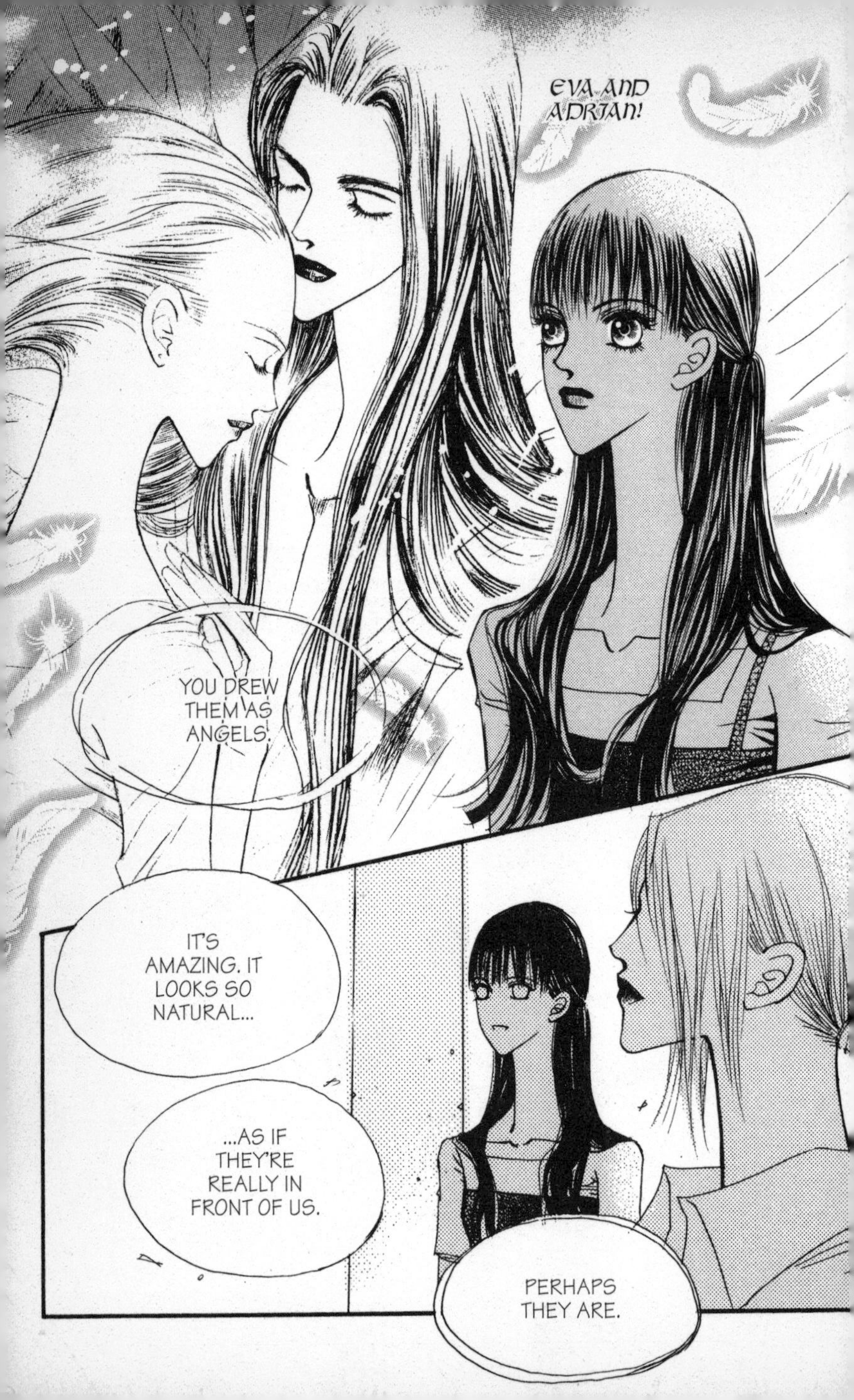
EVA AND ADRIAN!
YOU DREW THEM AS ANGELS.
IT'S AMAZING. IT LOOKS SO NATURAL...
...AS IF THEY'RE REALLY IN FRONT OF US.
PERHAPS THEY ARE.

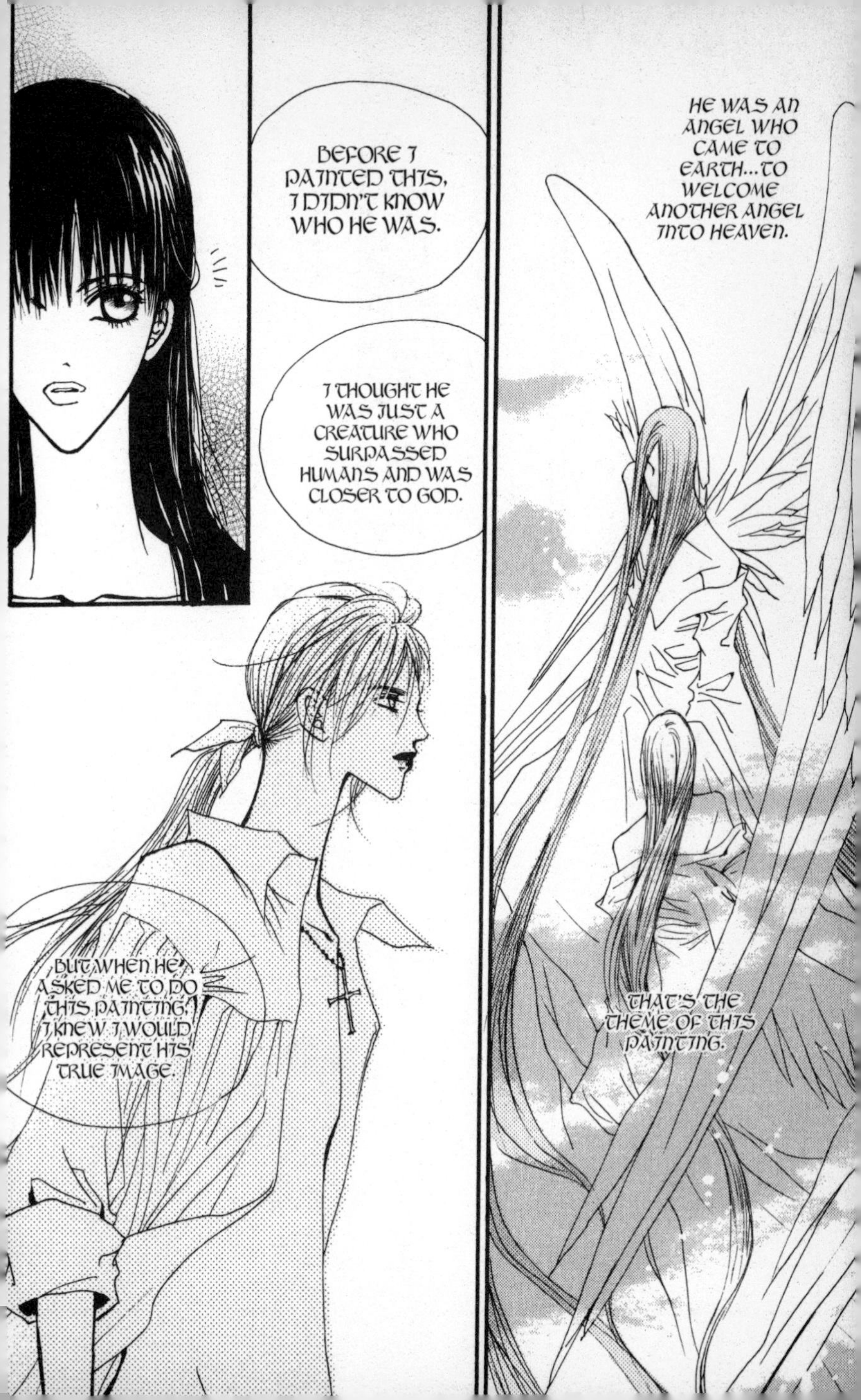
BEFORE I PAINTED THIS, I DIDN'T KNOW WHO HE WAS.
I THOUGHT HE WAS JUST A CREATURE WHO SURPASSED HUMANS AND WAS CLOSER TO GOD.
BUT WHEN HE ASKED ME TO DO THIS PAINTING, I KNEW I WOULD REPRESENT HIS TRUE IMAGE.
HE WAS AN ANGEL WHO CAME TO EARTH...TO WELCOME ANOTHER ANGEL INTO HEAVEN.
THAT'S THE THEME OF THIS PAINTING.

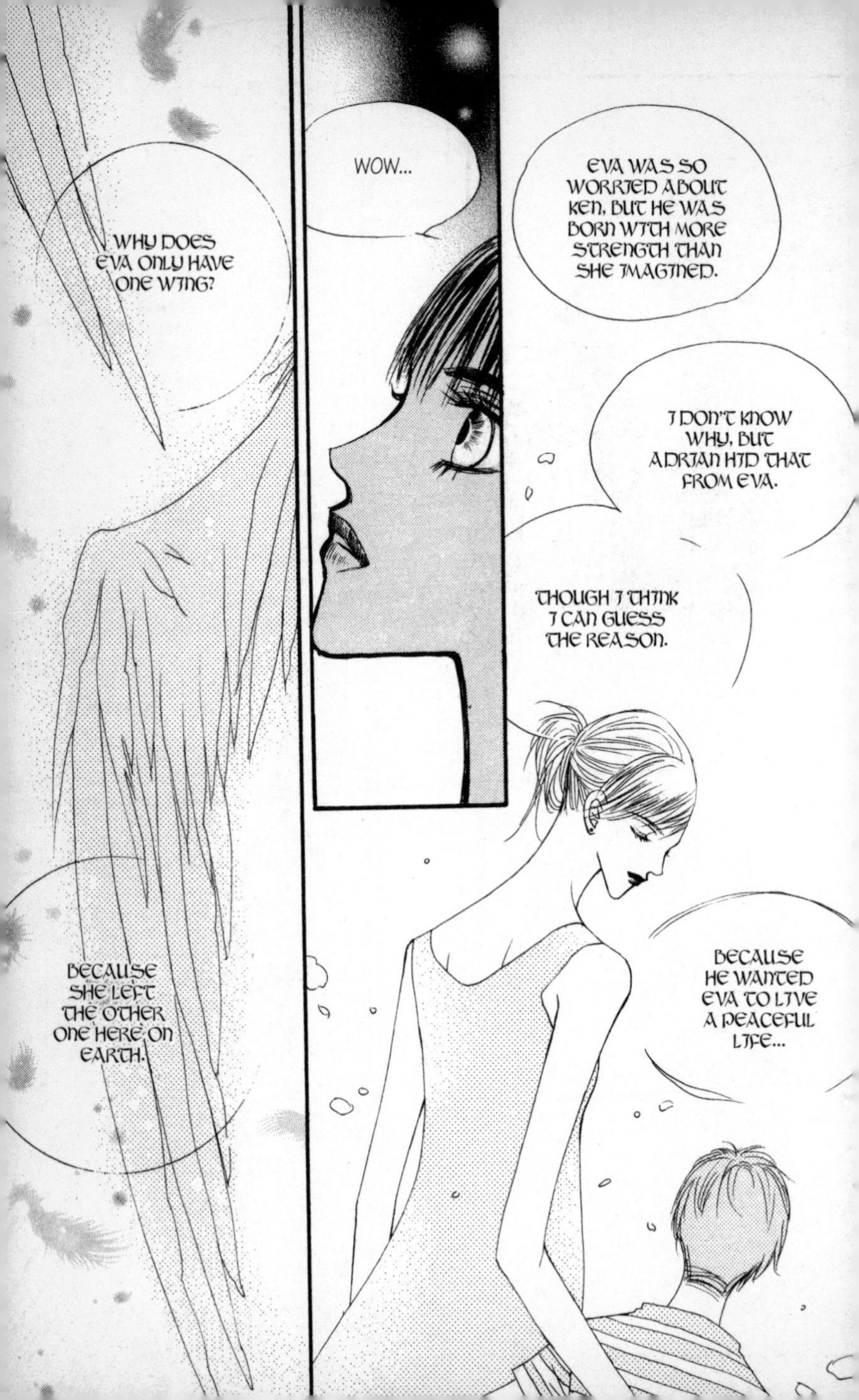
WHY DOES EVA ONLY HAVE ONE WING?
BECAUSE SHE LEFT THE OTHER ONE HERE ON EARTH.
WOW...
EVA WAS SO WORRIED ABOUT KEN, BUT HE WAS BORN WITH MORE STRENGTH THAN SHE IMAGINED.
I DON'T KNOW WHY, BUT ADRIAN HID THAT FROM EVA.
THOUGH I THINK I CAN GUESS THE REASON.
BECAUSE HE WANTED EVA TO LIVE A PEACEFUL LIFE...

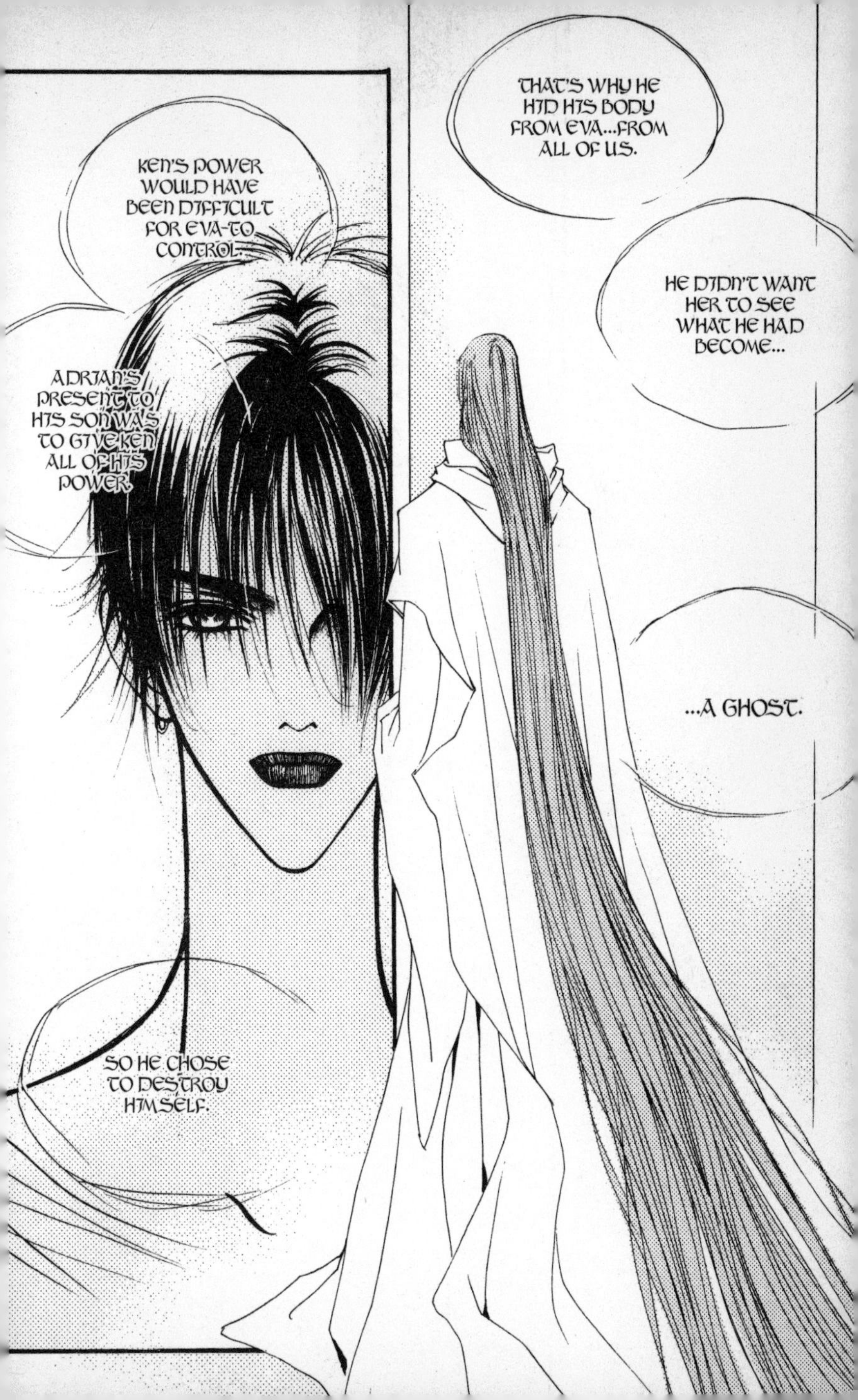
KEN'S POWER WOULD HAVE BEEN DIFFICULT FOR EVA TO CONTROL.
ADRIAN'S PRESENT TO HIS SON WAS TO GIVE KEN ALL OF HIS POWER.
SO HE CHOSE TO DESTROY HIMSELF.
THAT'S WHY HE HID HIS BODY FROM EVA...FROM ALL OF US.
HE DIDN'T WANT HER TO SEE WHAT HE HAD BECOME...
...A GHOST.

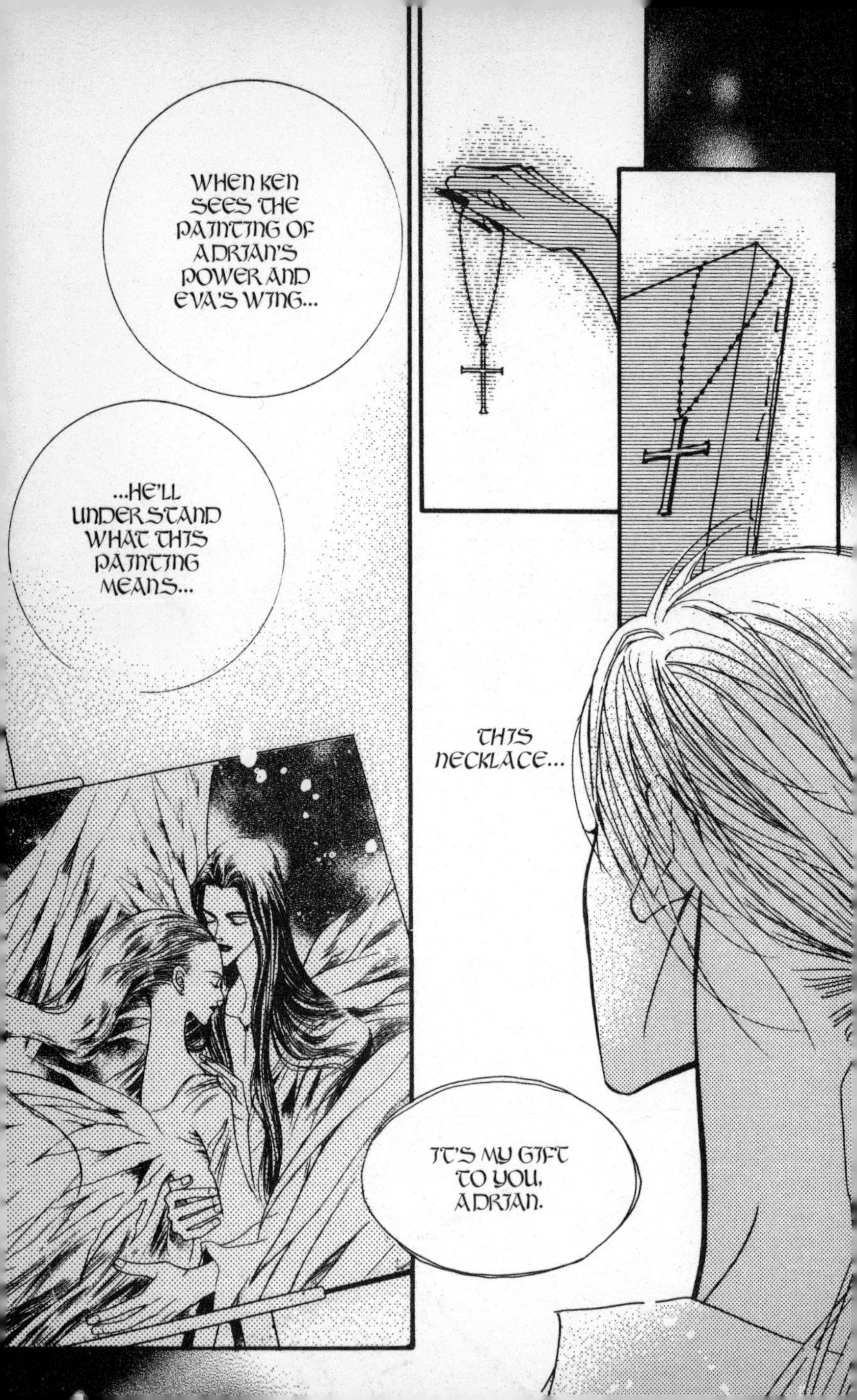
THIS NECKLACE...
IT'S MY GIFT TO YOU, ADRIAN.
WHEN KEN SEES THE PAINTING OF ADRIAN'S POWER AND EVA'S WING...
...HE'LL UNDERSTAND WHAT THIS PAINTING MEANS...

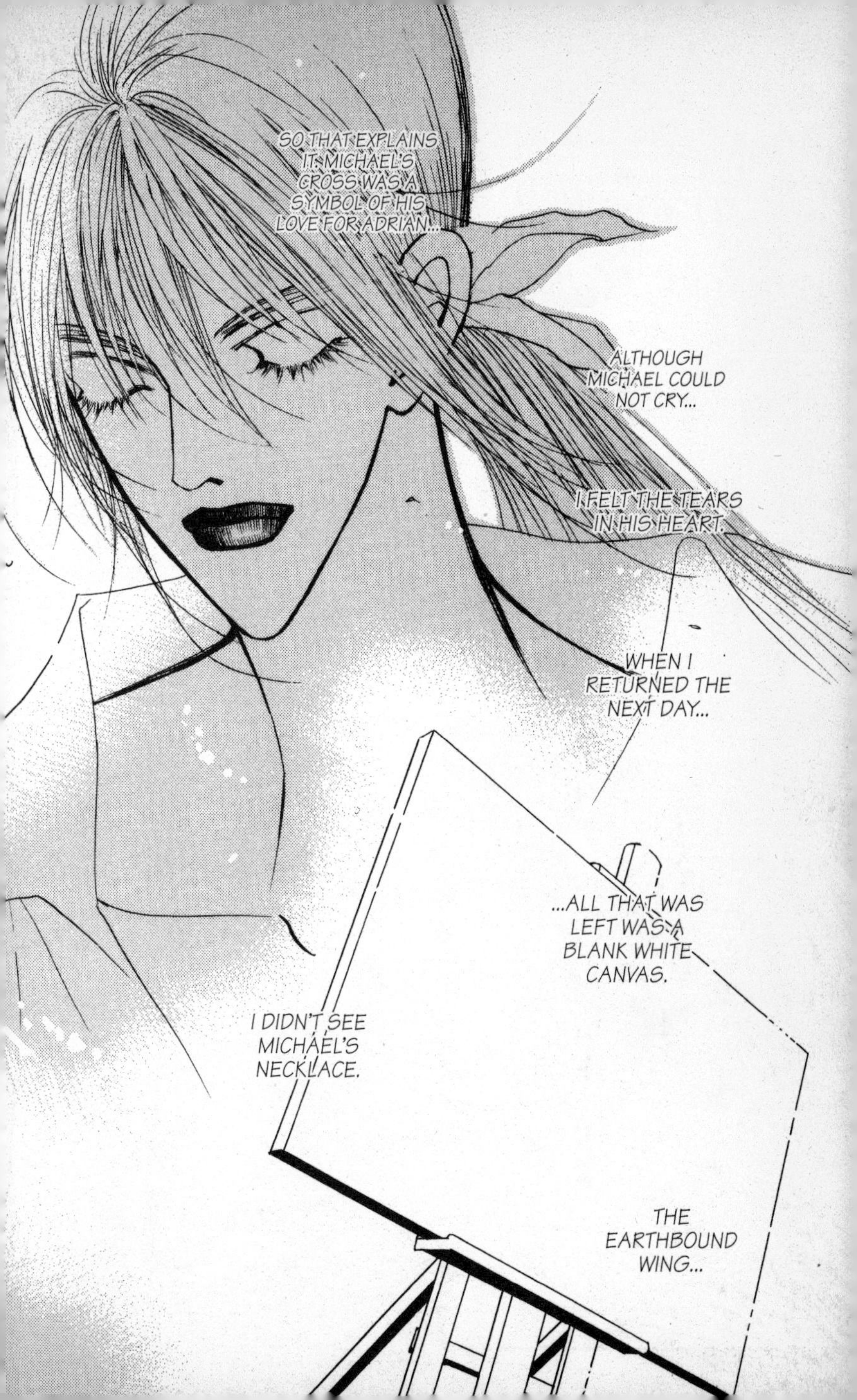
SO THAT EXPLAINS IT. MICHAEL'S CROSS WAS A SYMBOL OF HIS LOVE FOR ADRIAN...
ALTHOUGH MICHAEL COULD NOT CRY...
I FELT THE TEARS IN HIS HEART.
WHEN I RETURNED THE NEXT DAY...
...ALL THAT WAS LEFT WAS A BLANK WHITE CANVAS.
I DIDN'T SEE MICHAEL'S NECKLACE.
THE EARTHBOUND WING...

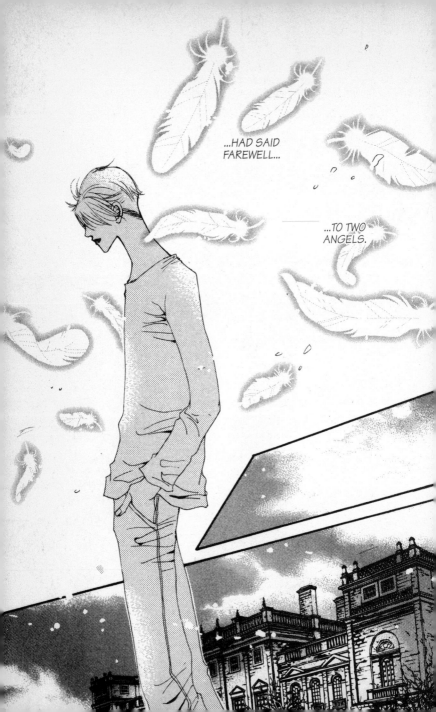

...HAD SAID FAREWELL...

...TO TWO ANGELS.

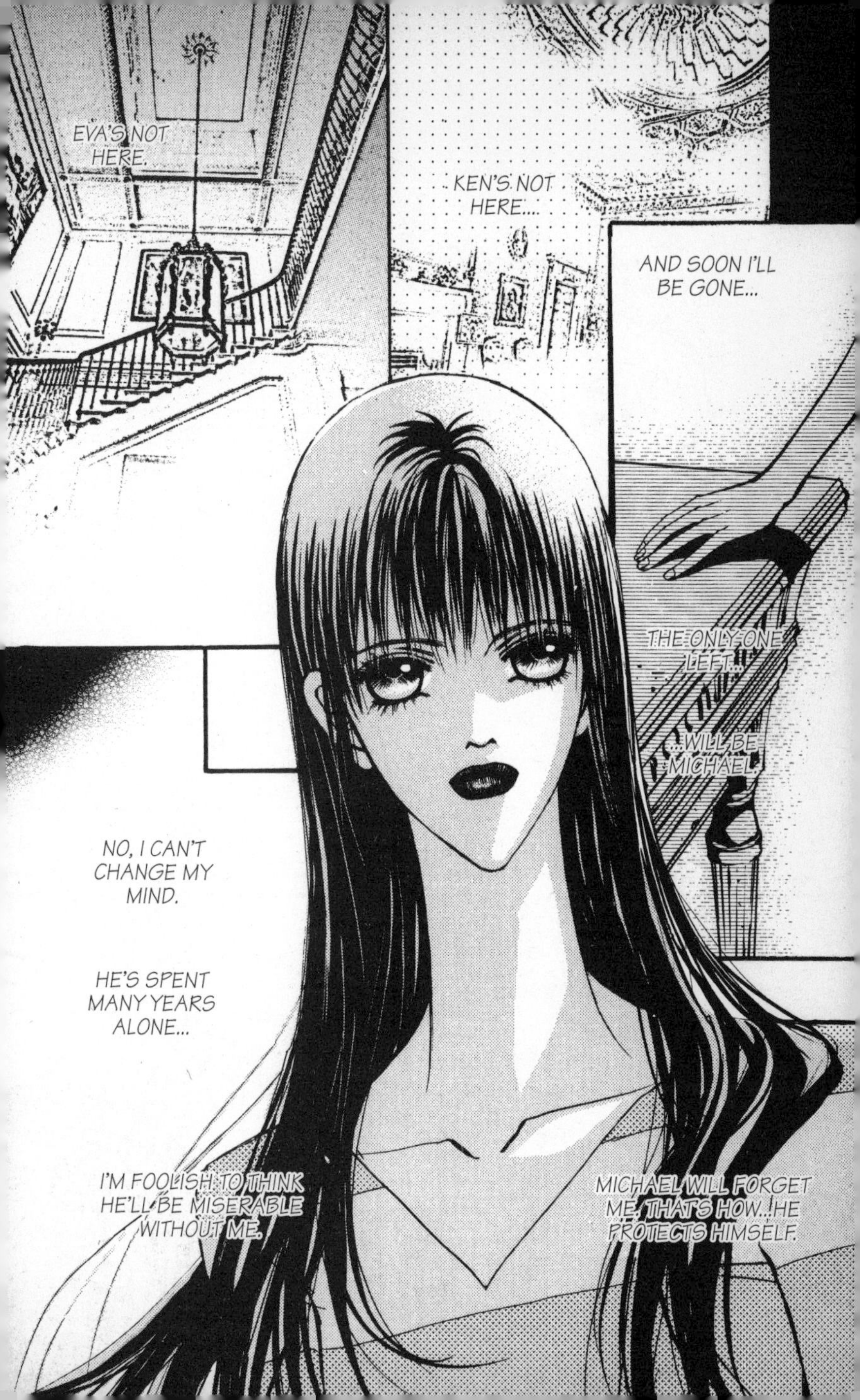
EVA'S NOT HERE.
KEN'S NOT HERE...
AND SOON I'LL BE GONE...
THE ONLY ONE LEFT...
...WILL BE MICHAEL.
NO, I CAN'T CHANGE MY MIND.
HE'S SPENT MANY YEARS ALONE...
I'M FOOLISH TO THINK HE'LL BE MISERABLE WITHOUT ME.
MICHAEL WILL FORGET ME. THAT'S HOW...HE PROTECTS HIMSELF.

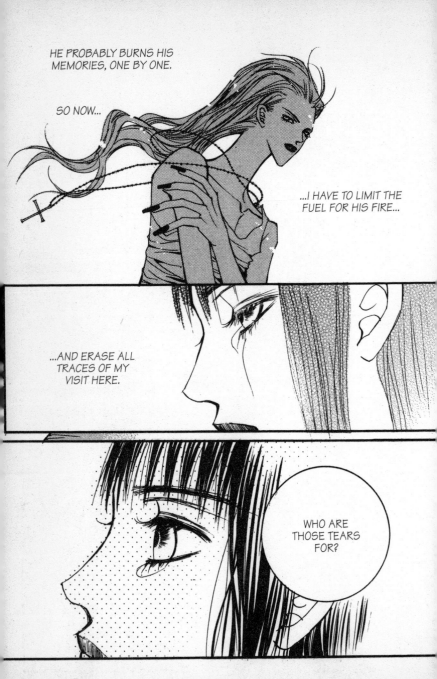

HE PROBABLY BURNS HIS
MEMORIES, ONE BY ONE.

SO NOW...

...I HAVE TO LIMIT THE
FUEL FOR HIS FIRE...

...AND ERASE ALL
TRACES OF MY
VISIT HERE.

WHO ARE
THOSE TEARS
FOR?

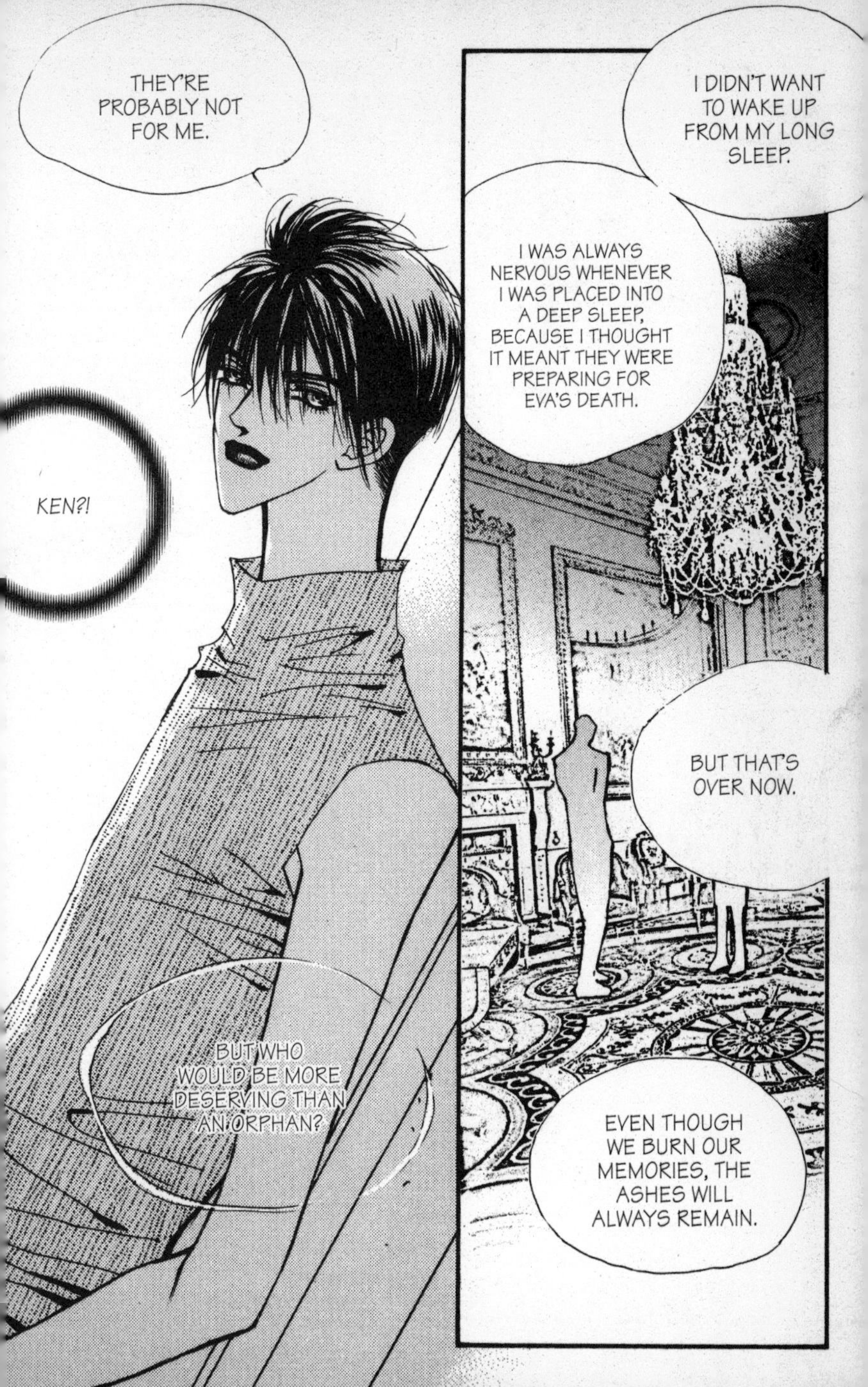
I DIDN'T WANT TO WAKE UP FROM MY LONG SLEEP.
I WAS ALWAYS NERVOUS WHENEVER I WAS PLACED INTO A DEEP SLEEP, BECAUSE I THOUGHT IT MEANT THEY WERE PREPARING FOR EVA'S DEATH.
BUT THAT'S OVER NOW.
EVEN THOUGH WE BURN OUR MEMORIES, THE ASHES WILL ALWAYS REMAIN.
THEY'RE PROBABLY NOT FOR ME.
KEN?!
BUT WHO WOULD BE MORE DESERVING THAN AN ORPHAN?

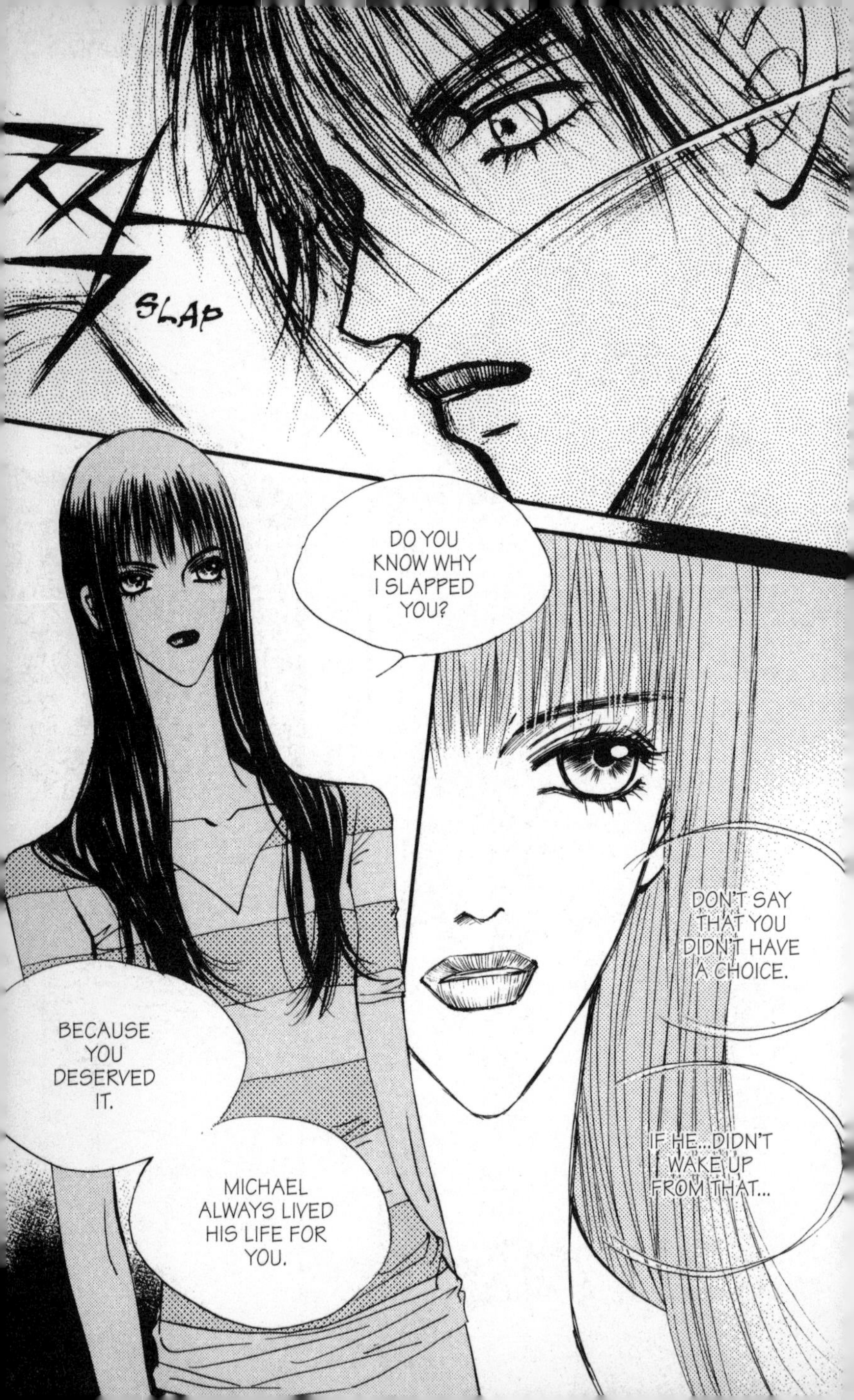
SLAP
DO YOU KNOW WHY I SLAPPED YOU?
BECAUSE YOU DESERVED IT.
MICHAEL ALWAYS LIVED HIS LIFE FOR YOU.
DON'T SAY THAT YOU DIDN'T HAVE A CHOICE.
IF HE...DIDN'T WAKE UP FROM THAT...

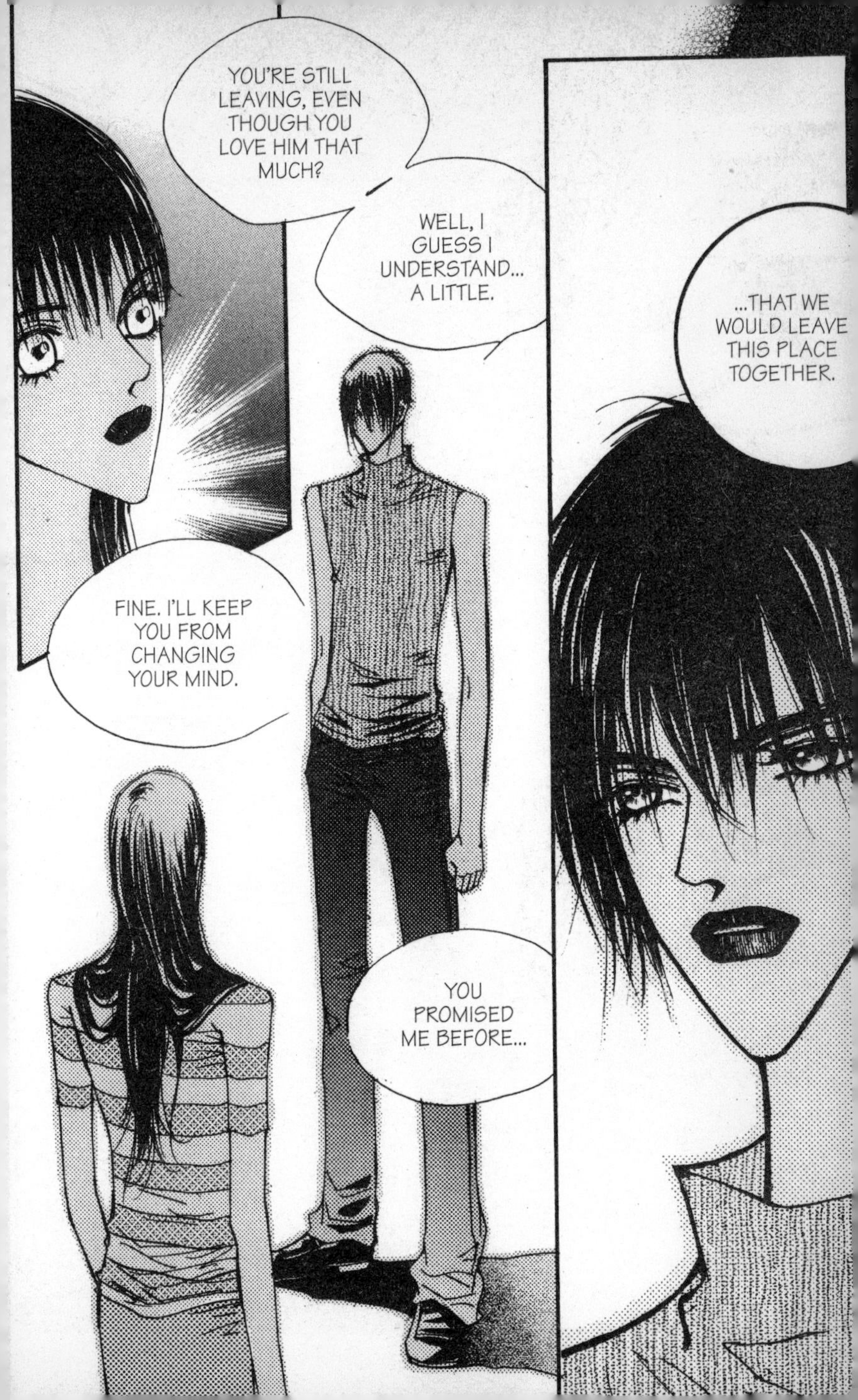
YOU'RE STILL LEAVING, EVEN THOUGH YOU LOVE HIM THAT MUCH?
WELL, I GUESS I UNDERSTAND... A LITTLE.
FINE. I'LL KEEP YOU FROM CHANGING YOUR MIND.
YOU PROMISED ME BEFORE...
...THAT WE WOULD LEAVE THIS PLACE TOGETHER.

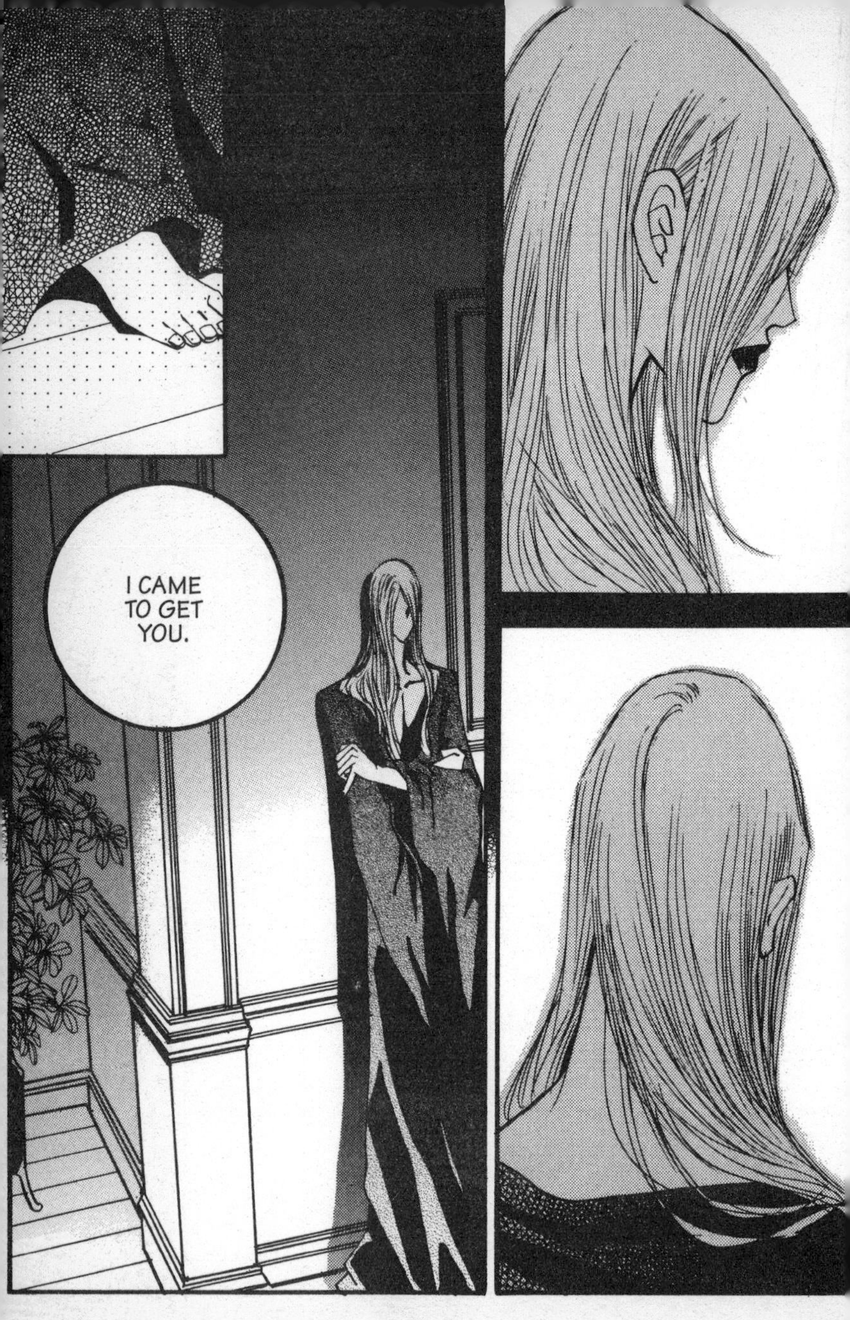
I CAME TO GET YOU.

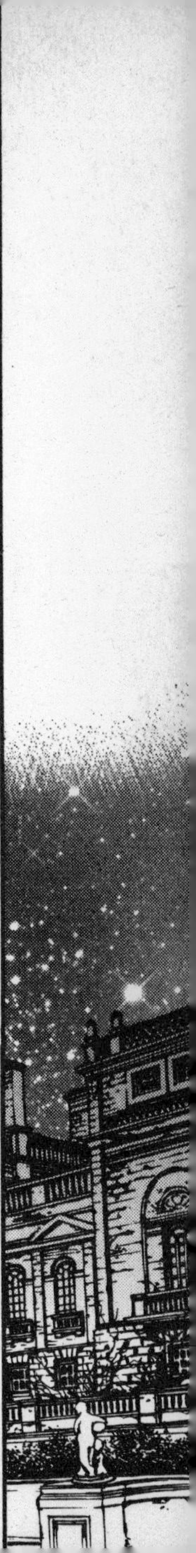
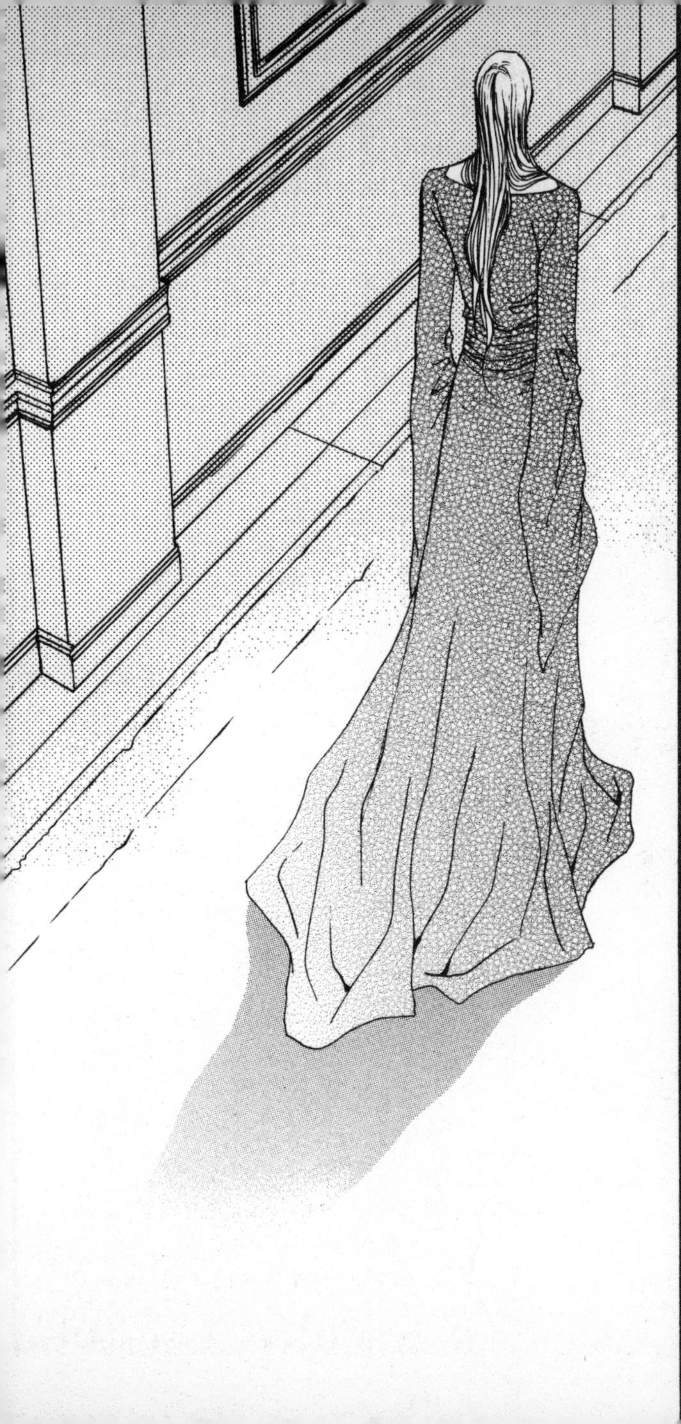

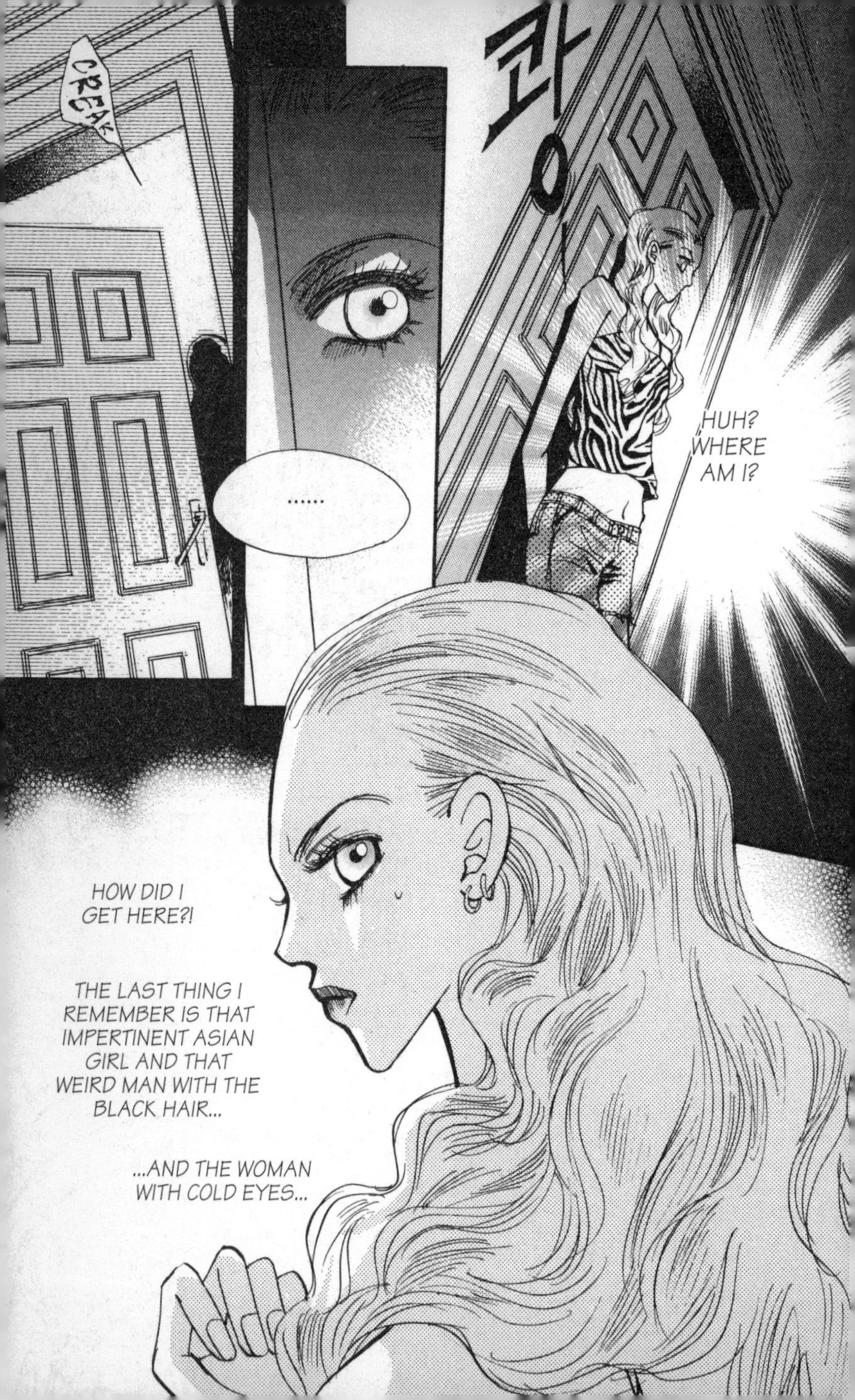
CREAK
......
쾅
HUH? WHERE AM I?
HOW DID I GET HERE?!
THE LAST THING I REMEMBER IS THAT IMPERTINENT ASIAN GIRL AND THAT WEIRD MAN WITH THE BLACK HAIR...
...AND THE WOMAN WITH COLD EYES...

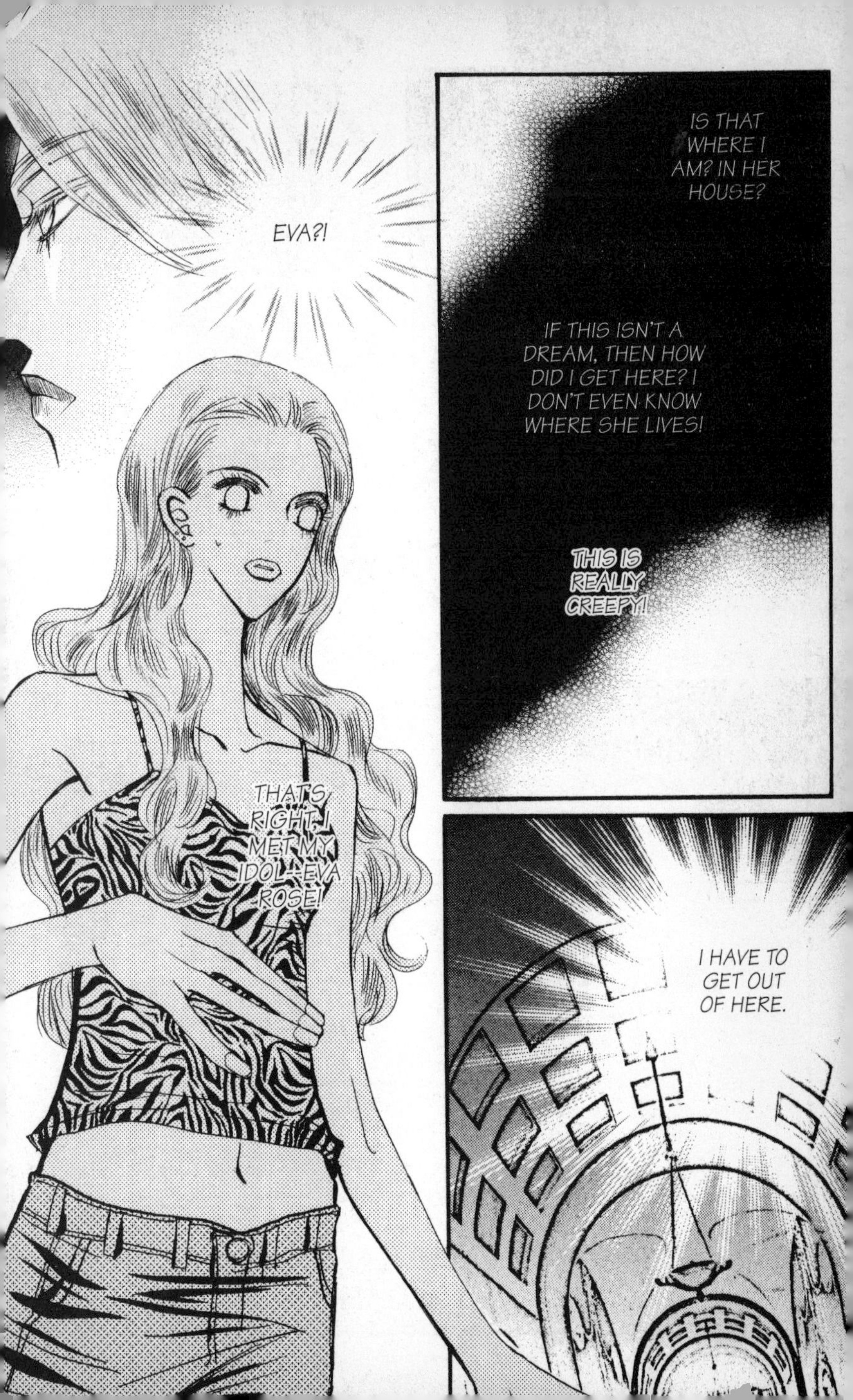
EVA?!
THAT'S RIGHT, I MET MY IDOL--EVA ROSE!
IS THAT WHERE I AM? IN HER HOUSE?
IF THIS ISN'T A DREAM, THEN HOW DID I GET HERE? I DON'T EVEN KNOW WHERE SHE LIVES!
THIS IS REALLY CREEPY!
I HAVE TO GET OUT OF HERE.

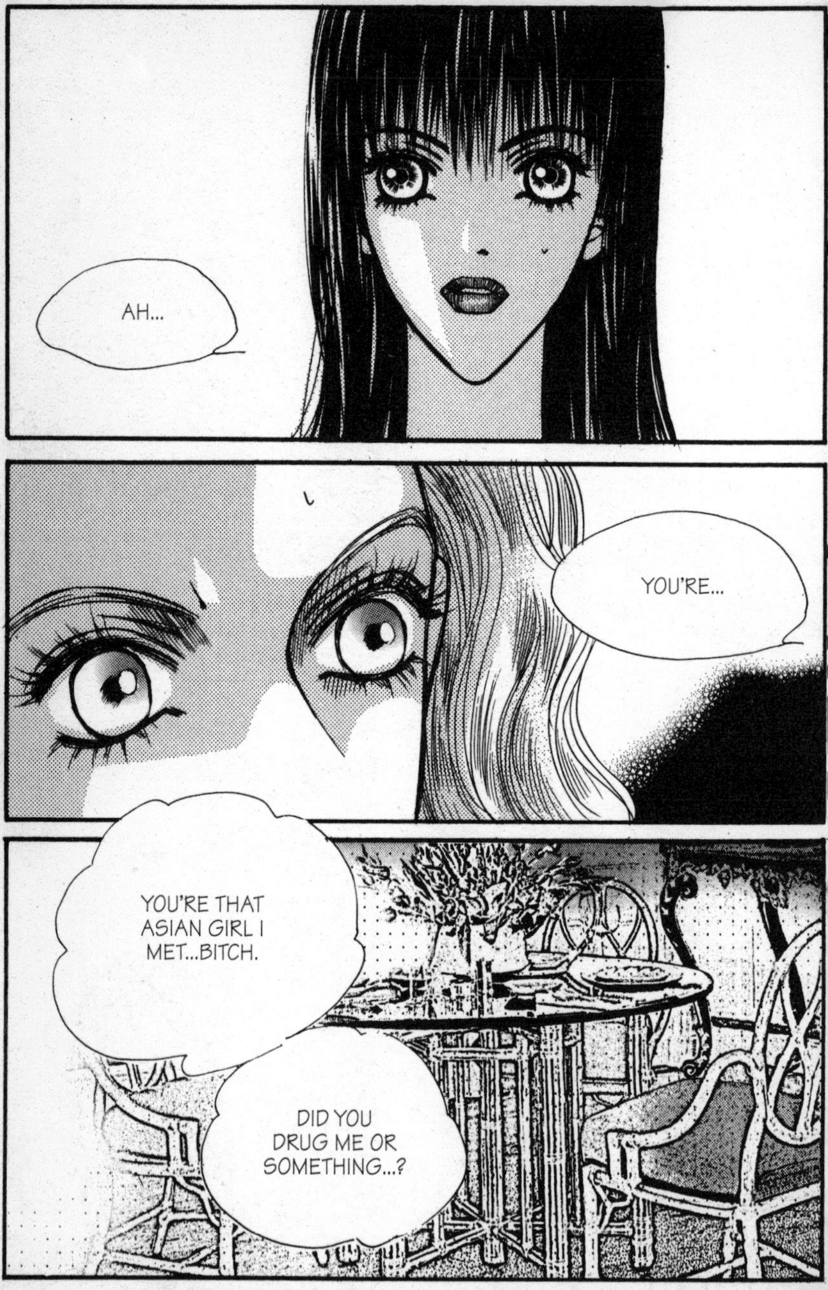
AH...
YOU'RE...
YOU'RE THAT ASIAN GIRL I MET...BITCH.
DID YOU DRUG ME OR SOMETHING...?

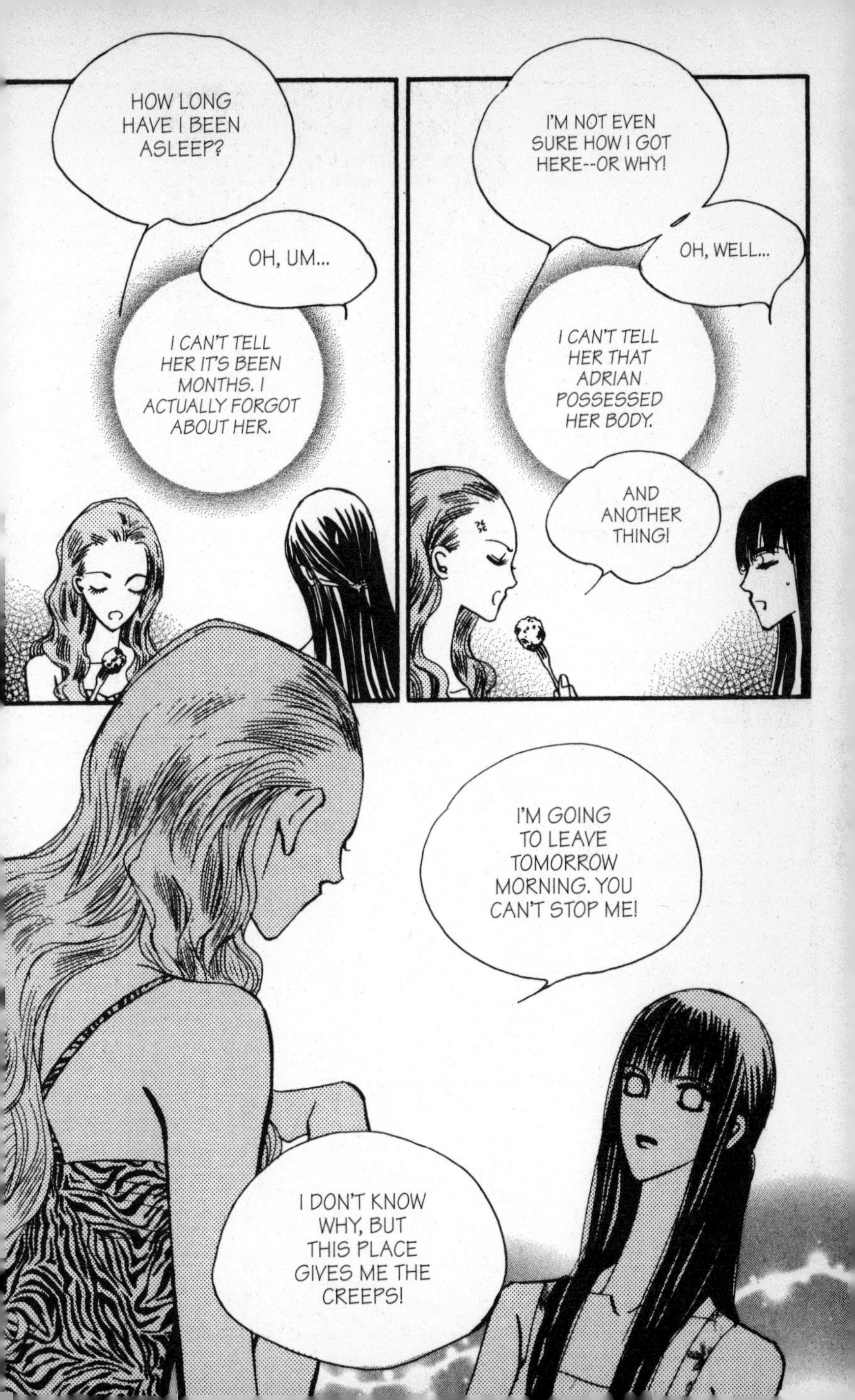
HOW LONG HAVE I BEEN ASLEEP?
OH, UM...
I CAN'T TELL HER IT'S BEEN MONTHS. I ACTUALLY FORGOT ABOUT HER.
I'M NOT EVEN SURE HOW I GOT HERE--OR WHY!
OH, WELL...
I CAN'T TELL HER THAT ADRIAN POSSESSED HER BODY.
AND ANOTHER THING!
I'M GOING TO LEAVE TOMORROW MORNING. YOU CAN'T STOP ME!
I DON'T KNOW WHY, BUT THIS PLACE GIVES ME THE CREEPS!

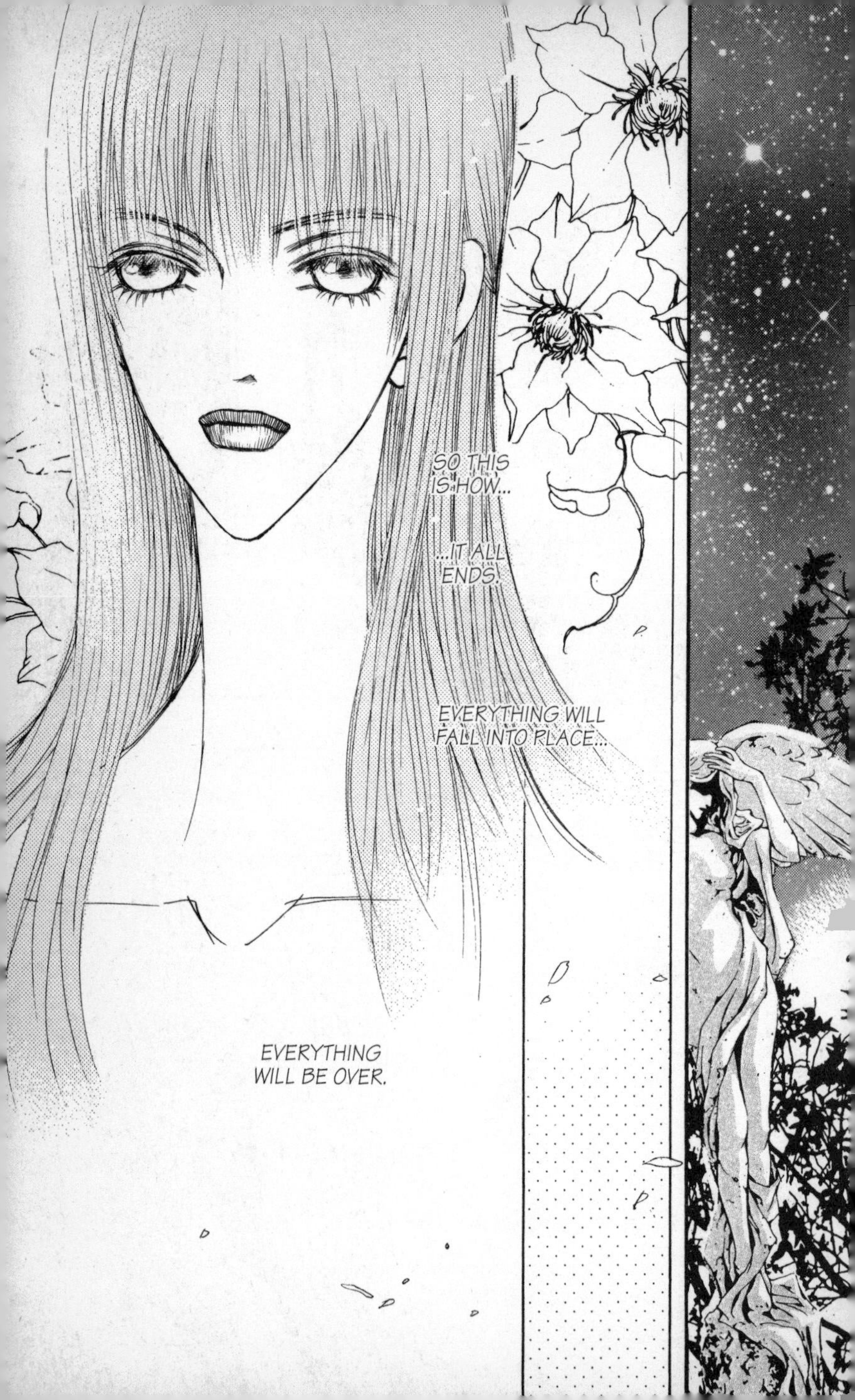
SO THIS IS HOW...
...IT ALL ENDS.
EVERYTHING WILL FALL INTO PLACE...
EVERYTHING WILL BE OVER.

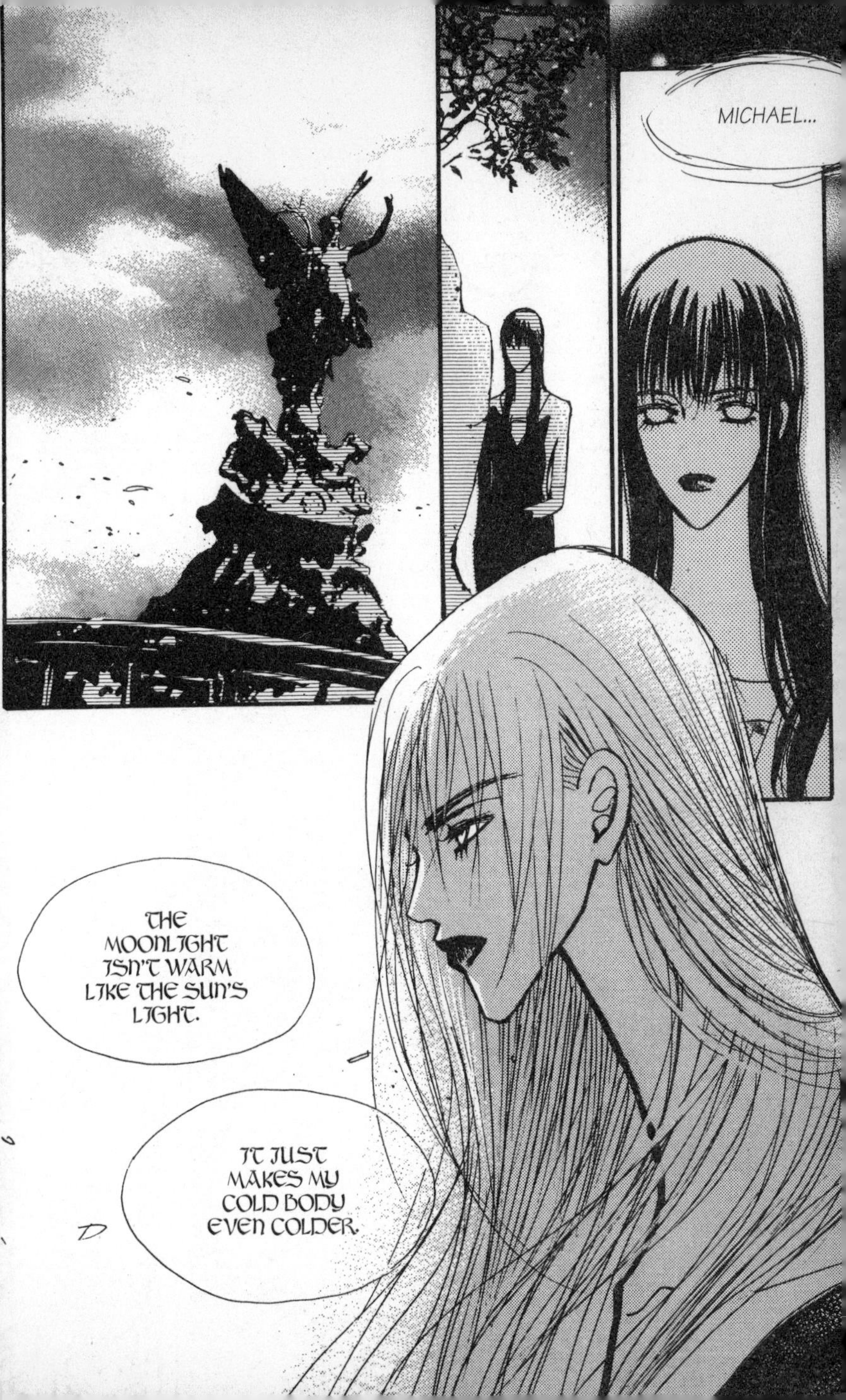
MICHAEL...
THE MOONLIGHT ISN'T WARM LIKE THE SUN'S LIGHT.
IT JUST MAKES MY COLD BODY EVEN COLDER.

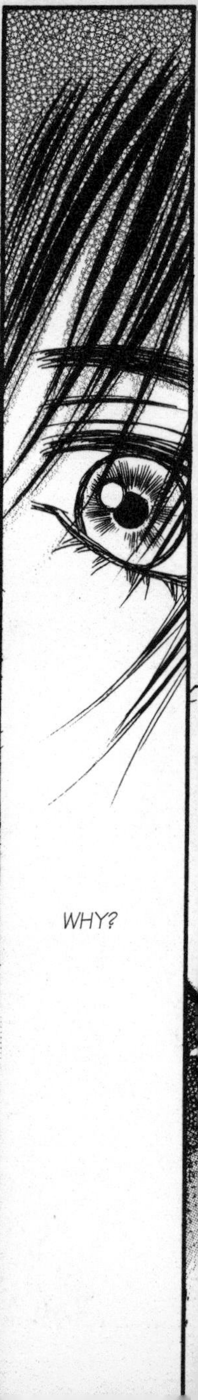
WHY?
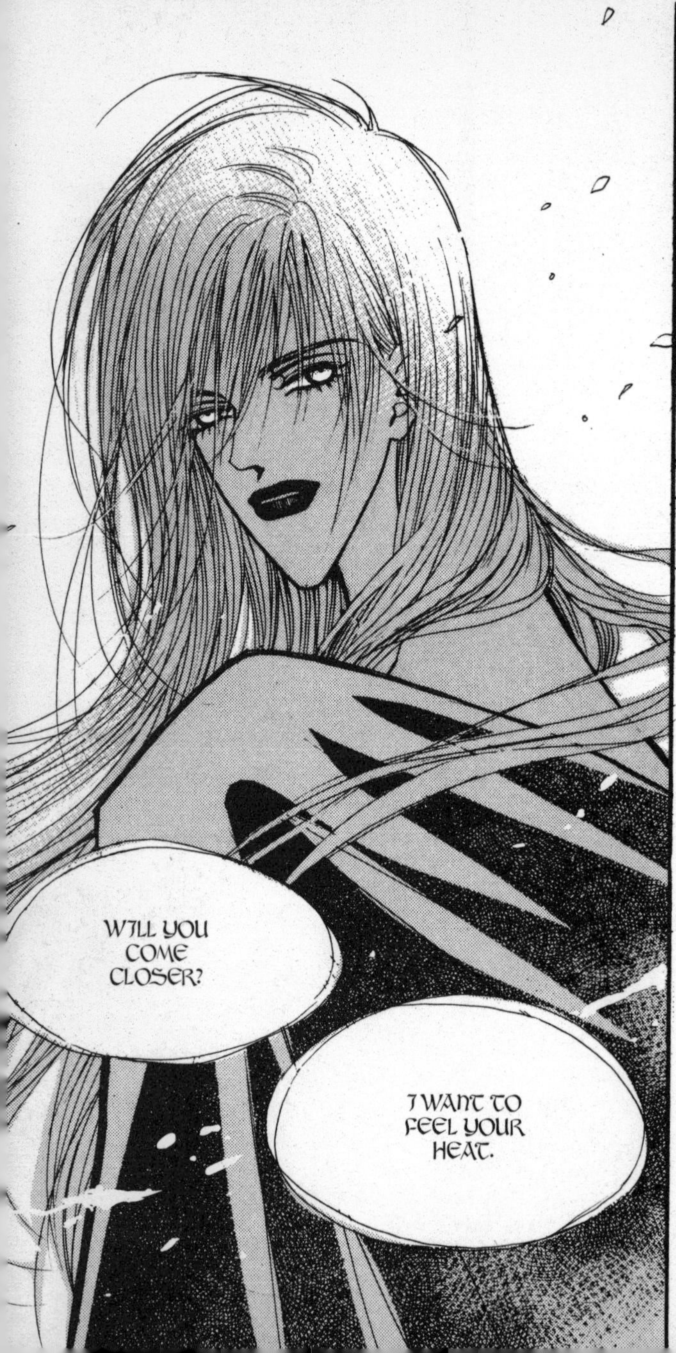
WILL YOU COME CLOSER?
I WANT TO FEEL YOUR HEAT.

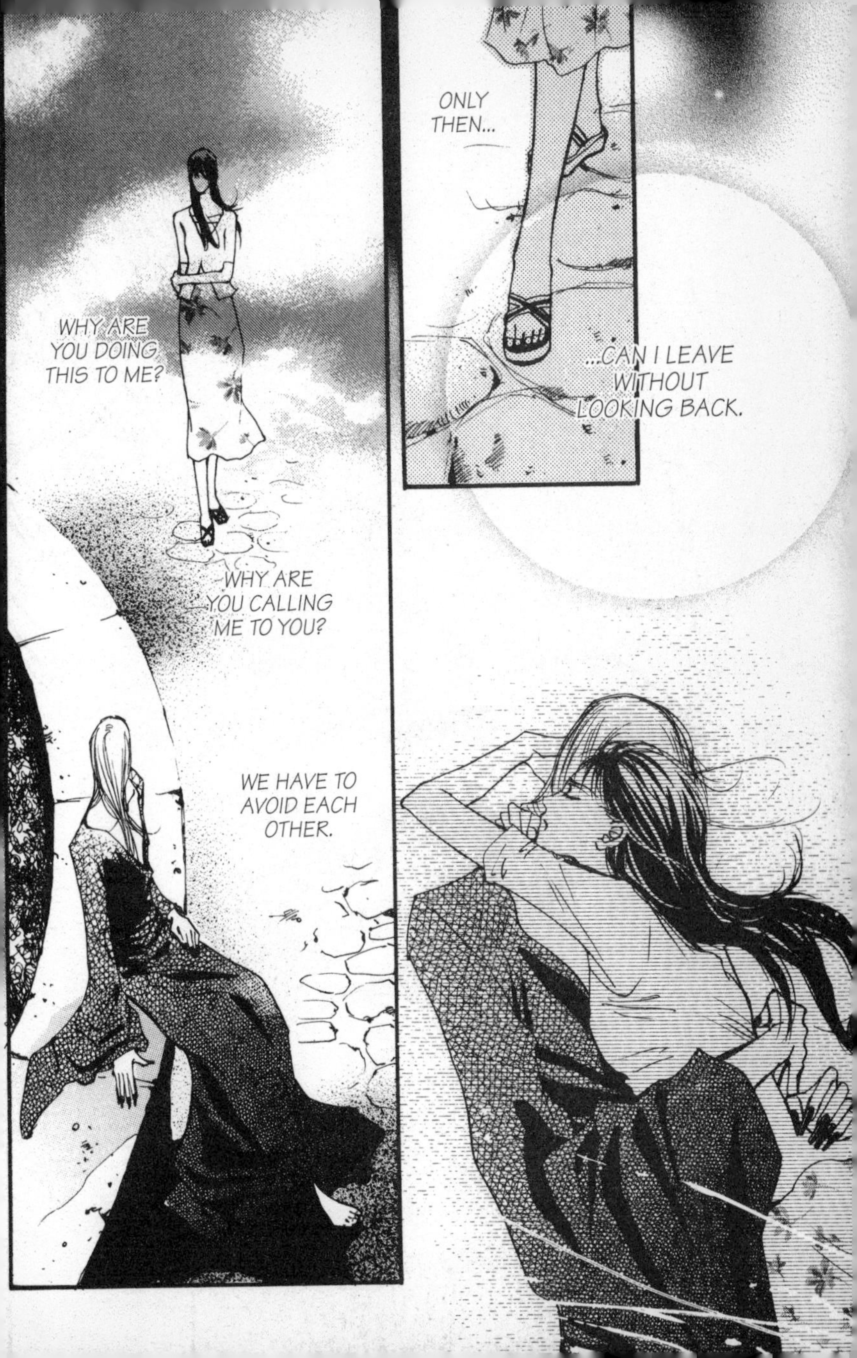
WHY ARE YOU DOING THIS TO ME?
WHY ARE YOU CALLING ME TO YOU?
WE HAVE TO AVOID EACH OTHER.
ONLY THEN...
...CAN I LEAVE WITHOUT LOOKING BACK.

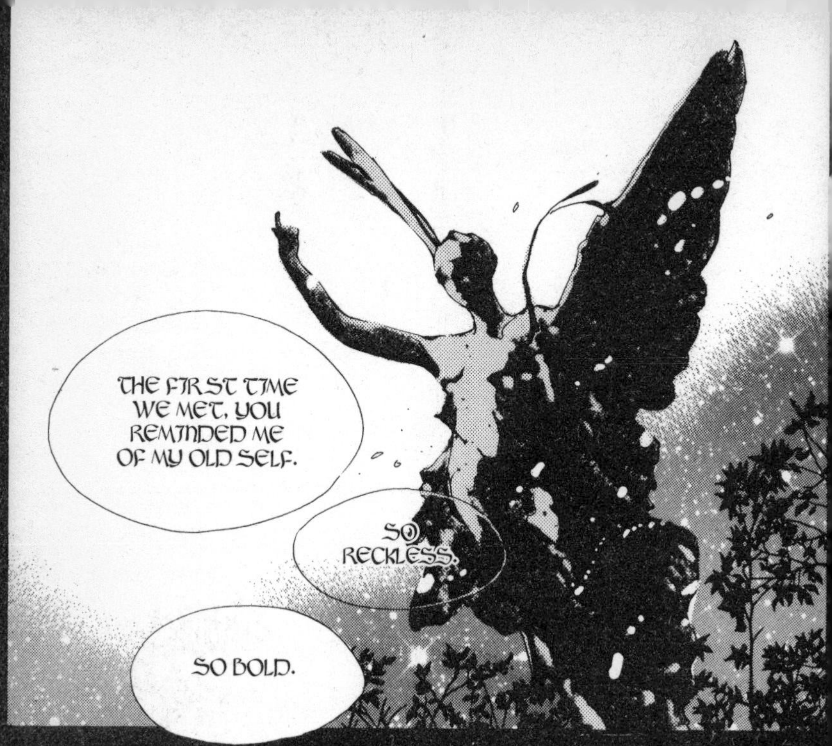
THE FIRST TIME WE MET, YOU REMINDED ME OF MY OLD SELF.
SO RECKLESS.
SO BOLD.

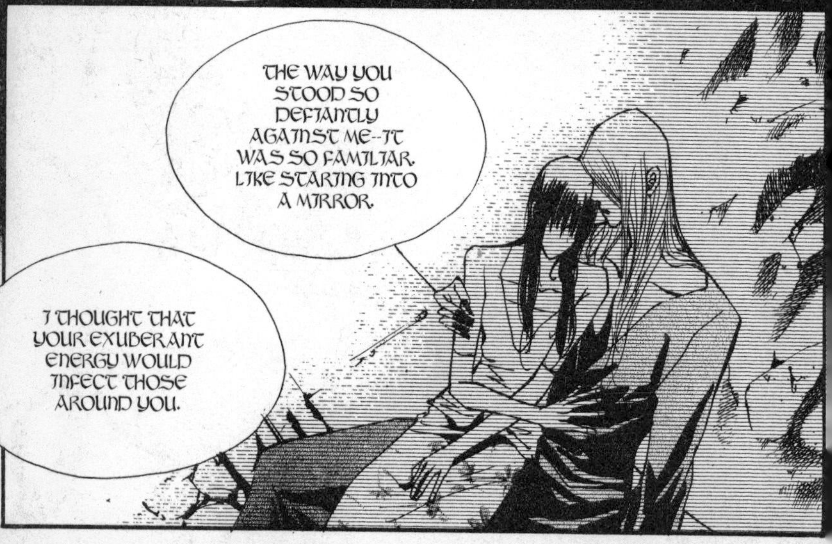
THE WAY YOU STOOD SO DEFIANTLY AGAINST ME--IT WAS SO FAMILIAR. LIKE STARING INTO A MIRROR.
I THOUGHT THAT YOUR EXUBERANT ENERGY WOULD INFECT THOSE AROUND YOU.

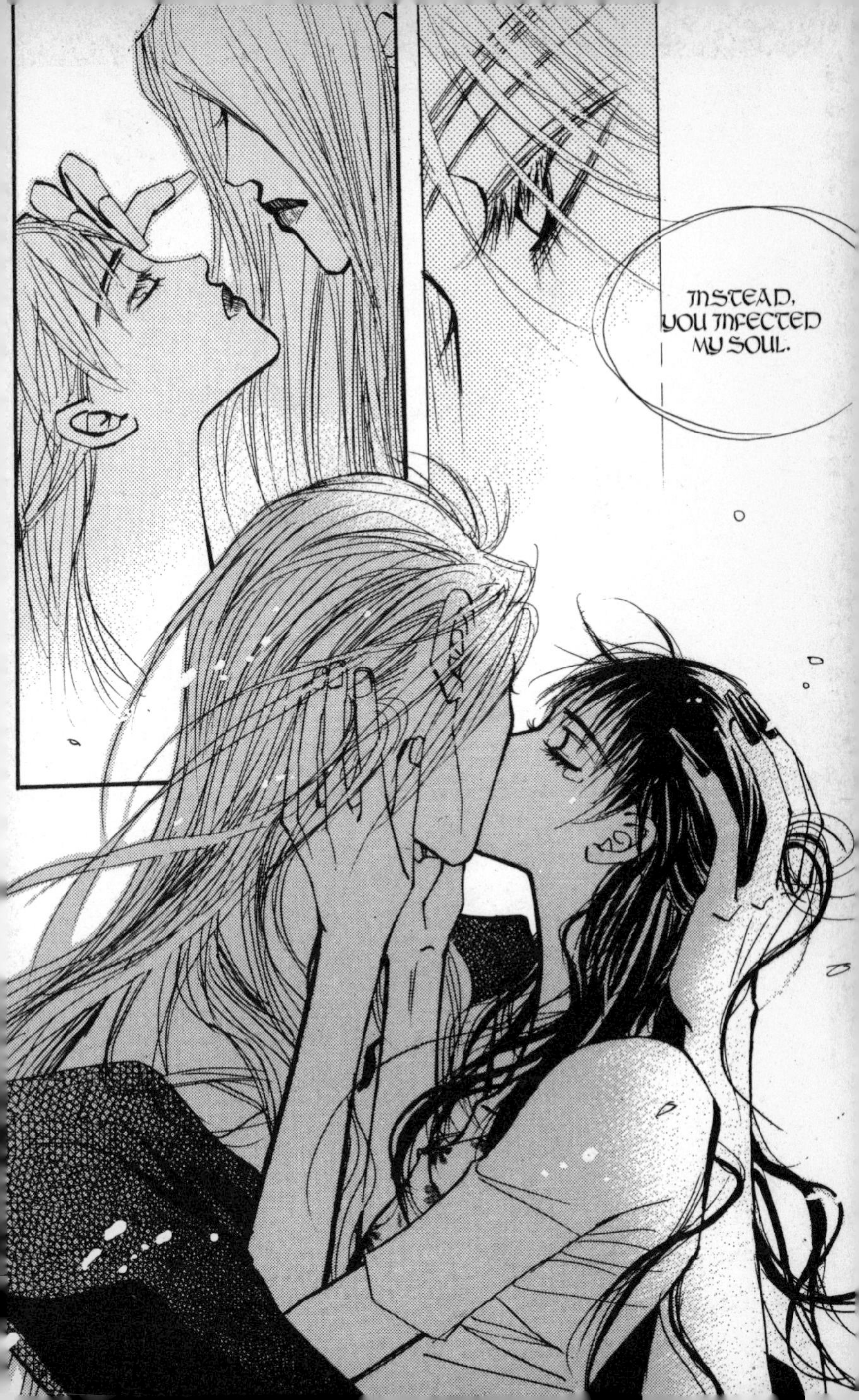
INSTEAD, YOU INFECTED MY SOUL.

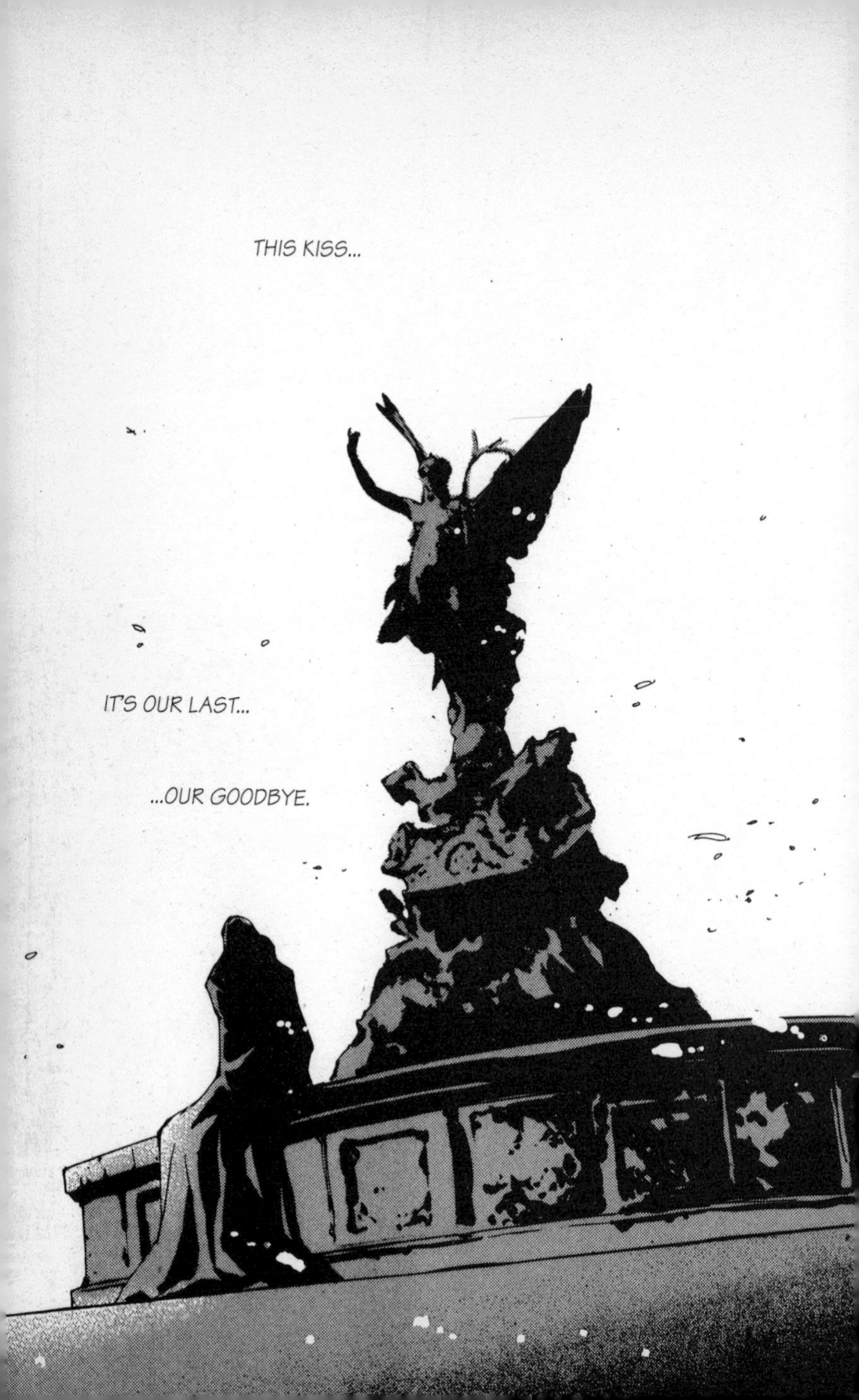
THIS KISS...
IT'S OUR LAST...
...OUR GOODBYE.

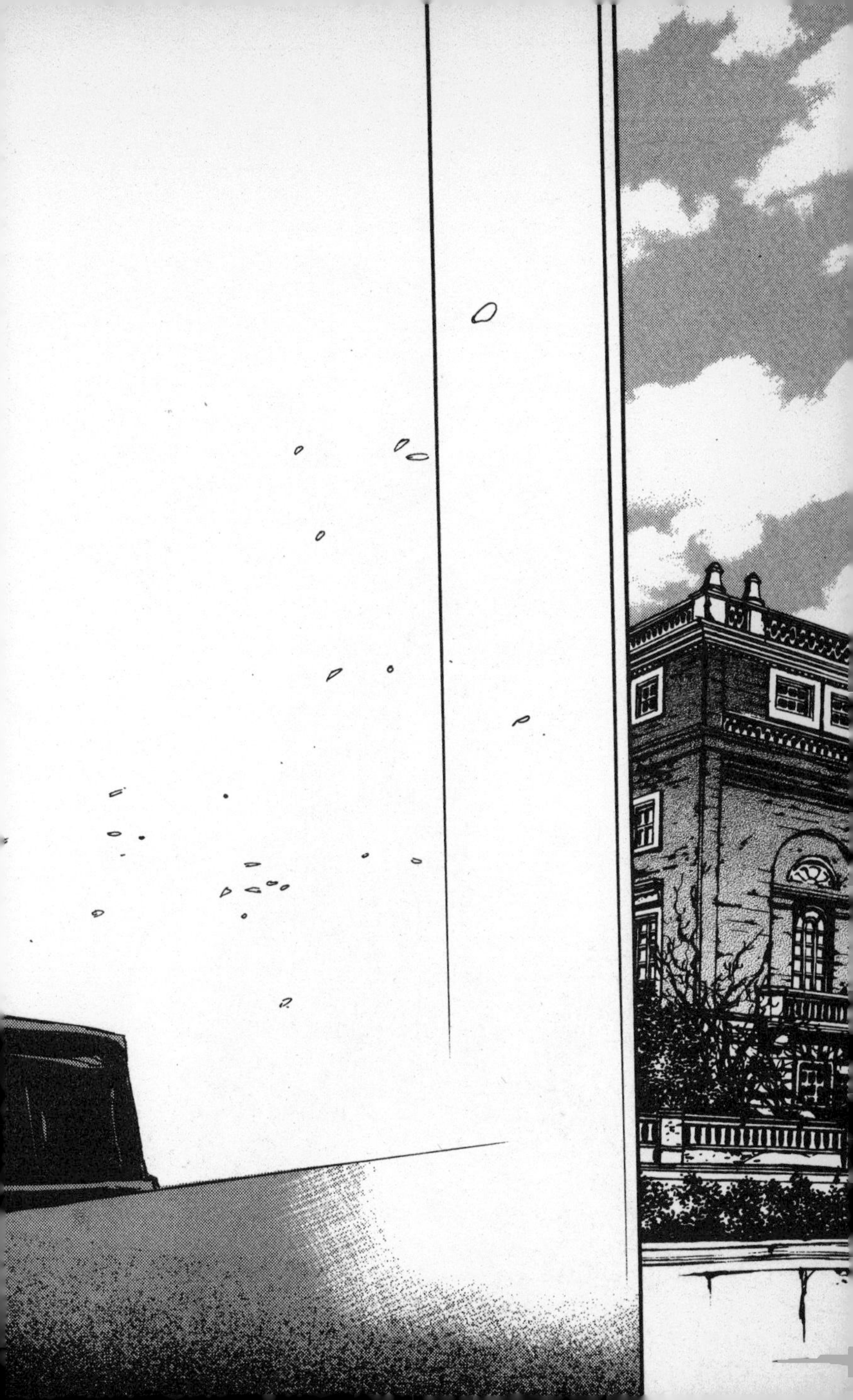

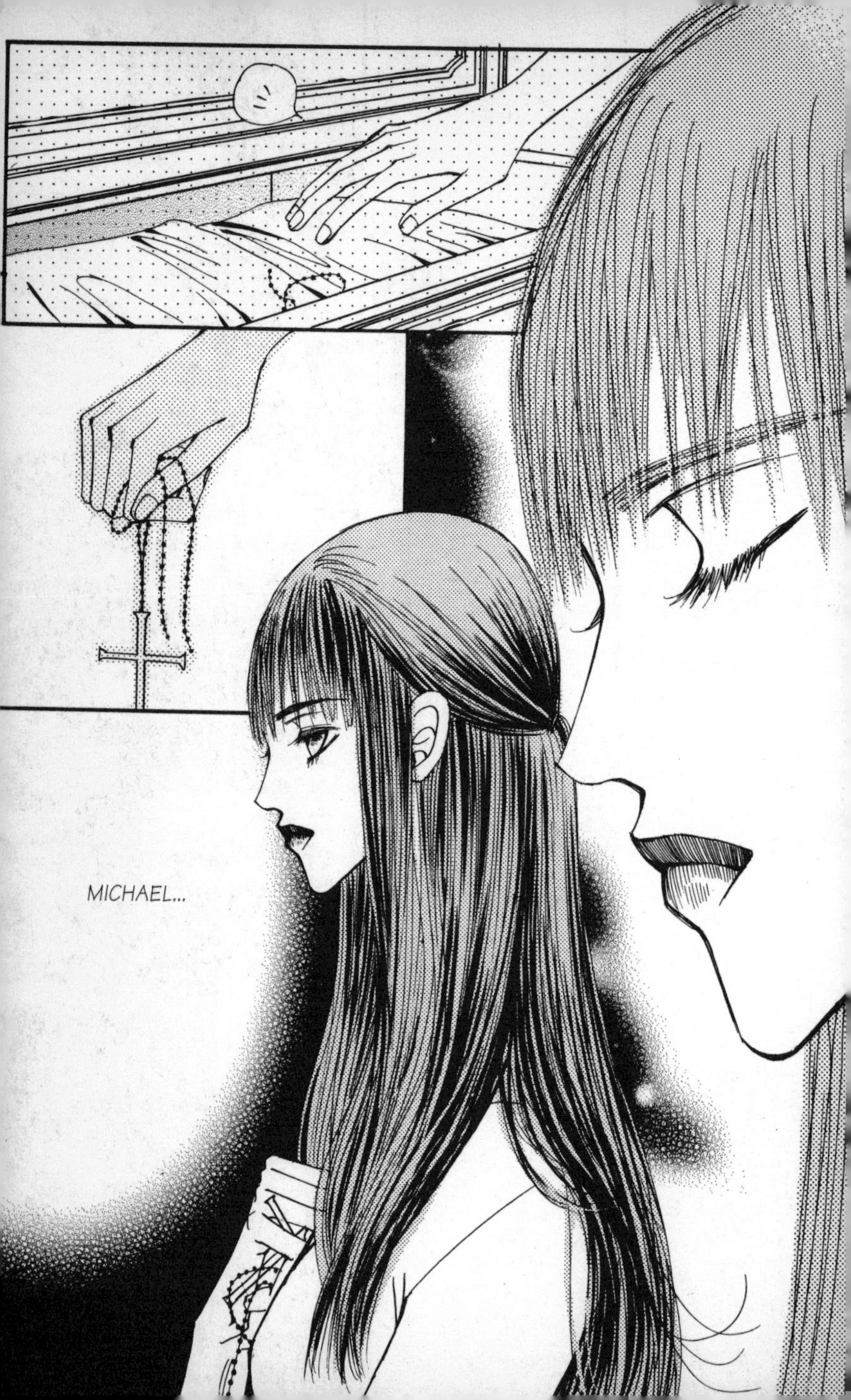
MICHAEL...

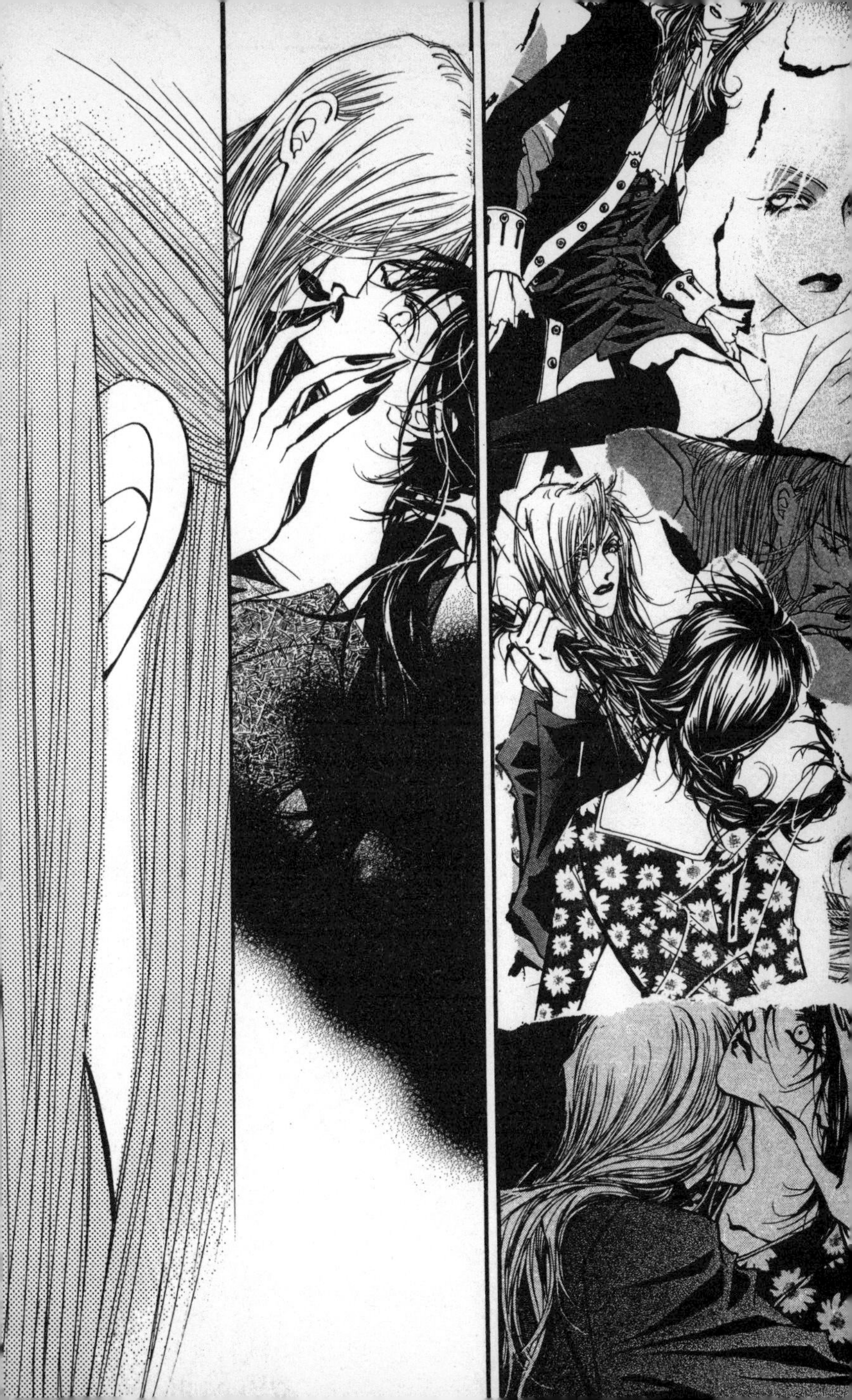

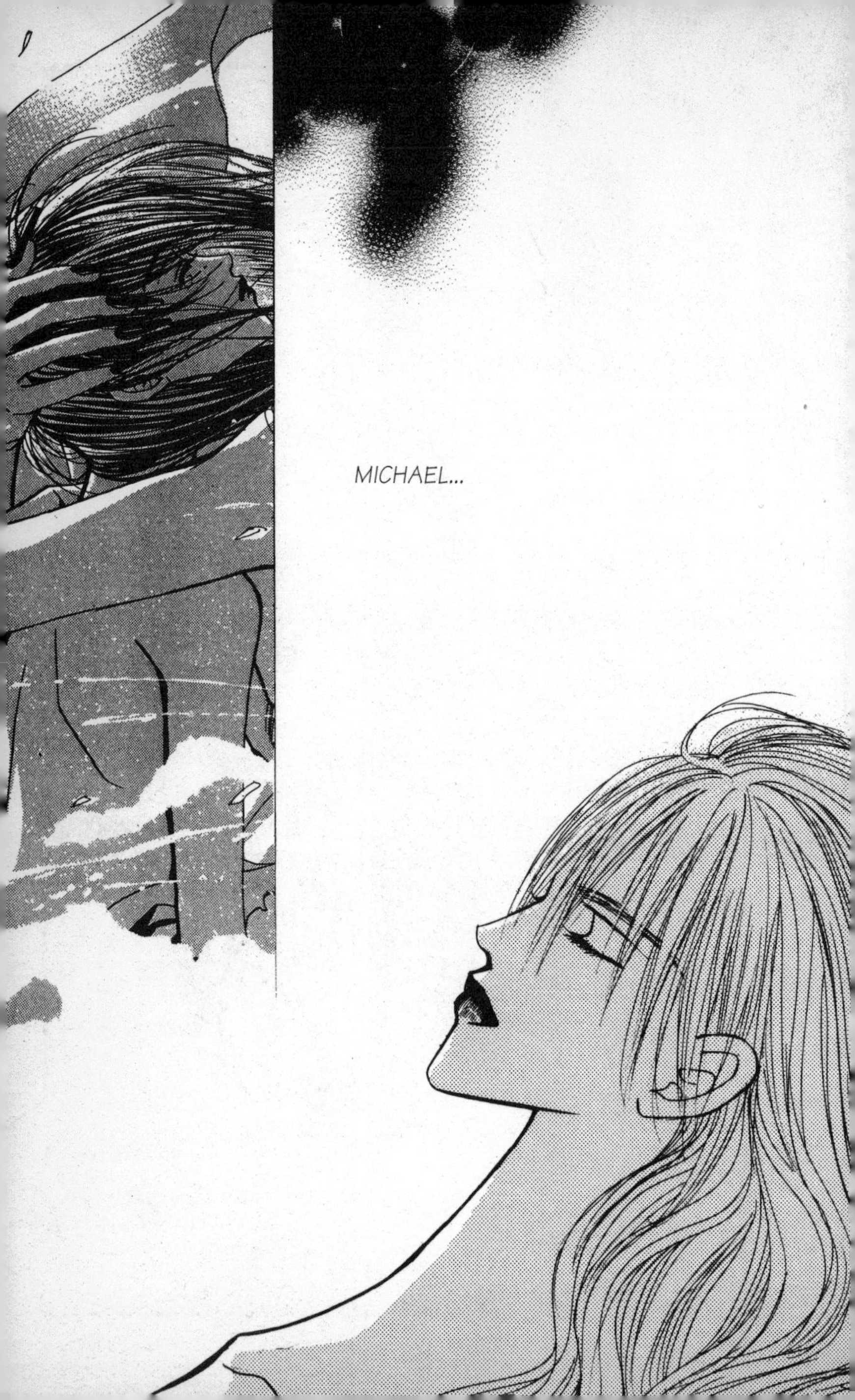
MICHAEL...

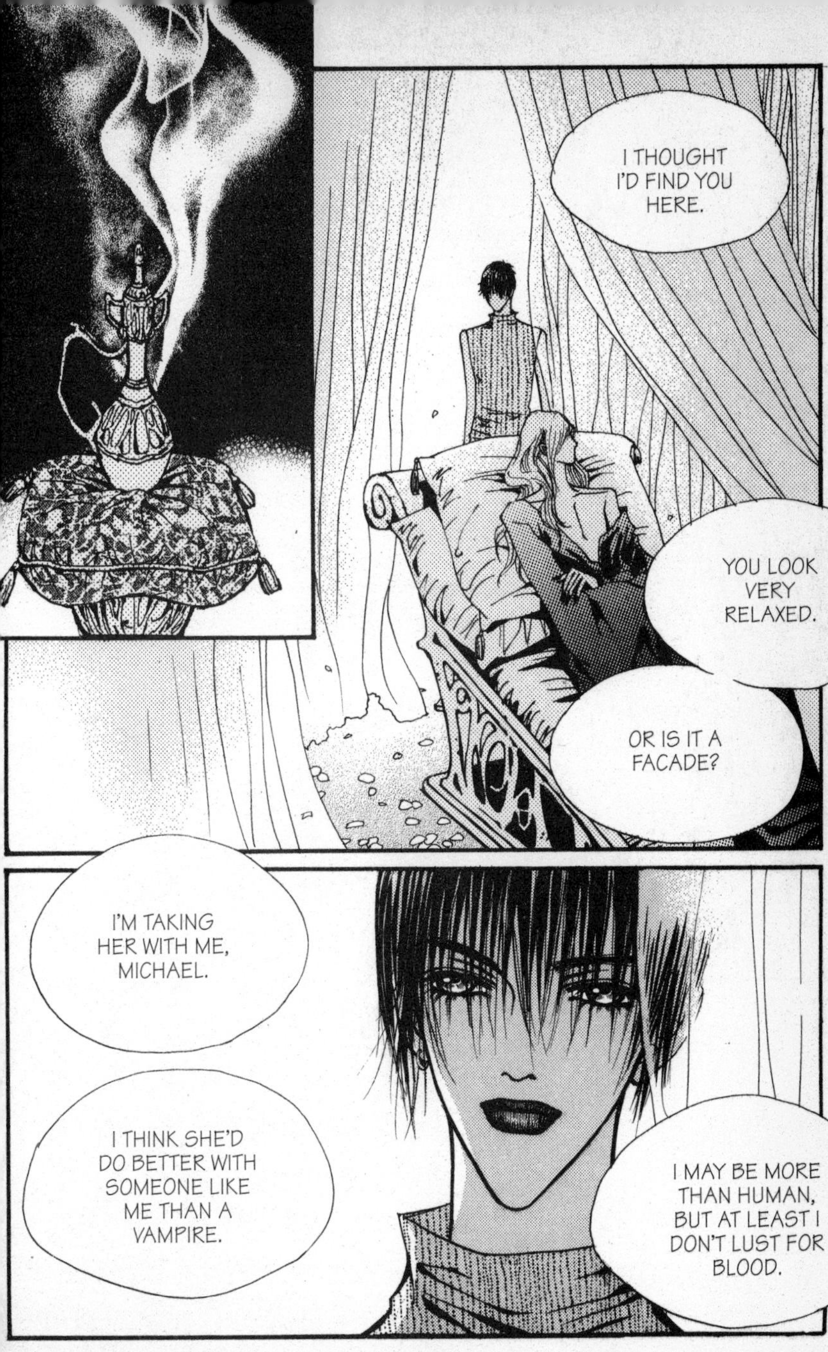
I THOUGHT I'D FIND YOU HERE.
YOU LOOK VERY RELAXED.
OR IS IT A FACADE?
I'M TAKING HER WITH ME, MICHAEL.
I THINK SHE'D DO BETTER WITH SOMEONE LIKE ME THAN A VAMPIRE.
I MAY BE MORE THAN HUMAN, BUT AT LEAST I DON'T LUST FOR BLOOD.

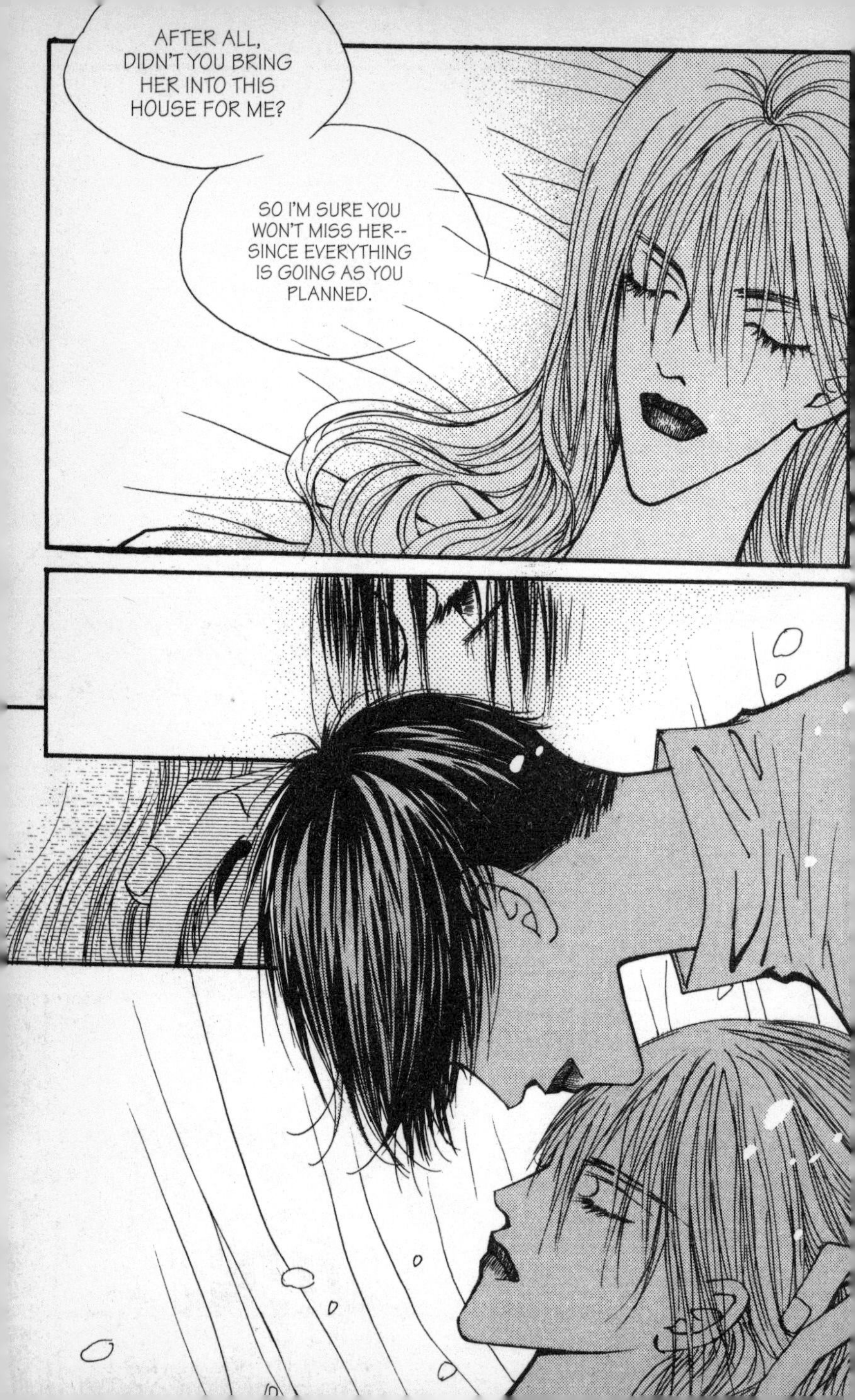
AFTER ALL, DIDN'T YOU BRING HER INTO THIS HOUSE FOR ME?
SO I'M SURE YOU WON'T MISS HER-- SINCE EVERYTHING IS GOING AS YOU PLANNED.

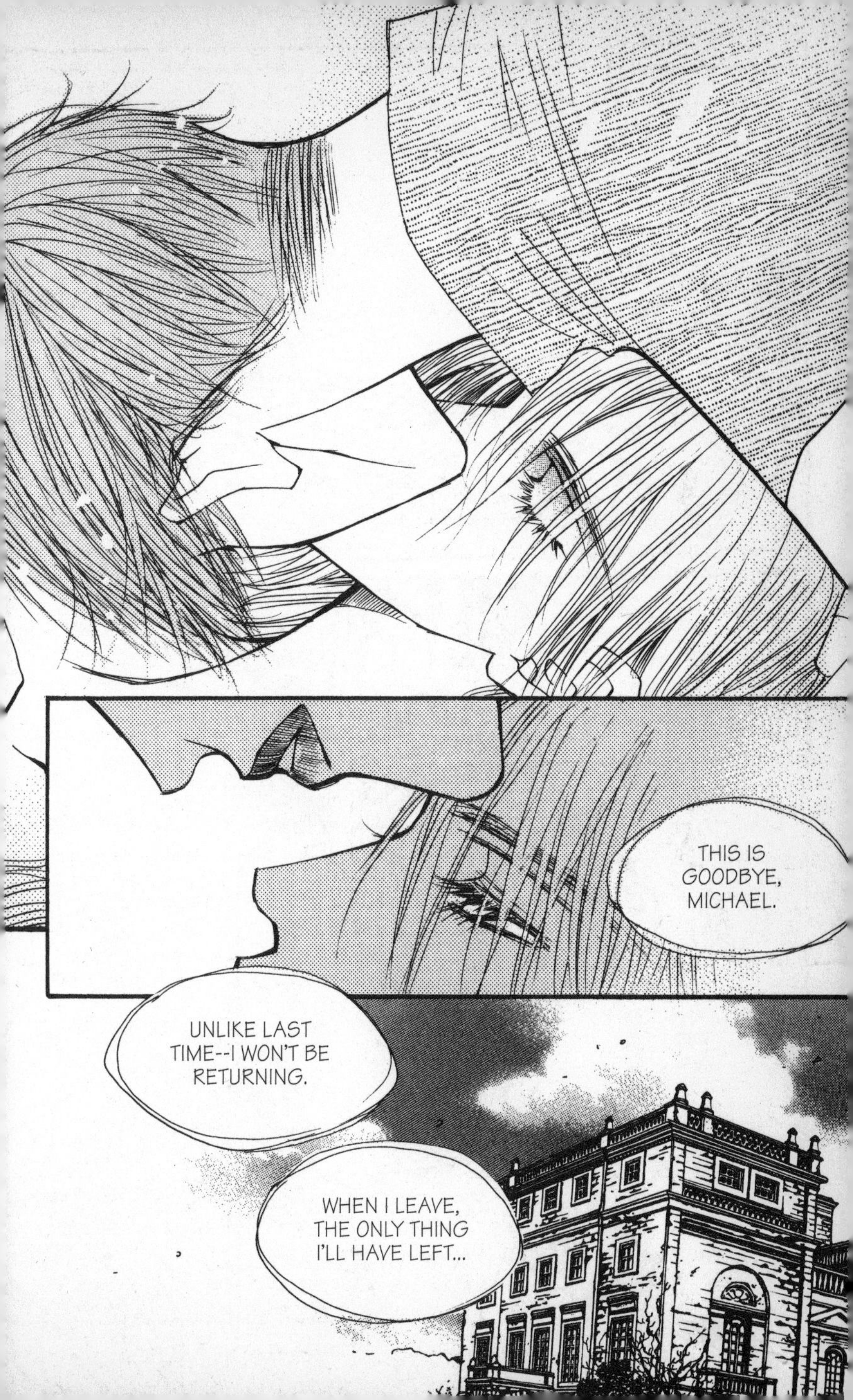
THIS IS GOODBYE, MICHAEL.
UNLIKE LAST TIME--I WON'T BE RETURNING.
WHEN I LEAVE, THE ONLY THING I'LL HAVE LEFT...

...ARE MY MEMORIES OF THIS PLACE.

THANK GOD! THE TAXI'S HERE. HURRY UP. I WANT TO GET OUTTA HERE.

THE SOONER THE BETTER.

IS THIS IT?

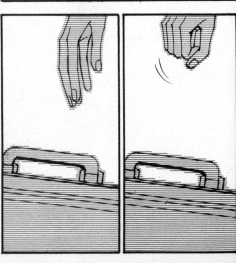

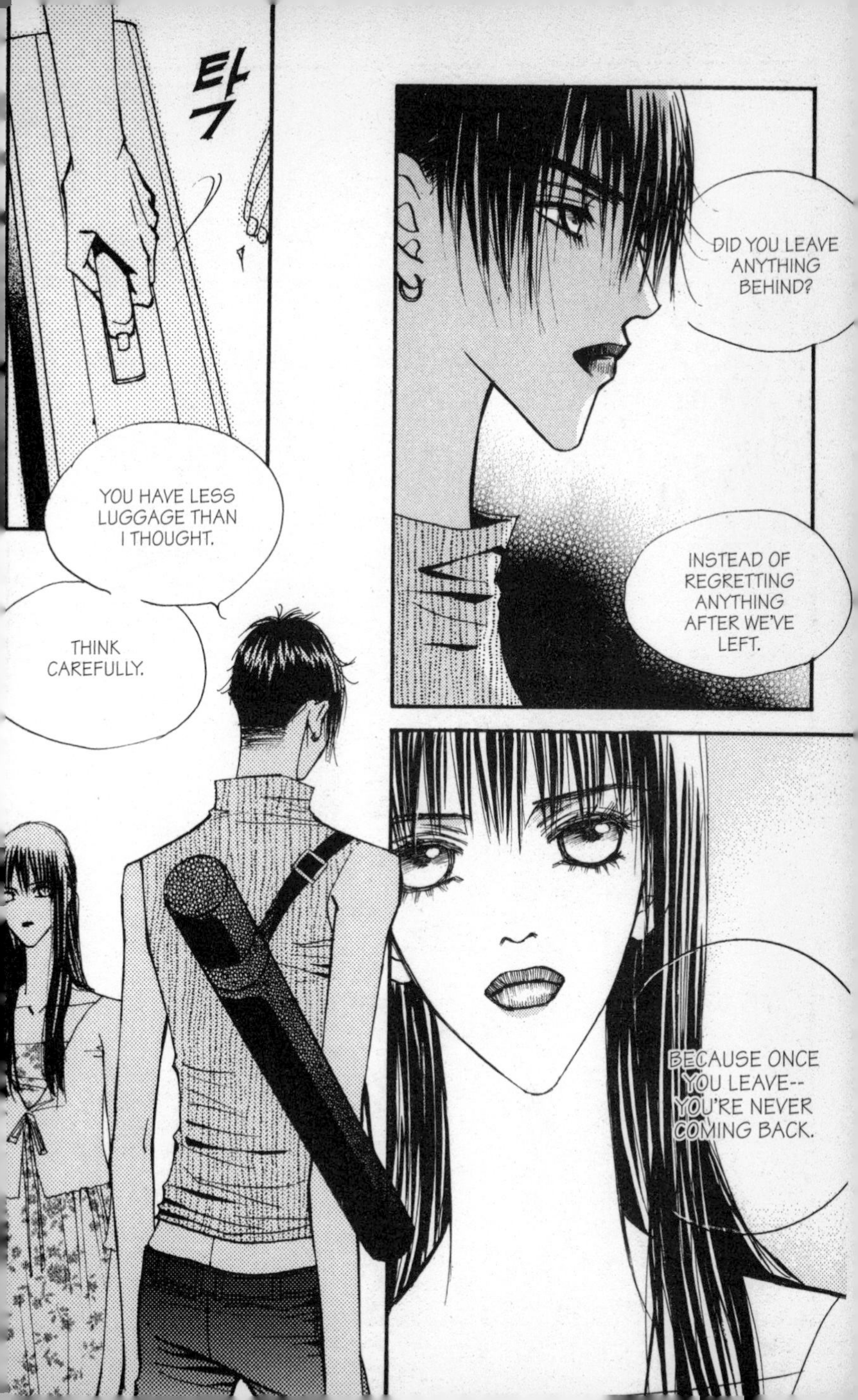
탁
YOU HAVE LESS LUGGAGE THAN I THOUGHT.
THINK CAREFULLY.
DID YOU LEAVE ANYTHING BEHIND?
INSTEAD OF REGRETTING ANYTHING AFTER WE'VE LEFT.
BECAUSE ONCE YOU LEAVE-- YOU'RE NEVER COMING BACK.

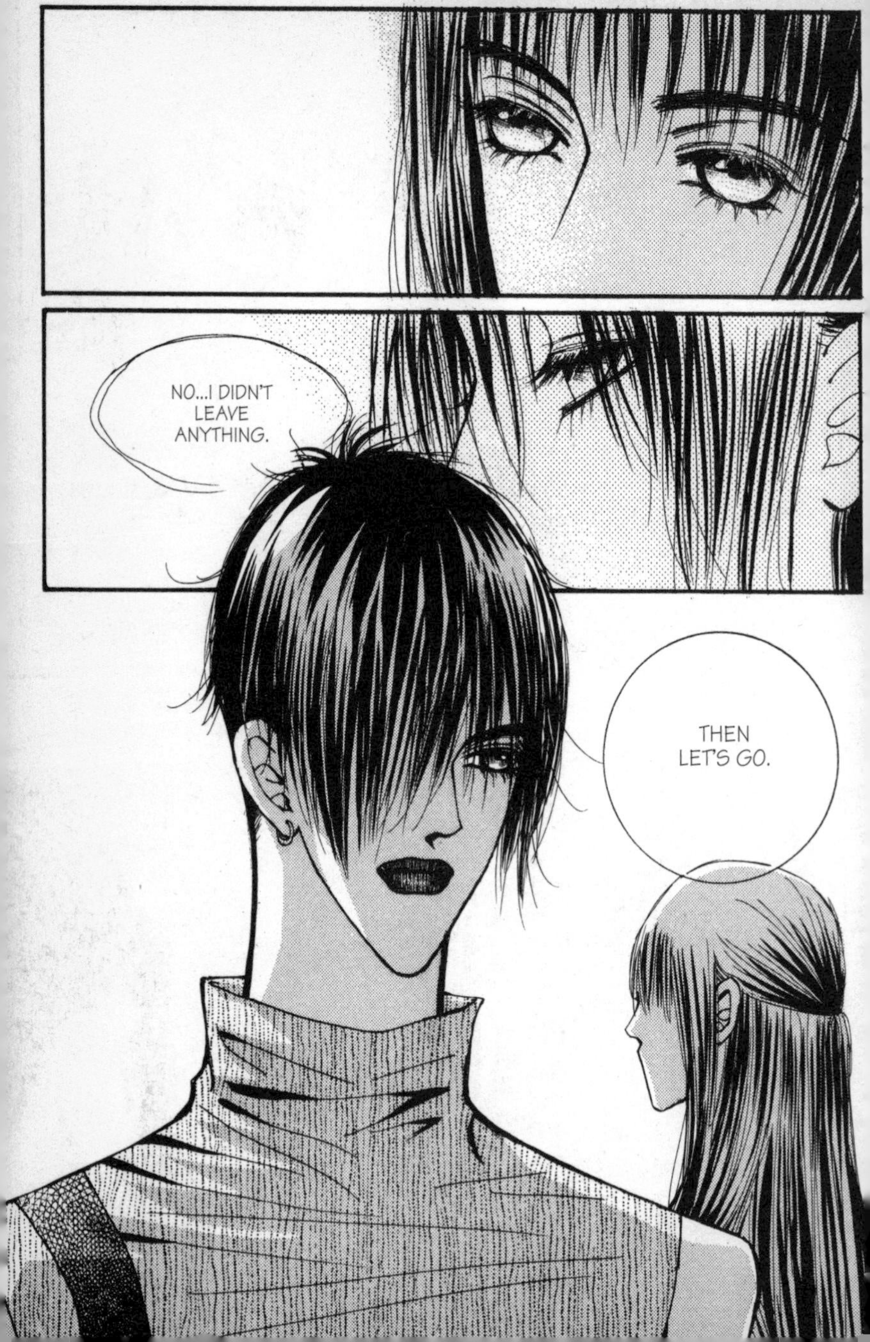
NO...I DIDN'T LEAVE ANYTHING.
THEN LET'S GO.

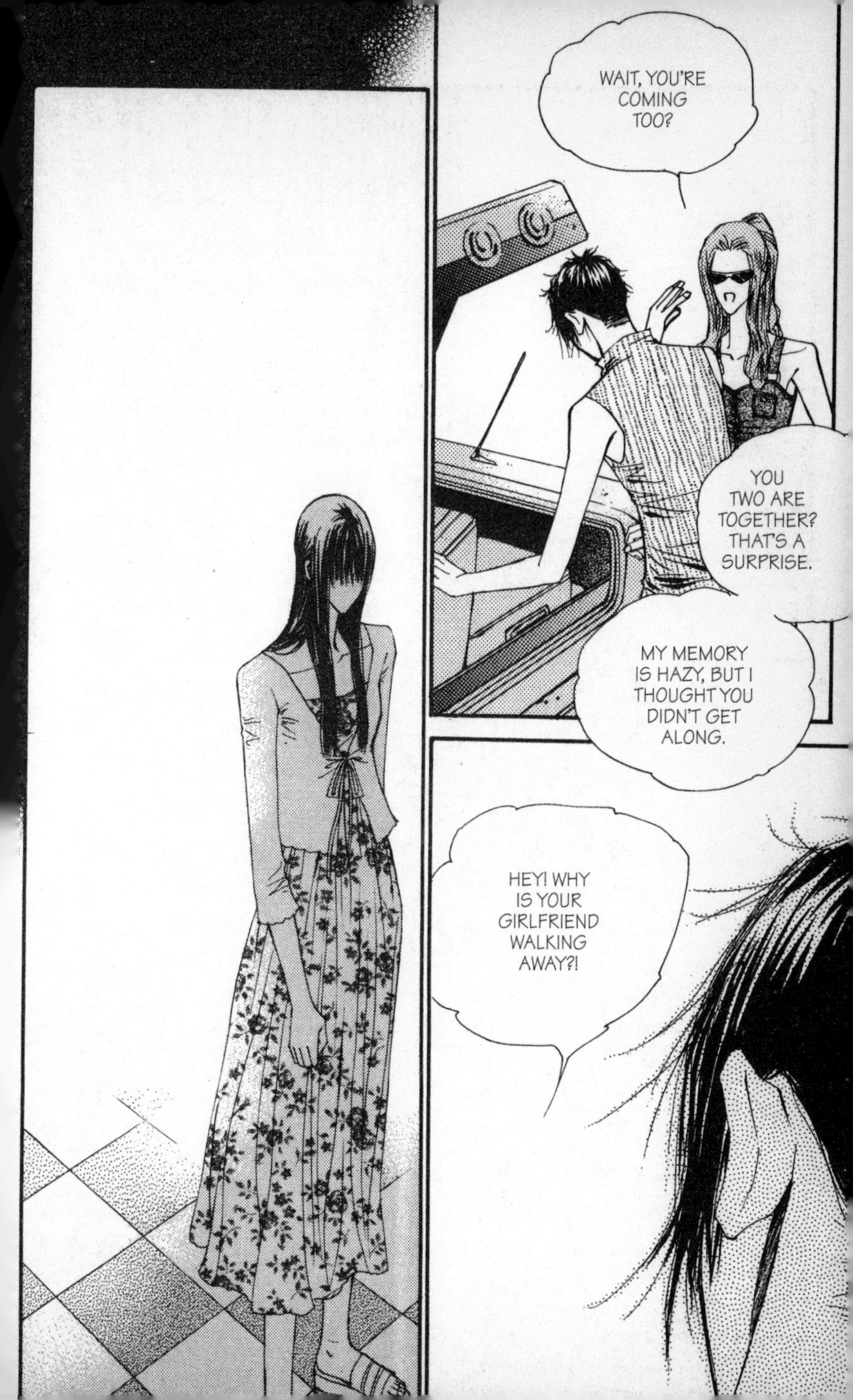
WAIT, YOU'RE COMING TOO?
YOU TWO ARE TOGETHER? THAT'S A SURPRISE.
MY MEMORY IS HAZY, BUT I THOUGHT YOU DIDN'T GET ALONG.
HEY! WHY IS YOUR GIRLFRIEND WALKING AWAY?!

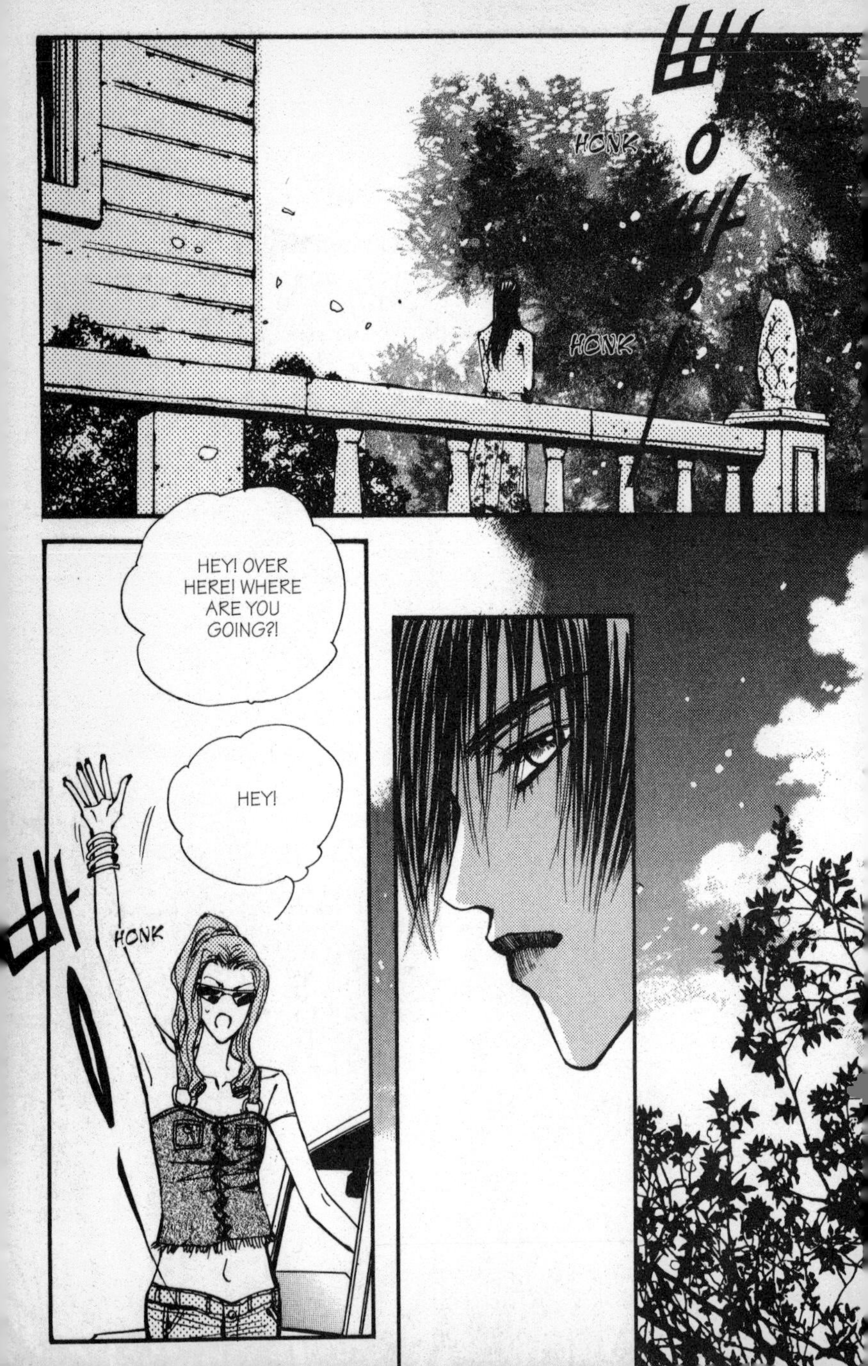
HONK
HONK
HEY! OVER HERE! WHERE ARE YOU GOING?!
HEY!
HONK

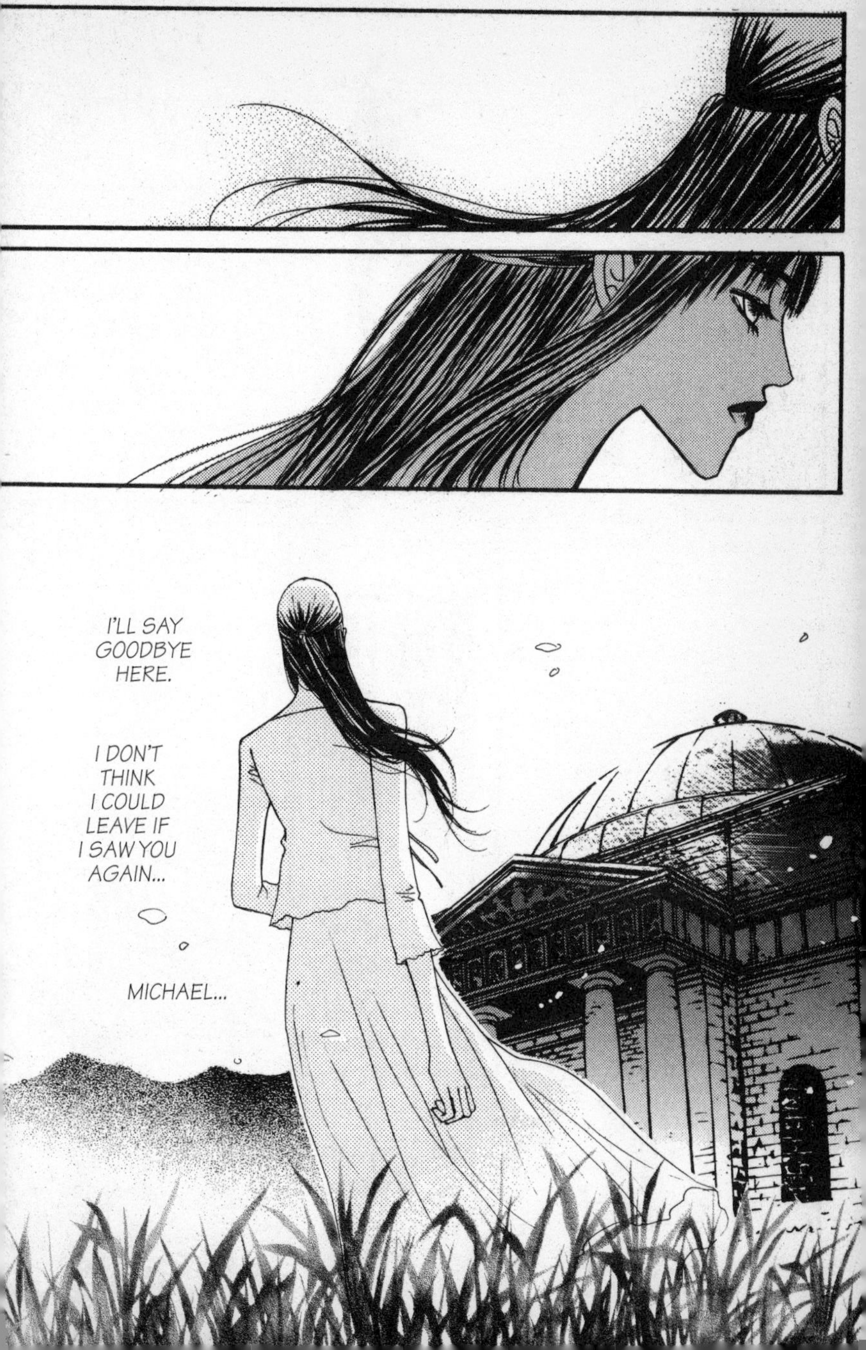
I'LL SAY GOODBYE HERE.
I DON'T THINK I COULD LEAVE IF I SAW YOU AGAIN...
MICHAEL...

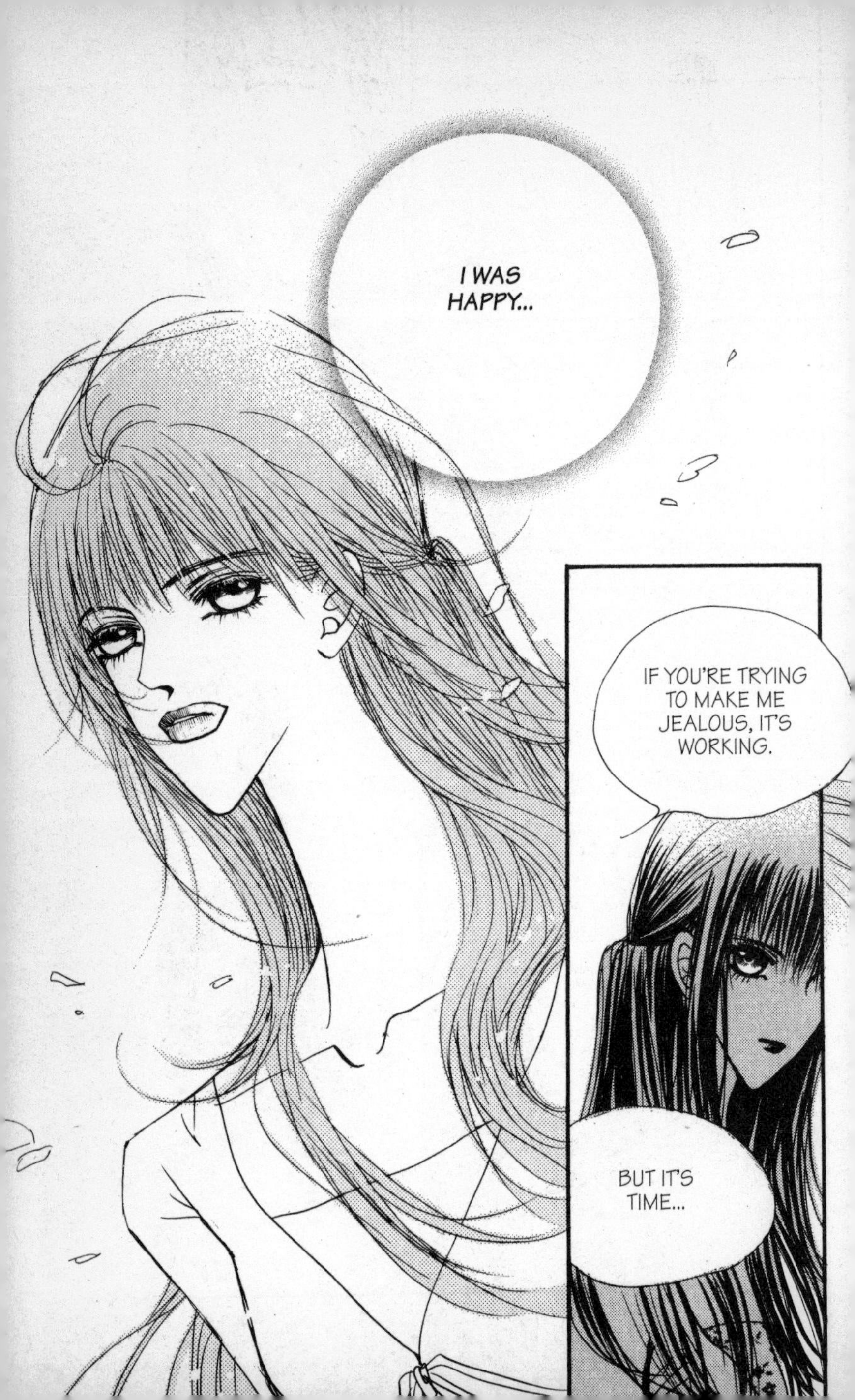
I WAS HAPPY...
IF YOU'RE TRYING TO MAKE ME JEALOUS, IT'S WORKING.
BUT IT'S TIME...

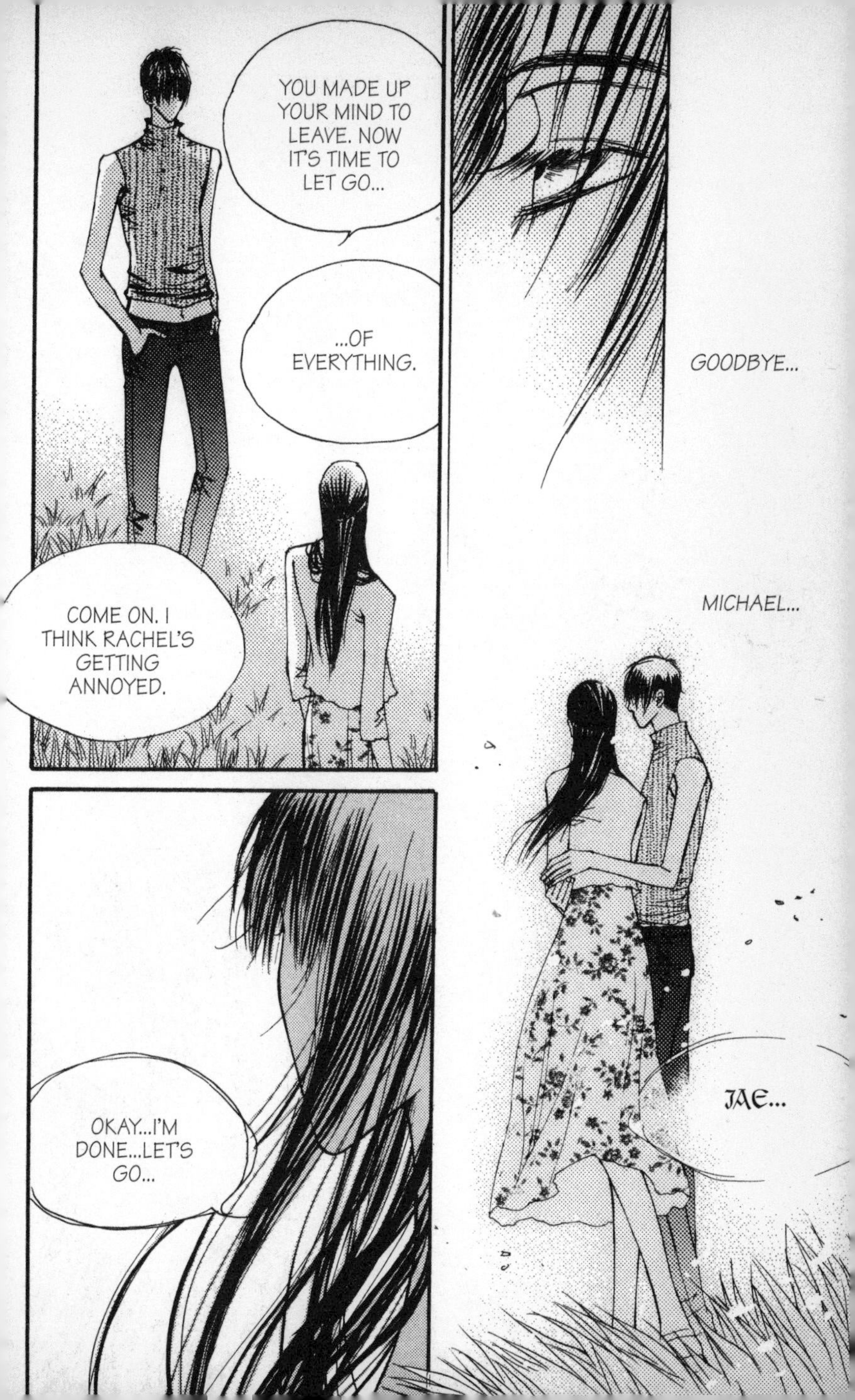
YOU MADE UP YOUR MIND TO LEAVE. NOW IT'S TIME TO LET GO...
...OF EVERYTHING.
COME ON. I THINK RACHEL'S GETTING ANNOYED.
OKAY...I'M DONE...LET'S GO...
GOODBYE...
MICHAEL...
JAE...

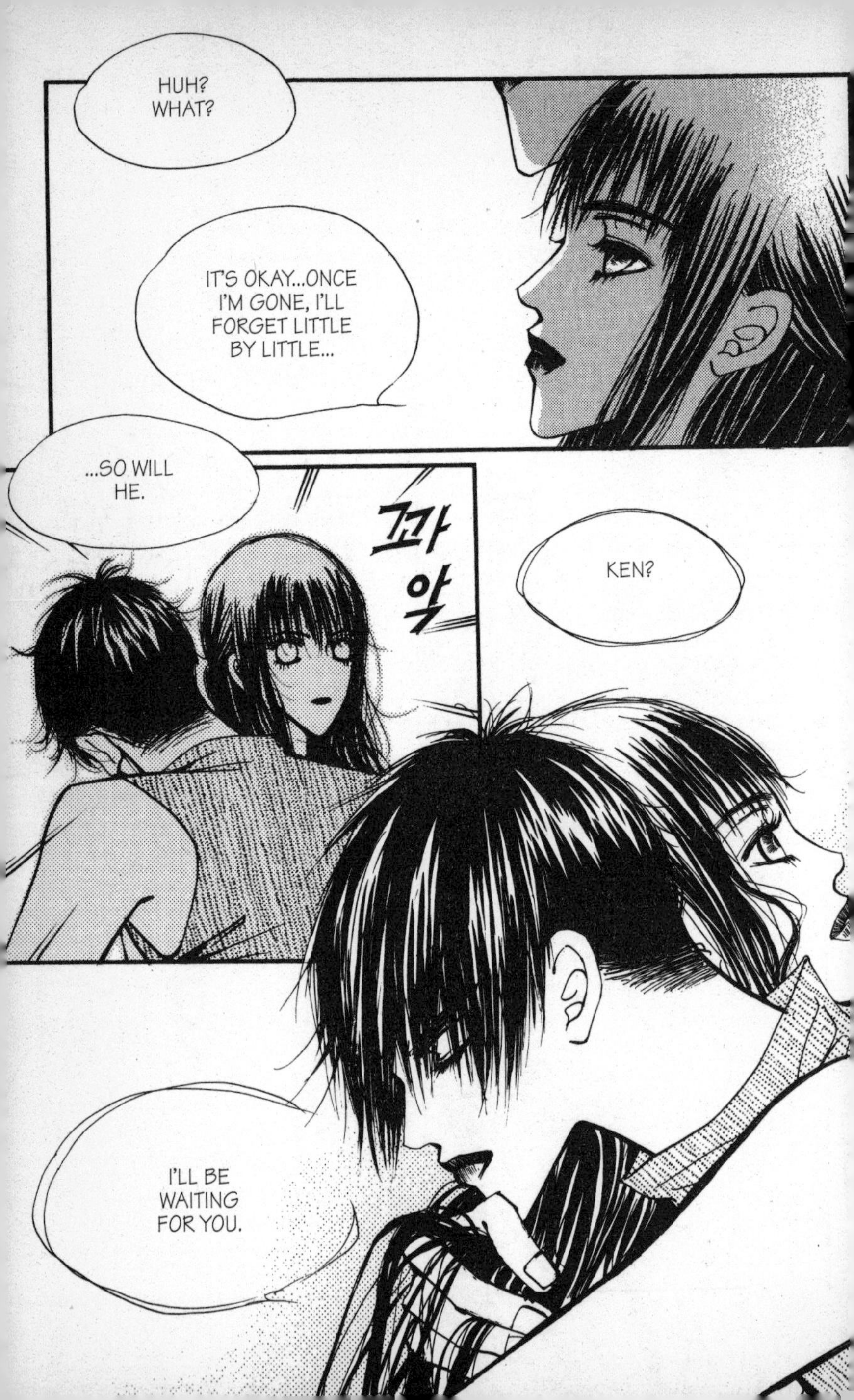
HUH? WHAT?
IT'S OKAY...ONCE I'M GONE, I'LL FORGET LITTLE BY LITTLE...
...SO WILL HE.
꽈악
KEN?
I'LL BE WAITING FOR YOU.

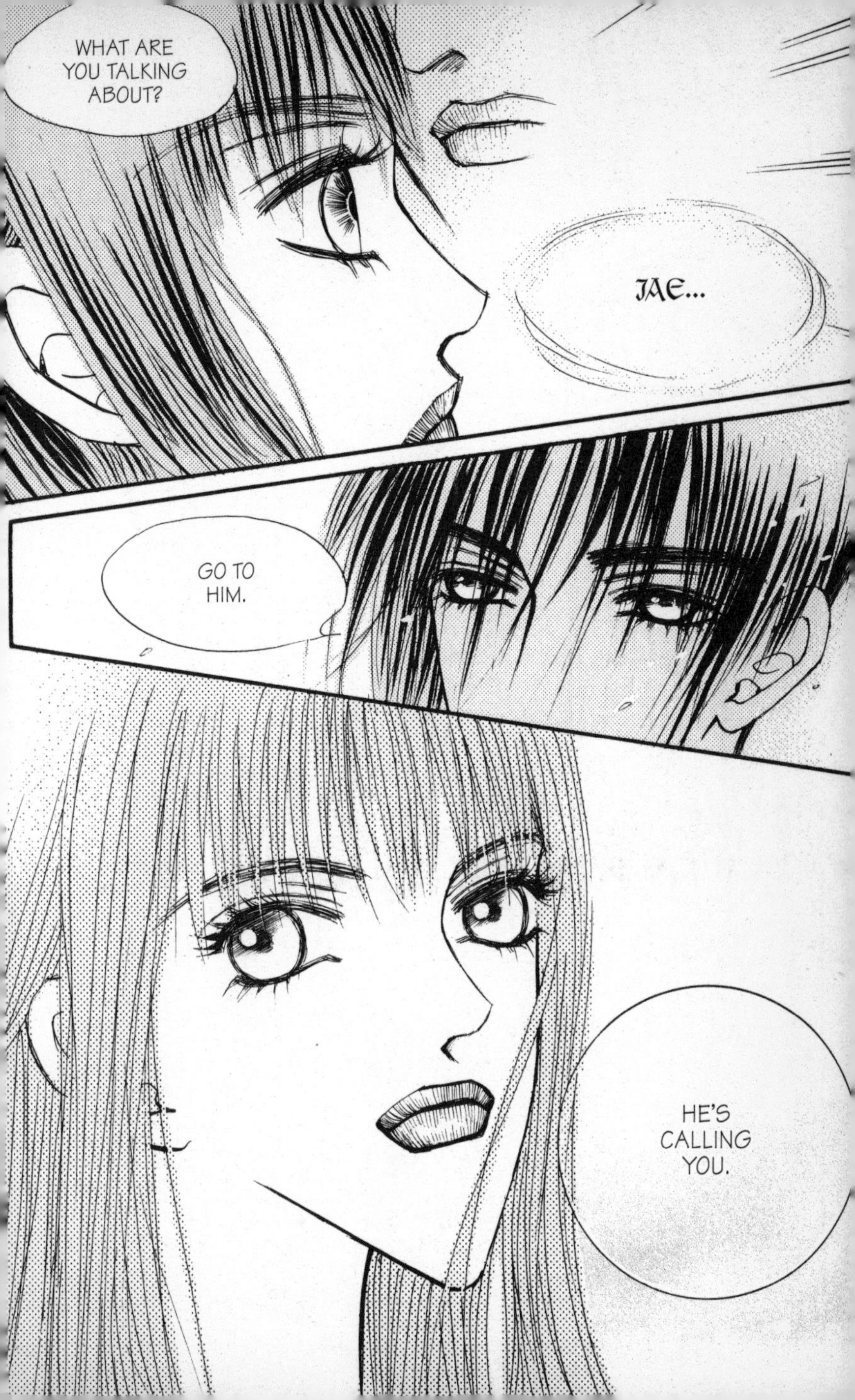
WHAT ARE YOU TALKING ABOUT?
JAE...
GO TO HIM.
HE'S CALLING YOU.

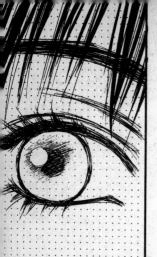

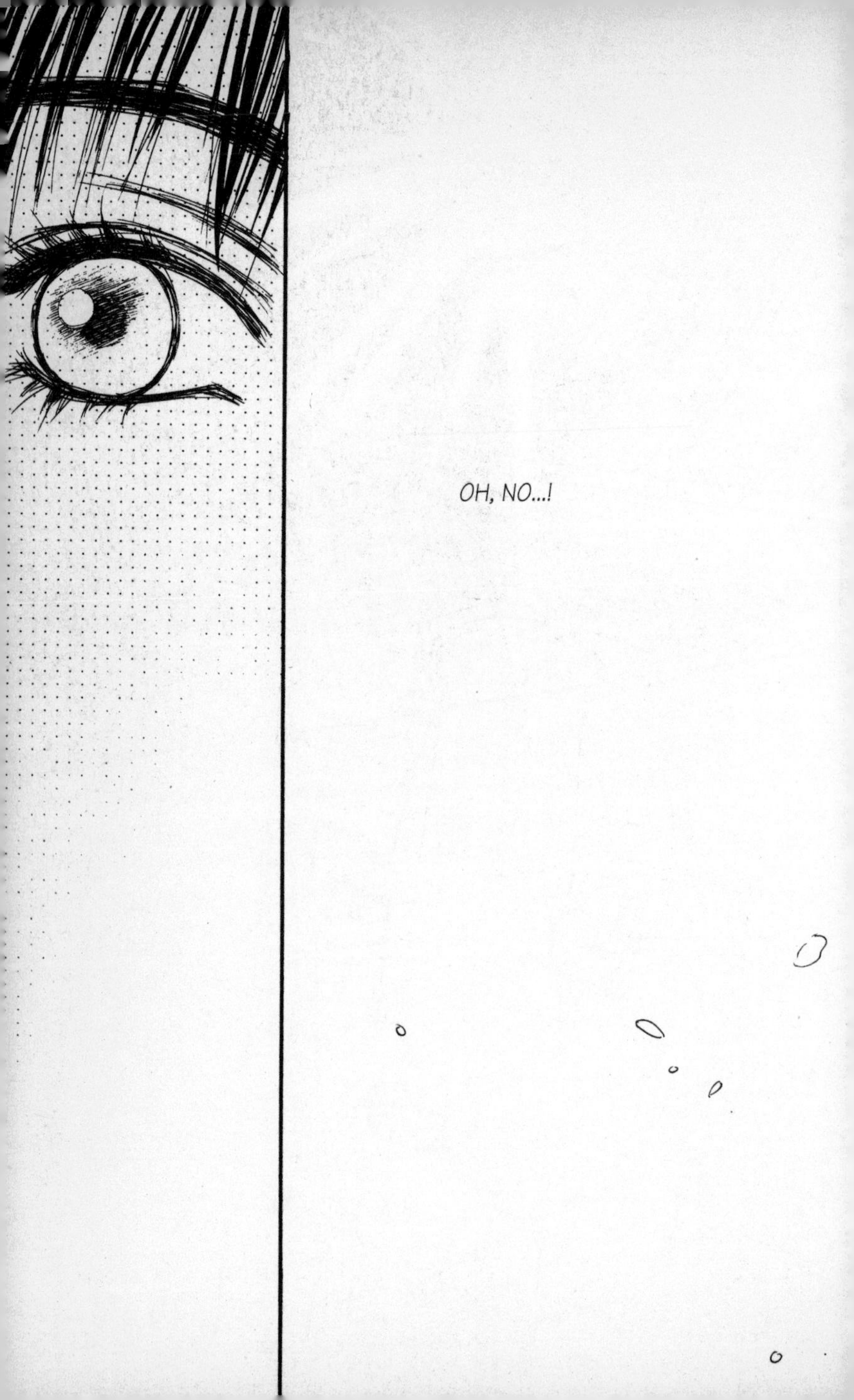

OH, NO...!

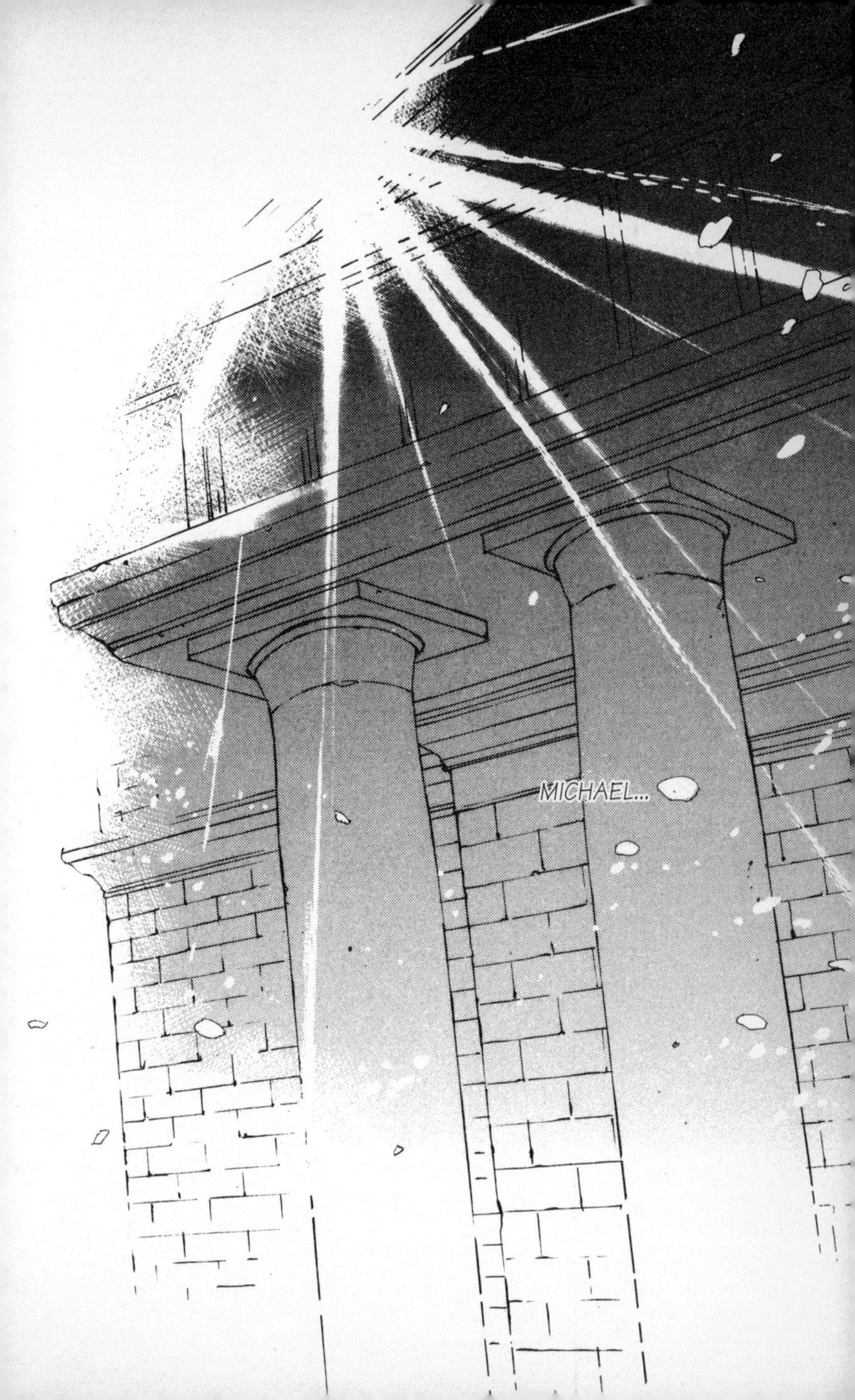
MICHAEL...

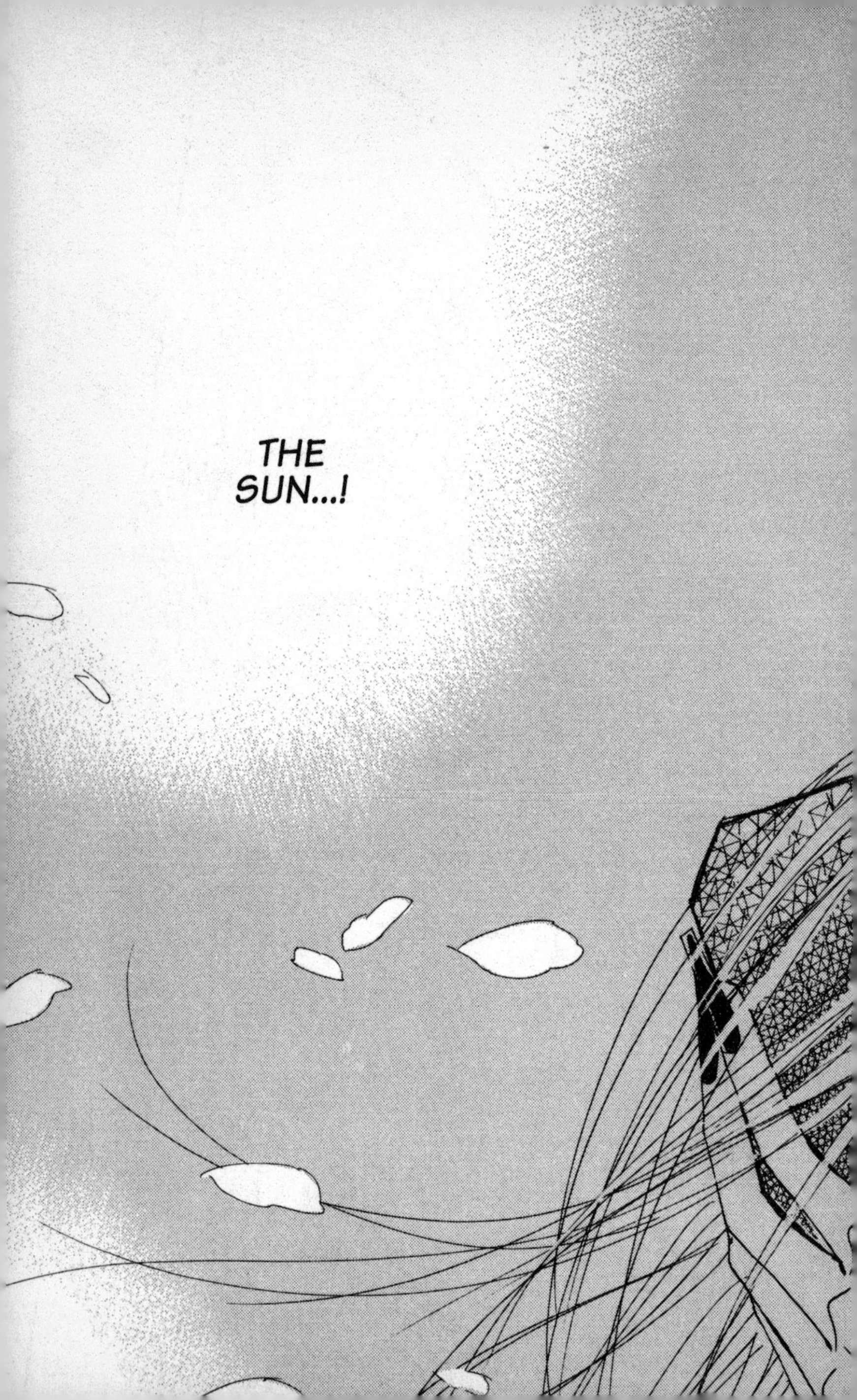
THE SUN...!

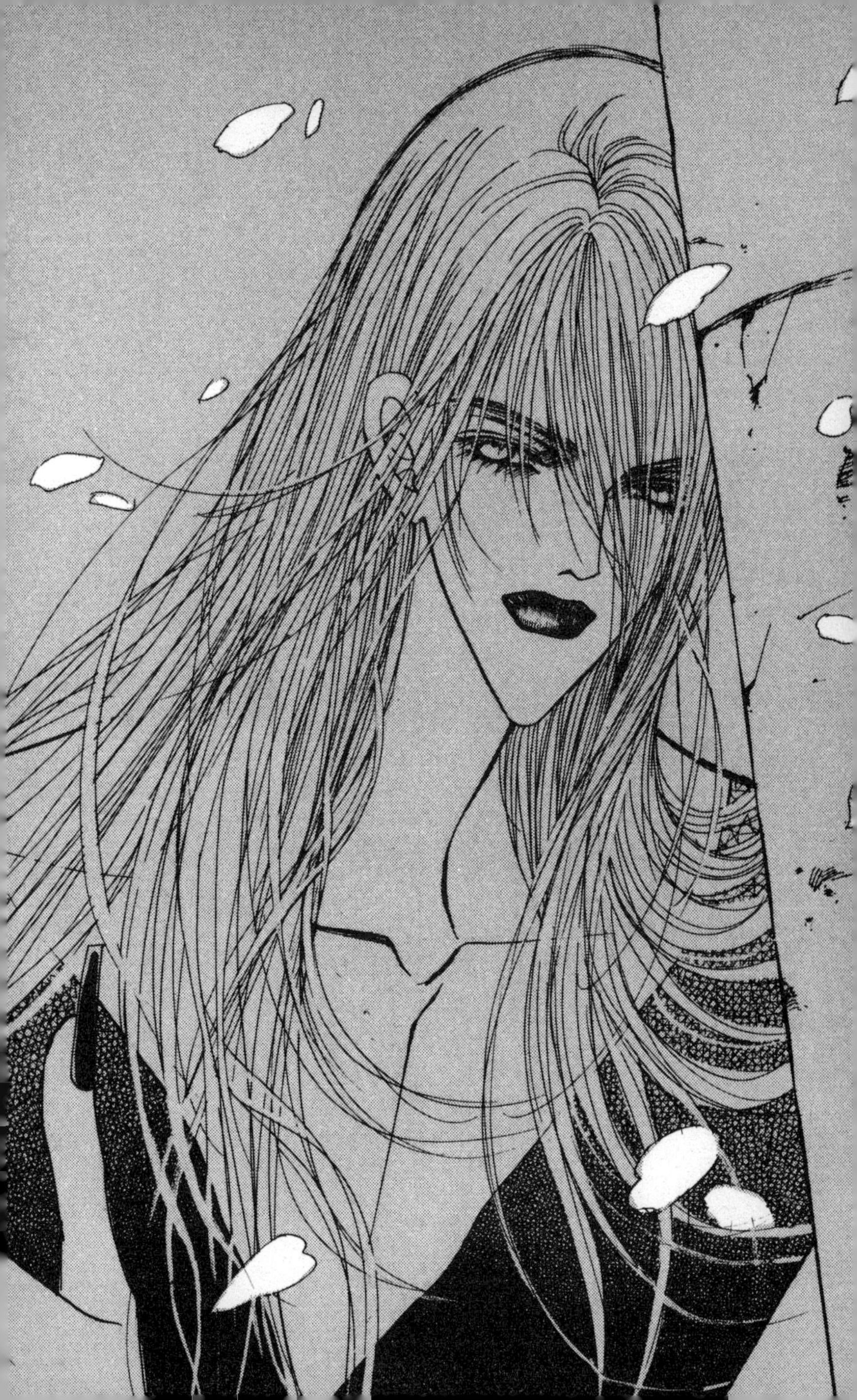

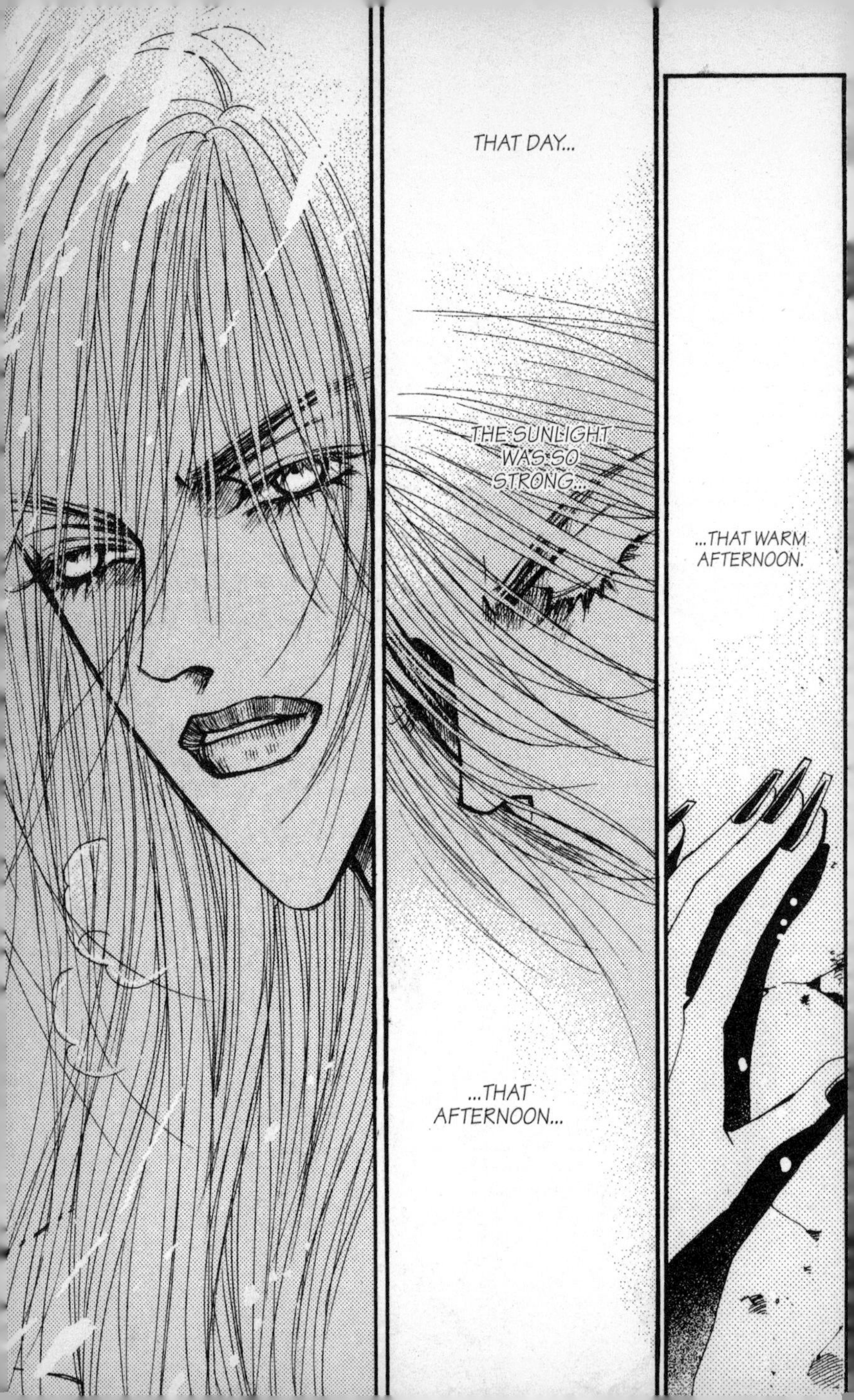
THAT DAY...
THE SUNLIGHT WAS SO STRONG...
...THAT AFTERNOON...
...THAT WARM AFTERNOON.

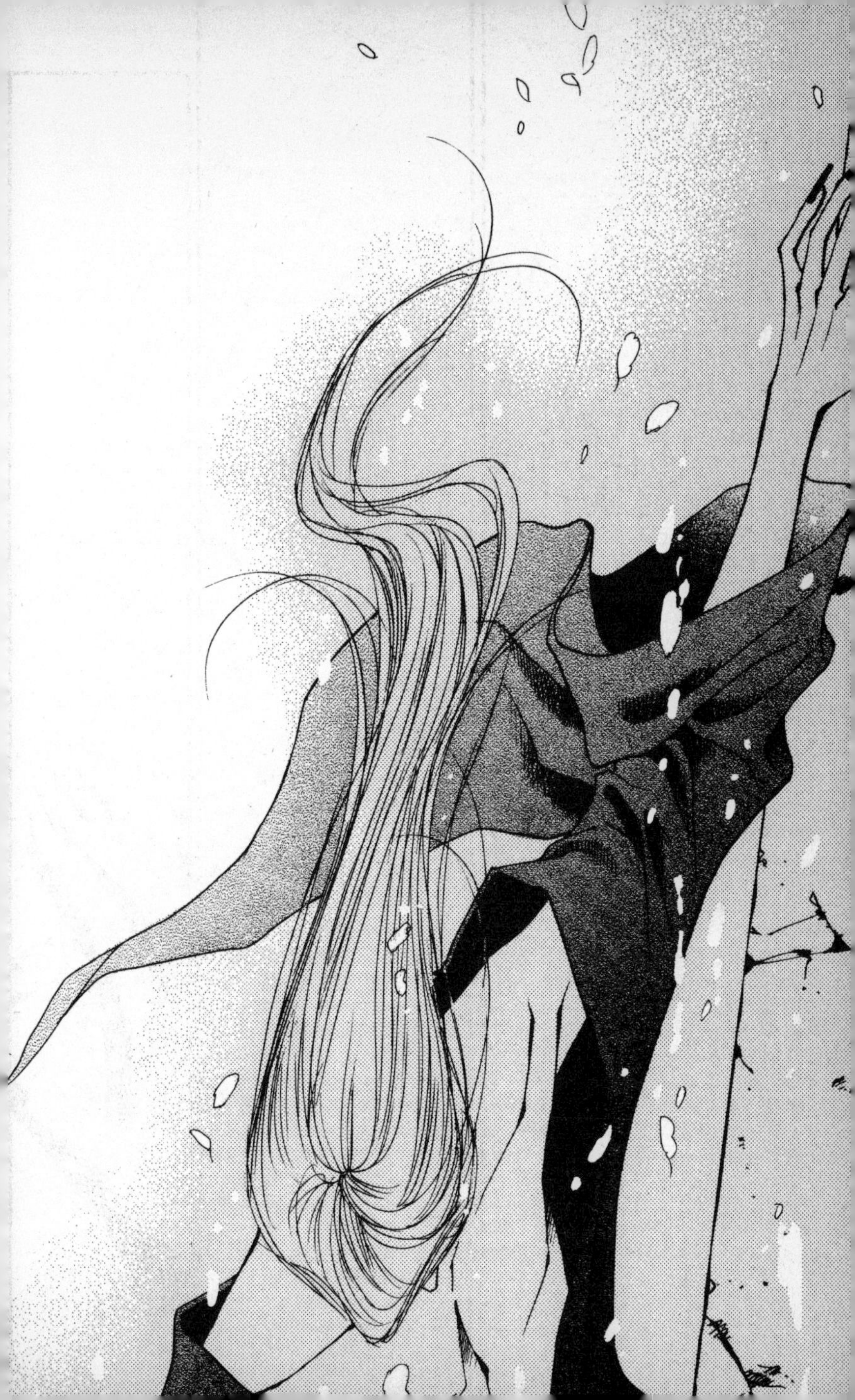

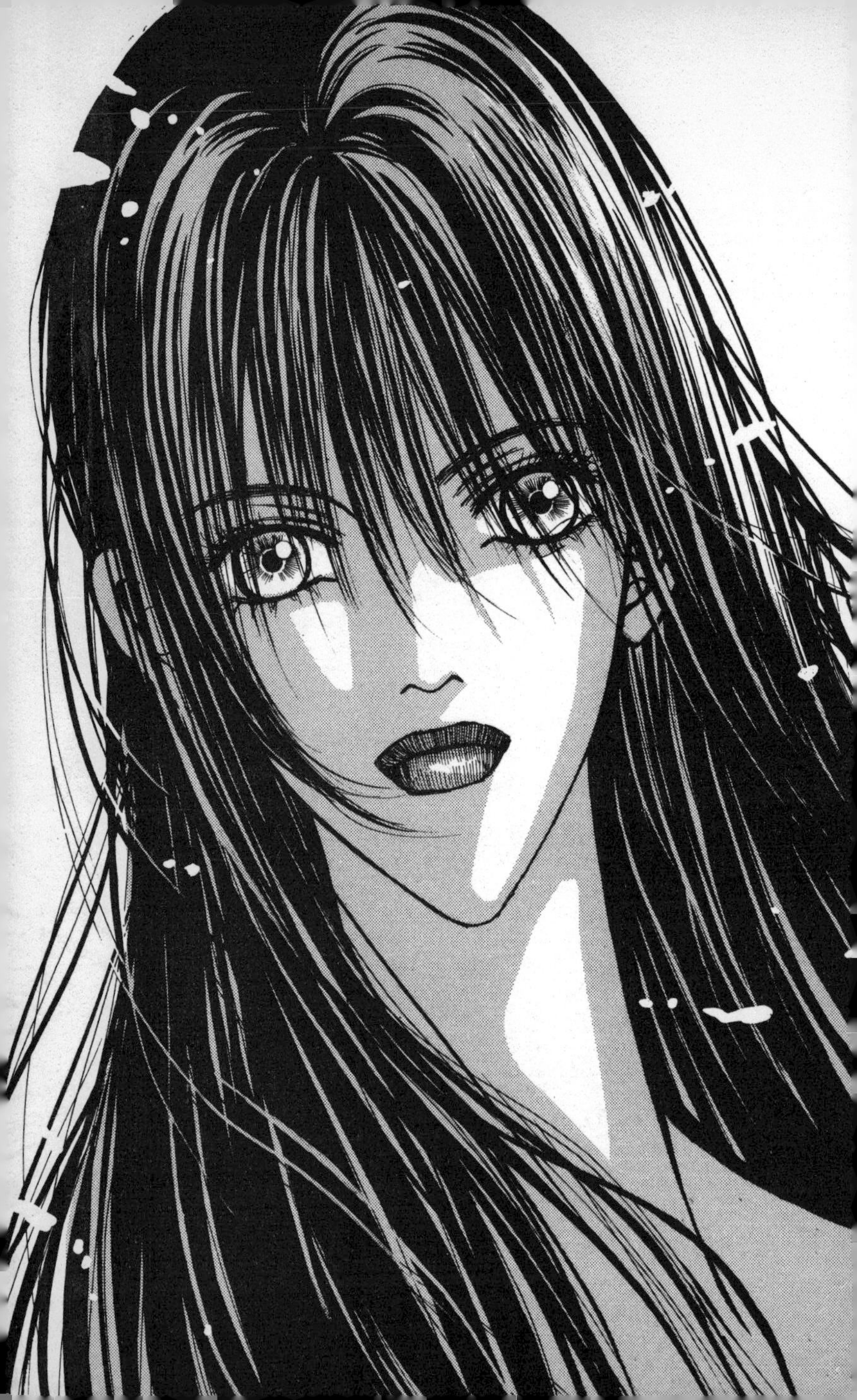

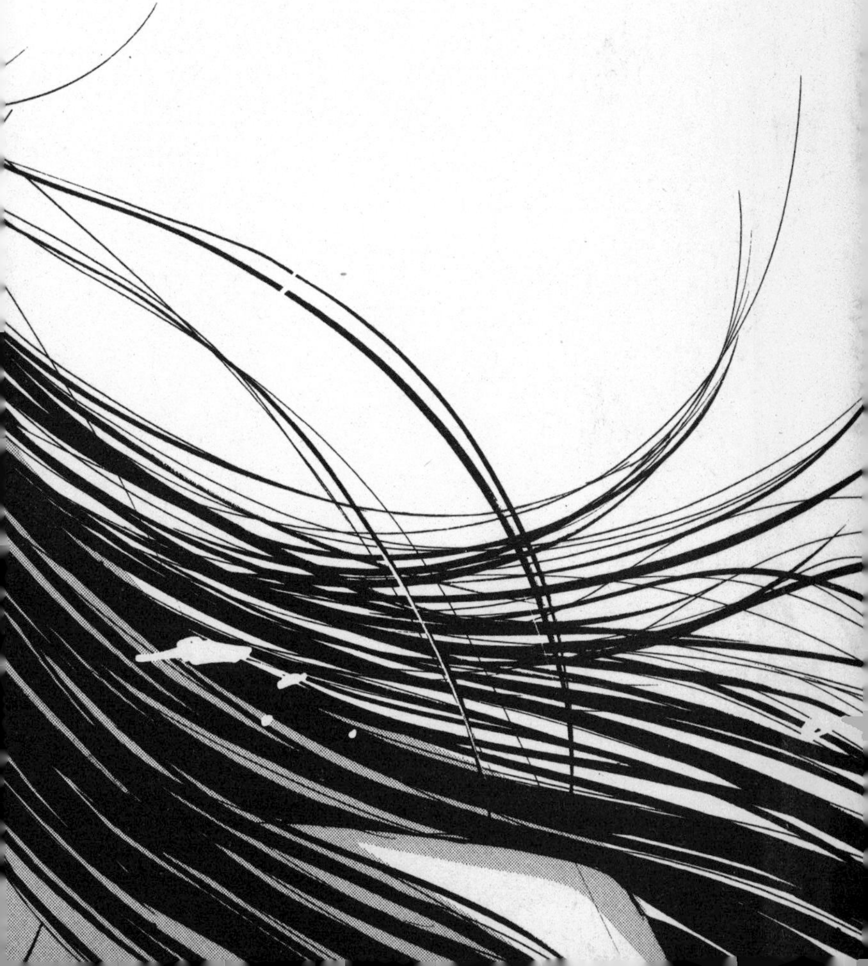

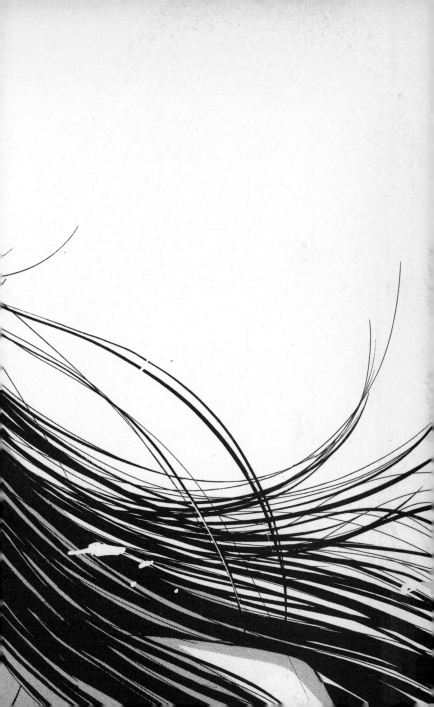

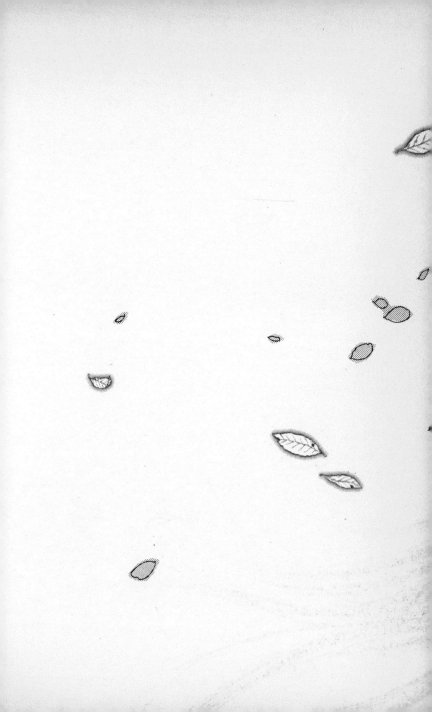

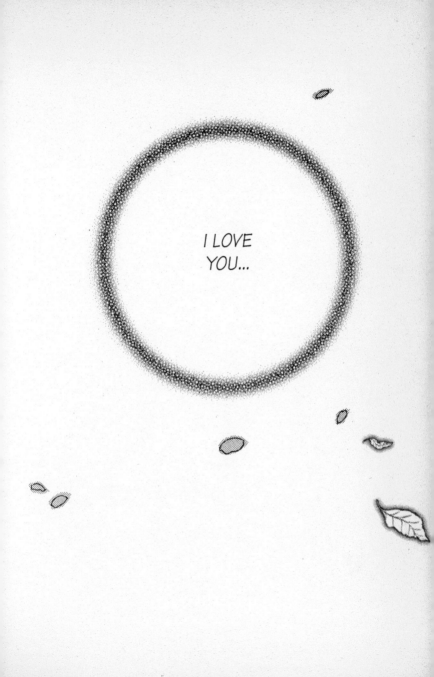

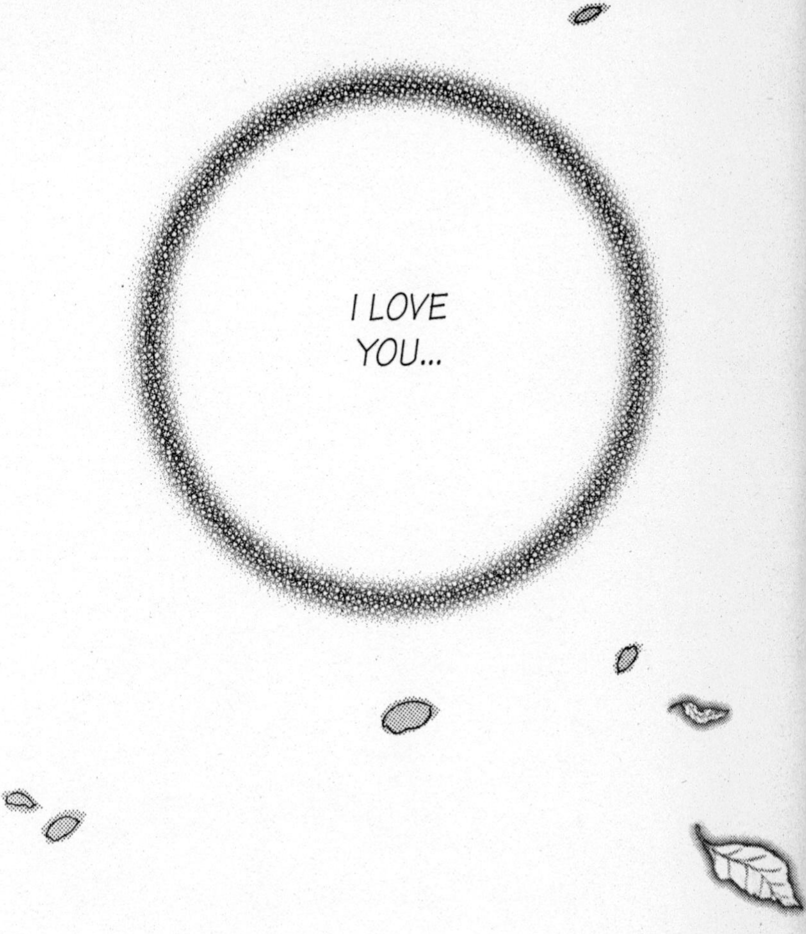
I LOVE YOU...

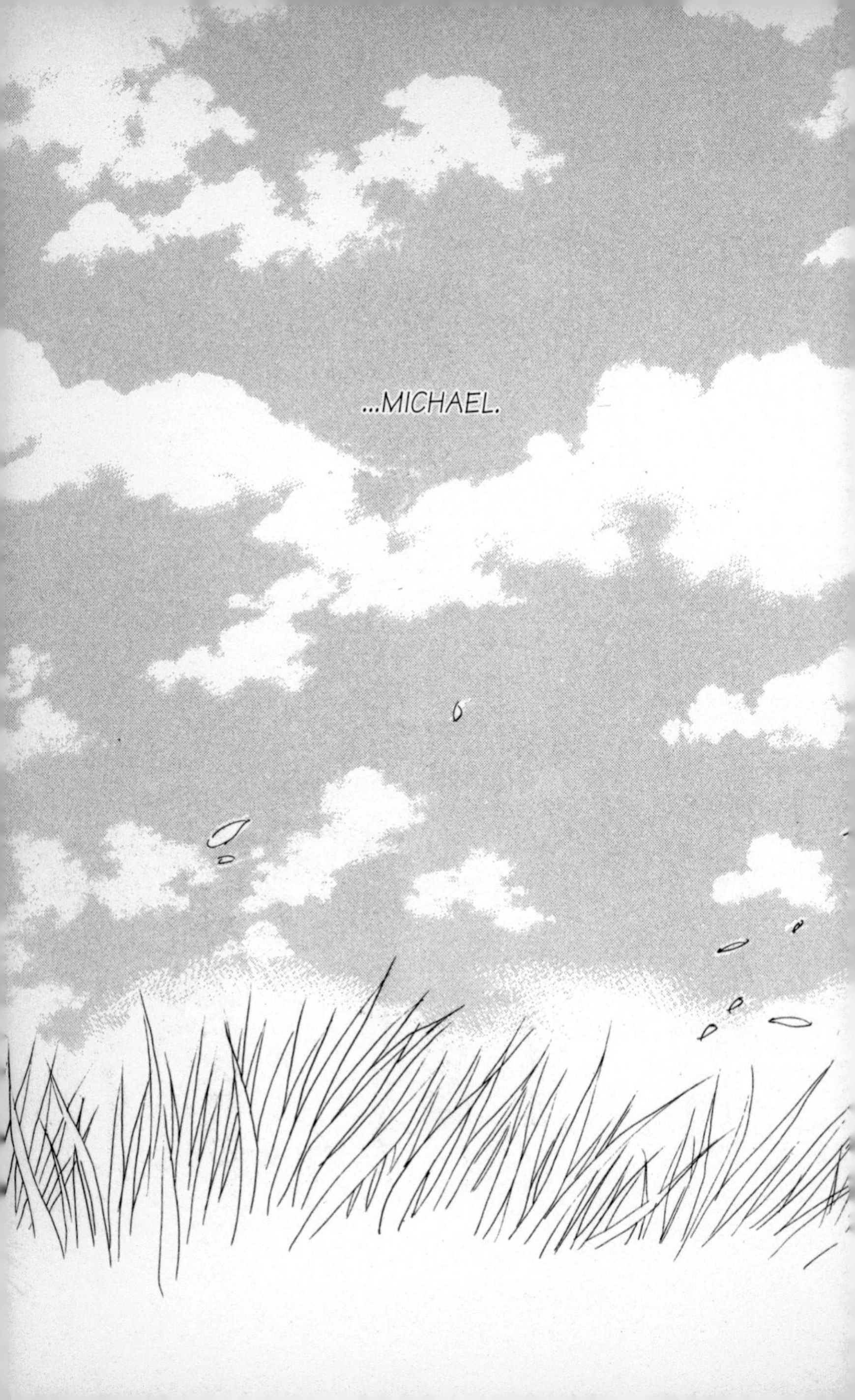
...MICHAEL.

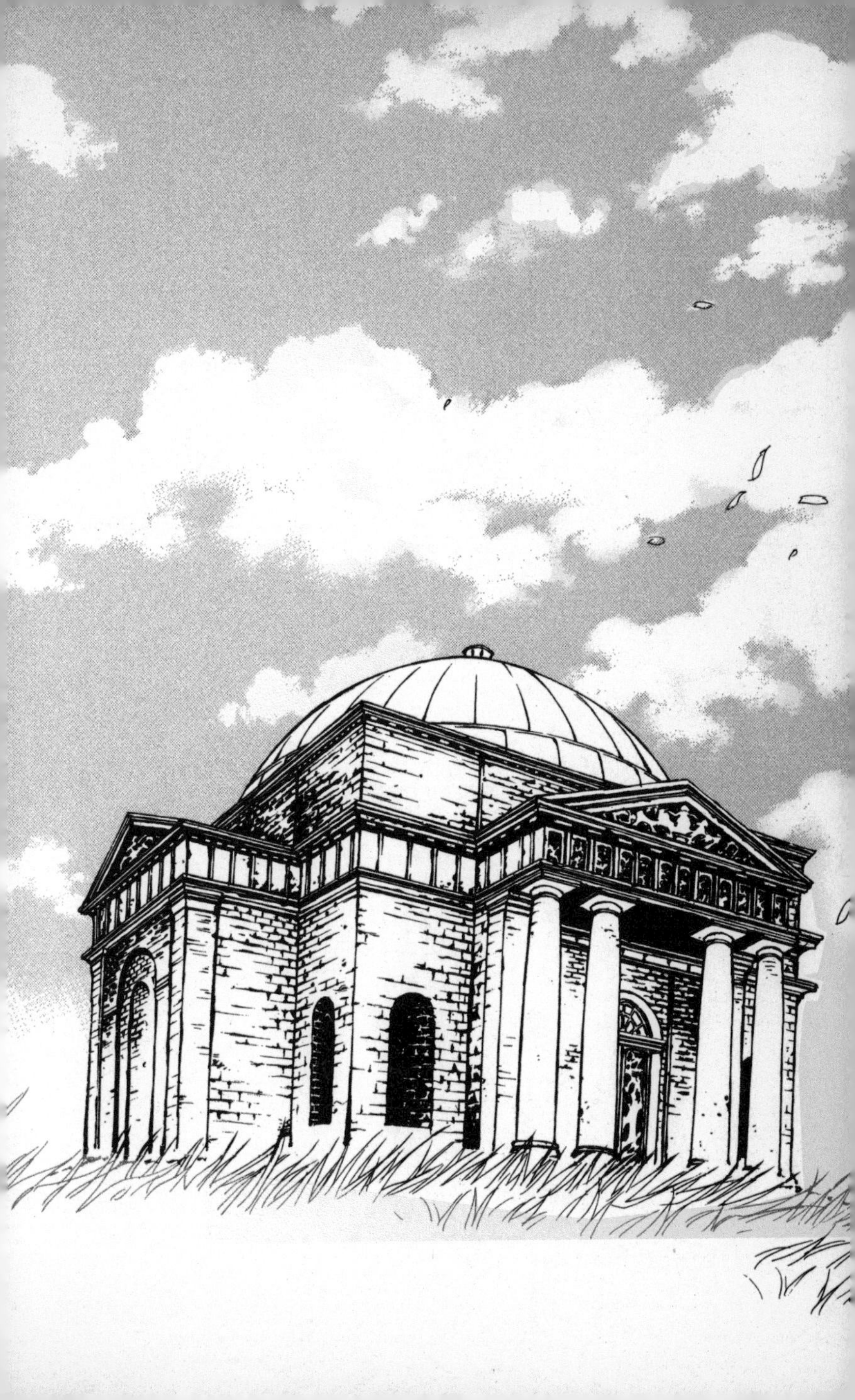

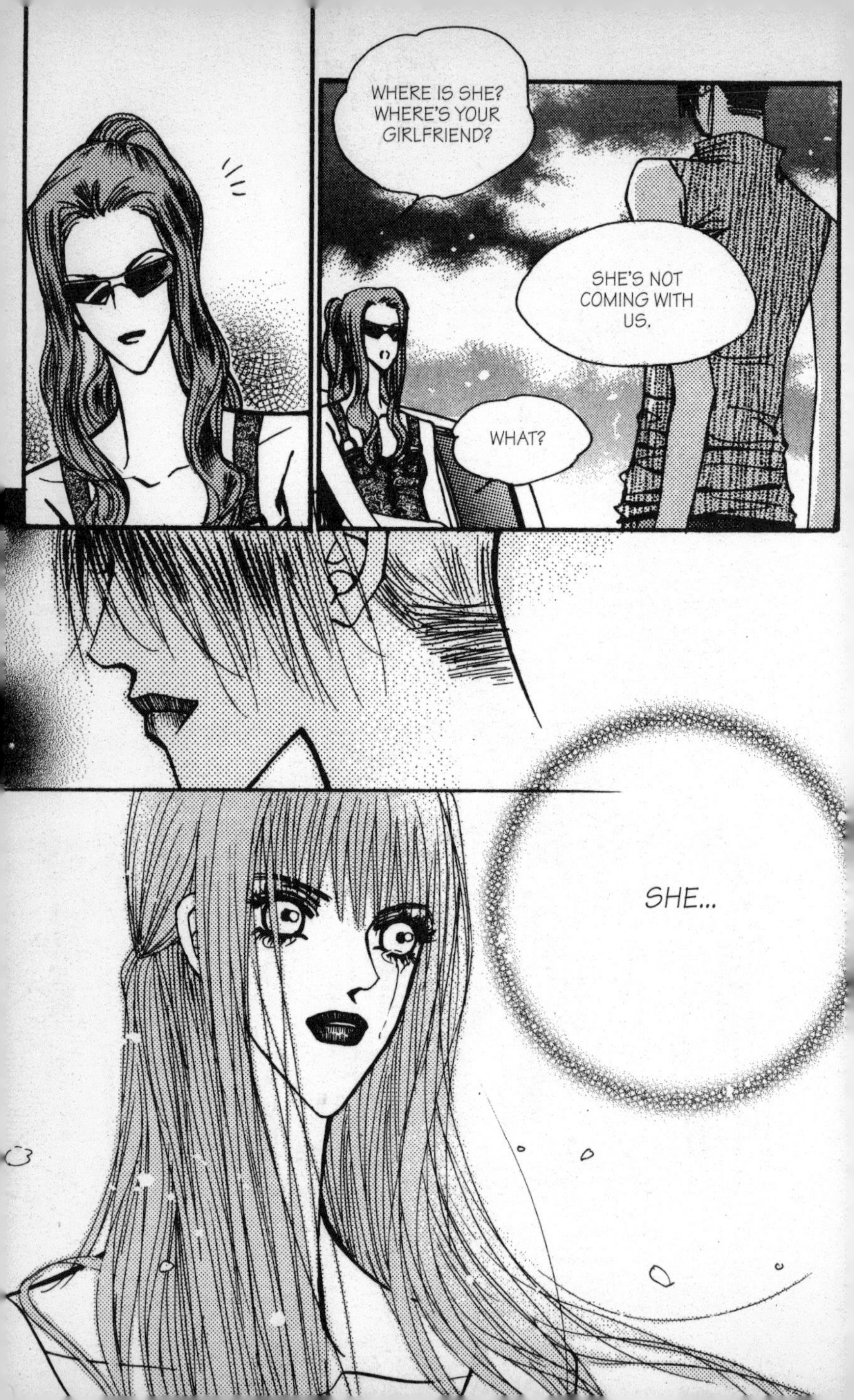
WHERE IS SHE? WHERE'S YOUR GIRLFRIEND?
SHE'S NOT COMING WITH US.
WHAT?
SHE...

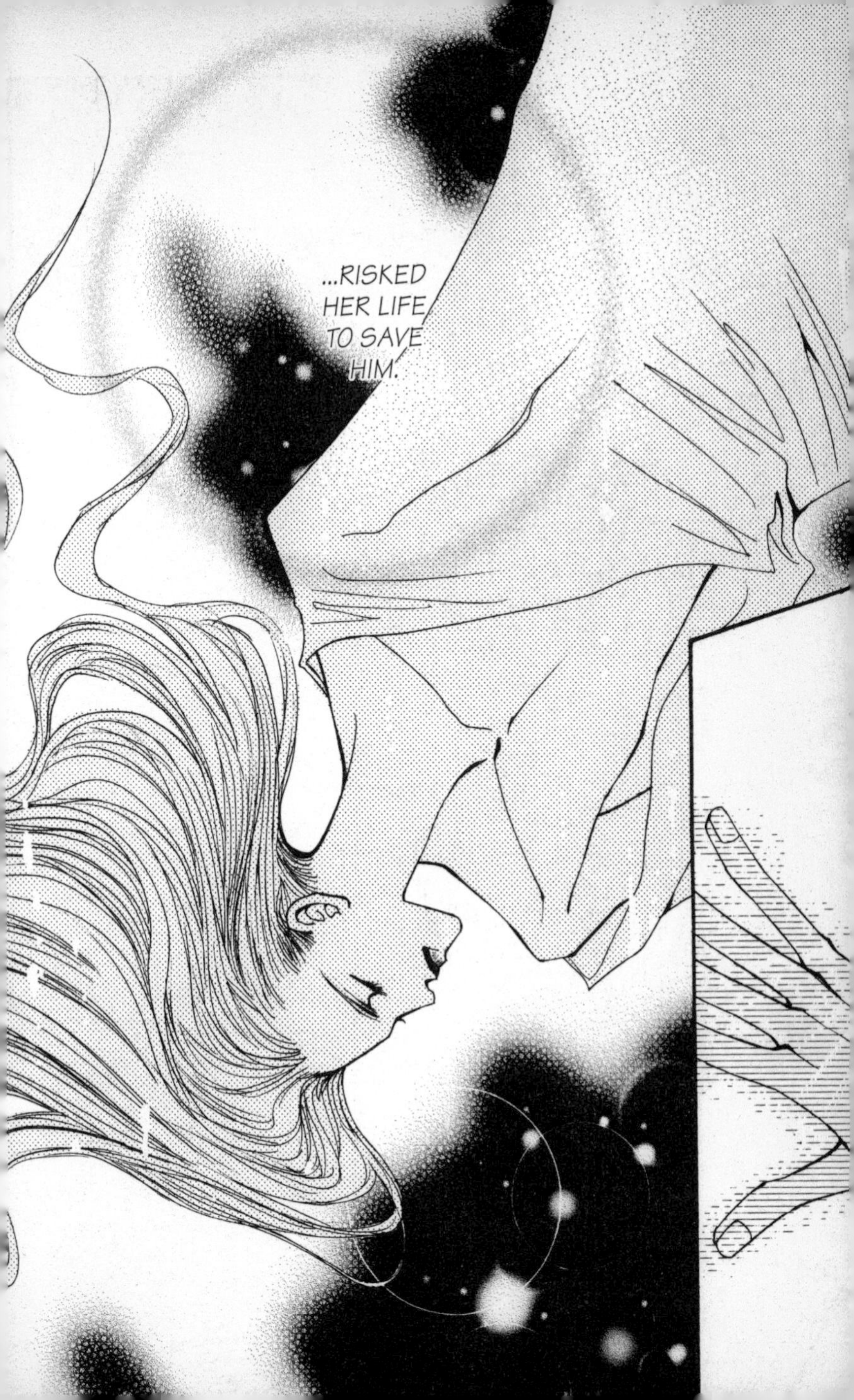
...RISKED HER LIFE TO SAVE HIM.

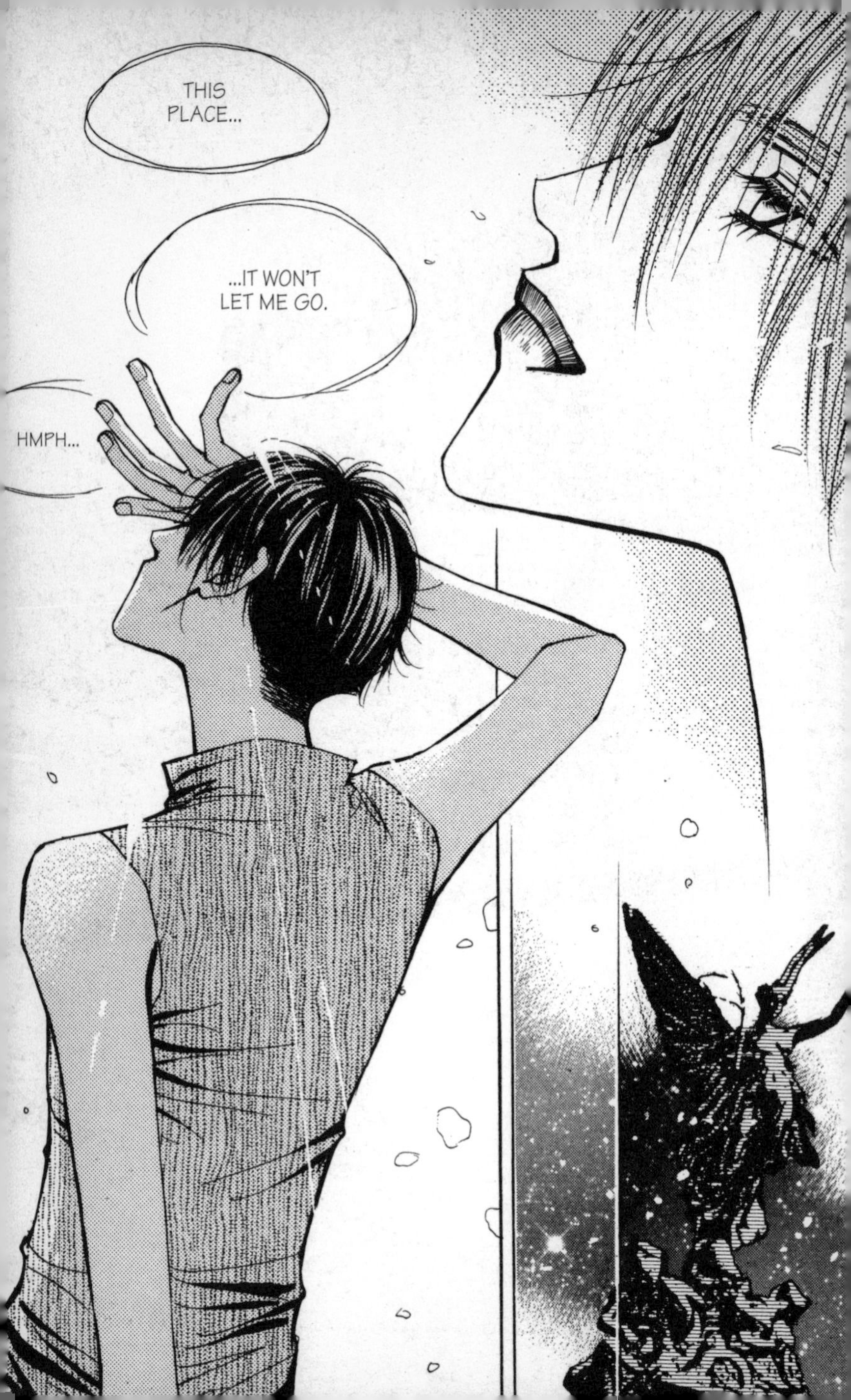
THIS PLACE...
...IT WON'T LET ME GO.
HMPH...

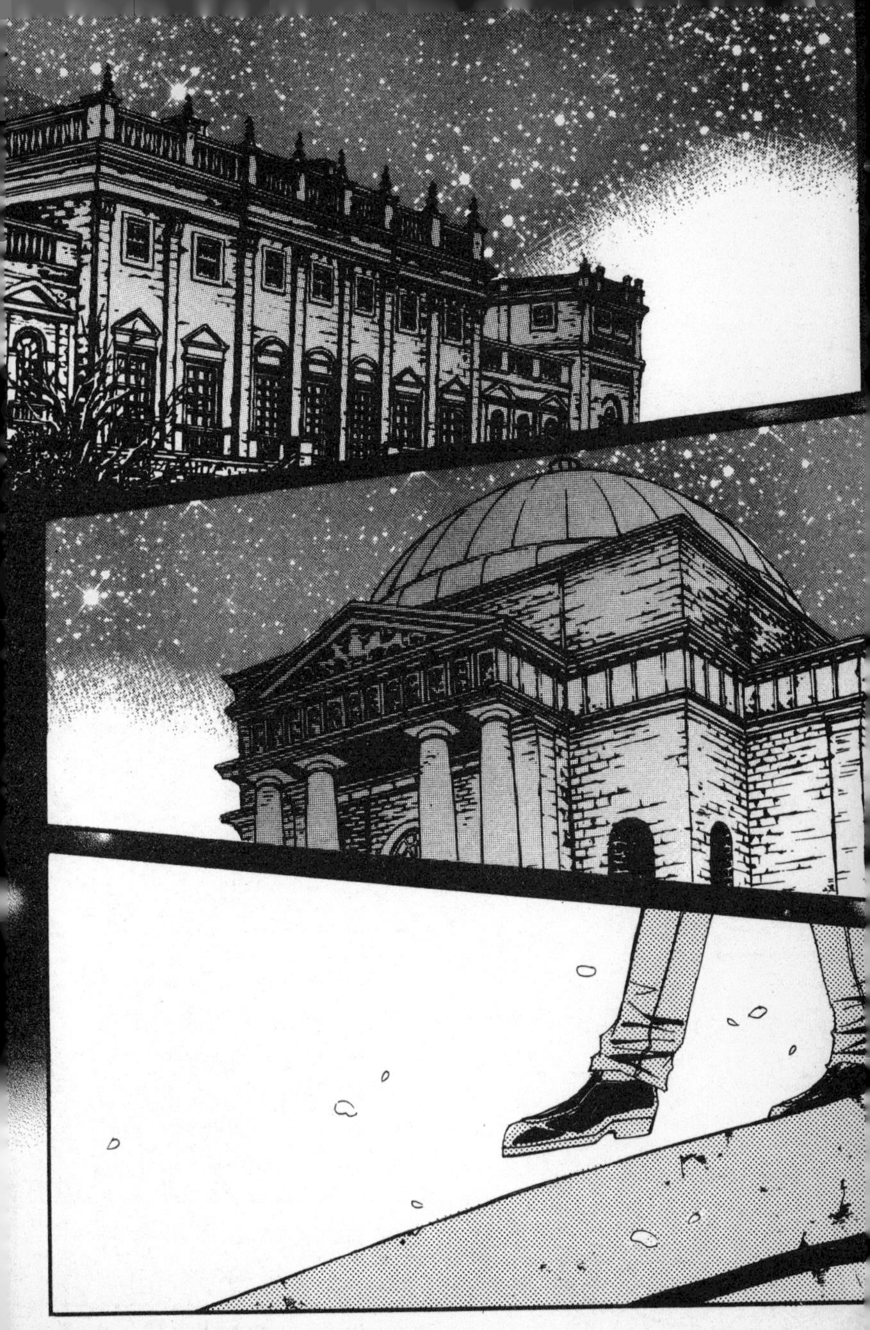

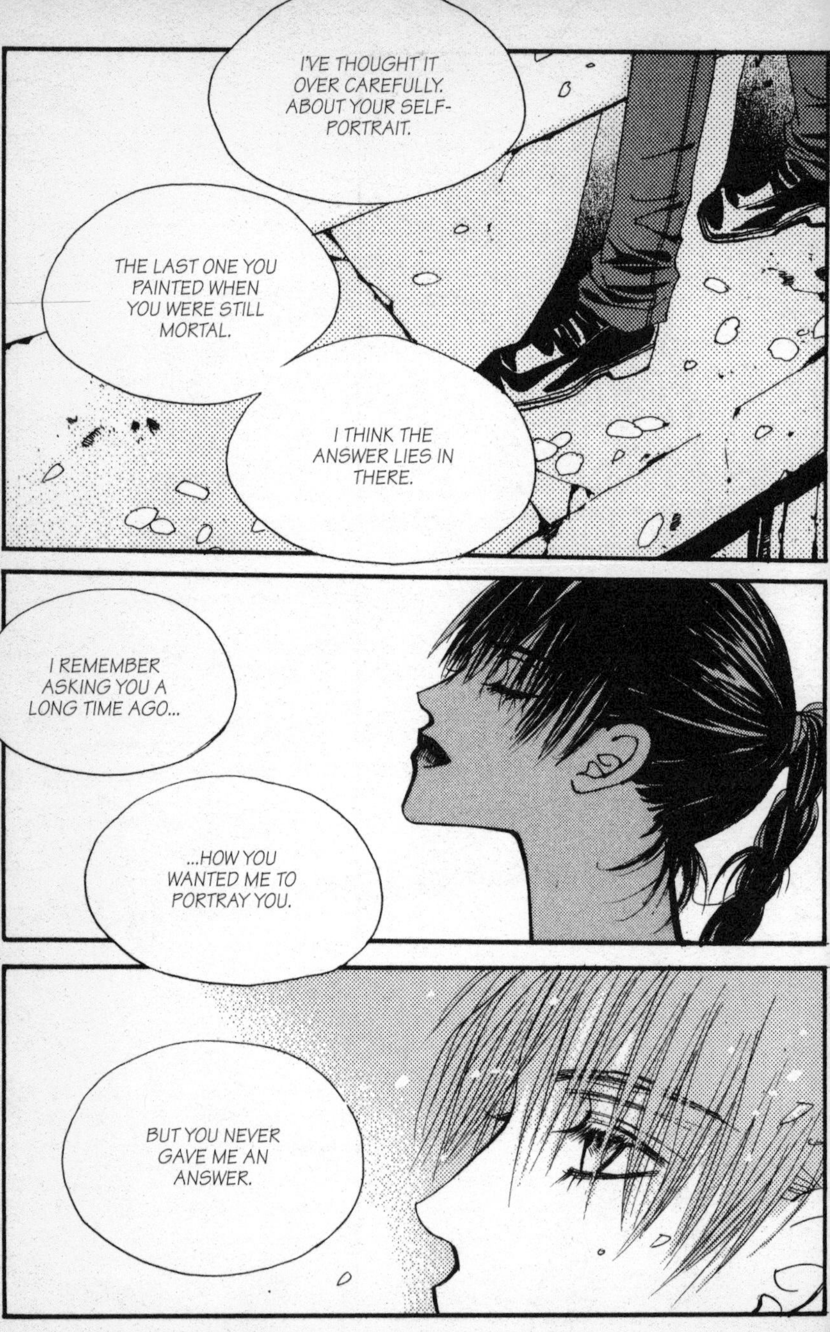
I'VE THOUGHT IT OVER CAREFULLY. ABOUT YOUR SELF-PORTRAIT.
THE LAST ONE YOU PAINTED WHEN YOU WERE STILL MORTAL.
I THINK THE ANSWER LIES IN THERE.
I REMEMBER ASKING YOU A LONG TIME AGO...
...HOW YOU WANTED ME TO PORTRAY YOU.
BUT YOU NEVER GAVE ME AN ANSWER.

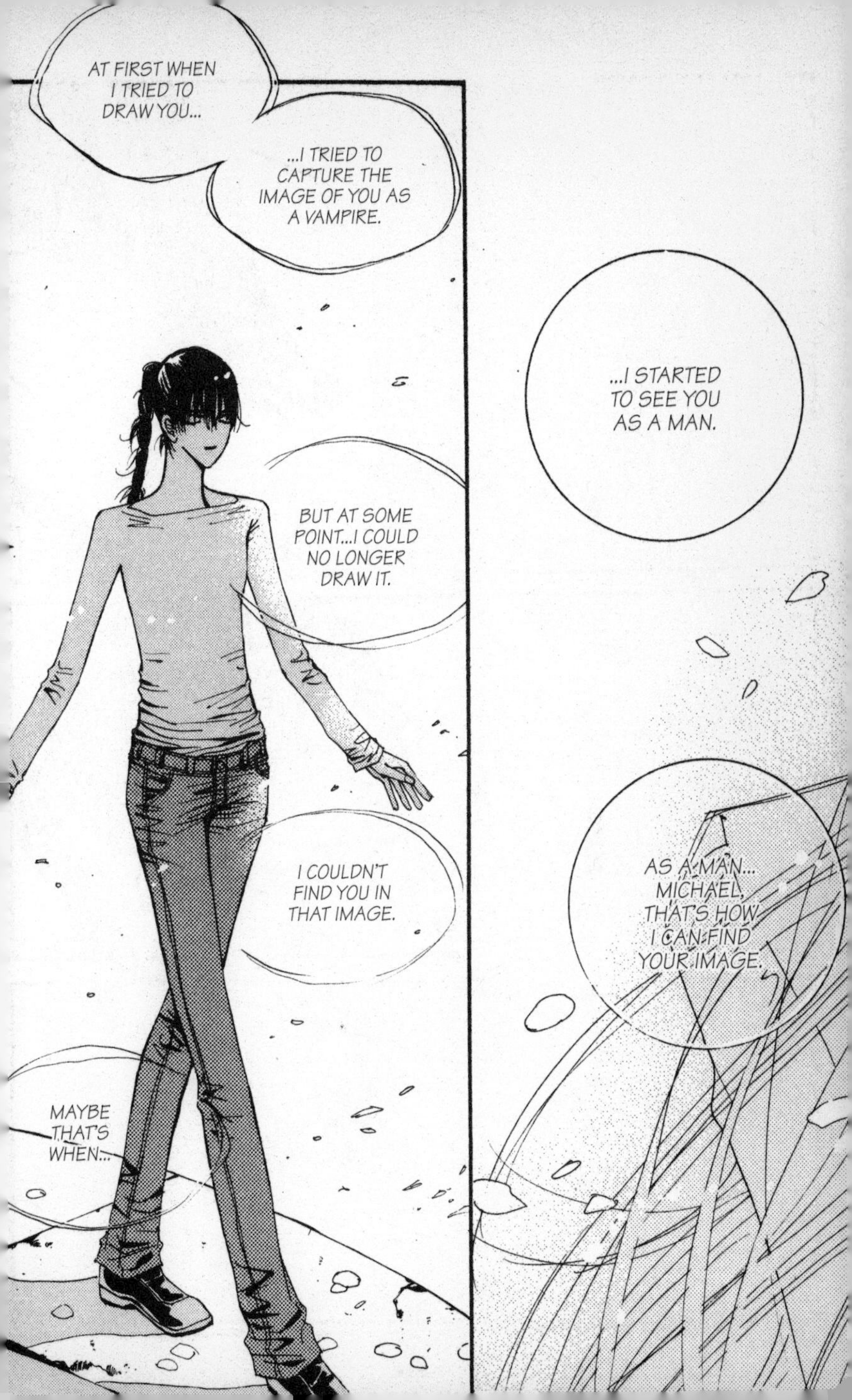
AT FIRST WHEN I TRIED TO DRAW YOU...
...I TRIED TO CAPTURE THE IMAGE OF YOU AS A VAMPIRE.
BUT AT SOME POINT...I COULD NO LONGER DRAW IT.
I COULDN'T FIND YOU IN THAT IMAGE.
MAYBE THAT'S WHEN...
...I STARTED TO SEE YOU AS A MAN.
AS A MAN... MICHAEL, THAT'S HOW I CAN FIND YOUR IMAGE.

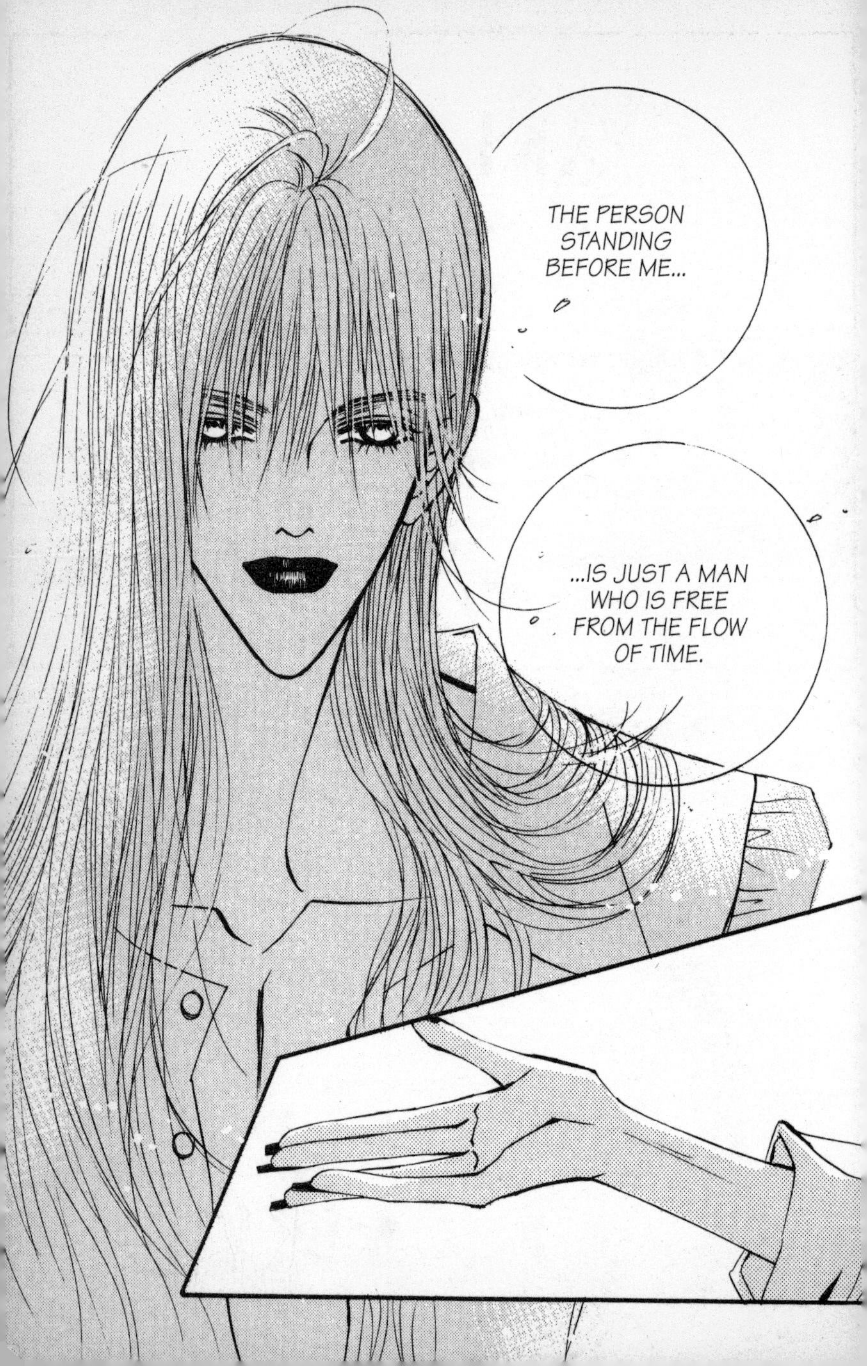
THE PERSON STANDING BEFORE ME...
...IS JUST A MAN WHO IS FREE FROM THE FLOW OF TIME.

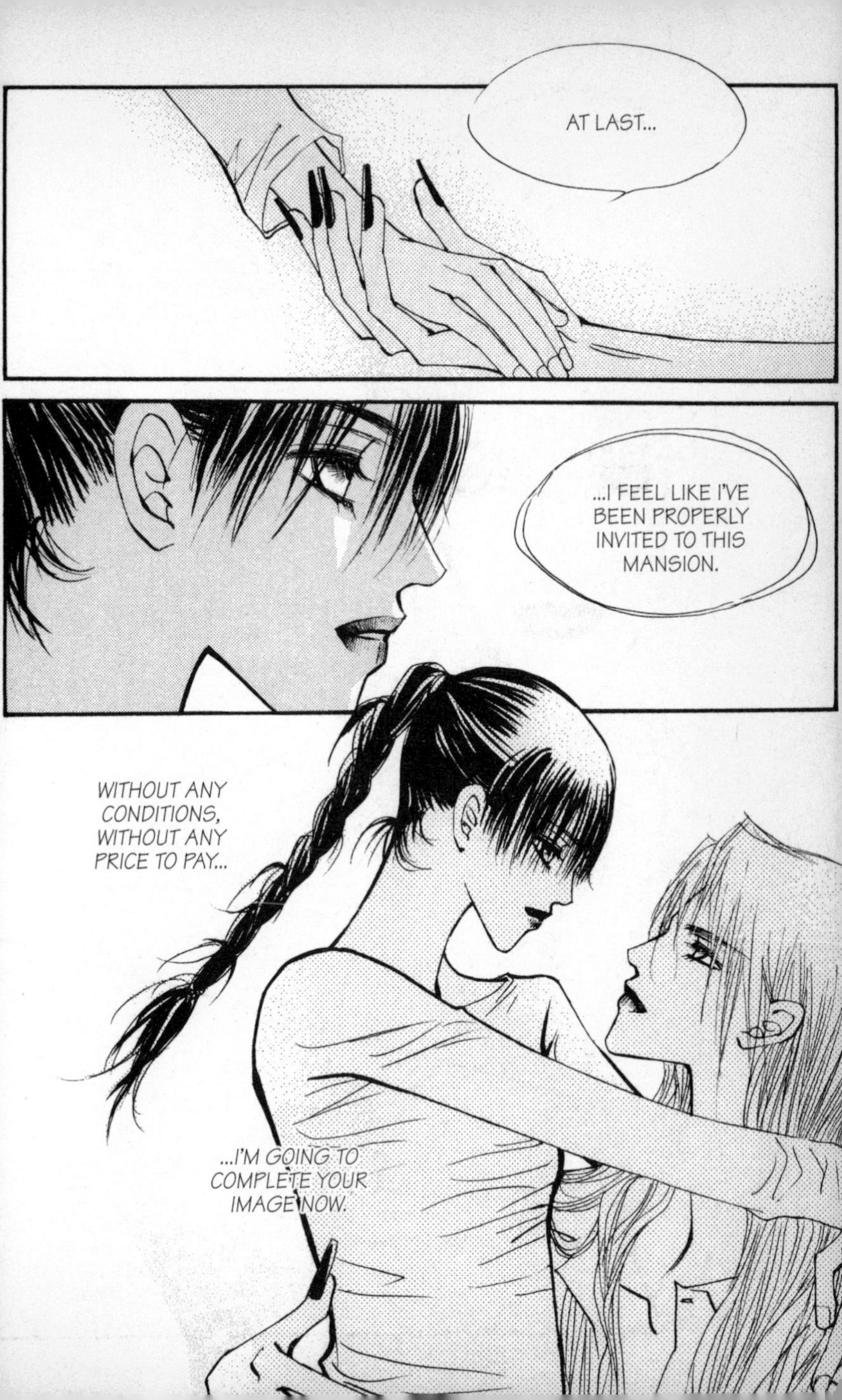
AT LAST...
...I FEEL LIKE I'VE BEEN PROPERLY INVITED TO THIS MANSION.
WITHOUT ANY CONDITIONS, WITHOUT ANY PRICE TO PAY...
...I'M GOING TO COMPLETE YOUR IMAGE NOW.

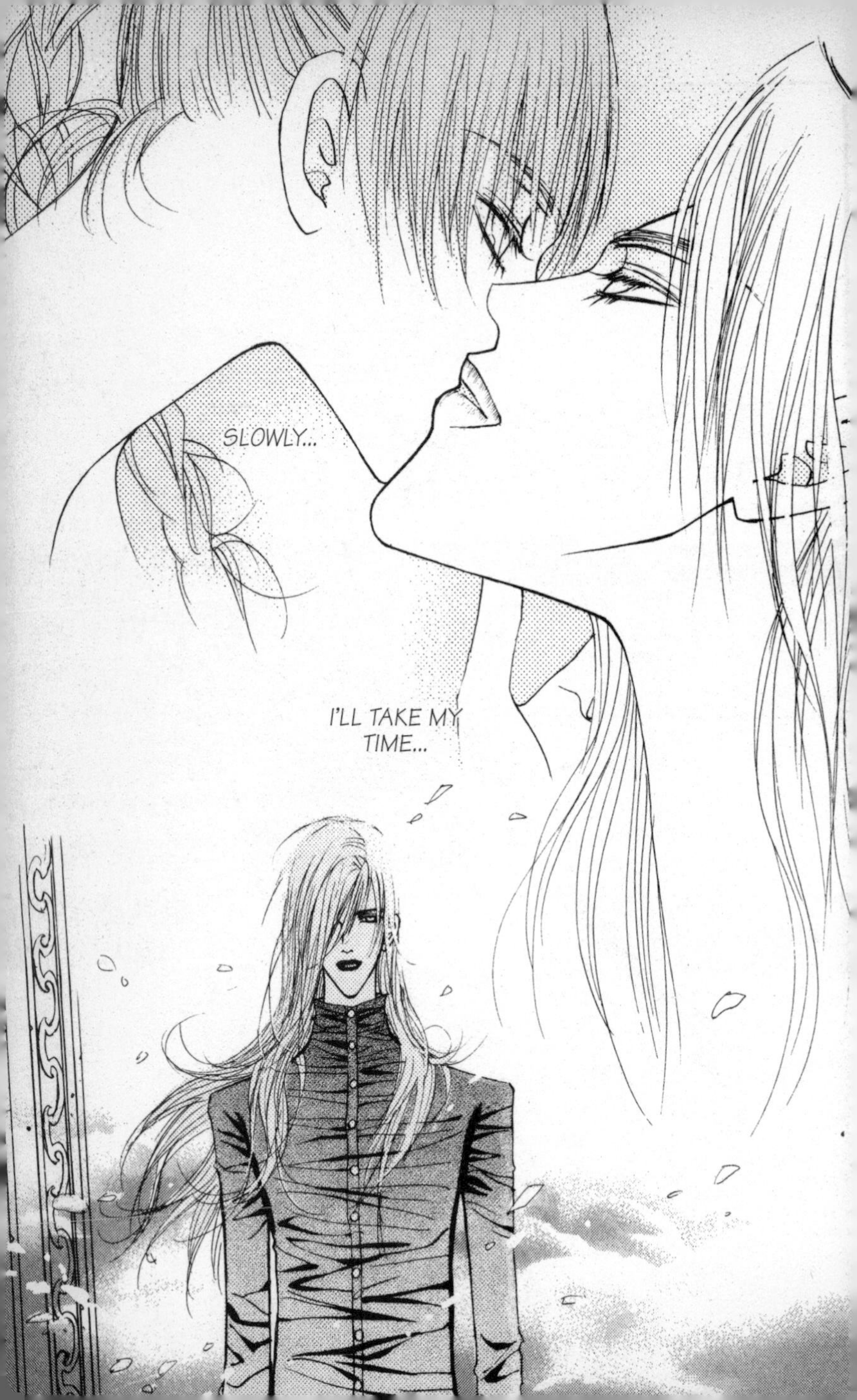
SLOWLY...
I'LL TAKE MY TIME...

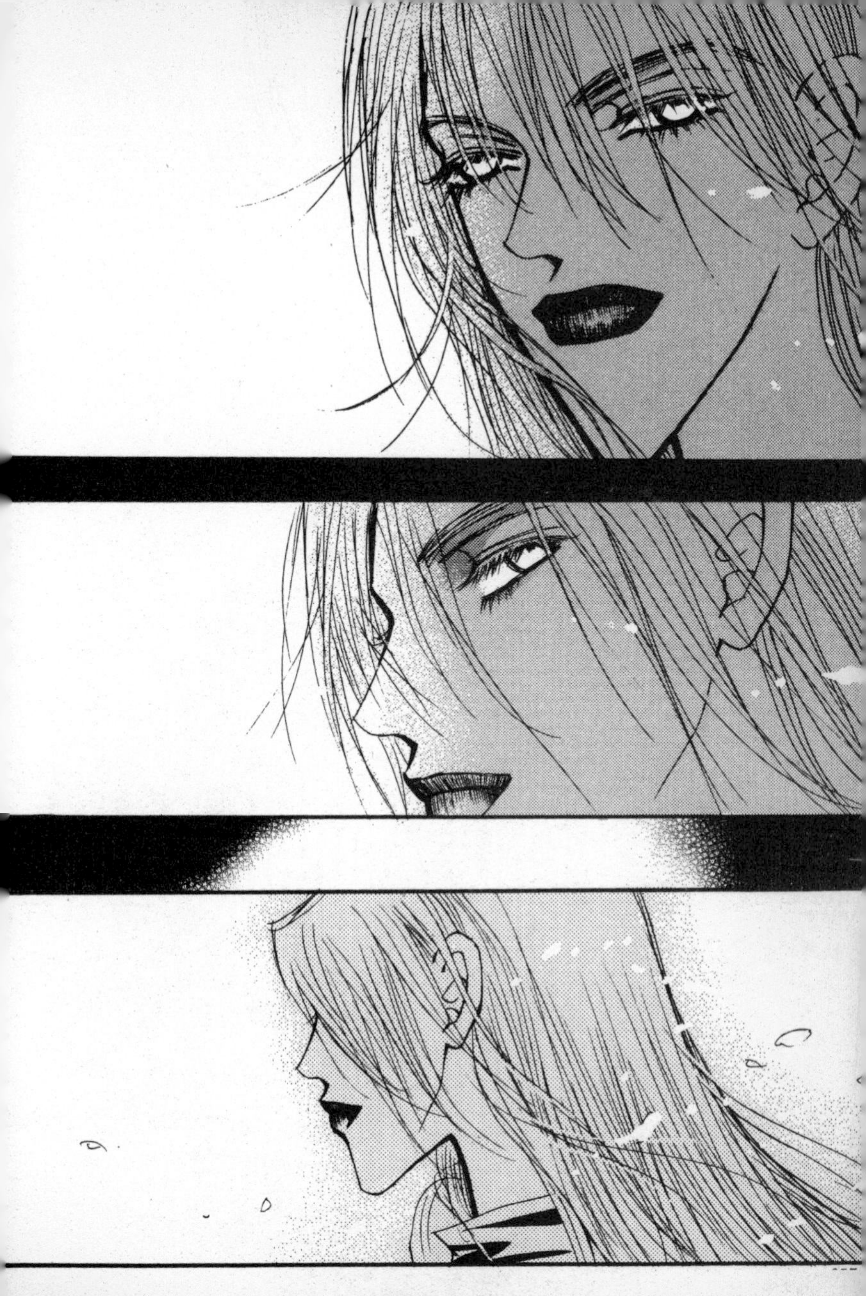

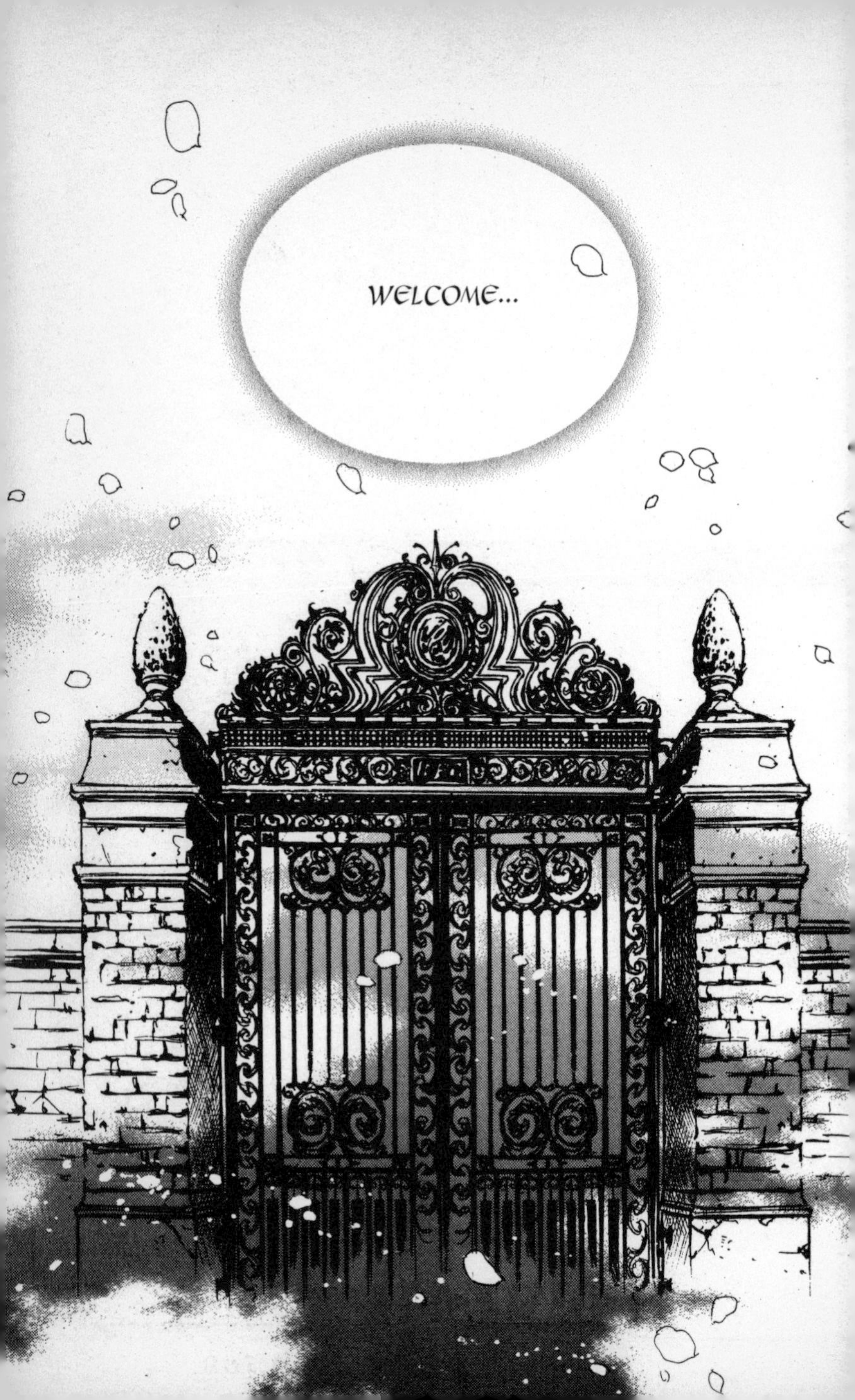
WELCOME...

MODEL — THE END

TOKYOPOP SHOP

WAR ON FLESH

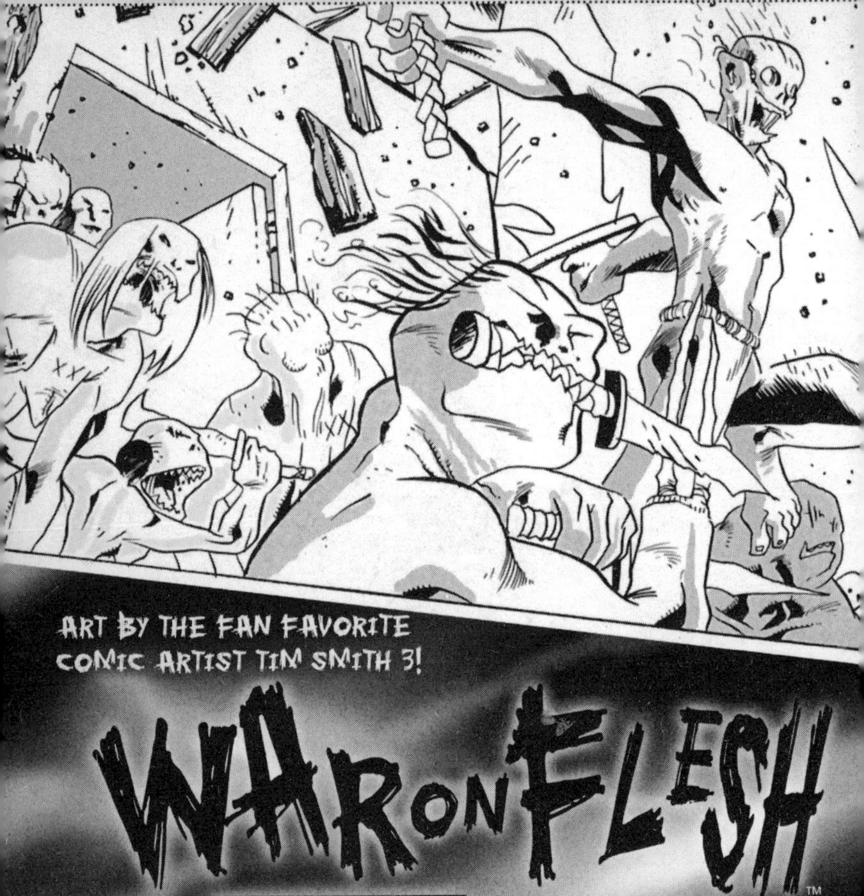

ART BY THE FAN FAVORITE
COMIC ARTIST TIM SMITH 3!

WAR ON FLESH™

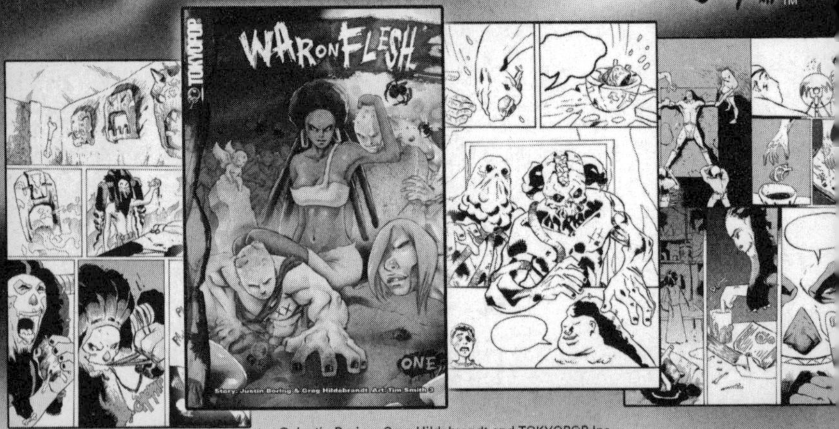
WAR ON FLESH
TOKYOPOP
ONE
Story: Justin Boring & Greg Hildebrandt Art: Tim Smith 3